SOMETHING ABOUT THE AUTHOR

ISSN 0276-816X

something ABOUT THE AUTHOR

**Facts and Pictures about Authors
and Illustrators of Books for Young People**

EDITED BY
ANNE COMMIRE

VOLUME 60

 **Gale Research Inc.** · *DETROIT* · *NEW YORK* · *LONDON*

Managing Editor: Anne Commire

Editors: Agnes Garrett, Helga P. McCue

Associate Editor: Elisa Ann Ferraro

Assistant Editors: Marc Caplan, Eunice L. Petrini, Linda Shedd

Sketchwriters: Peggy Boyer, Catherine Coray, Cathy Courtney, Johanna Cypis, Marguerite Feitlowitz, Mimi H. Hutson, Deborah Klezmer, Dieter Miller, Beatrice Smedley

Researcher: Catherine Ruello

Editorial Assistants: Joanne J. Ferraro, Marja T. Hiltunen, June Lee, Susan Pfanner

Production Manager: Mary Beth Trimper

External Production Assistant: Marilyn Jackman

Production Supervisor: Laura Bryant

Internal Production Associate: Louise Gagné

Art Director: Arthur Chartow

Keyliner: C. J. Jonik

Special acknowledgment is due to the members of the *Something about the Author Autobiography Series* staff who assisted in the preparation of this volume.

Library of Congress Catalog Card Number 72-27107

ISBN 0-8103-2270-6
ISSN 0276-816X

Printed in the United States

Contents

Introduction ix   **Acknowledgments xv**

Introduction

As the only annually published ongoing reference series that deals with the lives and works of authors and illustrators of children's books, *Something about the Author (SATA)* is a unique source of information. The *SATA* series includes not only well-known authors and illustrators whose books are most widely read, but also those less prominent people whose works are just coming to be recognized. *SATA* is often the only readily available information source for less well-known writers or artists. You'll find *SATA* informative and entertaining whether you are:

> —a student in junior high school (or perhaps one to two grades higher or lower) who needs information for a book report or some other assignment for an English class;

> —a children's librarian who is searching for the answer to yet another question from a young reader or collecting background material to use for a story hour;

> —an English teacher who is drawing up an assignment for your students or gathering information for a book talk;

> —a student in a college of education or library science who is studying children's literature and reference sources in the field;

> —a parent who is looking for a new way to interest your child in reading something more than the school curriculum prescribes;

> —an adult who enjoys children's literature for its own sake, knowing that a good children's book has no age limits.

Scope

In *SATA* you will find detailed information about authors and illustrators who span the full time range of children's literature, from early figures like John Newbery and L. Frank Baum to contemporary figures like Judy Blume and Richard Peck. Authors in the series represent primarily English-speaking countries, particularly the United States, Canada, and the United Kingdom. Also included, however, are authors from around the world whose works are available in English translation, for example: from France, Jean and Laurent De Brunhoff; from Italy, Emanuele Luzzati; from the Netherlands, Jaap ter Haar; from Germany, James Krüss; from Norway, Babbis Friis-Baastad; from Japan, Toshiko Kanzawa; from the Soviet Union, Kornei Chukovsky; from Switzerland, Alois Carigiet, to name only a few. Also appearing in *SATA* are Newbery medalists from Hendrik Van Loon (1922) to Lois Lowry (1990). The writings represented in *SATA* include those created intentionally for children and young adults as well as those written for a general audience and known to interest younger readers. These writings cover the spectrum from picture books, humor, folk and fairy tales, animal stories, mystery and adventure, science fiction and fantasy, historical fiction, poetry and nonsense verse, to drama, biography, and nonfiction.

Information Features

In *SATA* you will find full-length entries that are being presented in the series for the first time. This volume, for example, marks the first full-length appearance of David J. Darling, Paul Frame, J. D. Landis, Cin Forshay-Lunsford, and Mary Riskind.

Obituaries have been included in *SATA* since Volume 20. An Obituary is intended not only as a death notice but also as a concise view of a person's life and work. Obituaries may appear for persons who have entries in earlier *SATA* volumes, as well as for people who have not yet appeared in the series. In this volume Obituaries mark the recent deaths of Robert Bright, Daphne du Maurier, Don Dwiggins, and Noel B. Gerson.

Revised Entries

Since Volume 25, each *SATA* volume also includes newly revised and updated entries for a selection of *SATA* listees (usually four to six) who remain of interest to today's readers and who have been active enough to require extensive revision of their earlier biographies. For example, when Beverly Cleary first appeared in *SATA* Volume 2, she was the author of twenty-one books for children and young adults and the recipient of numerous awards. By the time her updated sketch appeared in Volume 43 (a span of fifteen years), this creator of the indefatigable Ramona Quimby and other memorable characters had produced a dozen new titles and garnered nearly fifty additional awards, including the 1984 Newbery Medal.

The entry for a given biographee may be revised as often as there is substantial new information to provide. In this volume, look for revised entries on Paula Fox, Penelope Lively, Mary Norton, Scott O'Dell, Cyndy Szekeres, and Geoffrey Trease.

Illustrations

While the textual information in *SATA* is its primary reason for existing, photographs and illustrations not only enliven the text but are an integral part of the information that *SATA* provides. Illustrations and text are wedded in such a special way in children's literature that artists and their works naturally occupy a prominent place among *SATA*'s listees. The illustrators that you'll find in the series include such past masters of children's book illustration as Randolph Caldecott, Walter Crane, Arthur Rackham, and Ernest H. Shepard, as well as such noted contemporary artists as Maurice Sendak, Edward Gorey, Tomie de Paola, and Margot Zemach. There are Caldecott medalists from Dorothy Lathrop (the first recipient in 1938) to Ed Young (the latest winner in 1990); cartoonists like Charles Schulz ("Peanuts"), Walt Kelly ("Pogo"), Hank Ketcham ("Dennis the Menace"), and Georges Rémi ("Tintin"); photographers like Jill Krementz, Tana Hoban, Bruce McMillan, and Bruce Curtis; and filmmakers like Walt Disney, Alfred Hitchcock, and Steven Spielberg.

In more than a dozen years of recording the metamorphosis of children's literature from the printed page to other media, *SATA* has become something of a repository of photographs that are unique in themselves and exist nowhere else as a group, particularly many of the classics of motion picture and stage history and photographs that have been specially loaned to us from private collections.

Index Policy

In response to suggestions from librarians, *SATA* indexes no longer appear in each volume but are included in each alternate (odd-numbered) volume of the series, beginning with Volume 58.

SATA continues to include two indexes that cumulate with each alternate volume: the **Illustrations Index,** arranged by the name of the illustrator, gives the number of the volume and page where the illustrator's work appears in the current volume as well as all preceding volumes in the series; the **Author Index** gives the number of the volume in which a person's Biographical Sketch, Brief Entry, or Obituary appears in the current volume as well as all preceding volumes in the series.

These indexes also include references to authors and illustrators who appear in *Yesterday's Authors of Books for Children* (described in detail below). Beginning with Volume 36, the *SATA* Author Index provides cross-references to authors who are included in Gale's *Children's Literature Review.* Starting with Volume 42, you will also find cross-references to authors who are included in the *Something about the Author Autobiography Series* (described in detail below).

What a *SATA* Entry Provides

Whether you're already familiar with the *SATA* series or just getting acquainted, you will want to be aware of the kind of information that an entry provides. In every *SATA* entry the editors attempt to give as complete a picture of the person's life and work as possible. In some cases that full range of information may simply be unavailable, or a biographee may choose not to reveal complete personal details. The information that the editors attempt to provide in every entry is arranged in the following categories:

1. The "head" of the entry gives

    —the most complete form of the name,
    —any part of the name not commonly used, included in parentheses,
    —birth and death dates, if known; a (?) indicates a discrepancy in published sources,
    —pseudonyms or name variants under which the person has had books published or is publicly known, in parentheses in the second line.

2. "Personal" section gives

    —date and place of birth and death,
    —parents' names and occupations,
    —name of spouse, date of marriage, and names of children,
    —educational institutions attended, degrees received, and dates,
    —religious and political affiliations,
    —agent's name and address,
    —home and/or office address.

3. "Career" section gives

    —name of employer, position, and dates for each career post,
    —military service,
    —memberships,
    —awards and honors.

4. "Writings" section gives

    —title, first publisher and date of publication, and illustration information for each book written; revised editions and other significant editions for books with particularly long publishing histories; genre, when known.

5. "Adaptations" section gives

    —title, major performers, producer, and date of all known reworkings of an author's material in another medium, like movies, filmstrips, television, recordings, plays, etc.

6. "Sidelights" section gives

    —commentary on the life or work of the biographee either directly from the person (and often written specifically for the *SATA* entry), or gathered from biographies, diaries, letters, interviews, or other published sources.

7. "For More Information See" section gives

    —books, feature articles, films, plays, and reviews in which the biographee's life or work has been treated.

How a *SATA* Entry Is Compiled

A *SATA* entry progresses through a series of steps. If the biographee is living, the *SATA* editors try to secure information directly from him or her through a questionnaire. From the information that the biographee supplies, the editors prepare an entry, filling in any essential missing details with research. The author or illustrator is then sent a copy of the entry to check for accuracy and completeness.

If the biographee is deceased or cannot be reached by questionnaire, the *SATA* editors examine a wide variety of published sources to gather information for an entry. Biographical sources are searched with the aid of Gale's *Biography and Genealogy Master Index*. Bibliographic sources like the *National Union Catalog*, the *Cumulative Book Index*, *American Book Publishing Record*, and the *British Museum Catalogue* are consulted, as are book reviews, feature articles, published interviews, and material sometimes obtained from the biographee's family, publishers, agent, or other associates.

For each entry presented in *SATA*, the editors also attempt to locate a photograph of the biographee as well as representative illustrations from his or her books. After surveying the available books which the biographee has written and/or illustrated, and then making a selection of appropriate photographs and illustrations, the editors request permission of the current copyright holders to reprint the material. In the case of older books for which the copyright may have passed through several hands, even locating the current copyright holder is often a long and involved process.

We invite you to examine the entire *SATA* series, starting with this volume. Described below are some of the people in Volume 58 that you may find particularly interesting.

Highlights of This Volume

PAUL FRAME......started drawing at the age of five and was strongly influenced by Howard Pyle's illustrations of *King Arthur and the Roundtable.* "I spent a good deal of time copying his pen and ink drawings, and for hours on end played at being King Arthur, Sir Lancelot, Sir Galahad, or any of the legendary characters of the Round Table....Throughout primary school I was a very average pupil always lost in my own dreams. It was not unusual for me to reply to a question I had been asked in class as though I was Sir Lancelot....I've always said that I drew my way through four years of Latin. I filled my notebooks with drawings of Roman fortifications, soldiers, and generals. My Latin teacher was intrigued by the kind of research I put into my drawings to make them as accurate as possible. Those drawings were quite real to me—I was there as far as I was concerned." Having illustrated over 200 children's books, including many Nancy Drew and Hardy Boys stories, Frame has found that in order to illustrate something he must have "a real understanding for the characters or feel a wonderful viral hate for them....If they are not my friends, it shows."

GARRY MARSHALL......was raised in the Bronx where "you were either an athlete or a gangster, or you were funny. We all grew up surrounded by the sense of laughter." Discovering that he was "a mediocre journalist, a mediocre musician, a mediocre actor, a mediocre athlete," Marshall began a career in comedy writing. From "The Odd Couple" to "Happy Days" and "The Flamingo Kid," he has made America laugh. "Funny is funny. On television, in a nightclub, in the theater, movies, no matter where, funny is funny. And the key is the audience. You're funniest when you use the audience. I use the audience as a barometer. I listen to the 300 people, and I can *hear* whether they laugh or don't laugh; so I don't need subjective opinions about what's funny....I've done...over a thousand situation comedies. I can't look you in the eye and say that every one of those episodes was brilliant and perfect. Some *were* perfect. Some were good. Some were pretty good. Some were a little embarrassing—but every piece I've tried to make professional....In the education of the American people, I am Recess. I do Recess well."

SCOTT O'DELL......was born near the turn of the century in Los Angeles, "a frontier town [with] more horses than automobiles, more jack rabbits than people....We turned over every likely rock, looking for small monsters. We thrust our hands down every squirrel and coyote hole in our path. Commonly we found an owl. This was the prize of all prizes....What did we do with this creature of the nocturnal air? We killed it, of course. We wrung its neck....I remember these depredations with horror." O'Dell began his first novel for young people "to say to the young and to all who wish to listen that we have a chance to come into a new relationship to the things around us....*Island of the Blue Dolphins* began in anger, anger at the hunters who invade the mountains where I live and who slaughter everything that creeps or walks or flies. This anger was also directed at myself, at the young man of many years ago, who thoughtlessly committed the same crimes against nature."

FRANK OZ......first learned the art of puppeteering from his parents. Jim Henson spotted seventeen-year-old Oz performing at the National Puppetry Festival and invited him to New York to join the crew of the Muppets. Originator of Fozzie Bear, Animal, Sam Eagle, Cookie Monster, Bert, and Grover, Oz is best known for his kinship with the legendary Ms. Piggy, a pig whom Oz considers "a character...not a caricature. She's full of complexities....She wants to have children, but at the same time she doesn't want to give up her career. Let's face it. She's a woman alone. She's not very attractive. She has an obsession with this frog....She wants her frog and her career. She's torn, like everyone else." After years of performing, Oz began directing Muppet feature films and has since directed a number of comedies including *Little Shop of Horrors.* He believes strongly in the importance of laughter: "You can always get a laugh....because you can always drop your pants and get a laugh....I'm not interested in just getting laughs. I want the *quality* of the laughs to be right."

CYNDY SZEKERES......grew up toward the end of the Depression when "treasures were not things that could be bought—they were made from things that ignited our imagination. Making 'secrets' meant going out in the woods, pulling up a tuft of grass and laying out flowers in a pattern, covering it with broken glass, making a picture, and then covering it up again with the grass. A 'best friend's gift' was to let her know your 'secret.'...Going into the woods was for us better than a trip to Tiffany's....The woods are vital to my work....In the winter, I bring inside frozen patches of leaves and bark. It thaws in the house, then the small creatures hibernating gradually awaken all over the studio." Szekeres can't remember a time when she didn't draw, when nature didn't affect her life. "It was a fascination with what I saw—simple things: flowers, grass, fog—the variety of details and differences in animals and people." She considers illustrating a form of communication, and "to communicate, one must have something to say and know one's audience. Achieving this end is about as complicated and difficult as qualifying for the cutting end of brain surgery....The learning never stops."

ERNEST THAYER......"was never a baseball fan," and considered his famous ballad, "Casey at the Bat," no better than the "large quantity of nonsense" he put out while with the *San Francisco Examiner*. "The poem has no basis in fact. The only Casey actually involved...was not a ball player. He was a big, dour Irish lad of my high school days." When "Casey" was first published by the *Examiner* in 1888, Thayer's byline read simply "E.L.T." and as a result many tried to claim authorship following actor De Wolf Hopper's acclaimed rendition of the poem. "The claimants to the authorship of "Casey" multiply through the years, and I am getting a little tired of the subject. I have heard of as many as three in as many weeks....It would be hard to say, all things considered, if it has given me more pleasure than annoyance. The constant wrangling about the authorship, from which I have tried to keep aloof, has certainly filled me with disgust." Considered an authentic American masterpiece, "Casey" is the only piece of Thayer's work that has not fallen into obscurity.

These are only a few of the authors and illustrators that you'll find in this volume. We hope you find all the entries in *SATA* both interesting and useful.

Yesterday's Authors of Books for Children

In a two-volume companion set to *SATA, Yesterday's Authors of Books for Children (YABC)* focuses on early authors and illustrators, from the beginnings of children's literature through 1960, whose books are still being read by children today. Here you will find "old favorites" like Hans Christian Andersen, J. M. Barrie, Kenneth Grahame, Betty MacDonald, A. A. Milne, Beatrix Potter, Samuel Clemens, Kate Greenaway, Rudyard Kipling, Robert Louis Stevenson, and many more.

Similar in format to *SATA, YABC* features bio-bibliographical entries that are divided into information categories such as Personal, Career, Writings, and Sidelights. The entries are further enhanced by book illustrations, author photos, movie stills, and many rare old photographs.

In Volume 2 you will find cumulative indexes to the authors and to the illustrations that appear in *YABC*. These listings can also be located in the *SATA* cumulative indexes.

By exploring both volumes of *YABC*, you will discover a special group of more than seventy authors and illustrators who represent some of the best in children's literature—individuals whose timeless works continue to delight children and adults of all ages. Other authors and illustrators from early children's literature are listed in *SATA*, starting with Volume 15.

Something about the Author Autobiography Series

You can complement the information in *SATA* with the *Something about the Author Autobiography Series (SAAS)*, which provides autobiographical essays written by important current authors and illustrators of books for children and young adults. In every volume of *SAAS* you will find about twenty specially commissioned autobiographies, each accompanied by a selection of personal photographs supplied by the authors. The wide range of contemporary writers and artists who describe their lives and interests in the *Autobiography Series* includes Joan Aiken, Betsy Byars, Leonard Everett Fisher, Milton Meltzer, Maia Wojciechowska, and Jane Yolen, among others. Though the information presented in the autobiographies is as varied and unique as the authors, you can learn about the people and events that influenced these writers' early lives, how they began their careers, what problems they faced in becoming established in their professions, what prompted them to write or illustrate particular books, what they now find most challenging or rewarding in their lives, and what advice they may have for young people interested in following in their footsteps, among many other subjects.

Autobiographies included in the *SATA Autobiography Series* can be located through both the *SATA* cumulative index and the *SAAS* cumulative index, which lists not only the authors' names but also the subjects mentioned in their essays, such as titles of works and geographical and personal names.

The *SATA Autobiography Series* gives you the opportunity to view "close up" some of the fascinating people who are included in the *SATA* parent series. The combined *SATA* series makes available to you an unequaled range of comprehensive and in-depth information about the authors and illustrators of young people's literature.

Please write and tell us if we can make *SATA* even more helpful to you.

Acknowledgments

Grateful acknowledgment is made to the following publishers, authors, and artists for their kind permission to reproduce copyrighted material.

ARBOR HOUSE PUBLISHING CO. Jacket illustration by George Barr from *Countersolar!* by Richard A. Lupoff. Copyright © 1987 by Richard A. Lupoff. Reprinted by permission of Arbor House Publishing Co.

ARO PUBLISHING CO. Illustration by Bob Reese from *Bubba Bear* by Bob Reese. Copyright © 1986 by Aro Publishing Co. Reprinted by permission of Aro Publishing Co.

ASHTON SCHOLASTIC PTY, INC. Illustration by Pamela Lofts from *Wombat Stew* by Marcia K. Vaughan. Copyright © 1984 by Marcia Vaughan. Reprinted by permission of Ashton Scholastic Pty, Inc.

ATHENEUM PUBLISHERS. Illustration by Cheng Mung Yun from *Heaven's Reward* by Catherine Edwards Sadler. Text copyright © 1985 by Catherine Edwards Sadler. Illustrations copyright © 1985 by Cheng Mung Yun./ Jacket illustration by Steve Senn from *Spacebread* by Steve Senn. Copyright © 1981 by Steve Senn./ Jacket illustration by Gros from *Napoleon/* by Manfred Weidhorn. Text copyright © 1986 by Manfred Weidhorn. Jacket design copyright © 1986 by Marilyn Marcus. All reprinted by permission of Atheneum Publishers.

BALLANTINE/DEL REY/FAWCETT BOOKS. Cover illustration by Darrell K. Sweet from *The Last Unicorn* by Peter S. Beagle. Copyright © 1968 by Peter S. Beagle./ Cover painting by Barclay Shaw from *The Folk of the Air* by Peter S. Beagle. Copyright © 1977, 1986 by Peter S. Beagle. Both reprinted by permission of Ballantine/Del Rey/Fawcett Books.

BRADBURY PRESS. Illustration by Paul Giovanopoulos from *How Many Miles to Babylon?* by Paula Fox. Copyright © 1967 by David White Co./ Illustration by Eros Keith from *The King's Falcon* by Paula Fox. Text copyright © 1969 by Paula Fox. Illustrations copyright © 1969 by Eros Keith./ Illustration by Arnold Lobel from *Good Ethan* by Paula Fox. Text copyright © 1973 by Paula Fox. Illustrations copyright © 1973 by Arnold Lobel./ Illustration by Rosemary Wells from *Hungry Fred* by Paula Fox. Text copyright © 1969 by Paula Fox. Illustrations copyright © 1969 by Rosemary Wells. All reprinted by permission of Bradbury Press.

CHIVERS PRESS. Jacket illustration by Malcolm Stokes from *Moon Tiger* by Penelope Lively. Copyright © 1987 by Penelope Lively. Reprinted by permission of Chivers Press.

COWARD-McCANN, INC. Illustration by Wallace Tripp from *Casey at the Bat: A Ballad of the Republic, Sung in the Year 1888* by Ernest Lawrence Thayer. Illustrations copyright © 1978 by Wallace Tripp. Reprinted by permission of Coward-McCann, Inc.

THOMAS Y. CROWELL. Illustration by Jerry Pinkney and Sidelight excerpts from *Childtimes: A Three-Generation Memoir* by Eloise Greenfield and Lessie Jones Little. Copyright © 1979 by Eloise Greenfield and Lessie Jones Little. Copyright © 1971 by Pattie Ridley Jones./ Illustration by Carole Byard from *I Can Do It by Myself* by Lessie Jones Little and Eloise Greenfield. Text copyright © 1978 by Lessie Jones Little and Eloise Greenfield. Illustrations copyright © 1978 by Carole Byard. All reprinted by permission of Thomas Y. Crowell.

DANDELION PRESS. Illustration by Paul Frame from *Horses* by Ruby E. McCreight. Reprinted by permission of Dandelion Press.

DELACORTE PRESS. Jacket illustration by Frank Morris from *Walk through Cold Fire* by Cin Forshay-Lunsford. Text copyright © 1985 by Cin Forshay-Lunsford. Illustrations copyright © 1985 by Frank Morris. Reprinted by permission of Delacorte Press.

J. M. DENT & SONS LTD. Sidelight excerpts from *Quite Early One Morning,* edited by Paul Ferris. Reprinted by permission of J. M. Dent & Sons Ltd.

DODD, MEAD & CO. Illustration by Susan Swan from *The Case of the Horrible Swamp Monster* by Drew Stevenson. Text copyright © 1984 by Drew Stevenson. Illustrations copyright © 1984 by Susan Swan. Reprinted by permission of Dodd, Mead & Co.

E. P. DUTTON. Illustration by Bert Dodson from *Nelson Malone Meets the Man from Mush-Nut* by Louise Hawes. Text copyright © 1986 by Louise Hawes. Illustrations copyright © 1986 by Bert Dodson./ Illustration by Antony Maitland from *The Ghost of Thomas Kempe* by Penelope Lively. Text copyright © 1973 by Penelope Lively. Illustrations copyright © 1973 by William Heinemann Ltd./ Jacket illustration by Larry Ross from *Uninvited Ghosts* by Penelope Lively. Copyright © 1974, 1977, 1981, 1984 by Penelope Lively./ Illustration by David Parkins from *A House Inside Out* by Penelope Lively. Text copyright © 1987 by Penelope Lively. Illustrations copyright © 1987 by David Parkins./ Jacket illustration by Richard Cuffari from *Going Back* by Penelope Lively. Copyright © 1975 by Penelope Lively./ Jacket illustration by David K. Stone from *The Driftway* by Penelope Lively. Copyright © 1972 by Penelope Lively./ Illustration by Anita Lobel from *Fanny's Sister* by Penelope Lively. Illustrations copyright © 1976 by Penelope Lively. Illustration copyright © by Anita Lobel./ Illustration by Chris Molan from *Hidden Treasures* by Geoffrey Trease. Text copyright © 1989 by Geoffrey Trease. Illustrations copyright © 1989 by Chris Molan. All reprinted by permission of E. P. Dutton.

FARRAR, STRAUS & GIROUX, INC. Jacket illustration by Robert Sabin from *A Place Apart* by Paula Fox. Copyright © 1980 by Paula Fox. Reprinted by permission of Farrar, Straus & Giroux, Inc.

FIVE OWLS PRESS LTD. Sidelight excerpts from *Children's Book Review*, winter, 1974-1975 by C. S. Hannabuss. Reprinted by permission of Five Owls Press Ltd.

FOUR WINDS PRESS. Illustration by Cyndy Szekeres from *The 329th Friend* by Marjorie Weinman Sharmat. Text copyright © 1979 by Marjorie Weinman Sharmat. Illustrations copyright © 1979 by Cyndy Szekeres. Reprinted by permission of Four Winds Press.

DAVID R. GODINE, PUBLISHERS, INC. Illustration by Barry Moser from *Casey at the Bat* by Ernest Lawrence Thayer./ Illustration by Edward Ardizzone from *A Child's Christmas in Wales* by Dylan Thomas. Text copyright 1954 by New Directions. Illustrations copyright © 1978 by Edward Ardizzone. Both reprinted by permission of David R. Godine, Publishers, Inc.

GREENWILLOW BOOKS. Illustration by Yossi Abolafia from *Poems* by Jack Prelutsky. Text copyright © 1985 by Jack Prelutsky. Illustrations copyright © 1985 by Yossi Abolafia. Reprinted by permission of Greenwillow Books.

HARCOURT BRACE JOVANOVICH, INC. Illustration by Erik Blegvad from *Bed-Knob and Broomstick* by Mary Norton. Copyright 1943, © 1957, 1971 by Mary Norton./ Illustrations by Beth and Joe Krush from *The Borrowers* by Mary Norton. Text copyright 1953 © 1981 by Mary Norton. Illustrations copyright © 1981 by Beth Krush and Joe Krush./ Illustration by Beth and Joe Krush from *The Borrowers Afield* by Mary Norton. Text copyright © 1955, 1983 by Mary Norton./ Illustration by Beth and Joe Krush from *The Borrowers Avenged* by Mary Norton. Text copyright © 1982 by Mary Norton. Illustrations copyright © 1982 by Beth and Joe Krush./ Illustration by Beth and Joe Krush from *Poor Stainless* by Mary Norton. Text copyright © 1966 by Hamish Hamilton Ltd. Illustrations copyright © 1971 by Harcourt Brace Jovanovich, Inc./ Sidelight excerpts from Introduction to *The Complete Adventures of the Borrowers* by Mary Norton. Copyright © 1967 by Harcourt Brace Jovanovich, Inc./ Sidelight excerpts from *Fiction! Interviews with Northern California Novelists* by Dan Tooker and Roger Hofheins. Copyright © 1972 by Harcourt Brace Jovanovich, Inc. All reprinted by permission of Harcourt Brace Jovanovich, Inc.

HARPER & ROW, PUBLISHERS, INC. Illustration by Arnold Lobel from *The Devil and Mother Crump* by Valerie Scho Carey. Text copyright © 1987 by Valerie Scho Carey. Illustrations copyright © 1987 by Arnold Lobel. Reprinted by permission of Harper & Row, Publishers, Inc.

HEADLINE BOOK PUBLISHING. Cover illustration by Neil Pinkett from *The Folk of the Air* by Peter S. Beagle. Copyright © 1977, 1986 by Peter S. Beagle. Reprinted by permission of Headline Book Publishing.

D. C. HEATH & CO. Sidelight excerpts from *The Story of the McGuffeys* by Alice McGuffey Ruggles./ Sidelight excerpts from *William Holmes McGuffey and His Readers* by Harvey C. Minnich. Both reprinted by permission of D. C. Heath & Co.

HODDER & STOUGHTON LTD. Cover illustration by Adrienne Kennaway from *Awkward Aardvark* by Mwalimu. Text copyright © 1989 by Peter Upton. Illustrations copyright © 1989 by Adrienne Kennaway. Reprinted by permission of Hodder & Stoughton Ltd.

HOLIDAY HOUSE, INC. Illustration by Trina Schart Hyman from *A Child's Christmas in Wales* by Dylan Thomas. Text copyright 1954 by New Directions. Illustrations copyright © 1985 by Trina Schart Hyman. Reprinted by permission of Holiday House, Inc.

HENRY HOLT & CO. Photograph by John E. Barrett from *Miss Piggy's Treasury of Art Masterpieces from the Kermitage Collection* by Henry Beard. Copyright © 1982, 1983, 1984 by Henson Associates, Inc./ Sidelight excerpts from *Caitlin: Life with Dylan Thomas* by Caitlin Thomas with George Tremlett./ Cover illustration by Daniel Maffia from *Catch a Fire: The Life of Bob Marley* by Timothy White. Copyright © 1983 by Timothy White. Cover illustration copyright © 1983 by Daniel Maffia. All reprinted by permission of Henry Holt & Co.

THE HORN BOOK, INC. Sidelight excerpts from *Illustrators of Children's Books: 1967-1976,* compiled by Lee Kingman and others. Copyright © 1978 by The Horn Book, Inc./ Sidelight excerpts from *Newbery and Caldecott Medal Winners: 1966-1975,* edited by Lee Kingman. Both reprinted by permission of The Horn Book, Inc.

HOUGHTON MIFFLIN CO. Illustration by Milton Johnson from *The Black Pearl* by Scott O'Dell. Copyright © 1967 by Scott O'Dell./ Jacket illustration from *Zia* by Scott O'Dell. Copyright © 1976 by Scott O'Dell./ Jacket illustration by Evaline Ness from *Island of the Blue Dolphins* by Scott O'Dell. Copyright © 1960 by Scott O'Dell./ Illustration by Lynd Ward from *The Treasure of Topo-El-Bampo* by Scott O'Dell. Text copyright © 1972 by Scott O'Dell. Illustrations copyright © 1972 by Lynd Ward./ Jacket illustration by Arvis Stewart from *The Hawk That Dare Not Hunt by Day* by Scott O'Dell. Copyright © 1975 by Scott O'Dell./ Jacket illustration by Ted Lewin from *Alexandra* by Scott O'Dell. Text copyright © 1984 by Scott O'Dell. Jacket illustration copyright © 1985 by Ted Lewin./ Jacket illustration by Ted Lewin from *Sarah Bishop* by Scott O'Dell. Copyright © 1980 by Scott O'Dell./ Jacket illustration by Ted Lewin from *Streams to the River, River to the Sea* by Scott O'Dell. Text copyright © 1986 by Scott O'Dell. Jacket illustration copyright © 1986 by Ted Lewin./ Jacket illustration by Julie Downing from *Follow That Mom!* by Mary Riskind. Text copyright © 1987 by Mary Riskind. Jacket illustration copyright © 1987 by Julie Downing./ Jacket illustration by James Shefcik from *Wildcat Summer* by Mary Riskind. Text copyright © 1985 by Mary L. Riskind. Jacket illustration copyright © 1985 by James Shefcik. All reprinted by permission of Houghton Mifflin Co.

HUMAN SCIENCES PRESS, INC. Sidelight excerpts from an article "Fifty Years On: A Writer Looks Back," by Geoffrey Trease, autumn, 1983 in *Children's Literature in Education,* Volume 14, number 3. Reprinted by permission of Human Sciences Press, Inc.

MICHAEL JOSEPH LTD. Sidelight excerpts from *Dylan Thomas: Poet of His People* by Andrew Sinclair. Reprinted by permission of Michael Joseph Ltd.

ALFRED A. KNOPF, INC. Illustration by Allen Atkinson from *The Velveteen Rabbit* by Margery Williams. Copyright © 1983 by Armand Eisen. Reprinted by permission of Alfred A. Knopf, Inc.

LADYBIRD BOOKS LTD. Illustration by Kathie Layfield from *All in a Day,* poems selected by Kaye Webb. Copyright © 1985 by Ladybird Books Ltd. Reprinted by permission of Ladybird Books Ltd.

DAVID S. LAKE PUBLISHERS. Cover illustration by Sara Boore from *The Cardiff Hill Mystery* by Janet Lorimer. Copyright © 1988 by David S. Lake Publishers. Reprinted by permission of David S. Lake Publishers.

LERNER PUBLICATIONS CO. Photograph by Tom Moran from *Kite Flying Is for Me* by Tom Moran. Copyright © 1984 by Lerner Publications Co. Reprinted by permission of Lerner Publications Co.

J. B. LIPPINCOTT. Illustrations by Vo-Dinh Mai from *The Brocaded Slipper and Other Vietnamese Tales* by Lynette Dyer Vuong. Text copyright © 1982 by Lynette Dyer Vuong. Illustrations copyright © 1982 by Vo-Dinh Mai./ Illustration by Jenny Williams from *The Boy with Two Shadows* by Margaret Mahy. Text copyright © 1971, 1987 by Margaret Mahy. Illustrations © 1987 by Jenny Williams. All reprinted by permission of J. B. Lippincott.

LITTLE, BROWN & CO., INC. Jacket illustration by Ted Lewin from *Pets* by Frances Chrystie. Copyright 1953, © 1964, 1974 by Frances N. Chrystie./ Illustration by Adrienne Kennaway from *Crafty Chameleon* by Mwenye Hadithi. Copyright © 1987 by Bruce Hobson and Adrienne Kennaway. Both reprinted by permission of Little, Brown & Co., Inc.

LONE EAGLE PUBLISHING CO. Sidelight excerpts "From the Director's Chair" by Michael Singer in *1987 5th Annual International Edition of Film Directors: A Complete Guide.* Reprinted by permission of Lone Eagle Publishing Co.

THE MACMILLAN PRESS. Sidelight excerpts from *A Whiff of Burnt Boats* by Geoffrey Trease. Reprinted by permission of The Macmillan Press.

MACMILLAN PUBLISHING CO. Illustration by Eric Stemp from *A Flight of Angels* by Geoffrey Trease. Copyright © 1988 by Geoffrey Trease./ Jacket illustration by Linda Benson from *It's About Time* by Bernal C. Payne, Jr. Text copyright © 1984 by Bernal C. Payne, Jr. and Macmillan Publishing Co. Jacket illustration copyright © 1983 by Linda Benson./ Cover illustration by Ellen Thompson from *Blowfish Live in the Sea* by Paula Fox. Copyright © 1970 by Paula Fox. Cover illustration copyright © 1986 by Ellen Thompson./ Illustration by Ingrid Fetz from *Maurice's Room* by Paula Fox. Copyright © 1966 by Paula Fox and Macmillan Publishing Co./ Illustration by Paul Frame from *Sara and the Winter Gift* by M. E. Mason./ Illustration by Paul Frame from *Key to the Treasure* by Peggy Parish. All reprinted by permission of Macmillan Publishing Co.

McGRAW-HILL, INC. Illustration by Cyndy Szekeres from *Long Ago* by Cyndy Szekeres. Copyright © 1977 by Cyndy Szekeres. Reprinted by permission of McGraw-Hill, Inc.

WILLIAM MORROW & CO. Jacket illustration by Michael and Peggy Garland from *Crazy Quilt* by Jocelyn Riley. Text copyright © 1984 by Jocelyn Riley. Jacket illustration copyright © 1984 by Michael and Peggy Garland. Reprinted by permission of William Morrow & Co.

NEW DIRECTIONS PUBLISHING CORP. Illustration by Ellen Raskin from *A Child's Christmas in Wales* by Dylan Thomas. Copyright 1954 by New Directions Publishing Corp./ Illustration by Fritz Eichenberg from *A Child's Christmas in Wales* by Dylan Thomas. Both reprinted by permission of New Directions Publishing Corp.

PADDINGTON PRESS. Sidelight excerpts from *The Pied Pipers: Interviews with the Influential Creators of Children's Literature* by Justin Wintle and Emma Fisher. Reprinted by permission of Paddington Press.

THE PUTNAM PUBLISHING GROUP INC. Jacket illustration by Toby Gowing from *The Elephant Man* by Frederick Drimmer. Copyright © 1985 by Frederick Drimmer. Reprinted by permission of The Putnam Publishing Group Inc.

SOUVENIR PRESS. Jacket illustration by I. Bite from *The Fantasy Worlds of Peter Beagle* by Peter Beagle. Copyright © 1960, 1963, 1974, 1978 by Peter S. Beagle. Reprinted by permission of Souvenir Press.

UNIVERSITY OF CHICAGO PRESS. Sidelight excerpts from *The Annotated Casey at the Bat: A Collection of Ballads about the Mighty Casey* by Martin Gardner. Reprinted by permission of University of Chicago Press.

VANGUARD PRESS, INC. Illustration by William Stobbs from *The White Nights of St. Petersburg* by Geoffrey Trease. Copyright © 1967 by Geoffrey Trease./ Jacket illustration by Louis Slobodkin from *A Thousand for Sicily* by Geoffrey Trease. Copyright © 1964 by Geoffrey Trease./ Jacket illustration by Rethi from *Victory at Valmy* by Geoffrey Trease. Copyright © 1960 by Geoffrey Trease./ Illustration by Rus from *Message to Hadrian* by Geoffrey Trease. Copyright 1955 by Geoffrey Trease. All reprinted by permission of Vanguard Press, Inc.

VAN NOSTRAND REINHOLD CO., INC. Sidelight excerpts from *The Annotated McGuffey: Selections from the McGuffey Eclectic Readers, 1836-1920* by Stanley W. Lindberg. Reprinted by permission of Van Nostrand Reinhold Co., Inc.

VIKING PENGUIN, INC. Jacket illustration by Mel Williamson from *The Last Unicorn* by Peter S. Beagle. New Introduction by Jean Tobin. Text copyright © 1968 by Peter S. Beagle. Introduction copyright © by Jean Tobin./ Cover illustration by Val Biro from *Cue for Treason* by Geoffrey Trease. Copyright 1940 by Geoffrey Trease./ Cover illustration by Antony Maitland from *I Like This Poem,* edited by Kaye Webb. Copyright © 1979 by Puffin Club. All reprinted by permission of Viking Penguin, Inc.

FRANKLIN WATTS, INC. Illustration by Leonard Everett Fisher from *Casey at the Bat* by Ernest Lawrence Thayer. Illustrations copyright © 1964 by Franklin Watts, Inc.

WESTERN PUBLISHING CO., INC. Illustration by Cyndy Szekeres from *Book of Fairy Tales,* adapted by Cyndy Szekeres. Copyright © 1988 Cyndy Szekeres./ Illustration by Cyndy Szekeres from *Hide-and-Seek Duck* by Cyndy Szekeres. Copyright © 1985 Cyndy Szekeres./ Illustration by Cyndy Szekeres from *The Night before Christmas* by Clement C. Moore. Text copyright © 1982 by Western Publishing Co., Inc. Illustrations copyright © 1982, 1985 by Cyndy Szekeres. All reprinted by permission of Western Publishing Co., Inc.

WHITMAN PUBLISHING CO. Illustration by Paul Frame from *The Adventures of Tom Sawyer* by Mark Twain. Copyright © 1955 by Whitman Publishing Co./ Illustration by Paul Frame from *The Adventures of Huckleberry Finn* by Mark Twain. Copyright 1949, 1951 by Whitman Publishing Co. Both reprinted by permission of Whitman Publishing Co.

Illustration by *Alton Telegraph* in *Born Different: Amazing Stories of Very Special People* by Frederick Drimmer. Copyright © 1988 by Frederick Drimmer. Reprinted by permission of *Alton Telegraph.*/ Sidelight excerpts from *The California Feeling* by Peter S. Beagle. Copyright © 1969 by Peter Beagle. Reprinted by permission of Peter S. Beagle./ Sidelight excerpts from an article "Penelope Lively," in *Publisher's Weekly.* Copyright © 1988 by R. R. Bowker Co. Reprinted by permission of R. R. Bowker Co./ Sidelight excerpts from an article "Garry Marshall: Television's Man with the Midas Touch Turns to Film," by Tom Hinckley, August, 1987 in *Cable Guide.* Reprinted by permission of *Cable Guide.*/ Sidelight excerpts from an article "On Being Man of the House," by Peter S. Beagle, December, 1966 in *The Saturday Evening Post.* Reprinted by permission of Curtis Publishing Co./ Sidelight excerpts from an article "A Childhood of Sermons and Sonnets," by Paula Fox, July 12, 1981 in *New York Times Book Review.* Reprinted by permission of Paula Fox./ Photograph of Ernest L. Thayer's graduation portrait, 1885. Courtesy of Harvard University Archives. Reprinted by permission of Harvard University Archives.

Sidelight excerpts from an article "Goodbye to the Bronx," by Peter S. Beagle, December, 1964 in *Holiday.* Reprinted by permission of *Holiday.*/ Sidelight excerpts from an article "My Last Heroes," by P. S. Beagle, August, 1965 in *Holiday.* Reprinted by permission of *Holiday.*/ Sidelight excerpts from an article "Children and the Art of Memory, Part I," by Penelope Lively, February, 1978 in *The Horn Book Magazine.* Reprinted by permission of The Horn Book, Inc./ Sidelight excerpts from an article "Newbery Award Acceptance," by Scott O'Dell, August, 1961 in *The Horn Book Magazine.* Reprinted by permission of The Horn Book, Inc./ Sidelight excerpts from an article "On Desperate Characters," by Irving Howe, April 19, 1980 in *New Republic.* Reprinted by permission of *New Republic.*/ Sidelight excerpts from an article "Books," September 27, 1976 in *Newsweek.* Reprinted by permission of *Newsweek.*/ Sidelight excerpts from an article "E. L. Thayer Dead; Author of 'Casey,'" August 22, 1940 in *New York Times.* Reprinted by permission of *New York Times.*/ Sidelight excerpts from an article "Acceptance Speech: Hans Christian Andersen Award," by Scott O'Dell, October, 1972 in *Horn Book Magazine.* Reprinted by permission of Scott O'Dell.

Sidelight excerpts from an article "Caricature: Frank Oz," by Ted Salter, March/April, 1981 in *Puppetry Journal.* Reprinted by permission of *Puppetry Journal.*/ Sidelight excerpts from an article "Of Puppets and People," by Paul Scanlon, February 3, 1983 in *Rolling Stone.* Reprinted by permission of *Rolling Stone.*/ Sidelight excerpts from an article "Muppets' Frank Oz Takes on 'Horrors,'" December 19, 1986 in *St. Louis Post Dispatch.* Reprinted by permission of *St. Louis Post Dispatch.*/ Sidelight excerpts from an article "Frank Oz: The Man beneath Yoda, behind Miss Piggy, and Slightly to the Left of Fozzie Bear," by David Hutchinson, July, 1984 in *Starlog.* Reprinted by permission of *Starlog.*/ Sidelight excerpts from an article "Frank Oz: 'Little Shop of Horrors,'" by Randy Lofficier and Jean-Marc Lofficier, April, 1987 in *Starlog.* Reprinted by permission of *Starlog.*/ Sidelight excerpts from an article "Kids and Kinkajous: The Special Blessings of Growing Up with Animals," by Peter S. Beagle, October, 1974 in *Today's Health.* Reprinted by permission of *Today's Health.*/ Sidelight excerpts from an article "There's More to Miss Piggy Than Meets the Eye!" by Edwin Miller, November, 1980 in *Seventeen.* Copyright © 1980 by Triangle Communications, Inc. Reprinted by permission of Triangle Communications, Inc./ Sidelight excerpts from *McGuffey and His Readers: Piety, Morality, and Education in Nineteenth-Century America* by John H. Westerhoff III. Reprinted by permission of John H. Westerhoff III.

PHOTOGRAPH CREDITS

Peter Beagle: copyright © 1986 by Andy Hagara; Gilbert Cross: Dick Schwarze; Paula Fox: copyright © 1984 by Thomas Victor; Penelope Lively: copyright © 1967 by Tara Heinemann; Elsie McCutcheon: Bury Free Press; Mary Norton: Cathy Courtney; Jocelyn Riley: Jeffrey Steete; Cyndy Szekeres: Marc Prozzo, 1981; Marcia Vaughan: Richard Vaughan; Marilyn Waniek: LSU Press; Nell Wise Wechter: Martin's Studio; Timothy White: Westwood One Radio Networks; Jack Ziegler: copyright © 1987 by Anne Hall.

Appreciation to the Performing Arts Research Center of New York Public Library at Lincoln Center for permission to reprint the program cover for "The Broken Banjo" and the still from "Under Milk Wood."

SOMETHING ABOUT THE AUTHOR

ABOLAFIA, Yossi 1944-

PERSONAL: Born June 4, 1944, in Tiberias, Israel; son of Jacob (a shopkeeper) and Aliza (a housewife; maiden name, Simana) Abolafia; married Irit Eliav (a lawyer), July 10, 1972; children: Michal, Tal, Itamar. *Education:* Attended Bezalel Academy of Arts and Design, Jerusalem, 1961-65. *Religion:* Jewish. *Studio:* 6 Hakarmel St., Jerusalem 94309, Israel. *Office:* c/o Greenwillow Books, 105 Madison Ave., New York, N.Y. 10016.

CAREER: Israeli Television Authority, Jerusalem, Israel, writer, editor, actor, on-camera political cartoonist, contributor to children's programs, 1968-76, 1978-80; Canadian Broadcasting Corporation, Toronto, Ontario, animation director, 1976; National Film Board of Canada, Montreal, Quebec, director of animation, 1977-78, 1980-84; author and illustrator, 1983—. *Awards, honors:* American Israel Cultural Foundation Fellowship, 1976; *Harry's Mom* and *My Parents Think I'm Sleeping* were both selected one of Child Study Association of America's Children's Books of the Year, 1986, and *Aviva's Piano,* 1987.

WRITINGS:

ALL SELF-ILLUSTRATED

My Three Uncles, Greenwillow, 1985, large print edition, 1985.
Yanosh's Island, Greenwillow, 1987.
A Fish for Mrs. Gardenia, Greenwillow, 1988.
Fox Tale, Greenwillow, 1989.

ILLUSTRATOR

Charlotte Pomerantz, *Buffy and Albert,* Greenwillow, 1982.
Jack Prelutsky, *It's Valentine's Day,* Greenwillow, 1983, large print edition, 1983.
Barbara Ann Porte, *Harry's Visit* (ALA Notable Book; Junior Literary Guild selection), Greenwillow, 1983.

B. A. Porte, *Harry's Dog* (ALA Notable Book; Junior Literary Guild selection), Greenwillow, 1984.
J. Prelutsky, *What I Did Last Summer* (poems), Greenwillow, 1984.
B. A. Porte, *Harry's Mom,* Greenwillow, 1985.
J. Prelutsky, *My Parents Think I'm Sleeping* (poems), Greenwillow, 1985.
Miriam Chaikin, *Aviva's Piano,* Clarion, 1986.
Susan Love Whitlock, *Donovan Scares the Monsters,* Greenwillow, 1987.
Franz Brandenberg, *Leo and Emily's Zoo,* Greenwillow, 1988.
SuAnn Kiser and Kevin Kiser, *The Birthday Thing,* Greenwillow, 1989.
B. Porte, *Harry in Trouble,* Greenwillow, 1989.

SIDELIGHTS: "I never thought I'd write and illustrate books. I always wanted to be a pilot. Until this day, when I doodle, I doodle planes. All kinds.

"I was born in Tiberias, on the Sea of Galilee, where I attended school. But mostly I doodled. My older sister, Chana, collected some drawings of mine and took them to a local artist—Mira Laufer. She expressed a desire to teach me drawing, and so, one afternoon, I found myself in her living room, staring at a vase full of flowers. Still-life drawing doesn't appeal to me now, and it didn't much then. The minute she left the room, I climbed out of the living room window, and ran for my life.

"I wasn't particularly successful where school was concerned, but in the middle of high school, I transferred to a Kibbutz. It was there, on the banks of the Jordan River, that I started to take my drawing more seriously. As I recall, two things affected my development there. The first was being put in charge of illustrating and designing the school's monthly paper. The second was Beefsteak. Beefsteak was a mule. Being an agricultural school, we had a large vegetable garden which supplied us with a good

(From *My Parents Think I'm Sleeping* by Jack Prelutsky. Illustrated by Yossi Abolafia.)

portion of our food. The students were in charge of picking them; Beefsteak was in charge of carting them; I was in charge of Beefsteak.

"It was a beautiful period in my life. I'd always been small, and in one year on the Kibbutz, I grew five inches taller.

"At the age of seventeen, I was accepted to the Bezalel Art Academy, where I studied graphic design for the next four years. It was after that, during my three years of army service, that I began to do illustrations and cartoons for the army news magazine. On occasion, I was sent on assignment, to cover stories—mostly humorous—on army life.

"It was clear in my mind that I would work in cartooning and illustration. There was one specific medium that fascinated and excited me—animation—where cartoons come to life.

"In those days, believe it or not, there was no television in Israel. Finally, in 1968, when the Israel Television Authority was born, I got my chance. I was hired as a cartoonist for the News Program, and took immediately to experimenting with animation. Since no one knew much about it then, they were overjoyed with my experiments, and luckily for me, most everything I did was aired. Even an animated weather report!

"For the next few years, I worked in Israel as an animator. In 1974 I was approached by Keter Books, an Israeli publishing house, who figured that if I could amuse adults with my drawings—children might enjoy them in books written *for* children. And so, alongside my work as an animator, which brought me to Canada and the United States. I began to illustrate other people's stories. It was Susan Hirshman, the chief editor of Greenwillow, who first suggested that I write my own stories. I protested, explaining that since Hebrew is my mother tongue, I was not really equipped to write stories in English. She insisted that there were stories hidden inside the illustrations, and that what I thought was a language problem was no big deal. (Since then, my English has gotten progressively better.)

"My time and energies are divided between writing and illustrating children's books in Israel and in New York, creating and drawing comic strips for Israeli newspapers, and most importantly, my three children and lovely wife."

ADAMS, Barbara Johnston 1943-
(Barbara Shiels)

PERSONAL: Born August 24, 1943, in Bronxville, N.Y.; daughter of Robert Cossin (a civil engineer) and Charlotte (a homemaker; maiden name, Shiels) Johnston; married Lawrence C. Adams (a telecommunications engineer), December 17, 1966; children: Hilary Shiels. *Education:* Connecticut College, B.A. (with honors), 1965. *Agent and office:* Ann Tobias, 307 South Carolina Ave. S.E., Washington, D.C. 20003.

CAREER: Appleton-Century-Crofts (publisher), New York, N.Y., staff editor, 1965-66; World Publishing Co., New York, N.Y., editorial assistant, 1967; University of Maryland, College Park, Md., faculty research assistant, 1967-69; Young Womens Christian Association, Washington, D.C., director of public relations, 1969-71; Goetz Printing Co., Washington, D.C., marketing representative, 1971-72; free-lance writer, 1974—; Fairfax County Public Schools, Fairfax, Va., consultant and writer, 1984, 1985-86; part-time medical assistant, 1987—. Volunteer at Reston Hospital Center and Reston Community Center. *Member:* Society of Children's Book Writers, Washing-

BARBARA JOHNSTON ADAMS

ton Independent Writers, American Association of University Women. *Awards, honors:* Research and Projects Grant from the American Association of University Women, 1985; *The Picture Life of Bill Cosby* and *Winners* were each chosen one of Child Study Association of America's Children's Books of the Year, both 1987.

WRITINGS:

(Editor) Rosemary Theroux and Josephine Tingley, *The Care of Twin Children: A Common Sense Guide for Parents*, Center for Study of Multiple Gestation, 1978.
(Under name Barbara Shiels) *Winners: Women and the Nobel Prize*, Dillon, 1985.
The Picture Life of Bill Cosby, F. Watts, 1986.
Crime Mysteries, F. Watts, 1988.
New York City, Dillon, 1988.

Contributor of over fifty articles to publications including *Cleveland, Topic, America,* and *George Mason.*

WORK IN PROGRESS: A book for six- to nine-year-olds that is fiction with some nonfiction elements; story of a dollar bill found on the street by a young boy and his friends.

SIDELIGHTS: "My first book for young people was written through a series of coincidences. For several years I'd been writing magazine articles for adults. At the same time I'd been under contract with Washington, D.C. private businesses as well as government agencies for various writing assignments.

"One of my clients asked me to provide the text for a series of twenty-one posters on Nobel Prize winners. As I researched the material, our daughter, then eight years old, asked me to tell her more about the Prizes. I found very little had been written for children on the Nobel winners, especially on women who had been honored.

"This was the genesis of *Winners: Women and the Nobel Prize* which I chose to write under a pen name, Barbara Shiels. (Shiels was my maiden middle name; all subsequent books have been written under my real name.) My second book was written at the request of an editor, as was the fourth. The idea for the third book, however, originated directly with children.

"Schools in the Washington, D.C. area often ask me to speak to their students. This has become a most enjoyable part of my career and one I never anticipated. Children's questions can be far more probing than those of adults. At the close of my workshops, I ask the young people for suggestions for future books. Quite a few times the idea for a book on 'real-life crimes' came up. So you might say *Crime Mysteries* was written by special request.

"Perhaps because I became an author after having earlier jobs in publishing, printing, and public relations, I find great joy in being able to write what I want when I want to write it. It seems each book makes its own demands. And, with each, I need to draw from past experiences. These range from the smells and sights of individual places to the hard-to-recall knowledge of college or even high school courses.

"Most of all, I guess, I enjoy the challenges of every new book—interviewing celebrities, struggling to understand concepts, and taking pleasure in an endlessly varied language. Books, whether I'm reading or writing them, continue to be the ultimate adventure.

"I supplement my writing income by working in a medical office, but hope someday to be able to write full time. The trips I've taken to Japan, Africa, Europe, and the Caribbean have been among the most enjoyable times of my life."

HOBBIES AND OTHER INTERESTS: Travel, ballet, theater.

FOR MORE INFORMATION SEE:

Reston/Herndon Times (Va.), December 27, 1984.
Connection (Va.), March 18, 1987.

ANDERSON, David Poole 1929-
(Dave Anderson)

PERSONAL: Born May 6, 1929, in Troy, N.Y.; son of Robert P. (an advertising executive) and Josephine (an insurance broker; maiden name, David) Anderson; married Maureen Ann Young (a homemaker), October 24, 1953; children: Stephen, Mark, Mary Jo, Jean Marie. *Education:* Holy Cross College, B.A., 1951. *Home:* 8 Inness Rd., Tenafly, N.J. 07670. *Office: New York Times,* 229 West 43rd St., New York, N.Y. 10036.

CAREER: Brooklyn Eagle, Brooklyn, N.Y., sports writer, 1951-55; *New York Journal-American,* New York City, sports writer, 1955-66; *New York Times,* New York City, sports writer, 1966—, author of column "Sports of the Times," 1971—. *Awards, honors:* New Jersey Authors Award from the New Jersey Institute of Technology, 1965, for *Great Quarterbacks of the NFL;* Best Sports Stories Award, 1965, for "The Longest Day of Sugar Ray," and 1972, for "Beaufort, S.C. Loves Joe Frazier . . . Now"; Page One Award from the New York Newspaper Guild, 1972, for "Beaufort, S.C. Loves Joe Frazier . . . Now"; Pro Football Writers Story of the Year Award, 1972; Nat Fleischer Award, 1974, for Distinguished Boxing Journalism; *The Yankees* was selected one of New York Public Library's Books for the Teen Age, 1980; Pulitzer Prize for Distinguished

Commentary, 1981; *The Story of Football* was selected one of Child Study Association of America's Children's Books of the Year, 1986; Golf Writers Award for Best Column, 1987; honorary Doctor of Letters, Iona College, 1988.

WRITINGS:

JUVENILE; ALL UNDER NAME DAVE ANDERSON

Great Quarterbacks of the NFL, Random House, 1965.
Great Pass Receivers of the NFL, Random House, 1966.
Great Defensive Players of the NFL, Random House, 1967.
The Story of Football, Morrow, 1985.
The Story of Basketball, Morrow, 1988.

OTHER

Countdown to Super Bowl, Random House, 1969.
(With Sugar Ray Robinson) *Sugar Ray,* Viking, 1970.
(With Larry Csonka and Jim Kiick) *Always on the Run,* Random House, 1973.
Pancho Gonzalez: The Golden Year, Prentice-Hall, 1974.
(With Frank Robinson) *Frank: The First Year,* Holt, 1976.
The Yankees, Random House, 1979.
Sports of Our Times, Random House, 1979.
(With John Madden) *Hey Wait a Minute (I Wrote a Book!),* Villard, 1984.
(With J. Madden) *One Knee Equals Two Feet,* Villard, 1986.
(With J. Madden) *One Size Doesn't Fit All,* Villard, 1988.

Contributor of more than three-hundred articles to magazines, including *Reader's Digest, Sports Illustrated,* and *Golf Digest.*

SIDELIGHTS: After the New York Jets' 1969 victory over the Baltimore Colts in Super Bowl III, quarterback Joe Namath announced that he would be interviewed only by New York reporters, and among them, Dave Anderson. Anderson had

DAVID POOLE ANDERSON

covered the Jets when they were first known as the Titans and was an admirerer of Namath's skill, in addition to harboring the idea that the Jets could beat Baltimore. *Countdown to Super Bowl,* Anderson's chronicle of the days prior to football's most prestigious event, was praised for its clear, concise, and unbiased sports presentation. Arthur Cooper of *Newsweek* noted that Anderson ''has written a day-by-day account in an understated style that is mercifully free of sport cliches.''

Pete Axthelm, in his review of *Countdown,* called Anderson ''a fine reporter with a spare, straightforward style, remarkably free of cliches of the all-out rooting for the home team that afflicts most football writers.'' It is ''the controlled narrative,'' noted Axthelm, ''that only increases the emotional impact of what the Jets were accomplishing. In addition to being great entertainment for football fans, the crisp and original account of the game should be a textbook for future sportswriters, as well as many of Anderson's present colleagues.''

With the 1981 Pulitzer Prize for Distinguished Commentary, Anderson joined two other *New York Times* columnists as the only sportswriters so honored.

In an interview with *Editor & Publisher,* Anderson was asked about sportswriting. ''I'd say it's generally good and sometimes excellent in the major cities and in many of the smaller cities,'' he said. ''There are more realists than romantics now. The best way to improve sportswriting is to hire the best writers and reporters available. Don't let them dismiss journalism as a profession because of its comparatively low pay scale. The better the pay, the better writers and reporters it will attract.''

Jim Scott praised Anderson for his professional attitude and noted that he ''has long been in demand by magazine editors for he always turns out a masterful job.''

Anderson's three books with television personality John Madden were on the *New York Times'* best seller lists, hardcover and paperback, for a total of sixty-one weeks.

HOBBIES AND OTHER INTERESTS: Golf.

ATKINSON, Allen 1953(?)-1987

PERSONAL: Born about 1953, in Norwalk, Conn.; died of a heart attack, June 22, 1987, in Danbury, Conn. *Education:* Graduated from Paire School of Art. *Residence:* Bethel, Conn.

CAREER: Illustrator. Designer of greeting cards and toys for children. *Awards, honors: Humpty Dumpty and Other Favorites* and *Mary Had a Little Lamb and Other Favorites* were each chosen one of Child Study Association of America's Children's Books of the Year, 1986.

WRITINGS:

Jack in the Green (self-illustrated), Crown, 1987.

ILLUSTRATOR

John Morressy, *The Windows of Forever,* Walker, 1975.
Beatrix Potter, *The Tale of Peter Rabbit and Other Stories,* Knopf, 1982.
Jacob Grimm and Wilhelm K. Grimm, *Grimm's Fairy Tales,* Wanderer Books, 1982.
Margery Williams, *The Velveteen Rabbit,* Knopf, 1983.
B. Potter, *Cecily Parsley's Nursery Rhymes,* Bantam, 1983.

And then, one day, the Boy was ill. (From *The Velveteen Rabbit* by Margery Williams. Illustrated by Allen Atkinson.)

B. Potter, *The Tale of Mr. Jeremy Fisher,* Bantam, 1983.
B. Potter, *The Tale of Tom Kitten,* Bantam, 1983.
B. Potter, *The Tale of Mrs. Tiggy-Winkle,* Bantam, 1984.
B. Potter, *The Tale of Peter Rabbit,* Bantam, 1984.
B. Potter, *The Tailor of Gloucester,* Bantam, 1984.
B. Potter, *The Tale of Benjamin Bunny,* Bantam, 1984.
B. Potter, *The Tale of Squirrel Nutkin,* Bantam, 1984.
Mother Goose's Nursery Rhymes, Knopf, 1984.
The Cat and the Fiddle and Other Favorites, Bantam, 1985.
Humpty Dumpty and Other Favorites, Bantam, 1985.
Little Boy Blue and Other Favorites, Bantam, 1985.
Mary Had a Little Lamb and Other Favorites, Bantam, 1985.
Ski Michaels, *Mystery of the Windy Meadow,* Troll Associates, 1986.
James Howe, *Babes in Toyland,* Harcourt, 1986.
Jack and Jill and Other Favorites, Bantam, 1986.
Little Bo-Peep and Other Favorites, Bantam, 1986.
Simple Simon and Other Favorites, Bantam, 1986.
Old King Cole and Other Favorites, Bantam, 1986.
David Eastman, *Peter and the Wolf,* Troll Associates, 1987.

Also illustrator of L. Frank Baum's *The Wizard of Oz,* 1985.

SIDELIGHTS: Born and raised in rural Connecticut, Atkinson's favorite subjects for his paintings were the well-known children's stories which he read as a child. Involved in theater as well as illustration, he has designed costumes and sets as well as acted in numerous productions. In illustrating *Babes in Toyland* he combined the enchantment of fairy tale with the drama of the stage.

Atkinson created toys for children, including four stuffed bean-bag toys based on his artwork for *Mother Goose's Nursery Rhymes.* He has also designed greeting cards.

FOR MORE INFORMATION SEE:

OBITUARIES

New York Times, June 24, 1987 (p. B-10).
New York Times Biographical Service, June, 1987 (p. 621).
Publishers Weekly, September 11, 1987 (p. 14).

BEAGLE, Peter S. 1939-

PERSONAL: Born April 20, 1939, in New York, N.Y.; son of Simon (a teacher) and Rebecca (a teacher; maiden name, Soyer) Beagle; married Enid Elaine Nordeen, May 8, 1964 (divorced July, 1980); married Padma Hejmadi (a writer), September 21, 1988; children: Vicki, Kalisa, Daniel. *Education:* University of Pittsburgh, B.A., 1959; Stanford University, graduate study, 1960-61. *Politics:* Anarcho/monarchist. *Religion:* Jewish animist. *Home and office:* 5517 Crystal Springs Dr. N.E., Bainbridge Island, Wash. 98110. *Agent:* McIntosh & Otis, Inc., 475 Fifth Ave., New York, N.Y. 10017.

CAREER: Writer. *Member:* American Civil Liberties Union (vice-chairman, Santa Cruz chapter, 1968-69). *Awards, honors:* Wallace Stegner Writing Fellowship, 1960-61; Guggenheim Foundation Award, 1972-73; NEA Grant, 1977-78; Guest of Honor, Seventh World Fantasy Convention, 1981.

WRITINGS:

FICTION

A Fine and Private Place, Viking, 1960.
The Last Unicorn, Viking, 1968 (published in England as *The Last Unicorn: A Fantastic Tale,* Bodley Head, 1968).
Lila the Werewolf (chapbook), Capra Press, 1974, revised edition, 1976.
The Fantasy Worlds of Peter S. Beagle (contains *A Fine and Private Place, The Last Unicorn, Lila the Werewolf,* and "Come, Lady Death"), Viking, 1978.
The Folk of the Air, Del Rey, 1987.

OTHER

I See by My Outfit, Viking, 1965.
(Author of introduction) J. R. R. Tolkien, *The Tolkien Reader,* Houghton, 1966.
The California Feeling (illustrated with photographs by Michael Bry and Ansel Adams), Doubleday, 1969.
American Denim: A New Folk Art, Abrams/Warner, 1975.
(With Pat Derby)*The Lady and Her Tiger,* Dutton, 1976.
(Author of foreword) Abraham Soyer, *Adventures of Yemima, and Other Stories,* translated by Rebecca Beagle and Rebecca Soyer, Viking, 1979.
(Author of foreword) Avram Davidson, *The Best of Avram Davidson,* Doubleday, 1979.
The Garden of Earthly Delights, Viking, 1981.

SCREENPLAYS

"The Zoo" (television script), Columbia Broadcasting System, 1973.
(With Adam Kennedy) "The Dove," E.M.I., 1974.
"The Greatest Thing That Almost Happened" (television script), Charles Fries, 1977.

(With Chris Conkling) "The Lord of the Rings, Part One," United Artists, 1978.
"The Last Unicorn," Marble Arch/Rankin-Bass, 1982.

WORK IN ANTHOLOGIES

William Abrahams and Richard Poirier, editors, *Prize Stories: The O. Henry Awards,* Dutton, 1965.
Terry Carr, editor, *New Worlds of Fantasy,* Ace Books, 1967.
T. Carr, editor, *New Worlds of Fantasy 3,* Ace Books, 1971.
Jane Mobley, editor, *Phantasmagoria,* Anchor Books, 1977.
Robert H. Boyer and Kenneth J. Zahorski, editor, *The Fantastic Imagination: An Anthology of High Fantasy,* Avon, 1977.
R. H. Boyer and K. J. Zahorski, editors, *Dark Imaginings: A Collection of Gothic Fantasy,* Dell, 1978.

Contributor of articles and fiction to periodicals, including *Holiday, Seventeen, Texas Quarterly, Harper's, Today's Health, Saturday Evening Post, Venture, West, Atlantic,* and *Ladies' Home Journal.*

WORK IN PROGRESS: The Innkeeper's Song, a fantasy novel based on a song Beagle wrote some years ago about three strange women who come to an inn; "A Fine and Private Place," a screen adaptation; "The Monster Garden," a television movie based on a novel by Vivien Alcock.

SIDELIGHTS: Born April 20, 1939, in New York, New York, the son of Simon and Rebecca Beagle. "As far as New York is concerned, I grew up at the end of the world. The subways end [in the Bronx], and the buses run by appointment only. The view from my bedroom window is still dominated by the trees of Woodlawn Cemetery and Van Cortlandt Park. I used to lie in bed and try to count them, but they're so thick that it's hard to make out single trees, and I always lost count. Beyond the trees there are hills and the horn of a church, and something that looks like a

PETER S. BEAGLE

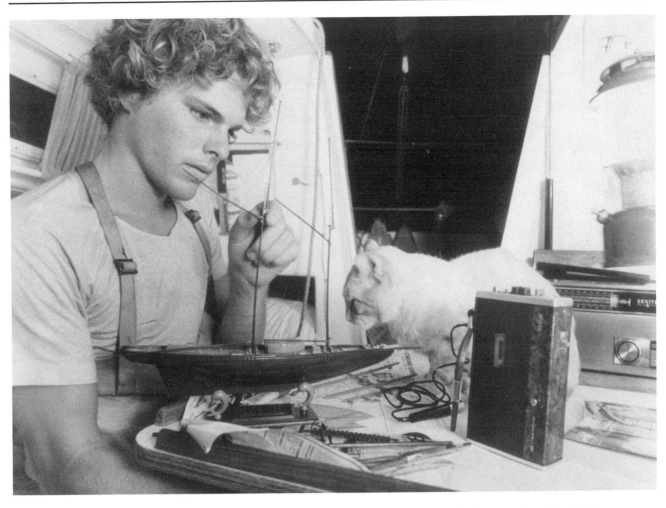

(Joseph Bottoms starred in the movie "The Dove." Screenplay by Peter Beagle. It was released in 1974.)

castle, and Yonkers . . . . When I was going to elementary school in the East Bronx, there was the ghost of a farm just across the street from us, a jungly, terrifying place owned by a half mad old man who threw stones at us when we tried to sneak up on him during lunch hour. Less and less these days, but still more than the rest of New York, the Bronx reminds you that it was wild country once."[1]

Beagle had a somewhat lonely childhood. "I was shy, over-weight, ill-coordinated, asthmatic, and allergic to everything. Even if our New York City apartment landlord had been complaisant about animals, I used to lose my voice within half an hour of being in a room with a cat or a dog. My parents gave me a great deal of affection, but not many other people did. I came home from school and read books. I remember that I had a long-lived fantasy about being a wolf—and, as late as high school, an imaginary lion friend named Cyrano.

"Thinking about that time now, I realize that in its own painful way, it was invaluable for me. I learned to be alone. Nobody who wants to be a writer can do without that skill. I learned to entertain myself and to look after myself, in a sloppily efficient sort of way. And I taught myself not to care what anyone else thought about me. I can remember making that decision, very consciously, around the sixth grade.

"I also lost the ability to cry; but you pay for everything, and that's an extremely common price for a man in America to pay.

You rarely even notice that it's missing, as used to be mentioned in stories about men who sold their souls."[2]

Inspired by his parents, a handful of established writers, and his love for animals, Beagle began writing early. "I started when I was seven, literally. My parents were remarkable. They never told me that writing was not a fit profession for a young man. I can remember writing stories in class. I wanted to imitate sounds. I love sounds. I was always excited by the sensuality of words and I wanted to copy that. I would imitate other writers. I haven't altogether lost that. *The Last Unicorn* starts off imitating half dozen people: James Stephens, Thurber, T. H. White. And Lord Dunsany is always somewhere in the background."[3]

"The friends and acquaintances I made when I was going to high school came mainly from the North and West Bronx, and we had a number of things in common. In the first place, we were almost all Jewish, children of Russian, German, and South European immigrants. (I didn't come in contact with the white Protestant America of television commercials until I went to college, and to this day I don't really believe that everybody in the world isn't Jewish. I pretend I do, but I don't.) We were intelligent, hungrily so, having been the family prodigies, the block's 'walking dictionaries' long enough to be sick of it, and, for many of us, high school was the first contact we had had with people like ourselves. We traded books and records back and forth; we showed each other our drawings and our poetry; we met informally to read plays aloud; we went out together, to concerts, to the theater, to ball games, to the movies, to museums, and to all

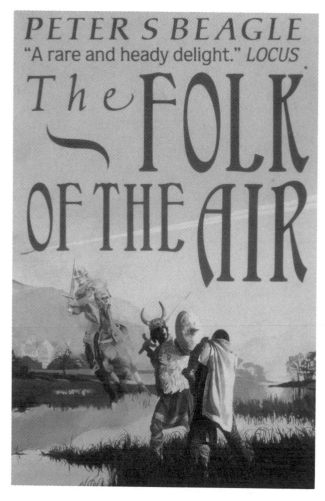

It was like being at a League tourney that went on forever. (Cover illustration by Neil Pinkett from *The Folk of the Air* by Peter S. Beagle.)

the places that had bored us so when our parents used to take us there.

"And we talked—lord, how we learned to talk!—constantly, perpetually, in the school cafeteria, on the stairs, in class, walking home, in candy stores and coffee shops, on buses, on subways, on the telephone—all as though conversation were a privilege that could be taken away from us at any moment, and probably would be. I don't know that we communicated more than other people do, but I think we tried more. We seemed to have so much to say.

"We all began running away from home about then; rarely in the classic sense—Tom Sawyer never had College Boards—but within ourselves. As middle-class children, we ate well, slept warmly, and knew nothing of real suffering; and we knew that we knew nothing when we looked around us with open eyes. When we forgot, our parents, most of whom had fought their way up from the Lower East Side to arrive at this quiet place, this narrow island in the middle of a dangerous street, were happy to remind us."[1]

As a young man, Beagle travelled to Europe where he was able to see in person a French performer named Georges Brassens, whose recordings he had heard, and whom he admired and tried to emulate. "Then suddenly I graduated from college, and I went to Europe for a year or so, Paris, mostly. It was a stupid time: it has that kind of flavor, anyway, when I think about it the taste

that makes you wriggle and spit. *Ah no, my God, was that me, that cold puppet? Oy, schmuck.* It was a lonesome, stupid time, and if I learned anything from it, it doesn't show. I would manage things better now, but not much better.

"I knew no French, and I had no friends. I could feel myself disappearing day by day, until it seemed to me that I was no more than a pair of eyes floating through the streets of Paris, speechless, shadowless, seeing some things but making no sense of them. But in the evenings I went to see Brassens at the Olympia or the Bobino, and when he came walking onstage, head down, clutching his guitar by the neck, his moustache like great wings, then somehow I had a voice again, and being. I even glanced around in my seat and smiled at the people sitting near me, certain that I could talk to them.

"He would take a drink from the carafe on the piano, put his left foot up on an old chair, and sing those songs in that voice, in this world. Graying, wild-haired, sweating in the lights, he had no stage presence: he was just *there,* like an animal, like the bear he is always compared to, like the sound of his voice and his guitar. Between songs he wandered in the space between the chair, the piano and his bass-fiddle accompanist, who always whispered the few words that seemed to turn him slowly back to the lights and the applause. When he was finished he walked off with the steps of a man trying not to run. He never gave encores, and he never bowed.

"Brassens was my bag, my bit, my thing, my hangup; as he still is, really. The sound of him on a record can still make me stop whatever I'm doing and say softly, 'Ah, that wicked old sonofabitch. That nut.' It can also make me feel like crying. I'll sing his complete works for anything that moves, translating each song carefully to explain the dislocated cliches, the quotations from Villon and the Pleiade and the other strange things that Brassens does with words. Sitting alone with my guitar, my fingers melt through the chord patterns that have never come to bore me, and I pick out his tunes to hear—almost to see—them cut their lean shapes into the air. And when I sing them, alone or for others, the special joy that is the other side of crying goes roaring around inside me, making me smile foolishly."[4]

In 1960, Beagle attended Stanford University in California, where he has continued to reside for many years. "Going to school here is an altogether different experience than in New York. People who went to bile-colored elementary schools that had numbers instead of names, and then on to slaggy, small-windowed high schools and sidewalk universities like office buildings are just not like people who grew up going to schools that looked like schools. This has nothing to do with the quality of the education received, which is about the same. But in New York, being educated isn't supposed to be a sensual business. So we come out to California to do graduate work, and of course we go crazy.

"Native Californians do look different. When I first came to Stanford I suffered from snowblindness and vertigo for some time, until I began to get used to all those clean teeth and clean limbs; the sunny skin, the friendly, untroubled faces, the air of being the people that the movies and advertisements were made for and about, and of knowing it. I used to suspect that they exposed all the ugly babies on hillsides. It was almost a relief to wander into Berkeley in the spring and discover the sallow, wary, messed-up New York faces there."[5]

By 1960, Beagle's first novel, *A Fine and Private Place,* had been published. Despite the author's youth, the book, whose central character is a fifty-three-year-old man, met with critical and popular success. The story concerns Jonathan Rebeck, a former Bronx druggist who, discouraged by encroaching commercialism in his neighborhood, takes to living in a mausoleum in the Yorkchester cemetery. There he encounters a middle-aged widow who comes to visit her dead husband, two young ghosts between whom a romance blossoms, and a talking raven who looks after Rebeck, even supplying him with food from a local deli. With this, Beagle established himself as a ''fantasy'' writer, creating animal characters with distinctly human qualities. ''The thing that interests me most is the line between fantasy and realism, because they're both so arbitrary. The books I like always seem to shimmer back and forth between one and the other. And many books that are presented as realistic novels I find utterly fantastic, and a lot of books that are listed as fantasy seem very normal to me.''[6]

''Many people, especially younger people, are coming to believe that there may be more than one reality. I remember a great line delivered by my younger brother who is a trained historian and a Marxist and an activist. He said, 'I'm slowly coming grudgingly to believe that there are some things in the universe that Dialectical Materialism doesn't cover.' I think people are less willing to accept flat definitions of what is real and what is not. There's that. The other thing, of course, is just plain desperation. You can hear it in the music. Suddenly there is a desperate swing back to the old styles of music. I know where it comes from. It comes from a hunger for that sort of time, walking down the street singing that sort of tune. Now you have all the

Cover of the 1978 reprint. (Cover illustration by Mel Williamson from *The Last Unicorn* by Peter S. Beagle.)

UFOs suddenly being seen. This time you can really smell the hunger. There's a desperation for somebody to come down and get us out of this.''[3]

In 1964, Beagle married Enid Elaine Nordeen, a mother of three. Until their divorce in 1980, they lived in the Santa Cruz Mountains, in a house filled with and surrounded by animals, both wild and tame. Beagle had outgrown his childhood allergies to animals. In 1966 he lovingly wrote of his new family. ''My wife Enid had been married twice before we met. She brought me two daughters and a son, a dying piano, six parakeets, a 1957 Chevrolet, and a reasonably complete set of Dostoevski. My own gift to the bride was an amiable young man who meant no one any harm, who had been to Europe, had published one book and read far too many and who had never in his life borne any greater responsibility than dressing himself and dodging traffic. In Las Vegas they were giving 18 to 1, and no takers—except Enid.''[7]

''Enid, Vicki, Kalisa, and Danny—my instant family—are my hold on the world, and the world's hold on me. Before they came, I think, I slept through my relationships with others, as I did through my childhood and my schooling. But their existence keeps me awake. There is no way to turn them off, to unplug them, to make them disappear. They will suffer if I don't take care of them, and so I will. This fact—and I possess few others—is simultaneously aggravating, frustrating, frightening, and dizzyingly sweet. I am very glad that I don't feel that

The unicorn lived in a lilac wood. (Cover illustration by Darrell K. Sweet from *The Last Unicorn* by Peter S. Beagle.)

way about any other people. What would the world be like for a man who felt that way about everybody?

"For, even at its kindest and deepest, it is a lonely feeling. Not until you want to help do you realize how little help you can give; not until you truly wish to pass into another person's skin can you know how separate even lovers are. Danny twists and moans inside a nightmare, sitting up with his eyes open, but still asleep, calling for his mother, who is holding him on her lap. Kalisa weeps over a clay sculpture that is impossible for an eight year old to make, but not to visualize. Vicki is a young girl now, and who can help a young girl except by checking over her homework, and making the house a good place for her? Enid is tired, and I cannot be tired for her; her back hurts, and I cannot take the pain into my own body. Loving makes you aware that the ones you love are suffering, and that love will not help, not just then. This awareness is the gift and the price tag together.

"Love and creativity are two of America's favorite fantasies; and, like most American dreams, they end at the real beginning. The girl and the publisher say *yes I will yes*. And then the wise alarm clock goes off. People dream of being writers, of being in love; but not of writing, not of loving. I dream of being a great guitarist, but never of studying scale patterns. In the dream I already know all that stuff.

"But I do know something about daily love, because it is not a dream for me. It is an atmosphere, a medium in which I move, and out of which I don't breathe well. In our house, the children and the cats have grown up being played with, being teased, being yelled at, being swatted, being threatened with sudden and permanent death—but always, always being handled, being held. And I have grown to recognize children—and adults, and cats—who have not been held enough; who may never have been obviously hurt or damaged, but who have never learned to love. They want to, very often, very much, but they don't know how."[7]

The animals, too, were valued members of the family. "When my wife and I moved into an unheated shack in the central California mountains, a dog and a pigeon were waiting for us. The dog had belonged to the owner's brother, but now he belonged to the pigeon. She ate his food, slept with him, followed him everywhere, and used to peck gently at him in a way that I always interpreted as hunting for ticks. It never occurred to me in those days that a bird would find it necessary to express affection for a dog. We were always taught not to anthropomorphize animals' emotions, when I was in school.

"Someone gave our oldest daughter a black and white kitten: stub-tailed, with malformed hip joints, mad eyes, and an inborn detestation of all other cats. None of this kept her from dropping a long line of kittens as wobbly and loony and tough as herself. With a little help from their friends and relations, they worked the cat population up into the twenties and thirties and kept it there pretty consistently. There was a high point of some fifty-three once, before several sets of kittens were old enough to give away. Another time, a distemper epidemic left us with five cats and the new experience of holding a convulsing animal close and praying for it to die. We didn't know anything about distemper, nor about the literally numberless varieties of pneumonitis that cats get; nor what you do when a kitten is being born the wrong way, or when its mother won't nurse it and keeps snapping at it, crying like a kitten herself. We learned about ticks, too—the dog died of a fairly rare fever caused by a tick bite. The pigeon died shortly afterward, apparently of natural causes.

"The more unusual of our seventy-five creatures came gradually, in between the generations of cats, dogs, and horses by which

we began in time to keep track of our own memories and adventures: A one-legged quail, doctored and brought to us by a neighbor's son; a golden-mantled squirrel; a gray African parrot who sits on the curtain rod all day and imitates cat fights; a myna bird who lived in the bathtub and scared visitors; a kestrel falcon named Cuchulain (cu-HOO-lin); a family of ferrets, never vicious but teasing and absolutely without fear; a desert chipmunk who suffered a heart seizure one evening, was revived by massage with a fingertip, and still lives; an iguana; a Bengali monitor lizard named Rabindranath; a tree shrew (not a true shrew at all, but a low form of primate); a timid bush baby like a living, wide-eyed feather; a nineteen-year-old kinkajou named Miss Lucy Brown, all golden brown fur and Victorian manners. There have been, and will be, many others: after a certain point, the only real limit has to do with one's capacity for caring and attention. Recently, we managed to say no to a wild-animal-raising friend's offer of a cougar kitten. It was the right decision; but the strain, as Mark Twain says, ruptured every cartilage in us, and I don't know how we'd respond to the gift of a coyote or a raccoon . . . . Yes, I do."[2]

In 1968, Beagle's best known book, *The Last Unicorn*, was published. It is the story of the last free unicorn's quest to find and rescue her fellow unicorns from imprisonment by an evil king. The novel is at once a traditional romantic fantasy, and a parody of such romances. Further, the dialogue is spiced with literary allusions, and contemporary colloquialisms, giving the story a pleasant air of absurdity. "I was deliberately taking the classic fairy tale structure, the classic fairy tale characters, and trying to do something else with them. I was saddling myself and aiding myself both with all the proper forms."[6]

The novel was a combination of research and daydreams. "It's funny. I know more about unicorns now than I did then. I have Odell Shepard's *The Lore of the Unicorn* which is the great work on unicorns. It compiles everything anybody's ever written or said about unicorns. But I didn't have it then. The novel might be different to some extent if I had. When I started the book, I was living with a friend in Cheshire, Massachusetts. I went to the library in Pittsfield to look things up. I discovered the Chinese had a unicorn. And in one funny encyclopedia there was just a line: 'Doctor Olfert Dapper saw a wild unicorn in the Maine woods in 1673.' It didn't say that he claimed to, but that he actually saw one. That's the reason for the dedication in the book. And that was about all I found. It wasn't much help.

"I make things up as I'm writing. There's a very odd relationship between me and a piece of paper. Very commonly I'll start a chapter without knowing what's in it. Things come to flower that I have no idea I'm thinking about. The pattern I keep turning back to is that I seem to write books to find out what it is I'm writing about. In each case, with every book I've done, I've been wrong about what I thought it was. About two-thirds of the way through, I find out what book I'm supposed to be doing and then I go back and make it look easy. My new book is taking me four years to find out what it's about and who's in it. It would be better I suppose if I could think these things out first and plan.

"Poul Anderson, the science fiction writer, once told me he knows everything in advance, that the actual writing is the shortest part of the process. Sometimes, I think he does better than that might suggest. He's done several books I really like. He almost *has* to outline to make a living writing science fiction. He has to be extremely prolific and has to know what he's doing. He can't afford to discover at the typewriter, as I do. I think Anderson and other people often have a lot of things knocking around in different stages of completion. I seem to do one thing at a time. It's a matter of energy. I'm slow and lazy about a lot of things. I really have to be forced into thinking more than

(From the 1982 animated movie "The Last Unicorn.")

superficially. If I don't have to think about a new character or situation, I won't. But if I get to a point where I've painted myself into six corners at once, I have to think, and something happens—some kind of concentration, dementia, or whatever—that I can't get unless there's that kind of insane pressure. Jim Houston says that writing novels is like juggling: you throw up one ball, then another, and another. The first one comes down, and then you're writing a novel."[3]

In 1969, Beagle published *The California Feeling,* a collaboration with photographer Michael Bry. "Much of this book is based on a series of voyages up and down California that Michael Bry and I made during the course of a year. Mike is German and Chilean and American—not in neat geological strata, but all together, the way children roll different colors of clay into each other. He is an artist, a solid harmonica player (with a natural country sound), and one of the world's great improvisational cooks, given a couple of cans and a few onions. Mike is also very comfortable to be quiet with, late in the day, with fifty miles still to go, everything discussed, and the five-thirty gloomies coming on. He comes into this book much more often than he is mentioned.

"We did our traveling in a 1957 Volkswagen bus named Renata Tebaldi. She went everywhere, *andante* and in 4/4 time, but she got where she was going, and she put up graciously with the erratic tenors. Mike built a bed in the back, which turned out to be so comfortable, and Renata herself so self-sufficient, that he said with a sigh, 'It's sure too bad both of us are a fella.' She smelled of dust and cheese and unwashed sleeping bags, and at

night she made small creaking, pinging noises as everybody settled down.

"I think this book is a letter to New York. I can't imagine what else it could possibly be. It isn't a travel guide, and it isn't any sort of serious analysis of the state; and it certainly isn't that much-needed work on the way it really is to live in California. It's a grab-bag; a shapeless, disorderly rummage of scenes, impressions, memories, digressions, people, prejudices, days, places, misunderstandings, and mostly what I happened to be thinking about on that particular afternoon. As Thorne Smith said of his own books, you can probably start reading at any random page or section and 'be equally mystified, if not revolted. I am myself.' But if it were to be decoded and distilled, the message might run something like this:

"See, they don't have winter here. I mean, they have *a* winter— where I live, it's liable to rain any time between November and June, or all the time—but they don't have winter. The idea of it isn't carved into them right down to the chromosomes, the way it is with us. It makes a difference. I'm going to write a book about that difference one day, when I understand it better. It'll be called *The Social, Political, and Cultural Importance of Being Warm.*

"You have to have a car. I don't mean to get from one town to another, but just to get around—to go shopping, to visit friends, to go to a movie, to school, anywhere. California is flying slowly apart into things that aren't exactly towns, but more like the medieval feudal arrangements of houses ranged in the shadow of some local lord's thatched castle and paling of sharpened stakes. The lord, in this case, usually being a big shopping center. They don't have subways, of course; though there will eventually be one in the Bay Area, in spite of the people who are doing it. But one of the really serious problems in Watts, for instance, is that you can spend a couple of dollars and a couple of hours a day riding the buses to work in Los Angeles. The great urban areas move and feed like gigantic one-celled creatures, responding to needs and tropisms; but distances seem to be increasing. You know the way your body is disoriented by long jet flights from one time zone to another? There's a sense of that here all the time.

"The coffee isn't nearly as good as New York coffee, but it's the spirit that counts, unless you really wanted coffee. Californians are friendlier than New Yorkers. Granted, so is the average Mexican bandit, but it's interesting to compare the two defense mechanisms. In New York, people go around like clenched fists, blind and furious, because they have to. Everything crowds in too closely—everything is screaming out there in the street. If you let your eyes focus on somebody, he'll come up to you and mug you, or proposition you, or breathe his hard luck, his death, all over you. Californians can still afford to smile and give a stranger directions. I don't think they give anything else any more freely than New Yorkers, but it sure looks like more. It's a matter of distance again.

"It's no easier to be poor out here than it is in the East—just warmer. One thing, though: garbage cans generally contain much more edible stuff than New York garbage cans. People throw things away earlier; supermarkets have big boxes of slightly stale vegetables sitting out in back, and they're usually grateful if you come around and pick over them. I also have it on excellent authority that the shoplifting scene is much better in California. I know several people who ate their way through four years of college for no more than the Army Surplus price of a very long overcoat."[5]

Beagle collaborated again in 1975, for the first time since *The California Feeling,* on *The Lady and Her Tiger,* with author Pat Derby. "A lot of it had to do with just having known Pat for a long time, having some idea of the way she thinks. There are people—fictional or real—into whose heads I can think myself. And then there are people whose heads, for one reason or another, are inaccessible, and I can't imagine what it is to be like that. What would happen is that I would visit Pat for several-day stretches, during which time I'd be at the place helping with the animals and talking to Pat. She also sent me tapes on a steady basis. She is a good storyteller, an articulate woman, and I would work from the tapes and from my own experiences with Pat and try to put the chapters as much in her voice and with her locutions and phrasing as I could. I'd send each chapter to her and wait for her to make any corrections she wanted to. That worked. It's probably the only book I'll ever do like that, but it worked. I think all the years I had spent doing magazine journalism helped a good deal."[8]

"I think eighty-five percent of what I do is craft. I've been doing this a long time. I spend eight hours a day down here. You learn things. But fifteen percent, or ten percent, or whatever, is what I call the swamp. I don't understand the swamp, but I believe it's there. There's a point where I will have come as far as I can by craft. I'll walk around this office and tell the swamp aloud sometimes, 'All right, I'd appreciate it if you'd gurgle something up, because I can't do any more by myself.' I've come to believe that in a day, or two days, or when it damn well feels like it, the swamp will burp up a character I've never met or something that's never happened to me, because it's done it before. In that

sense all those strange images and metaphors come out of the swamp.

"If I've done two pages [in a day] that's a lot. I put down a sentence and look at it for a while and push it around some and then add another sentence to it and see how that looks. I work a sentence at a time and then look at the paragraph. Jim Houston is the only person who ever picked up on my paying a lot of attention to the last lines of my paragraphs. I seem to think in terms of paragraphs, and they're like building blocks. After a while, there's a point where I finally know what I'm doing and then I don't think in terms of paragraphs, but just write. So much of it is instinct and learning to trust your instincts. A Hungarian poet once gave me a poem which goes, 'Being a poet is an act of faith and great memory, like digging a ditch.' And that is really all I do. It is faith, pure faith.

"I [revise] as I go along, but still have to revise again at the end of the book. Sometimes at night I come half awake realizing, 'Oh shit, I knew that was a lousy adjective. I can't stand it. Damn. I should go down to the barn and change it right now. It's a lousy adjective. I should have done better. Dummy!'

"When I'm finished with the draft, I'll go back through it. It will be at least fifty pages too long, and I'll take fifty pages out a sentence at a time. That's slow and hard, but I don't mind doing it."[3]

Fantasy novelist, journalist, essayist, Beagle has added screenwriting to his credits over the last twenty years. "When the work's coming in, it's possible finally for me to do one or two film things a year and write fiction the rest of the time.

"I've been very lucky in the sense that I've made my living in one way or another off my writing. That's almost impossible. For all that you read about the seven-figure contracts for the Sidney Sheldons of this world, the other extreme of making a hundred to two thousand dollars a year off your work is vastly more common. There is almost no middle ground. I don't live off my fiction, and if it hadn't been for my nonfiction and my screen work, I would have been in trouble. The thing that upsets me is that the climate is so bad right now for fiction writers. I have a friend my age, a novelist and poet whom I've known for over twenty years; he's published four novels and three books of poetry. He taught at Stanford and he's done some screen work. All his stuff is out of print and there's no assurance that he'll get anything else published—he can never take it for granted. The seven-figure contracts that Sidney Sheldon gets come directly from the contracts of people like this who are lucky to get ten or fifteen thousand in advance, and they come in such small fractions that they're spent before they come in. My friend's last book got a rave review in the *New York Times* but didn't go into paperback because there was no assurance that it would sell. He's a splendid writer, one of the best I know.

"So I'm genuinely concerned about what is happening to the structure of publishing in America. I'm very alarmed that a lot of good writers are going to be driven away from it in the coming years by economics and, worse, by lack of any real recognition. That frightens me and angers me when I think of people who are as good as I am who haven't been anywhere near as lucky."[8]

"My life is a slow process of making things real, making them continue to exist when my back is turned. It is my worst failing, this dangerous solipsism, but it is also one reason why I write: to create the world line-by-line, to find a way in, a handhold. For all I know, no one else in the world has this problem, but I wonder. Could we all go on treating people the way we do if we believed that they were real?"[7]

Beagle co-authored the screenplay for the animated film "Lord of the Rings" in 1978.

"Lizard and louse, man and tiger, we are all here together, barely alive in the dark, clinging to the earth and trying to stay warm. Either we all have souls, or none of us do."[2]

FOOTNOTE SOURCES

[1] Peter S. Beagle, "Good-bye to the Bronx," *Holiday,* December, 1964.
[2] P. S. Beagle, "Kids and Kinkajous: The Special Blessings of Growing Up with Animals," *Today's Health,* October, 1974.
[3] Dan Tooker and Roger Hofheins, *Fiction! Interviews with Northern California Novelists,* Harcourt, 1972. Amended by P. Beagle.
[4] P. S. Beagle, "My Last Heroes," *Holiday,* August, 1965. Amended by P. Beagle.
[5] P. S. Beagle, *The California Feeling,* Doubleday, 1969.
[6] David Van Becker, "Time, Space, and Consciousness in the Fantasy of Peter S. Beagle," *San Jose Studies,* February, 1975.
[7] P. S. Beagle, "On Being the Man of the House," *Saturday Evening Post,* December, 1966.
[8] *Contemporary Authors New Revision Series,* Volume 4, Gale, 1981.

FOR MORE INFORMATION SEE:

Kirkus, March 15, 1960.
Library Journal, May 1, 1960, June 1, 1960, February 15, 1968.
Time, May 23, 1960.
Saturday Review, May 28, 1960 (p. 18), March 30, 1968 (p. 21ff).
New York Herald Tribune Book Review, May 29, 1960.
San Francisco Chronicle, June 2, 1960.
Chicago Tribune, June 5, 1960, November 26, 1978.

New York Times Book Review, June 5, 1960, March 24, 1968, September 23, 1979.
Christian Century, August 31, 1960.
Galaxy, April, 1961, June, 1977.
Holiday, June, 1965 (p. 35ff).
Hollins Critic, April, 1968 (p. 1ff).
Best Sellers, April 1, 1968, September, 1976.
Chicago Tribune Book World, April 7, 1968 (p. 13).
Christian Science Monitor, May 9, 1968.
Commonweal, June 28, 1968.
Books and Bookmen, October, 1968.
New Worlds, December, 1968.
Locus, November 18, 1972, June 30, 1976.
Raymond M. Olderman, *Beyond the Waste Land: A Study of the American Novel in the Nineteen-Sixties,* Yale University Press, 1972.
Lin Carter, *Imaginary Worlds: The Art of Fantasy,* Ballantine, 1973.
P. S. Beagle, "Maya's Christmas," *Today's Health* December, 1975.
Contemporary Literary Criticism, Volume VII, Gale, 1977.
Algol, spring, 1977.
Critique: Studies in Modern Fiction, Volume XIX, number 2, 1977 (p. 93ff).
Frank N. Magill, *Survey of Contemporary Literature,* Volume 6, revised and enlarged edition, Salem Press, 1977.
Contemporary Literary Criticism, Volume VII, Gale, 1977.
Peter S. Beagle, *The Fantasy Worlds of Peter S. Beagle,* Viking, 1978.
Science Fiction Review, February, 1978, March-April, 1979.
Marshall B. Tymn, Kenneth J. Zahorski, and Robert H. Boyer, *Fantasy Literature: A Core Collection and Reference Guide,* Bowker, 1979.

Dust jacket from the 1978 hardcover edition. (Jacket illustration by I. Bite from *The Fantasy Worlds of Peter Beagle* by Peter S. Beagle.)

R. Reginald, *Science Fiction and Fantasy Literature: A Checklist, 1700-1974*, Volume 2: *Contemporary Science Fiction Authors II*, Gale, 1979.
Fantasiae, November/December, 1979.
Extrapolation, fall, 1979 (p. 230ff), spring, 1980 (p. 5ff).
Dictionary of Literary Biography Yearbook, Gale, 1980.
Ina Rae Hark, "The Fantasy Worlds of Peter Beagle," *Survey of Modern Fantasy Literature*, edited by Frank N. Magill, Salem Press, 1983.
Robert H. Boyer and Kenneth J. Zahorski, editors, *Fantasists on Fantasy: A Collection of Critical Reflections*, Avon, 1984.
E. F. Bleiler, editor, *Supernatural Fiction Writers*, Scribner, 1985.
K. J. Zahorski, *Peter S. Beagle*, Starmont House, 1988.

BODE, Janet 1943-

PERSONAL: Surname is pronounced *Boe*-dy; born July 14, 1943, in Penn Yan, N. Y.; daughter of Carl J. (a writer and professor) and Margaret (Lutze) Bode. *Education:* University of Maryland, B.A., 1965; graduate study at Michigan State University, and Bowie State College. *Agent:* Kevin McShane, Fifi

Oscard Associates, Inc., 19 West 44th St., New York, N.Y. 10036.

CAREER: Writer, 1975—. Has worked in Germany, Mexico, and the United States as a personnel specialist, program director, community organizer, public relations director, and teacher. *Member:* Authors Guild, Authors League of America, American Culture Association, Popular Culture Association. *Awards, honors: Rape* was selected an Outstanding Social Studies Book by the National Council for Social Studies and the Children's Book Council, 1979; *Kids Having Kids* was selected one of American Library Association's Best Books for Young Adults, and a Notable Children's Trade Book in the Field of Social Studies from the National Council for Social Studies and the Children's Book Council, both 1980; *Rape* was selected one of New York Public Library's Books for the Teen Age, 1980, and *Kids Having Kids*, 1981, and 1982.

WRITINGS:

Kids School Lunch Bag, Children's Foundation, 1972.
View from Another Closet: Exploring Bisexuality in Women, Hawthorn, 1976.
Fighting Back: How to Cope with the Medical, Emotional and Legal Consequences of Rape, Macmillan, 1978.
Rape: Preventing It; Coping with the Legal, Medical and Emotional Aftermath (young adult), F. Watts, 1979.
Kids Having Kids: The Unwed Teenage Parent (young adult), F. Watts, 1980.
Different Worlds: Interracial and Cross-Cultural Dating (young adult), F. Watts, 1989.
New Kids on the Block: Oral Histories of Immigrant Teens (young adult), F. Watts, 1989.
Real-Life Rape (young adult), F. Watts, 1990.

Co-author of "Women against Rape" (television documentary film), 1975. Contributor of articles to periodicals, including *Cosmopolitan, Redbook, New York, Medica, Glamour, Village Voice, Realist, New York Woman, Savvy,* and *Mademoiselle.*

WORK IN PROGRESS: Kids in Crisis: Siblings with Serious Problems, and *You Can't Tell Me What To Do: Living in Remarried Families,* both for young adults, both to be published by F. Watts.

BRIGHT, Robert 1902-1988 (Michael Douglas)

OBITUARY NOTICE—See sketch in *SATA* Volume 24: Born August 5, 1902, in Sandwich, Mass.; died of cancer, November 21, 1988, in San Francisco, Calif. Administrator, educator, illustrator, journalist, and author. Bright, whose books were published beginning in the 1940s, was most widely known as the author and illustrator of more than twenty books for children. His first books were primarily for adults—including such novels as *The Life and Death of Little Jo* and *The Intruders*—but he turned to children's literature to help support his family. Bright wrote numerous stories for children about the adventures of Georgie the ghost, ranging from *Georgie* in 1944 to *Georgie and the Baby Bird* in 1983. Two books from this series, *Georgie* and *Georgie to the Rescue*, were made into movies. His other juvenile titles include a book of poetry, *Round, Round World*, published under the name Michael Douglas. At the beginning of his career in the 1920s Bright worked briefly as a reporter for the Baltimore *Sun* and the Paris *Times*. He became assistant to the president of Conde Nast Publications in 1927, but left the next year to work as advertising manager of Revillon Freres until 1936. He was also a teacher in Boston in the 1950s, and music and art critic for the Santa Fe *New Mexican* from 1964 to 1965. In later years, he lived in La Jolla, California.

FOR MORE INFORMATION SEE:

D. L. Kirkpatrick, editor, *Twentieth-Century Children's Writers*, 2nd edition, St, Martin's, 1983.
Contemporary Authors, Volumes 73-76, Gale, 1978.

OBITUARIES

New York Times, December 3, 1988 (p. 33).
Washington Post, December 5, 1988.
Publishers Weekly, December 23, 1988 (p. 36).

BROOKS, Terry 1944-

PERSONAL: Born January 8, 1944, in Sterling, Ill.; son of Dean O. (a printer) and Marjorie (a housewife; maiden name, Gleason) Brooks; married Judine Elaine Alba (a bookseller) December 11, 1987; children: (previous marriage) Amanda Leigh, Alexander Stephen. *Education:* Hamilton College, B.A., 1966; Washington & Lee University, LL.B., 1969. *Address:* c/o Ballantine/Del Rey, 201 E. 50th St., New York, N.Y. 10022.

CAREER: Besse, Frye, Arnold, Brooks & Miller, Attorneys at Law, Sterling, Ill., partner, 1969-86; writer, 1977—. *Member:* American Bar Association, Illinois State Bar Association, Author's Guild. *Awards, honors: The Elfstones of Shannara* was selected one of American Library Association's Best Young Adult Books, and one of *School Library Journal*'s Best Books for Young Adults, both 1982; *Magic Kingdom for Sale—Sold* was selected one of *School Library Journal*'s Best Books for Young Adults, 1986.

WRITINGS:

FANTASY NOVELS

The Sword of Shannara, Random House, 1977.
The Elfstones of Shannara (illustrated by Darrell K. Sweet), Del Rey, 1982.
The Wishsong of Shannara (illustrated by D. K. Sweet), Del Rey, 1985.
Magic Kingdom for Sale—Sold, Del Rey, 1986.
The Black Unicorn, Del Rey, 1987.
Wizard at Large, Del Rey, 1988.
The Scions of Shannara, Del Rey, 1990.

ADAPTATIONS:

"The Sword of Shannara" (cassette), Caedmon, 1986.

WORK IN PROGRESS: Additional books in the "Shannara" series; a new fantasy novel.

SIDELIGHTS: "I grew up in a small midwestern steel town situated in the middle of farm country. Much of my time was spent reading and creating imaginary worlds in which to play. I went through stages in my reading from first grade to eighth: *Hardy Boys* and *Black Stallion* to Burroughs, Heinlein, Bradbury, and Del Rey to Walter Scott, Conan Doyle, Dumas, and James Fenimore Cooper. The European adventure story writers probably influenced me the most. I began writing when I was about ten. I was published for the first time in eighth grade when I

wrote a short story for an Illinois State Historical Society competition on Lincoln.

"I began experimenting with novels in high school, trying my hand at the great white whale story and others. I finished a science-fiction novel, now too awful to contemplate, but it was the first piece of long work that I had completed and I managed to wrangle a review out of a children's book editor working out of Detroit who was a friend of a friend. That encouraged me to continue writing. I wrote on and off through college, finally beginning work on *The Sword of Shannara* when I started law school. The book took me seven years to complete—due in no small part to the fact that I had accepted a job as an attorney after graduating law school, determined that I would not starve to death while trying to write.

"Like most writers, I am asked where I get my ideas. I still do not have a satisfactory answer to that question; somehow they are just always there. I am a writer who is compelled to write; I am not complete without my work. The writing of the book is the best part of the process. Once a book is done, I have a tendency to put it aside and forget about it. I believe that telling a good story is a fantasy writer's first obligation to his readers. I was first told that by my editor, and it is the best piece of advice I ever received about writing. I also believe in writing for myself; that is, if I write something that I would enjoy reading, it will find an audience."

BROW, Thea 1934-

PERSONAL: Born July 23, 1934, in Rhinelander, Wis., daughter of Frederick Lee (in the navy) and Inger Johanna (an office manager; maiden name, Christiansen) Corbett; married Edwin D. Brow (a major in the U.S. Army; deceased), December 29, 1958; children: John, Peter, Jill. *Education:* Attended San Diego State University, 1952-54; University of California at Los Angeles, B.A., 1957. *Home:* 4110 Miller St., San Diego, Calif. 92103.

CAREER: Writer, 1950—; U.S. Government, Bar-le-Duc, France, U.S. Army special services, 1957-58; *Union/Tribune*, San Diego, Calif., archival editing and research, 1986—. *Member:* Society of Children's Book Writers.

WRITINGS:

The Secret Cross of Lorraine (juvenile novel; illustrated by Allen Say), Houghton, 1981.

Author of "Teen Talk" column, *San Diego Union*, 1950.

WORK IN PROGRESS: Three juvenile mysteries; an adult mystery.

SIDELIGHTS: "I was born in Rhinelander, Wisconsin—home of my Norwegian immigrant grandparents—though I feel like a native of California since I moved, with my parents, to Long Beach when I was one month old.

"I received most of my schooling in San Diego public schools and attended San Diego State University and UCLA, where I graduated in 1957 with a degree in English literature. I took every course in writing offered. Writing was always my first love.

THEA BROW

"After graduating, I worked in Eastern France for the U.S. Government. During my year there I discovered a France much different from the Paris and Riviera shown on travel posters. Some villages and farms seemed untouched by the events of the twentieth century. Others, such as those around Verdun, were torn and changed by the ravages of modern—and ancient—wars.

"My novel, *The Secret Cross of Lorraine*, had its beginnings during a visit I made to a crumbling Maginot Line bunker in 1958. Years later I read that the French government was selling the bunkers to private citizens, to be converted to summer homes and museums. With this news, a plot took shape in my imagination. The result: my first juvenile novel, *The Secret Cross of Lorraine*.

"It is really a mystery story. It wasn't until after I had completed the writing and was rereading it that I realized it contains a rather strong anti-war statement in the plot. Also, there is a lot of history of that area reflected in the story. I write mysteries exclusively because I love reading and writing mystery stories. My favorite book as a child was *The Secret Garden*. That book started me off on a life of pursuing the mysterious!

"My marriage to a career Army officer whose speciality was military intelligence afforded a life of travel and a front-line view of world affairs. I lived at two different times in France and Germany. My first child was born in Stuttgart.

"Now a widow, I live in San Diego. My grown children are interested in writing too. John, the oldest, is serving with the U.S. Army in Nuernberg, Germany. Peter has finished his second science-fiction novel. Jill is working at the NBC affiliate station in San Diego.

"I share my desk with a very old calico cat the family adopted in Hawaii in 1969. That cat knows all the family secrets—if she could only talk!"

HOBBIES AND OTHER INTERESTS: Travel, vintage and classic movies, theater.

CAREY, Valerie Scho 1949-

PERSONAL: Scho is pronounced like "show"; born August 6, 1949, in Pittsburgh, Pa.; daughter of Ira Cass (a watchmaker) and Zelda (a homemaker; maiden name, Markowitz) Scho; married Brent L. Carey (a dentist), August 6, 1972; children: Kimberly, Allison, Jeffrey. *Education:* University of Michigan, B.A. (with distinction), 1971, M.A., 1973, doctoral pre-candidate, 1973-74.

CAREER: Genesee Merchants Bank, Flint, Mich., substitute bankteller, 1968-72; Flint Public Schools, Flint, Mich., substitute teacher, 1969-72; State of Michigan, Department of State, history division, Brooklyn, Mich., student curator, 1974; writer, 1979—. *Member:* Society of Children's Book Writers, Detroit Women Writers, Amnesty International. *Awards, honors: Harriet and William and the Terrible Creature* was chosen one of Child Study Association of America's Children's Books of the Year, 1986; Parents' Choice Award from the Parents' Choice Foundation, 1987, and Children's Choice from the International Reading Association and the Children's Book Council, 1988, both for *The Devil and Mother Crump*.

WRITINGS:

Harriet and William and the Terrible Creature (illustrated by Lynne Cherry), Dutton, 1985.
(Reteller) *The Devil and Mother Crump* (illustrated by Arnold Lobel), Harper, 1987.

Contributor of numerous stories to children's magazines, including *Noah's Ark, Young Judean, Shofar,* and *World Over.*

WORK IN PROGRESS: Tsugele's Broom, a picture book, for Harper Junior Books; *Quail Song,* a picture book retelling of a Pueblo tale, for Putnam; *Maggie Mab and the Bogey Beast,* a picture book retelling of a Northumbrian tale, for Arcade Books.

SIDELIGHTS: "I was the oldest of two children. Both my sister and I were born in Pittsburgh, Pennsylvania. Many of my most vivid childhood recollections are of those first five years when my family lived in Pittsburgh. I remember riding my tricycle along our street past the neighborhood grocery store with its fascinating collection of sweets (candy buttons on a paper backing and Turkish taffy being two of my favorites) and the shoemaker's shop (I could stop in front of this shop and see the cobbler busy at his bench working with a shoe on a wooden form) all the way to where the street ended at a fence which kept people from going off a cliff with the railroad running far below. The sound of trains in the distance and the image of steel mill flames reflected in the river at night are memories that stay with me from those early years.

"We lived on the first floor of a three-story house. I remember playing 'pirates' with neighborhood children in the alley behind that house. I remember the carousel truck—a tiny carousel mounted on the back of a small truck which drove through the streets offering rides in the summertime. I don't remember how much those rides cost, except that it must have been a good deal less extravagant than the cost of a trip to Kennywood (the local amusement park). I remember the mounted policemen, the fruit and vegetable venders who shouted their wares as they drove along either on a truck or on a horse-drawn wagon, the University of Pittsburgh campus with its towering Cathedral of Learning, the natural history museum (with its dinosaur skeletons that terrified me so that I had to fumble my way past them with my eyes closed), and the botanical garden building which fascinated me with its array of exotic plants (our own yard was extremely small and the landlady kept all of us children out of the garden by telling us that poison ivy grew there). I remember laying in bed at night listening to the train whistles in the distance, and again hearing them far below in the ravine which ran alongside my maternal grandmother's house.

"And I remember the day when one of those trains carried my mother, my sister, and me away from Pittsburgh, its hills, bridges, tunnels, and rivers—all of which I dearly loved—to join our father in Michigan. He had gone ahead of us a short time to look for work and prepare the way for our move from Pennsylvania. He took work in one of the auto factories in Flint, and later set up his own watchmaker's shop. We had many relatives in Flint (just as we had had in Pittsburgh), and we grew to have many friends and good times—but I think that much of what I am was imprinted early on in those first years which I carry so vividly with me.

"Almost as clear in my mind are the tales my parents' told of their childhoods. I loved to listen to the recollections of their

VALERIE SCHO CAREY

growing up years. There were my mother's stories of her girlhood in Pittsburgh and of her father's produce market-on-wheels (he'd set his store up in a converted bus), and the tales my father told of life in the 'shtetl' in the Ukraine around World War I and of life as an immigrant in America in the 1920s. And of course, every night before my sister and I went to sleep, our mother read to us. My favorite stories and poems were in *The Tall Book of Make-Believe* illustrated by Garth Williams. (That book, I am happy to say is still available and was among the earliest to be bought for our own children.) The stories that were told and read to us fired my imagination. I could never get enough—even if it meant hearing the same ones over and over again. I loved the repetitions. Before I could read, I had started making up my own stories to entertain first myself when I was alone, and then my younger sister. Sometimes, when I was sick and had to stay in bed or early in the morning before getting up, I would gaze intently at the linoleum floor in the bedroom my sister and I shared. This linoleum was patterned with splotches of irregular shapes of color and I would imagine these splotches into the shapes of characters and strange beasts and I would make up stories about them. I never told those stories to anyone. They were for me alone.

"I don't think that I actually learned to read until I started school—but somehow I can't remember not being able to read. It seems as though one day I couldn't, and then suddenly the next thing I knew—I could! Probably it was a more gradual process than that, but if it was, the recollection of the time it took certainly escapes me. I read avidly. Frequently I got into trouble with my teachers because we were supposed to take turns reading aloud in our reading groups while silently following the words of the child whose turn it was to do the reading. I usually had read well on ahead so that when I was called upon to take my turn, I had not the slightest notion of where I was supposed to start. By fourth grade I was particularly interested in animal stories like *Black Beauty, Big Red, Call of the Wild,* and *Lassie Come Home.* My mother sometimes became irritated and asked when I was going to start reading about something besides animals. I, however, enjoyed what I was reading and kept right on with it. One day, I believe it was in sixth grade, I checked out a copy of *Anna and the King of Siam.* I liked it a lot and so embarked on a trend of reading biographies which continued through much of junior high school. I especially liked to read about queens like Catherine the Great and Mary, Queen of Scotts.

"In the fourth grade, our music teacher gave us an assignment of writing verses. I liked doing that assignment and continued trying to write poems even after going on to junior high school. One of those early efforts was revised by me many years later (about twenty years later), and was published as 'Nuthatch' in a magazine.

"In junior high, I continued to write. But instead of verses, I was determined to write a novel. Partly I wrote because I liked to write, and partly I wrote because I was extremely shy and writing was a way for me to carve a place for myself in the classroom hierarchy. Classmates, when they learned that I was writing a 'novel,' became interested in reading what I was writing. I passed the chapters around the classroom in installments and this was how I supported my fragile, adolescent ego. I also loved to draw and spent a good deal of time sketching. While I never seriously thought of making a career in the arts, I did serve for a while as our junior high school newspaper's editor.

"Throughout high school and my undergraduate years in college (at the University of Michigan in Ann Arbor), I continued writing and I occasionally sent something out to one literary magazine or another. I never succeeded in getting anything published, and my stint working on a campus literary magazine

Her husband and children ran away from home just to get shut of her. (From *The Devil and Mother Crump* by Valerie Scho Carey. Illustrated by Arnold Lobel.)

was half-hearted and short-lived. I concentrated much more on my course work in history, political science, and sociology than on writing. It was also the time of the Vietnam War. There was a good deal of turmoil on the campus and in most people's minds. My writing efforts took a back seat to the importance of events going on around me.

"In the fall of 1971, I began a course of graduate study at the University of Michigan. I hoped to earn a doctoral degree in East European and Balkan history with a minor in cultural anthropology. I found myself far too busy with studying to continue writing. Through an anthropology professor, I learned that a course was being taught on American folklore. I had already become interested in East European folktales, so I decided to audit the course. It was fascinating. From then on I was hooked on folklore. I enjoyed browsing through the folktale books at the library and reading whatever appealed to me. I became especially interested in British and Celtic tales and in the Arthurian legends. In the meanwhile, I had also begun work toward a degree in museum practice with the intention of becoming a curator if I did not go on to teach history in a college.

"In 1972, I married my husband. We had attended the same high school in Flint and had seen each other in the school hallways, but had not really met until we were both at the University of Michigan. I left school in December, 1974 after earning an M.A. in history (1973) and completing the course work for the Ph.D. The record stated that I was officially a 'pre-candidate' for the doctoral degree. I was preparing to take the preliminary examinations before beginning to write a dissertation. I stopped because my husband and I were expecting our first child and I decided that the time was right for me to take a break from the world of academics. After all, I had been going to school since kindergarten with no breaks save for summer vacation! To write my dissertation I thought I might have to go to Europe, and to complete my second master's degree (the one in museum practice) I would have to do a full-time internship in a museum. Rather than do either, I preferred to stay home and take care of our baby while my husband got his dental practice established. In May, 1975, our beautiful baby girl was born. Three years later, she was joined by another equally beautiful sister.

"As my mother had read to my sister and me, my husband and I read to our daughters. One day, a lucky juxtaposition of events occured. Our oldest daughter (then three years old) observed a rainbow shimmering in a puddle. 'It looks,' she said, 'like a rainbow that died and fell from the sky.' I thought at the time that I had never heard anything put quite so beautifully. A short time later, we were reading some of Hans Christian Andersen's tales aloud. Something about my daughter's remark connected with the way Andersen wrote life into inanimate objects in 'The Steadfast Tin Soldier,' and I wanted to write a story about raindrops and snowflakes and clouds and rainbows that were alive and animate. I made up the story. Later I wrote it down. It worked nicely as a story to tell to my daughters. It was less successful written down. But it sparked my interest in renewing long abandoned efforts at writing.

"I wrote and wrote and wrote some more. Eventually I had some stories and a few poems published in magazines. In 1983, *Harriet and William and the Terrible Creature* was accepted for publication by Ann Durell at E. P. Dutton. I had begun that story in 1979. It had taken four years from the time I began work on it, to the time it earned a contract. It began as a book which was supposed to be a space adventure for the very young. Watching the 'Star Wars' movie had inspired me to want to write a space adventure. The more I worked on the story, the less it became what it had been intended to be and the more it became a story about siblings who, while very different from each other, still

deeply respect and love each other. I deliberately chose to make Harriet the more adventurous of the pair, imbuing her with a gift for mechanical aptitude and a certain wanderlust, while William is a gentle soul who enjoys gardening and a quiet home life, yet is just as strong as Harriet when strength and courage are needed to face a situation. I experienced a feeling of elation almost like that of giving birth when the book was accepted for publication. Two months later, our son was born. It was 1985 when *Harriet and William* at last appeared in the bookstores.

"In the meanwhile, my husband and I took a cruise along the Maine coast aboard a wooden, three-masted schooner. It was a marvelous experience made even better by returning home to learn that Harper & Row Junior Books had accepted not one, but two of my manuscripts for publication. *The Devil and Mother Crump* (a retelling of a folktale found in many versions around the world) was published in 1987. I was deeply honored to have had Arnold Lobel do the illustrations for that book. At the same time, Laura Geringer at Harper sent me a contract for a book which will be published as *Tsugele's Broom*. It draws its setting from the stories my father told me of his life in the 'shtetl' in the Ukraine.

"In recent years, I have traveled twice to the British Isles. Both trips have further encouraged my interest in Celtic and British folklore, in the Arthurian stories and the tales of the Mabinogion from Wales. Folklore, fantasy, and fairy tales enthrall me. I continue in my current writing to work with retellings of old tales that have particular meaning for me, and with the creation of new stories that draw their inspiration from elements of the old (stories my parents told of their childhoods and stories I have read or heard from other folk traditions)."

HOBBIES AND OTHER INTERESTS: Travel, reading, crosstitch.

CARTER, Samuel III 1904-1988

OBITUARY NOTICE—See sketch in *SATA* Volume 37: Born October 6, 1904, in New York, N.Y.; died of cancer, December 28, 1988, in Southbury, Conn. Advertising executive, scriptwriter, and author. After a varied career in the advertising and entertainment industries, Carter retired in the 1960s to write a series of books about American history. In the 1930s and again in the 1960s he worked at advertising agencies, writing radio commercials for the J. Walter Thompson firm and later serving as vice-president in charge of television at Sullivan, Stauffer, Colwell & Bayles. During the intervening years Carter wrote for radio, in Hollywood, and for television, contributing to shows such as "Philco Television Playhouse," "Chevrolet on Broadway," and "Celanese Theatre" and writing and editing for the National Broadcasting Company. Carter also wrote the screenplay for the film "I Love You Truly." His books for children include *The Story of the Atlantic Cable, The Happy Dolphins, Vikings Bold: Their Voyages and Adventures,* and *Cowboy Capital of the World: Dodge City.*

FOR MORE INFORMATION SEE:

Contemporary Authors, Volume 57-60, Gale, 1976.
Who's Who in America, 45th edition, Marquis, 1988.

OBITUARIES

New York Times, January 6, 1989.

(Jacket illustration by Ted Lewin from *Pets* by Frances Chrystie.)

CHRYSTIE, Frances N(icholson) 1904-1986

PERSONAL: Born in 1904, in New York, N.Y.; died of cancer, November 27, 1986; daughter of Thomas Ludlow and Sallie Hooper (Morrow) Chrystie. *Education:* Attended Bryn Mawr College; graduated from Columbia University School of Journalism, 1928.

CAREER: Worked for over thirty years as a buyer of children's books for F. A. O. Schwarz, New York, N.Y.; editor for Viking Press. *Awards, honors: Pets* was selected one of New York Public Library's Books for the Teenage, 1980, 1981, and 1982.

WRITINGS:

(With Marion B. Lowndes) *Traffic* (illustrated with photographs by John F. Floherty and others), Doubleday, Doran, 1936.
(Compiler) *Riddle Me This* (illustrated by Elizabeth B. Ripley), Oxford University Press, 1940, reissued, Walck, 1968.
The First Book of Jokes and Funny Things (illustrated by Ida Scheib), F. Watts, 1951.
Pets: A Complete Handbook on the Care, Understanding, and Appreciation of All Kinds of Animal Pets (illustrated by Gillett Good Griffin), Little, Brown, 1953, 3rd revised edition, 1974.
The First Book of Surprising Facts (illustrated by Don Phillips), F. Watts, 1956, new edition, Grolier, 1967.

SIDELIGHTS: Chrystie's book *Pets,* a comprehensive book on pet care, has been in print more than thirty-five years. Herbert Zim commented that the author of *Pets* "is constantly aware of the fine relationship that can exist between a child and its pet."

FOR MORE INFORMATION SEE:

Martha E. Ward and Dorothy A. Marquardt, *Authors of Books for Young People,* Scarecrow, 1964.

CROSS, Gilbert B. 1939-
(J. C. Winters, Jon Winters)

PERSONAL: Born May 2, 1939, in Walkden, near Manchester, England; son of Gilbert Edward (a borough treasurer) and Doris (a secretary) Cross; married Peggy Boswell (a schoolteacher), December, 1966; children: two. *Education:* Manchester University, B.A., 1961; London University, post-graduate certificate in education, 1962; University of Louisville, M.A., 1965; University of Michigan, Ph.D., 1971. *Politics:* Democrat. *Home:* 1244 Ferdon Rd., Ann Arbor, Mich. 48104. *Agent:* Harold Ober Associates, Inc., 40 East 49th St., New York, N.Y. 10017. *Office:* Department of English Language and Literature, Eastern Michigan University, Ypsilanti, Mich. 48197.

CAREER: Eastern Michigan University, Ypsilanti, professor of English language and literature, 1966—; writer. *Member:* Society of Children's Book Writers.

WRITINGS:

CHILDREN'S BOOKS

A Hanging at Tyburn, Atheneum, 1983.
Mystery at Loon Lake, Atheneum, 1986.
Terror Train!, Atheneum, 1987.
A Witch across Time, Atheneum, 1989.

ADULT

(Editor with Alfred Nelson) *Drury Lane Journal: Selections from James Winston's Diaries, 1819-1827,* Society Theatre Research, (London), 1974.
Next Week East Lynne: Domestic Drama in Performance, Bucknell University Press, 1976.
(Under pseudonym Jon Winters) *The Drakov Memoranda,* Avon, 1979.
(Editor with Atelia Clarkson) *World Folktales: A Scribners Resource Collection,* Scribner, 1980.
(Under pseudonym Jon Winters) *The Catenary Exchange,* Avon, 1983.
(Under pseudonym J. C. Winters) *Berlin Fugue,* Avon, 1985.

SIDELIGHTS: "One thing I know about writers is they read a lot as children; I certainly did, and I realize many writers now dismissed as second rate had one undeniable talent. They could tell a good story. It should be obvious story is very important where children's books are concerned. A college student will read the dullest books if they are assigned—children will not. This fact must never be forgotten by prospective writers.

"I didn't start writing fiction until later in life. I had not the slightest intention of being a full time writer, and I still don't. I write when I think I have something to communicate.

"My first children's book, *A Hanging at Tyburn* grew directly from my experience as a child in Worsley, near Manchester, in England. Everyone was familiar with the stories of the eccentric Duke of Bridgewater and his attempt to build the first canal in England. His success ushered in the Industrial Revolution. I combined history with fiction, adding a hero, George Found, a strolling actor. Since my specialty is theatre history, and as co-

GILBERT B. CROSS

editor of James Winston's diaries, I had a lot of off-beat knowledge at my disposal.

"After the publication of *Tyburn*, a librarian asked me if I could write a book that would appeal to 'reluctant' readers. She pointed out there was very little material, especially with a boy as the central character, for the eight to twelve age range that combined literary merit with a high level of excitement. At this time, Atheneum asked me to write a mystery for the same age range. The result was *Mystery at Loon Lake*. Its sequel, *Terror Train!* continues the adventures of Jeff and Nguyen. I want very much to spread the joy of reading. If these mysteries prove successful, I shall write more of them."

HOBBIES AND OTHER INTERESTS: Golf, theater history, movie-going.

FOR MORE INFORMATION SEE:

Detroit Free Press, April 23, 1987.

DARLING, David J. 1953-

PERSONAL: Born July 29, 1953, in Glossop, England; son of Bernard Eric (a general store manager) and Marjorie (Dixon) Darling; married Jill Varie Case, 1978; children: Lori-An Varie, Jeffrey Alan. *Education:* University of Sheffield, B.Sc., 1974; University of Manchester, Ph.D., 1977. *Home:* Kirkby Thore, Cumbria, England. *Office:* c/o Dillon Press, Inc., 242 Portland Ave. S., Minneapolis, Minn. 55415.

CAREER: Cray Research, Minneapolis, Minn., manager of applications software, 1978-82; free-lance author, 1983—. *Awards, honors: Comets, Meteors, and Asteroids, The Galaxies, The New Astronomy, The Stars, The Universe, Where Are We Going in Space?*, and *The Planets* were each chosen one of Child Study Association of America's Children's Books of the Year, 1986.

WRITINGS:

JUVENILE

Diana: The People's Princess (biography), Dillon, 1984.

*"DISCOVERING OUR UNIVERSE" SERIES; JUVENILE; ALL
    ILLUSTRATED BY JEANETTE SWOFFORD*

The Moon: A Spaceflight Away, Dillon, 1984.
The Sun: Our Neighborhood Star, Dillon, 1984.
Comets, Meteors, and Asteroids: Rocks in Space, Dillon, 1984.
Where Are We Going in Space?, Dillon, 1984.
The Planets: The Next Frontier, Dillon, 1984.
The Stars: From Birth to Black Hole, Dillon, 1985.
Other Worlds: Is There Life Out There?, Dillon, 1985.
The New Astronomy: An Ever-Changing Universe, Dillon, 1985.
The Galaxies: Cities of Stars, Dillon, 1985.
The Universe: Past, Present, and Future, Dillon, 1985.

DAVID J. DARLING

"THE WORLD OF COMPUTERS" SERIES; JUVENILE; ALL ILLUSTRATED BY TOM LUND, EXCEPT AS NOTED

Computers at Home: Today and Tomorrow (illustrated by T. Lund and Billy Fugate), Dillon, 1986.
Fast, Faster, Fastest: The Story of Supercomputers, Dillon, 1986.
Inside Computers: Hardware and Software, Dillon, 1986.
The Microchip Revolution, Dillon, 1986.
Robots and the Intelligent Computer, Dillon, 1986.

ADULT

Deep Time: The Journey of a Single Subatomic Particle from the Moment of Creation to the Death of the Universe and Beyond, Delacorte, 1989.

Contributor of articles to periodicals, including *Astronomy* and *Odyssey.*

WORK IN PROGRESS: A new science series for grades five and up called "Could You Ever . . . ?"

SIDELIGHTS: "I was born and grew up in the Peak District of Derbyshire, England, a picturesque region of wild moors and limestone caverns. An only child, I had a passion for reading anything on science or science fiction. As far back as I can remember my overriding interest was always astronomy and space travel; the idea of becoming a writer never entered my head until much later.

"At university, I first studied physics and then spent three years doing research for my doctorate in astronomy. In all that time I never looked through the eyepiece of a telescope—the one thing that most people assume all astronomers do! Instead I worked with the University's large computers, programming them to show what happens when a star like the sun grows old.

"It was in my last year as a student that I met my future wife, Jill, an American then on vacation in Britain. A few months later we were married, and I found myself living in Jill's home town, Minneapolis, Minnesota—very happy but with no idea about what job I wanted to do!

"It was then that the notion of writing for a living first seriously occurred to me. I had done no writing to speak of before, but I thought I could write reasonably well and, just as importantly, I felt an urge to share my interest in space with other people.

"I applied for an editorial position at *Astronomy* magazine in Milwaukee, and to my great surprise, was offered it. At the same time, because of my background in computing, I had applied for a post with Cray Research, a recently-formed company in Minneapolis that built supercomputers. Cray also offered me a job, which for various reasons I accepted, having reached an agreement with *Astronomy* to supply them with articles on a free-lance basis. My first published piece, called 'How Stars Lose Their Cool,' appeared in the March, 1979 issue.

"So, my writing career began. Over the next few years, on weekends and in the evenings, I wrote several more articles on stars, galaxies, and black holes, and steadily came to the realization that I enjoyed writing much more than working with computers. Finally, at the start of 1983, after a lot of encouragement from my wife, I took the plunge and became a full-time, free-lance writer.

"By now, we had two lively young children, Lori-An and Jeffrey, who were fortunate enough to be citizens of both the United States and Britain. We took the opportunity of my job change to move across the Atlantic for a while and educate the children in British schools.

"So much of a writer's success depends on luck and good timing. I was lucky enough to send in a proposal for a series of childrens' books on astronomy to a small publishing house, Dillon Press, in Minneapolis at just the time they happened to be considering such a project. The outcome was 'Discovering Our Universe,' a ten-volume series intended for young readers.

"Following this, I completed another juvenile series with Dillon Press about computers, entitled 'The World of Computers.' Dillon also asked me if I would consider doing a short biography of Princess Diana for children, since being in England I could presumably find out more about her! Thus I penned my first non-scientific book to date, *Diana: The Peoples' Princess.*

"Unpredictability is one aspect of being an author that I really enjoy! You never know what lies around the next bend. I certainly could never have guessed that I would have had published a book about the British royalty. Nor could I have foretold that a marvellous up-and-coming literary agent, Patricia Van der Leun, of Southport, Connecticut, would have contacted me after reading one of my articles in *Astronomy.*

"The computer series for Dillon was just nearing completion when Patricia wrote to ask me if I had any ideas for an *adult* book on astronomy. That was to mark a new turning point in my career. Within a few months I had sent to her a proposal, with a sample chapter, for *Deep Time,* a book that deals with the origins, evolution, and final fate of the Universe. It was published by Delacorte followed by editions published in Britain, Italy, Germany, and Japan.

"I have begun a new childrens' science series for Dillon Press with the title 'Could You Ever . . . ?' This series tries to answer young peoples' questions about whether things like journeys to the stars, time travel, meeting aliens, and communicating with other animal species will ever be possible. Indeed it tries to answer the very questions that my children are always asking me!"

HOBBIES AND OTHER INTERESTS: Classical guitar.

Di CERTO, Joseph J(ohn) 1933-

PERSONAL: Born February 27, 1933, in New York, N.Y.; son of Rocco (a barber) and Severina (a dressmaker; maiden name, Basile) Di Certo; married Josephine Valle (a nursery school teacher), September 5, 1964; children: Lisa Ann, David, Jennifer Ann. *Education:* Hunter College of the City University of New York, B.A., 1968. *Politics:* Independent. *Religion:* Roman Catholic. *Address:* 1646 First Ave., New York, N.Y. 10028.

CAREER: Writer, 1955—; Curtiss Wright Corp., Woodridge, N.J., senior technical writer, 1956-59; American Machine & Foundry, Greenwich, Conn., technical writer and editor, 1959-62; Sperry Gyroscope, Great Neck, N.Y., publication engineer, 1962-66; Sylvania Electric Products, New York City, advertising supervisor, 1966-72; Al Paul Lefton Co., Inc. (advertising agency), account supervisor, 1972-73; Marstella Advertising Agency, senior account executive, 1973; Sperry Rand Corp., New York City, manager of special projects, 1974-78; CBS Television, N.Y., director of world wide communications.

Military service: U.S. Air Force, 1952-56. *Awards, honors:* Best Magazine Series of the Year from the Association of Technical Writers and Editors, 1960; *Star Voyage* was chosen one of Child Study Association of America's Children's Books of the Year, 1981; *From Earth to Infinity* was named one of New York Public Library's Books for the Teen Age, 1981.

WRITINGS:

Planning and Preparing Data Flow Diagrams, Hayden, 1963.
Missile Base beneath the Sea, St. Martin's, 1967.
The Electric Wishing Well, Macmillan, 1976.
From Earth to Infinity: A Guide to Space Travel, Messner, 1980.
Star Voyage, Messner, 1981.
Looking into T.V., Messner, 1983.
The Wall People: In Search of a Home (novel; illustrated by Frederic Marvin), Atheneum, 1985.
Hoofbeats in the Wilderness: The Story of the Pony Express, F. Watts, 1988.

Also author of six audiovisual training programs published by Educational Activities. Contributor to *Electronic Design.*

WORK IN PROGRESS: The Prime Time Emmy Award Book, with Gene Barnes, to be published by Abbeville Press.

SIDELIGHTS: "Life in the 1930s in East Harlem, New York City was bitter-sweet. Times were hard and our family was very poor. But it was a close ethnic (Italian) neighborhood and a time of strong family values. We never heard of drugs and the church was open all night. Interestingly, I had absolutely no interest in writing (that came much later). I was interested in aviation and music. Later my brother Dominick and I formed a country-western band and singing group.

"After high school (where I studied aviation mechanics) I entered the Air Force, attended several schools to study jet engines and electronics, and became an instructor. Leaving the Air Force I went to work at American Machine & Foundry, working on the Titan missile launching systems. I also attended college at night, studying mathematics.

"While in the Air Force, I was approached one day by an officer who asked me (for some strange, unknown reason) if I would be interested in writing a monthly column for the base magazine. And for some strange, unknown reason, I said yes. From that day on (in 1955) I never stopped writing.

"A former singer in a band, I have written songs and produced three albums of songs for children entitled 'My Favorite Planet,' 'What Will I Be When I Grow Up,' and 'Songs about Peter Paintbrush.'"

HOBBIES AND OTHER INTERESTS: Music (big bands, Sinatra), golf.

JOSEPH J. Di CERTO

DRIMMER, Frederick

PERSONAL: Born in Brooklyn, N.Y.; son of John (a restaurant owner) and Mina (Lichtenberg) Drimmer; married Evelyn Laderman (a librarian), August 24, 1940; children: John Andrew, Jean Louisa. *Education:* City College (now City College of the City University of New York), B.A. (magna cum laude), 1938; Columbia University, M.A., 1940; New School for Social Research, additional graduate study, 1947-48. *Home:* 281 Grumman Ave., Norwalk, Conn. 06851.

CAREER: Writer. Greenberg (publishing house), New York City, editor-in-chief, 1940-46; City College (now City College of the City University of New York), English instructor, 1946-47; Greystone Press, New York City, editor-in-chief, 1946-56; Famous Artists Schools, Inc., Westport, Conn., editor-in-chief, 1956-72; Norwalk Community College, Norwalk, Conn., English instructor, 1966-67; *Funk and Wagnalls Encyclopedia,* New York City, writer and editor, 1974-78. *Military service:* U.S. Naval Reserve, 1943-46; in naval intelligence. *Member:* Phi Beta Kappa. *Awards, honors: The Elephant Man* was named a Notable Children's Trade Book in the Field of Social Studies by the National Council for Social Studies and the Children's Book Council, 1985.

WRITINGS:

Very Special People: The Struggles, Loves and Triumphs of Human Oddities (nonfiction), Crown, 1973, revised edition, Bantam, 1976, new edition, Bell, 1985.
In Search of Eden (nonfiction), C. R. Gibson, 1973.
Daughters of Eve (nonfiction), C. R. Gibson, 1975.
Body Snatchers, Stiffs, and Other Ghoulish Delights (nonfiction), Fawcett, 1981, new edition, 1987.

FREDERICK DRIMMER

The Elephant Man (young adult fictional biography), Putnam, 1985.

Born Different: Amazing Stories of Very Special People (young adult nonfiction), Atheneum, 1988.

FILMS

"Some Call Them Freaks," Home Box Office, 1981.

EDITOR

The Knapsack Book (anthology), Greenberg, 1942.

The Animal Kingdom, three volumes, Greystone, 1953.

Scalps and Tomahawks (nonfiction), Coward-McCann, 1961, revised editon published as *Captured by the Indians,* Dover, 1985.

A Friend Is Someone Special (anthology), C. R. Gibson, 1975.

Prayer (anthology), C. R. Gibson, 1978.

How to Draw and Paint Landscapes, Cortina, 1983.

Contributor to books, including *Complete Book of Mothercraft,* Greystone, 1952; *People's Almanac; Reader's Digest Family Health Guide,* and *You and the Law,* both published by Reader's Digest Press.

ADAPTATIONS:

RECORDINGS

"Scalps & Tomahawks: Journals of the Pioneers," Recorded Books, 1981.

"Born Different," Talking Books for the Blind, 1990.

WORK IN PROGRESS: An adult book tentatively titled *Blood for Blood: The Story of Executions in America,* for Lyle Stuart.

SIDELIGHTS: "I began to write in childhood. My first literary effort was a poem on the benefits of saving, written for a savings bank. My reward was a pencil with my name on it in gold letters and seeing the poem in print. The praise I received convinced me this was the way to go.

"As a teenager I wrote a good deal of poetry, as well as romantic stories about ancient Egypt and archaeologists. Many of these were published in newspapers. My first book was a little pamphlet of my poems that was published by a friend who had a print shop. At college I wrote for the school magazine and won awards for poetry and essays. My aim was to write and teach

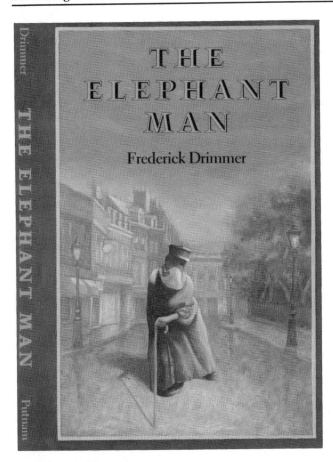

Only the eyes seemed fully human. (Jacket illustration by Toby Gowing from *The Elephant Man* by Frederick Drimmer.)

after college, but I graduated in the hard times of the Depression and opportunities were nonexistent.

"My first real job was as an editor with a book publisher. I could hardly believe my good luck. I quickly learned that editing was more than finding a good manuscript and seeing it through the press. If it was lacking in any way, I was expected to provide the remedy. Often this required writing thousands of words that the author had failed to furnish. With the help of careful research I found myself writing competently in many fields—medicine, law, animal life, baby care, child psychology, art, and anything else. To paraphrase Moliere, by hammering at the anvil I became a blacksmith, able to write in any area. I was a published and paid writer before I realized it. In the Navy, during World War II, between stints as a teacher and a Naval intelligence officer in the oriental languages branch, I wrote countless articles for a Navy newspaper. Later I was an editor of books for many years.

"I have written a number of assigned books for publishers, but the ones that mean the most to me are books that spring out of my imagination or are born of my personal interests. I try to write the kind of book I would like to read. One of these is *Captured by the Indians*. This was inspired by seeing a row of books at the Smithsonian Institution written by Indian captives about their adventures. I proceeded to compile, edit, and condense the best of these accounts. That my work was sound is proved by the book's being in print thirty years after it was first published.

"My book *Very Special People*, which sold over a million copies, told the stories of the struggles and triumphs of people born with birth defects, a subject that moved me deeply. The

reputation this book brought me led to a series of lectures in colleges around the country. Home Box Office commissioned me to write a television movie entitled 'Some Call Them Freaks,' starring Richard Kiley, and was considered by HBO as one of its best productions.

"My search for pictures to illustrate my college lectures brought me into contact with a North Carolina showman who owned a large collection. He also owned two dead bodies that he exhibited around the country, and he suggested there might be enormous interest in a book about 'stiffs,' as he called them. Research led me into the whole fascinating story of body snatching in Britain and the United States as well as such curious incidents as the theft of Charlie Chaplin's body and the bizarre attempt to steal Abraham Lincoln's. I was intrigued by such strange people as Martin Van Butchell, who embalmed his wife and kept her in the parlor, and Elmer McCurdy, the long-dead outlaw who turned up on a television movie set. Readers seem to find them just as memorable.

"Seeing the interest of young people in human oddities, I wondered why no one had ever told the story of the Elephant Man for teenagers; I was sure it would appeal to them. That my hunch was correct was proved by the success of my young adult book *The Elephant Man*, published by Putnam in 1985. I did the book as fiction because this technique allowed me to get inside the Elephant Man and show young people how he thought and felt, so that they could identify with him. The book was singled out for praise by many librarians and teachers, who viewed it as a

Robert [Wadlow, center] poses with his two brothers. (From *Born Different: Amazing Stories of Very Special People* by Frederick Drimmer.)

moving biography rather than fiction. In part this was because I had studied the Elephant Man's life so closely, visiting the London Hospital where his relics are kept, and conferring with medical authorities about the nature of his disease, which affects 100,000 Americans today. I have lectured about the Elephant Man in local schools and libraries in an effort to strengthen young people's sympathy with the handicapped.

"It was with this same purpose that I wrote my most recent young adult book, *Born Different: Amazing Stories of Very Special People*. I chose as my subjects some of the most fascinating human oddities of all time—including Chang and Eng, the original Siamese twins; Robert Wadlow, the tallest man that ever lived; Herrmann Unthan, born without arms, who taught himself to play the violin with his feet, and others. My aim was to show, first, that even people with severe birth defects, who may look very different from the rest of us, have exactly the same feelings as anybody else, and should be treated not as curiosities but as fellow human beings. Secondly, my aim was to show how the people in my book, although burdened with great handicaps, managed to overcome them or compensate for them so well that they won the respect and admiration of everyone who saw them. Their lives are splendid examples of the axiom 'Where there's a will, there's a way.'"

Of *Born Different* the *Kirkus* reviewer said, "The author of an adult book on 'human oddities' now brings the same respect, scientific knowledge, sense of history, and awe to a book for young readers . . . . The only surprise here is that it took so long before someone realized that kids would be as fascinated by Drimmer's stories as adults are. This one will be hard to keep on the shelf."

"I am nearing completion an adult book tentatively titled *Until You Are Dead: The Story of Executions in America*. I have planned the book not just to appeal to everyone who enjoys true crime stories and wonders what happens to the criminal after he (or she) has been found guilty, but to be a meaningful contribution to the literature of capital punishment. From the days of the Pilgrims to the latest execution in Texas or North Carolina, the book tells the stories of the most notorious criminals in our history—their life in crime, how they were captured and convicted, how they spent their days on death row, and finally how they faced death when executed. This has required endless research into old newspapers and magazines and correspondence with penologists and departments of correction all over the country. I'm paying special attention to how each successive technology—hanging, firing squad, electrocution, lethal gas, lethal injection—was developed, the first person put to death by it (when known), and the problems that arose in carrying out the execution. The book also includes chapters on presidential assassins and on people who were executed and were later found innocent. It will have many astonishing illustrations."

HOBBIES AND OTHER INTERESTS: Travel, music, languages.

FOR MORE INFORMATION SEE:

Bridgeport Sunday Post, November 24, 1974, September 22, 1985.
Sunday Advocate (Stamford, Conn.), October 25, 1981.
Hour (Norwalk, Conn.), October 30, 1981, October 5, 1985.

THEA DUBELAAR

DUBELAAR, Thea 1947-

PERSONAL: Born January 26, 1947, in Den Ilp, Holland; daughter of Hendrikus (a banker) and J. A. (a couturier; maiden name, Mul) Dubelaar; married Maurice Balzamont, January 1, 1972. *Education:* Attended journalism schools. *Office:* c/o Uitg. Ploegsma, Postbus 19857, 1000 GW Amsterdam, The Netherlands.

CAREER: Journalist; free-lance writer, 1973— . Worked at an insurance company for one year, and on a woman's magazine for seven years, both in Holland. *Member:* Dutch Writers Trade Union. *Awards, honors:* Silver Plaque Award from the Committee for the General Promotion of the Dutch Book, 1980, for *Sjanetje.*

WRITINGS:

FOR CHILDREN

Sjanetje (illustrated by Mance Post), Ploegsma (Amsterdam), 1979, published as *Maria,* translated by Anthea Bell, Morrow, 1982.
Liegbeest (title means "You're a Liar"), Ploegsma, 1980.
Zand in je limonade (title means "Sand in Your Lemonade"), Ploegsma, 1982.
Een beetje leeuw (title means "A Little Lion"), Ploegsma, 1983.
Het bontje van Betsie (title means "Betsy's Fur"), Ploegsma, 1983.
Drie in de put (title means "Three in a Hole"), Ploegsma, 1983.
Gevecht om een glimlach (title means "Battle for a Smile"), Ploegsma, 1984.
De grap (title means "The Joke"), Ploegsma, 1985.
Kom erin, zei de spin, Ploegsma, 1986.
Een ander verhaal (title means "Another Story"), Ploegsma, 1987.
Mijn pappa is een prins (title means "My Father Is a Prince"), Ploegsma, 1988.

Het wonder van Ron (title means "Ron's Miracle"), Ploegsma, 1989.
Gouden Vleugels, (title means "Golden Wings"), Ploegsma, 1989.
Op zoek naar Vincent (title means "Looking for Vincent"), Ploegsma, 1989.

WORK IN PROGRESS: A children's book telling the story of the life of Vincent van Gogh with thirty-two reproductions of his paintings as well as other illustrations by Ruud Bruyn.

SIDELIGHTS: "Traveling, creating and writing are equally important to me. I need nature very badly and the most awful time of my life was the eleven years that I lived in an apartment in Paris. Human contact is essential to me. In big cities there are too many people. Human contact is almost impossible. The fewer people there are in a place the more contact you have.

"I started to write books when I lived in Paris to compensate for the lack of nature and human contact. I continue to live in the country because I am addicted to writing."

HOBBIES AND OTHER INTERESTS: Gardening, silk painting.

FOR MORE INFORMATION SEE:

Jeugboekengids (Antwerpen, Belgium), January, 1988.

du MAURIER, Daphne 1907-1989

OBITUARY NOTICE—See sketch in *SATA* Volume 27: Born May 13, 1907, in London, England; died April 19, 1989, in Par, Cornwall, England; cremated. Editor, and author of nonfiction, plays, and novels. Du Maurier is widely remembered for her best-selling Gothic novel *Rebecca,* which was first published in 1938 and was later made into an Academy Award-winning film by director Alfred Hitchcock. Regarded as a gifted storyteller, she wrote suspenseful fiction with a mixture of romance, mystery and violence. Du Maurier's fifty-year writing career began in the late 1920s with short stories sold to magazines; later these were published in collections, and one became the classic Hitchcock film "The Birds." The first of her novels, *The Loving Spirit,* was published in 1931, and led to her meeting her husband, Frederick A. M. Browning. Upon reading her book, he vowed to meet the author, and they married soon after. In addition to her fiction, du Maurier wrote plays such as "The Years Between" and an adaption of *Rebecca,* and historical and scholarly works including a biography of her father, *Gerald: A Portrait,* and her own autobiography, *Myself When Young: The Shaping of a Writer.* She also edited *The Young George du Maurier: A Selection of His Letters, 1860-1867.* In 1969 she was named a Dame Commander of the Order of the British Empire.

FOR MORE INFORMATION SEE:

Daphne du Maurier, *Gerald: A Portrait,* Gollanz, 1934, Doubleday, 1935, reissued, Richard West, 1978.
D. du Maurier, *Myself When Young: The Shaping of a Writer,* Doubleday, 1977 (published in England as *Growing Pains: The Shaping of a Writer,* Gollanz, 1977).
D. du Maurier, *The Rebecca Notebooks and Other Memories,* Doubleday, 1980.
Contemporary Authors New Revision Series, Volume 6, Gale, 1982.

Who's Who, 141st edition, St. Martin's, 1989.
The Writer's Directory 1988-90, St. Martin's, 1988.

OBITUARIES

Chicago Tribune, April 20, 1989.
Detroit Free Press, April 20, 1989.
Los Angeles Times, April 20, 1989.
New York Times, April 20, 1989.
Times (London), April 20, 1989.
Washington Post, April 20, 1989.

DWIGGINS, Don 1913-1988

OBITUARY NOTICE—See sketch in *SATA* Volume 4: Born November 15, 1913, in Plainfield, N.J.; died in an automobile accident, December 10, 1988, in Malibu, Calif. Aviator, businessman, journalist, editor, and author. Dwiggins was a renowned pilot who flew with the Royal Canadian Air Force during World War II. Later, he briefly operated his own plane rental business. In 1947 he became aviation editor for the *Los Angeles Daily News,* where he remained until 1954. Two years later, Dwiggins assumed the same post with the *Los Angeles Mirror,* and stayed there until commencing his writing career in the early 1960s. In 1965 he worked for Disney Studios as editor of "Mickey Mouse Newsreel." He eventually wrote more than thirty works, several of them for children, including *Famous Flyers and the Ships They Flew, The Asteroid War, Jimmy Fox and the Mountain Rescue, Flying the Space Shuttles,* and *Hello? Who's Out There?: The Search for Extraterrestrial Life.* His children's book, *Eagle Has Landed,* was selected one of the Child Study Association of America's Children's Books of the Year in 1970. In addition, Dwiggins was senior editor of the magazine *Plane and Pilot* from 1974 to 1987.

FOR MORE INFORMATION SEE:

Horn Book, December, 1969.
Contemporary Authors New Revision Series, Volume 23, Gale, 1988.

OBITUARIES

Los Angeles Times, December 13, 1988.

FORSHAY-LUNSFORD, Cin 1965-

PERSONAL: Born May 2, 1965, in Syosset, N.Y.; daughter of Raymond Gordon (a vice-president of an insurance agency) and Elizabeth Louise (an English teacher; maiden name, Forshay) Lunsford. *Education:* Attended Queens College of the City University of New York, 1985-88. *Home and office:* 2929 Longbeach Rd., Apt. A., Oceanside, N.Y. 11572.

CAREER: Writer. Valley Stream Adult School, Valley Stream, N.Y., teacher of English as a second language, 1986-87, 1989. Lecturer. *Awards, honors:* Delacorte Press Prize for an Outstanding First Young Adult Novel, 1984, exhibited at the Bologna International Children's Book Fair, 1985, and named an Outstanding Book for Young Adults by the College of Education, University of Iowa, 1987, all for *Walk through Cold Fire;* named one of the top one hundred teens in America by *Teen Age* magazine, 1985; named an American Teen "Most Likely to Succeed," by *Seventeen,* 1987.

WRITINGS:

Walk through Cold Fire (young adult novel), Delacorte, 1985.

Contributor of short story "Saint Agnes Sends the Golden Boy" to anthology, *Visions,* edited by Don Gallo, Delacorte, 1987; and of "Love Potion" to anthology *Connections,* edited by D. Gallo, Bantam, 1989. *Walk through Cold Fire* has been published in England, Canada, and Denmark.

ADAPTATIONS:

"Walk Through Cold Fire" (cassette), Listening Library.
"Visions" (cassette; includes "Saint Agnes Sends the Golden Boy"), Listening Library, 1988.

WORK IN PROGRESS: The Emerald Sea Princess, a novel; "Riding Out the Storm," a play to be included in a collection of short plays for young adults edited by Don Gallo, for Harper.

SIDELIGHTS: "I began writing the first draft of *Walk through Cold Fire* when I was a seventeen-year-old high school senior. All my life I had enjoyed storytelling, whether it was telling ghost stories at slumber parties or escaping into my creative imagination to tell my own self tales. Just after my eighteenth birthday and prior to my high school graduation, I moved out of my parents' house to a studio in Long Beach where, eight months after it was begun, I finished the manuscript. Written in the first person, *Walk through Cold Fire* deals with the mental, emotional, and spiritual transformation of a sixteen-year-old girl over the course of one tender, pivotal, and tragic summer. Drawing on autobiographical details from my life experiences, the book reflects my vision of a segment of American youth whose motivations are misunderstood, actions condemned, and dreams

CIN FORSHAY-LUNSFORD

denied by society. Recurring themes in my work include the search for personal freedom, creative force in youth subculture, and the struggle to discover and maintain a unique sense of self.

"For eight months the book simultaneously tormented and sustained me. I became thoroughly obsessed with the characters and themes. Putting my characters into the kinds of situations that their personalities dictated they might become involved with, they inherited the strength and sensitivity to survive without selling out, to grow up but not give up.

"My characters were real to me. I constructed a town for them. I lent them the railroad tracks and the woods where I'd meet my friends on warm summer nights. I haunted them with the same fears, the same joys I was experiencing. I threw them the shadows of my life, stripping away my own defenses to breathe life into them.

"At one point I gave so much that I hurt. While they could not be more than I gave them, one day I realized the extent to which I had brought my characters. Instead of my leading them to make certain decisions, their fate became clear according to their individual personalities.

"It seemed that within the context of the novel they had grown stronger than I would ever be. When it dawned on me that I had made them what they were, I knew I could make myself what I wanted to be. I drew fortitude from them like blood.

"I believe that a unique human being, no matter how pressed to conform to society, to abandon a great dream for simple goals and easy victories, must turn up his collar and blink back the tears and fight. I have composed a statement that speaks for my people—that element of society too proud, too passionate to choke down lies; people who are punished for wanting more than the scraps thrown to them, for taking more than what is given.

"'Saint Agnes Sends the Golden Boy' is an odd tale. The story melds romance, fantasy, folklore, and dream; and involves ancient ritual, modern relationships, and a touch of magic. I was inspired to write it after I had a particularly vivid dream involving

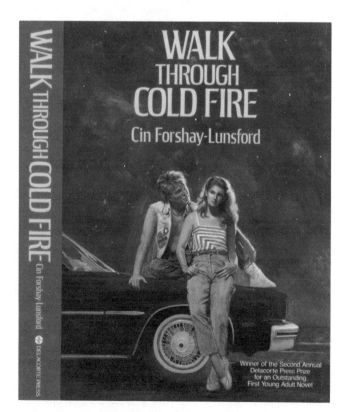

I am what is called an anomaly, which means I don't fit in. (Jacket illustration by Frank Morris from *Walk through Cold Fire* by Cin Forshay-Lunsford.)

a creature part boy, part lion, and part fish. I enjoy interpreting my dreams and often find material for my stories in them.

"'Love Potion' is the story of a classic love triangle, with one small hitch, one of the corners is a modern day witch. Also featuring teenage characters, this tale is one of my favorites, since I indulge myself and my readers with a happy ending.

"'Riding Out the Storm' is a fast-paced play wherein the siblings, girlfriend, and friends of a critically wounded young man wait out the time before his surgery is over by recalling fond memories of him, and discussing quite passionately: life and death, religion, relationships, eternity, and faith. Though it deals with a powerful and unnerving subject, teenage suicide, the play is not without humour, warmth, and hope.

"At Queens College, I studied literature and communication arts, while working on *Shards*, an as yet unpublished novel about a young artist. I lectured extensively across the United States at conferences, creative writing workshops, schools, and universities.

"The ocean has always endowed upon me a sense of serenity, beauty, and purpose, and so the days I spent living at the beach were for the most part fruitful. Before moving to my current residence in Oceanside, I traveled cross-country as a passenger on my friend's motorcycle. It is important for a writer to experience different people and places.

"'Daughters of the Moon and Other Poems' is a book-length collection of original poems I wrote between 1979 and 1988. Currently, I am living in a sunny apartment over a store in Oceanside. My studio is draped with plants and cluttered with books, sea shells, crystals, candles, and small animals. My current project is a novel called *The Emerald Sea Princess*, which falls into the realm of fantasy.

"Being a published author at nineteen is a great victory for me. I was expecting—and was willing—to spend my life struggling to pay the rent, stealing moments away from the grind to create something of worth and beauty out of the poet's life of loneliness and want. I've been desperate to reach the root of a reader's heart, to give myself away under the thin guise of my characters. I have been given that chance, and it is worth one hundred times over the sacrifices I made in choosing this road."

HOBBIES AND OTHER INTERESTS: Theater, music, film, ballet, mystic arts.

FOR MORE INFORMATION SEE:

Newsday, January 30, 1985.
Book Alert, May, 1985.
Children's Book Review Service, June, 1985.
Publishers Weekly, June 21, 1985.
Voice of Youth Advocates, August, 1985.
Teenage, September, 1985.
New York Times Book Review, September 22, 1985.
New York Times, October 6, 1985.
Book Report, November/December, 1985.
"Fire and Ice," *Top of the News,* winter, 1986.
Seventeen, September, 1987.

FOX, Paula 1923-

PERSONAL: Born April 22, 1923, in New York, N.Y.; daughter of Paul Hervey (a writer) and Elsie (de Sola) Fox; married Richard Sigerson, 1948 (divorced, 1954); married Martin Greenburg (a professor), June 9, 1962; children: (first marriage) Adam, Gabriel. *Education:* Columbia University, 1955-58. *Residence:* Brooklyn, N.Y. *Agent:* Robert Lescher, Lescher & Lescher, 67 Irving Place, New York, N.Y. 10003.

CAREER: Author. Worked as a teacher at the Ethical Culture School in New York, N.Y.; University of Pennsylvania, Philadelphia, professor of English literature, 1963—. *Member:* P.E.N., Authors League of America, Authors Guild.

AWARDS, HONORS: Portrait of Ivan was selected one of Child Study Association of America's Children's Books of the Year, 1969, *Blowfish Live in the Sea,* 1970, *The Slave Dancer,* 1973, and *The Moonlight Man,* 1987; *The King's Falcon* was selected one of the American Institute of Graphic Arts Children's Books, 1970; National Book Award Finalist, Children's Book Category, 1971, for *Blowfish Live in the Sea,* and 1979, for *The Little Swineherd and Other Tales;* National Institute of Arts and Letters Award, 1972; Guggenheim Fellow, 1972; one of *School Library Journal's* Best Books of the Year, 1973, Newbery Medal from the American Library Association, 1974, and Special Hans Christian Andersen Honor List, 1979, all for *The*

PAULA FOX

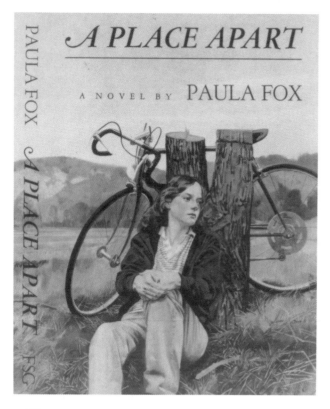

When my father died . . . I knew there would never be anyone who could tell me anything. (Jacket illustration by Robert Sabin from *A Place Apart* by Paula Fox.)

Slave Dancer; Hans Christian Andersen Medal for Writing, 1978.

A Place Apart was selected one of *New York Times* Outstanding Books, and one of *School Library Journal*'s Best Books of the Year, both 1980, one of New York Public Library's Books for the Teen Age, 1981, and American Book Award for Children's Fiction Paperback, 1983; Brandeis Fiction Citation, 1984; Rockefeller Foundation Fellowship Grant, 1984; Child Study Children's Book Award from the Bank Street College of Education, one of *New York Times* Notable Books, and one of American Library Association's Best Books for Young Adults, all 1984, Newbery Honor Book, and Christopher Award, both 1985, and International Board on Books for Young People Honor List for Writing (USA), 1986, all for *One-Eyed Cat*; *The Moonlight Man* was selected one of *New York Times* Notable Books, 1986; Silver Medallion from the University of Southern Mississippi, 1987; *Boston Globe-Horn Book* Award for Fiction, 1989, for *The Village by the Sea*.

WRITINGS:

Maurice's Room (illustrated by Ingrid Fetz), Macmillan, 1966, reissued, 1985.
A Likely Place (illustrated by Edward Ardizzone), Macmillan, 1967.
How Many Miles to Babylon? (ALA Notable Book; illustrated by Paul Giovanopoulos), David White, 1967, reissued, Bradbury, 1980.
Poor George (adult), Harcourt, 1967.
The Stone-Faced Boy (ALA Notable Book; illustrated by Donald A. Mackay), Bradbury, 1968.

Dear Prosper (illustrated by Steve McLachlin), David White, 1968.
Portrait of Ivan (ALA Notable Book; illustrated by Saul Lambert), Bradbury, 1969, reissued, 1985.
The King's Falcon (*Horn Book* honor list; illustrated by Eros Keith), Bradbury, 1969.
Hungry Fred (illustrated by Rosemary Wells), Bradbury, 1969.
Blowfish Live in the Sea, Bradbury, 1970.
Desperate Characters (adult), Harcourt, 1970, reissued, Nonpareil, 1980.
The Western Coast (adult), Harcourt, 1972.
Good Ethan (Junior Literary Guild selection; illustrated by Arnold Lobel), Bradbury, 1973.
The Slave Dancer (ALA Notable Book; illustrated by E. Keith), Bradbury, 1973.
The Widow's Children (adult), Dutton, 1976.
The Little Swineherd and Other Tales (illustrated by Leonard Lubin), Dutton, 1978.
A Place Apart, Farrar, Straus, 1980.
One-Eyed Cat (ALA Notable Book), Bradbury, 1984, large print edition, Cornerstone Books, 1987.
A Servant's Tale (adult), North Point Press, 1984.
The Moonlight Man, Bradbury, 1986.
Lilly and the Lost Boy, Orchard Books, 1987.
The Village by the Sea, Orchard Books, 1988.

Has also written for television.

ADAPTATIONS:

''Desperate Characters'' (motion picture), Paramount, 1970.
''One-Eyed Cat'' (cassette; filmstrip with cassette), Random House.

WORK IN PROGRESS: Two adult books—one entitled *The God of Nightmares*, takes place in New Orleans during the 1940s.

SIDELIGHTS: Paula Fox is one of the most highly-regarded writers currently working in the United States. Her books for children and young adults are regularly cited for their intelligence, originality, and social consciousness. Her adult novels have been praised for their exquisite craftsmanship, keen observations and uncompromising integrity. Critic Irving Howe has written that *Desperate Characters* is a masterpiece in a major line of American fiction, along with *Billy Budd, The Great Gatsby, Miss Lonelyhearts*, and *Seize the Day*.

''There are a good many autobiographical details in my books, mostly having to do with place: the Cuban sugar plantation where I spent part of my childhood with my grandmother; Spanish Harlem, where my cousins lived; the Hudson Valley and Brooklyn Heights, where I have lived. I have never written—and do not intend to write—the 'story of my life.' Yet my childhood was in many ways uncommon, and I have written about parts of that.

''My father was an itinerant writer. In the 20s, when I was born, he was trying to earn a living as a play fixer, which meant that he was hired to rewrite ailing plays so that they could open in New York City. In one tryout in Boston, he told me years later, a play he had 'fixed' opened and closed the first night. The cast, which included Louis Calhern, realized in the middle of the first act that there were only three people in the audience. Calhern advanced to the proscenium and suggested they join the cast so they wouldn't feel so lonely.

"My father wrote several plays of his own, one of which ran for nine months, a fairly respectable run for that period. At some point, he went to Provincetown, where he was part of a group of writers and actors who established the Provincetown Theater. Then he and my mother went to Hollywood, where he worked for M-G-M, and after that to the British-Gaumont studios in England."[1]

But Fox did not live with her parents. "As for me, my home for the first six years of my life was with a Congregational minister who had been a newspaperman . . . before he had found his vocation in the ministry. He was an ardent historian of the Revolutionary period in American history, particularly as it unfolded in the Hudson Valley, where he spent a large part of his life. Every morning he went to his study, and over the years there issued from his Remington typewriter sermons, items for a column he wrote for a local newspaper called 'Little-Known Facts about Well-Known People,' essays on battles that had taken place in defense of the Hudson Heights and a book on George Washington. A volume of his poems had also been published—mostly sonnets, a form for which he felt a special

Ethan took hold of the brown television wires and climbed straight up the side of his house. (From *Good Ethan* by Paula Fox. Illustrated by Arnold Lobel.)

reverence. He wrote his poems by hand. In the nursing home where he spent his last days, the old Remington was close by on the floor next to his bed, and there was writing paper and pen on the bedside table along with the paraphernalia of sickness.

"I lived with him and his invalided mother in a Victorian house on a hill that overlooked the Hudson River . . . . The house had been built by the minister's father in the 1890s on a site he had picked out as he stood at the bow of an Albany-bound boat on his first trip through the Hudson Highlands. Like other houses of that period, it seemed to unfurl from its own turreted roof. Its exterior had a massive, brooding air, a look of depth and temperament. In strong winds, the outer branches of surrounding trees scraped against the upper windows, making a sound as evocative as certain strains of music and which still, for me, is somehow bound up with history, with the past. When there was an electric storm, of which there were many during the humid Hudson Valley summers, the three of us would sit in the front hall near the entrance doors so that if lightning struck and set the house on fire, we could escape quickly . . . . While his mother dozed in her wheelchair, and the storm roared and wheeled around us, he told me stories.

"Often he would read something to me from his own work. He talked of the difficulties of writing a sonnet. I could hardly have understood, but the word sonnet itself stirred me. He knew many poems by heart and would recite them to me before I went to sleep. He taught me to read, and I memorized a poem myself, 'If' by Rudyard Kipling.

"There were books in nearly every room of that house. Even in the bathroom, on a shaky small rattan table, there was a volume of poems by Eugene Field. Among them was 'Little Boy Blue,' which when he read it to me, caused me to grieve so he would not read it again. Gingerly, I would open the book; an intimation of the power of words had touched me.

"When I was five, I had my first experience of being a ghost writer—of sorts. I was on my way outdoors one day when, as I passed his study, the minister called out to ask me what he should preach about the following Sunday. 'A waterfall,' I said, because at that moment I had been thinking about a picnic we had recently had on the banks of a stream fed by a cascade whose spray had dampened us and our lunch.

"I can still recollect the startled pleasure I felt that Sunday when, sitting in the corner of a pew, I realized that his sermon was, indeed, about a waterfall. Of course I knew nothing of metaphors or themes. But, for an instant, I grasped consciously what had been implicit in every aspect of my life with the minister—that everything could count, that a word, spoken as meant, contained in itself an energy capable of awakening imagination, thought, emotion, just as in the Chinese soapstone I often held in my hand, there was the concentrated essence of an earthquake.

"I think it was soon after the minister had preached his sermon on a waterfall that I told him I hoped I would be a writer when I grew up. He told me, with great seriousness, that he hoped so, too.

"When I left the minister's care, I was taken first to California for a couple of years, then to a sugar plantation in central Cuba. I didn't think about becoming a writer for a very long time, and I didn't find much to read. But he had given me substantial provisions, and they helped me through lean years."[2]

In Cuba, Fox attended a one-room school and learned to speak Spanish fluently. When Batista began his revolutionary rise to power, Fox was sent to New York. She rarely lived in one place

The rabbit leaned against Fred. Fred smiled. (From *Hungry Fred* by Paula Fox. Illustrated by Rosemary Wells.)

for more than a year and hardly ever saw her parents. By the time she was twelve she had gone to a total of nine schools. "I learned young that public libraries are places of refuge and stability amid chaos and confusion."[1]

Fox went to work at a variety of jobs, including machinist for Bethlehem Steel, reader for a movie production company, and punctuator of fifteenth-century Italian madrigals for a music publisher. "I knew I wanted to travel and was able to find jobs that would enable me to do so. In London I read manuscripts for Victor Gollancz, mostly novels by Irish mythologists that were so terrible they defy description. Right after the war, I became a 'stringer' for a small leftist, labor-oriented British news agency and covered Poland: the devastation wrought by the war, the concentration camps, the first efforts at recovery, the first elections. I remember meeting with the group of architects charged with rebuilding Warsaw, of which scarcely anything remained. I was taken to the concentration camp in Breslau. I remember taking a Polish aristocrat to lunch one day (it took me a month to pay off that bill!). He had been in one of the camps; his wife had lost her mind there and did not survive. 'Let me tell you a story about class,' he said with light irony. 'I tried to escape and was shot in the leg. The first thing I asked when I came out of the anesthetic was, "Will I be able to ride a horse again?"'

"I had the opportunity then to expatriate, but somehow couldn't face the enormity and finality of such an act. Not that I'm in the least bit nationalistic, but I couldn't see giving up my citizenship or leaving the States definitely.

"Eventually I returned to New York, married, had two sons, attended Columbia University and taught at a school for emotionally disturbed students, and then English to Spanish-speaking children. I also taught for a few years at Ethical Culture. I had wanted to be a writer, but for a long time it remained a shining, but elusive, goal. When my kids were about four months and two years old, my first husband and I divorced. I was teaching, and when my children were beyond the kind of constant custodial care they required when they were young, and I found myself with the time to write."[1]

Maurice's Room, Fox's first book tells the story about a boy who is such an avid collector that only he and one friend can enter his bedroom safely. Essentially Maurice succeeds in creating a world apart. "I was off and running. The books just seemed to pour out of me."[1]

How Many Miles to Babylon? was in many ways a breakthrough book for Fox. It was one of the first contemporary books for young adults to deal with the harsh realities of life for a black child in the inner city. Margot Hentoff of the *New York Times Book Review* wrote: "There is a dual sense of isolation; both the isolation of a lonely childhood and the further isolation of an impoverished urban existence. And like the hero of a *nouveau roman*, James moves through this dream city, accepting what he sees.

"There is a plot. Perhaps too dense a plot . . . . But what is rare and valuable about this book is its unblunted vision of the way things are, and its capacity to evoke the sense of what it is to live as so many do live in this city, in this time."[3]

Ruth Hill Viguers of *Horn Book* felt that the writing was "subtle, making the understated story almost nightmarish in its excitement. Against the background, suggested rather than described, Jimmy is a small bewildered victim of an almost overwhelming situation. A story with great impact, it is far more important for young people who have no knowledge of Negro ghettos than it is for children for whom the setting may be all too familiar."[4]

The readership of *The King's Falcon* about a monarch who had no desire to rule, included college students, particularly those engaged in anti-Vietnam protests and the "counter-culture." "Of course they read it as a pacifist allegory, which in many ways, I suppose, it is. It goes to show that one can not always accurately predict what age-groups will be attracted to a given book. I thought I had written *The King's Falcon* for younger readers. It pleases me greatly that it has drawn readers of different ages."[1]

Fox is frequently asked to differentiate between literature intended for adults and literature intended for children. "That is a difficult and teasing question. As Coleridge said, 'difference is not division.' But there is a perfectly apparent difference between children and adults: whereas we all live in time, children haven't lived in time as long. Children have everything adults have, with the exception of judgment, which comes only over the course of time. So there are certain things you don't write about for children, because it does not conform to the knowledge they have acquired. I would not write an explicitly detailed sexual book for children, or one about dismembering a corpse. 'Appropriate' is a word that has currency here; and by 'appropriate' I do not mean 'prudish.' It means that you don't write about teenage pregnancies in a book for six-year-olds. Because those readers simply cannot understand.

"And yet, children know about pain and fear and unhappiness and betrayal. And we do them a disservice by trying to sugarcoat dark truths. There is an odd kind of debauchery I've noticed, particularly in societies that consider themselves 'democratic' or 'liberal': they display the gory details but hide meaning, especially if it is ambiguous or disturbing."[1]

Fox's recent book *The Moonlight Man* for young readers is a good case in point. The book takes place over a summer vacation during which a teenager lives with her divorced father. A "n'er-do-well" by his own standards, "the moonlight man" is nevertheless a beguiling, even seductive, person. After a very difficult, disillusioning visit, father and daughter take their leave of one another. "See you," says the girl. "Not if I see you first," replies her dad.

"Oh, I hope no one ever asks me the precise meaning of that last line. But it seemed to me the absolute sum of everything that is true about that man. The line has that wicked charm he radiates, and like many of his actions, is nearly impossible to 'read.' Given those characters, how on earth could I have written a 'happy' story about them? It would have rung completely false."

"One thing is certain: the criteria for artistry and integrity must be every bit as high in books for children as for adults. We must never, ever try to pull the wool over children's eyes by 'watering down' powerful stories. Contrary to popular belief, children are not easily fooled; they know if a story is authentic, or not. And for this they deserve our respect and the best literature that can be made available."[1]

Fox published *Desperate Characters*, her first book intended for adults, in 1970. The reviews were admiring, calling attention to Fox's craftsmanship, subtlety, grasp of complex and sometimes contradictory relationships, and extraordinary powers of observation. The book gained readers slowly and steadily, and ten years after its initial publication was reissued with an afterword by Irving Howe, who placed the book in a line of masterpieces in the American short-novel genre.

Howe explains: "The strength of [the book] lies in its prose, which we should see not as some autonomous beauty or pretty decoration, but sentence by lapidary sentence as the realization of a mind committed to the hardness of its own truth . . . . *Desperate Characters* is a book about civilization, its fragility, and its costs—I should add that, in its hard way, it is also about injustice. It captures, to some extent, a mood of the late 1960s, the anxiety of cultivated liberated people that 'everything is going to hell' and the threatening hordes are at the gate. Those who felt this were far from right, yet not entirely wrong, either; and it is the complicatedness, perhaps even the hopelessness, of the Bentwoods' responses, shown as settling into no easy formulas of acceptance or rejection, that may be one reason for Paula Fox's severity of tone. Some readers have spoken of that tone as one of resignation, but I would call it a gritty stoicism, a determination to fight for one's morale. The civilization depicted here is flawed, and without sufficient joy or energy. But it is a civilization, and even with its quotient of middle-class guilt and failure, it embodies the achievement of generations in giving us whatever it is we have."[5]

The years during which Fox wrote *Desperate Characters* were a time of explosive experimentation in fiction, indeed in all the arts. Yet in writing her novel about creeping social chaos, she chose to observe the classical unities and to make a strictly linear narrative. "I've never been part of any trend. I don't think I ever could be, or in fact would I wish to be. In the case of *Desperate Characters*, I think that the very stern simplicity allows for much more drama than what Coleridge called the 'madness pretense of

pseudo-poesy.' Raging and screaming hasn't nearly the intensity for me that George Eliot has, for example. I think too that the classical form throws the contemporary setting into relief. As far as I'm concerned, an artist preoccupied with being 'modern' is well on the road to an early death. To be 'modern' is to be dead. But you can be at once classical and new.

"Story remains critical for me. Stories last—just think of the old, in fact ancient, tales that are so central a part of our lives. Style is ephemeral, and the more it calls attention to itself for its own sake, the more ephemeral it usually is."[1]

Fox may be most widely known for *The Slave Dancer*, easily her most controversial work. It is an historical novel about a white thirteen-year-old street musician who is kidnapped and forced to work on a slave ship. Jessie, the protagonist, is confronted with a series of moral tests on board ship, and although he never willingly commits any wrongful act toward the slaves, the experience profoundly, and even tragically, changes him. *The Slave Dancer* received the coveted Newbery Medal for the most distinguished work of fiction for young people published in a given year. However, the reviews were far from unanimous, and there were demonstrations against the book on the evening of the awards ceremony.

My brother, Ben, says that blowfish live in the sea. He says it in many ways. (Cover illustration by Ellen Thompson from *Blowfish Live in the Sea* by Paula Fox.)

Among the book's supporters was C.S. Hannabuss, writing in *Children's Book Review:* "In a concise and carved style, Paula Fox once again gets into a child and looks out on a harsh and dangerous world. For the nightmare of the voyage is shown in the very moments of realisation, growing fear and panic and disgust gripping the reader too at deep levels of consciousness. The ship is an evil place, and cruelty and degradation and fever and greed are its crew. The boy's groping understanding and the power of suggesting by few words both generate involvement to an unusual degree, involvement which like life itself has to be worked at and worked through. Jesse's horror of the fetid hold, the hatreds among the crew, the hypocrisy of the Mate and the crazed bravado of the Captain, and the terribly just fate of the ship build on one another to a crescendo that must be resolved . . . . This story . . . extends the belief that [Paula Fox] is one of the most exciting writers practising for children and young people today.''[6]

Anita Moss, one of the most highly-respected scholars in the field of children's literature writes in the same vein: "*The Slave Dancer* is historical fiction at its finest, for Fox has meticulously researched every facet of the slave trade and of the period. More important she allows the reader to perceive the true horror of showing the sights, sounds, and details of it as they are filtered through Jesse's consciousness. Like Joseph Conrad's *Heart of Darkness, The Slave Dancer* takes the reader on a voyage that reveals a haunting glimpse into the abyss of human evil . . . *The Slave Dancer* is clearly Fox's masterpiece, and it is fast becoming a classic in American children's literature.''[7]

A number of critics who attacked *The Slave Dancer* did so out of a belief that the story was racist and/or promoted racist viewpoints. Albert Schwartz of *Interracial Books for Children* said, "The Black people *are* only pathetic sufferers. No 'fight back' qualities whatever are found in these characterless, chained objects on the ship . . . . For them the author presents no balance . . . . White readers who empathize with the misery of the Black Experience can feel virtuous. To feel virtuous is to feel superior. To put it into the terms of an R. D. Laing 'Knot' or paradox: 'I feel bad that this is happening to them. I feel good that I feel bad.' But by thus feeling compassion, whites are relieved of the need to change society.''[8]

"No matter what the author's intent," says Binnie Tate of *Interracial Books for Children*, "[*The Slave Dancer*] presents grave problems for those of us concerned with eliminating children's materials which help perpetuate racism.

"As the story develops the author attempts to portray the slave ship's captain and crew as villains, but through the characters' words, she excuses the captors and places the blame for the slaves' captivity on Africans themselves. The author slowly and systematically excuses almost all the whites in the story for their participation in the slave venture and by innuendo places the blame elsewhere.''[9]

Julius Lester, writing in the *New York Times Book Review*, took a slightly different approach in his attack. "What saves [this] book from being a failure is the quality of [the] writing, which is consistently excellent. With such good writing, it is too bad that the book as a whole does not succeed. This novel describes the horrors of The Middle Passage, but it does not re-create them, and if history is to become reality, the reader must live that history as if it were his own life. In *The Slave Dancer* we are only spectators and we should have been fellow sufferers—as slave traders and slaves.''[10]

"I was under the impression that the reception of *The Slave Dancer* was an unmitigated success. Not long after the book

The stern was smashed and the mainmast tilted. (From *Maurice's Room* by Paula Fox. Illustrated by Ingrid Fetz.)

came out I was at a party when a woman approached and said, 'My goodness, you're calm! I'd be a total wreck.' Well, I was a total wreck when I found out what was going on. And on the evening of the Newbery Award, when I learned that there were plans for a sort of demonstration, I literally thought I would die. There I was in my evening gown, shaking like a leaf. But I gave my speech, and afterwards one or two of the previously hostile critics approached me, to let me know I was 'forgiven.''[1]

Fox's Newbery Award acceptance speech may be considered an important part of her literary oeuvre, so lucidly, profoundly, and elegantly does she analyze the writer's task. "Nearly all the work of writing is silent. A writer does it alone. And the original intention—that first sudden stirring of one's imagination—is made up of many small, almost always humble, things. Because a major effort of writing is reflection, which is silent and solitary, I place thought under the heading of the experiences I had while I was writing *The Slave Dancer*.

"By thought, I do not mean the marshalling of one's intellectual forces to refute an argument or to bring about a temporary victory over what agitates and bewilders us. All such victories are, I believe, transient. By thought, I mean that preoccupation with what we feel and why we feel it, and the enormous effort we must make to educe from a tangle of impressions and fleeting images the nature of those feelings. In this sense, thought is the effort to recognize.

"It is an effort carried about against formidable enemies: habit; inertia; the fear of change and what it will entail; the wish to preserve our idiot corners of safety, of being 'right' and self-righteousness—the most dangerous enemy of all, full of a terrible energy that would turn us away from pondering the mystery of existence towards its own barren pleasures.

"This effort to recognize is an effort to connect ourselves with the reality of our own lives. It is painful; but if we are to become human, we cannot abandon it. Once set on that path of recognition, we cannot forswear our integral connections with other people. We must make our way towards them as best we can, try to find what is similar, try to understand what is dissimilar, try to particularize what is universal.

"Once we accept the responsibility of our connection with others, we must accept that we are like them even in our differences; and if in one instance, we are not a victim, we can be in another. And if in one instance we do not persecute, in another we will. And if we have not experienced the ultimate shame and anguish of captivity, of utter helplessness, we have experienced—at some time in our lives—something approximate to it, something from which we can construe a sense of what it is like to be other than ourselves . . . . I write to discover, over and over again, my connections with myself, with others. Each book deepens the question. It does not answer it.

"There are those who feel that slavery debased the enslaved. It is not so. Slavery engulfed whole peoples, swallowed up their lives, committed such offenses that in considering them, the heart falters, the mind recoils. Slavery debased the enslavers.

"There are others who feel that black people can be only humiliated by being reminded that once they were brought to this country as slaves. But it is not the victim who is shamed. It is the persecutor, who has refused the shame of what he has done and, as the last turn of the screw, would burden the victim with the ultimate responsibility of the crime itself.

"I wrote *The Slave Dancer* as a never-quite-to-be-freed captive of a white childhood in a dark condition. When I read a footnote in a book, the title of which I can't now recall, that said that slaver crews often kidnapped youthful street musicians and signed them on ships as slave dancers—for such were they called—something consonant with, or peculiar to, my own sense of myself set me on the course of writing my book.

"Writing *The Slave Dancer* was the closest I could get to events of spirit and flesh which cannot help but elude in their reality all who did not experience them. Still, the effort to draw nearer is part of the effort of writing. It is not so different from the effort to understand our own infancies which become fictions because we cannot consciously recall them. Yet a few powerful images maintain their grip on our imaginations for all of our lives. If we are able to invoke even fragments of those images, we can, sometimes, despite formidable differences in circumstance, rouse them up in others. Little though we may have in common, there is enough for us to take on the truest obligation we have—recognition of the existence of that which is other than ourselves."[11]

"This notion that we must 'identify' with characters in books, that we must be able to see the particulars of our lives in their lives and vice versa—which Julius Lester affirms—drives me up a wall. It is tantamount to saying we are unable to feel compassion, unable to bear witness, and unable to register feelings about what we have seen. This mania for identifying is right out of the sentimental slop jar of American culture. The whole point of reading is to find out about others. This insistence on always finding evidence and reflections of oneself is a result of a deep-seated denial of the reality of others. My thoughts go immediately to Maxim Gorki's three-volume autobiography, *My Life*, in which he says outright and repeatedly that reading saved his life, that had he not read about *other lives, other places, other options,* and *other ambitions,* he never would have survived the horrible, dank interiors he lived in with his violent relatives. Books may well be the best way to surmount the physical, economic, social, and spiritual confines of a given individual life."[1]

Fox's next book, *The Widow's Children*, drew admiring, if not altogether enthusiastic reviews. As the reviewer for *Newsweek* put it in a little vignette:

> "Here. Read this novel. Please."
> "Is it any good?"
> "First rate."
> "Will I like it?"
> "Not a chance. It's for admiring, not liking."
> "Oh. Well, I like to like a book."[12]

The Widow's Children takes place over the course of one evening and the following day. The "widow" of the title is the grandmother who has that afternoon died in a nursing home. The widow's daughter, the redoubtable Laura, knows and tells no one at the family dinner cum farewell party for her and her husband, who are leaving on an extended trip. It is an evening of heavy liquor, ancient rivalries, and high domestic theatre. Laura's secret lends an extraordinary charge to the dinner, even by the melodramatic standards of the family.

The *Newsweek* reviewer goes on to say: "Mortification, humiliation, unattended gasps for recognition—Fox spares her characters no distress . . . but how is a reader to rise to this story? Fox's brilliance has a masochistic aspect: I will do this so well, she seems to say, that you will hardly be able to read it. And so she does, and so do I, who admire her work, find myself muttering in the street—'admirable, not likable.'"[12]

"People are always saying my work is 'depressing.' But what does that mean? They said *Desperate Characters* was depressing too, and it's been reissued twice. I'm so used to having the word *'depressing'* tied to me I feel like a dog accustomed to the tin can around its neck. The charge can still make me angry, not because of how it might reflect on my work, but because of what it tells me about reading in this country. Is *Anna Karenina* depressing? Is *Madame Bovary*? 'Depressing,' when applied to a literary work is so narrow, so confining, so impoverished and impoverishing. This yearning for the proverbial 'happy ending' is little more than a desire for oblivion."[1]

Ten years (and several books) after the publication of *The Slave Dancer*, Fox published *A Servant's Tale*, and in the process was once again exposed to the racism and ethnic bias ingrained in American culture. "There are two stories connected to this novel. *A Servant's Tale* is set on a sugar plantation in Cuba. Many of the events are entirely invented, but the place, and a good deal of the history is not, including the sorry attempt at revolution there. The book was rejected by an editor at Farrar, Straus because he said he had 'never heard of a revolution like that.' Well, I lived through that revolution! I was there! The point here is that the editor could not allow for what he didn't know. The irony is that the very arrogant position he took was really born of ignorance. We're back to that characteristically American mania for identification with books: the editor was saying, 'If this book isn't about me and what I know, it can't be any good. So I'll banish it.'

"The second story takes place immediately after *A Servant's Tale* was published and was being circulated for reviews. It happened that I knew someone on the editorial board of the *New York Times Book Review*, and he told me the following story. At the weekly book review meeting, the editor-in-chief said, 'There's a book by a very fine black writer I think we should review. It's called—, the author is—, the editor at this point fumbled around in his pockets, fishing for a little piece of paper. Oh yes, *A Servant's Tale* by Paula Fox.' Well, my friend had all he could do not to burst into loud guffaws. The editor-in-chief had jumped to the conclusion that a book about a servant would perforce be written by a black. Particularly if that author had

HOW MANY MILES TO BABYLON?

a novel by PAULA FOX

illustrations by
PAUL GIOVANOPOULOS

Bradbury Press   Scarsdale, N.Y.

James didn't like dogs. They made faces at him and got in his way. (From *How Many Miles to Babylon?* by Paula Fox. Illustrated by Paul Giovanopoulos.)

previously written something about slaves. It's a funny story, but its message is very discouraging.

"It seems that American consciousness is completely bound up with real estate; we have no pre-capitalist history here. The first thing the European settlers did upon arriving was to 'strike a deal' with the Indians for land. The American spirit, if you will, derives from that original real estate transaction. The recent trend in so-called minimalist writing reflects this perfectly. I do not hold with those critics who affirm that the minimalism in recent fiction is an important philosophical statement. I am not convinced that so-called minimalist writers have chosen to use a limited part of the language. Rather, I think the work is semi-literate and that those authors are using as many words as they know.

"A favorite American myth is that we have an open, democratic society. I think our society is rigidly divided. The vignette about the *Times Book Review* illustrates it. The perception is that there are black writers who write about such-and-such, white writers who would never write about what the black writers do, Spanish-American writers who have their territory, and on and on. And of course, 'white knight' publications who in their infinite bounty deign to favor with a review a few authors out of the so-called mainstream.

"In our culture, writers increasingly 'make it' on the basis of being 'personalities.' Reading and writing take time, quiet and

solitude, all of which are grossly devalued in this country. It isn't merely that ours is a visual culture: look at the horrendous quality of visual imagery on television. I could accept, I think, that the visual was becoming a pre-eminent form of literacy. But the common fund of visual imagery that pervades television and the media is execrable and lacks complexity and resonance. It consists mostly of flashes, demanding mere seconds of our attention.

"This was really brought home to me when I was teaching in the early and mid-seventies. My students were of the first generation to be raised on television. Because our classes were three hours, which I found impossibly long, I spent a good deal of time reading to them. And they were mesmerized, they couldn't get enough. For they had not been read to. They'd been plunked down in front of the TV instead. They had very little in the way of a common literary currency, their cultural points of reference were not tales, myths, poems, novels, or plays—they were TV shows and, especially, TV commercials.

"It isn't like this everywhere. In Europe, for example, writers are held in great esteem. The assumption is that good writing, in and of itself, has value. I remember when I was finally able to quit my teaching job and devote myself full-time to writing. People asked me, 'But what will you do?'

"'I'm going to write books,' I would say. And they would reply, 'Yes, but what will you DO?'

"People have this idea that a life spent writing is essentially a life of leisure. Writing is tremendously hard work. There is nothing more satisfying, but it is work all the same. Even after years of experience and a good number of books published, it can still be painfully difficult.

"I generally don't work from an outline (although for *A Servant's Tale* I had a kind of blueprint), but do keep notebooks. I write down everything that comes to mind in no apparent order. I dream a lot, and everything I see, dream, feel, and think seems to relate to the book. I keep pads all over the house, so that even when I'm chopping onions, if something occurs to me, I can easily jot it down. It is very easy to lose ideas and impressions—writing them down 'solidifies' them. I work every day, starting in the morning because that's when my energy is best. Usually I put in about four hours of writing, though when I'm finishing a book I'll work straight through until evening. I need a lot of time around my writing periods. If I know I have an afternoon appointment, for example, I'm somewhat distracted all morning and don't work as well as I might."[1]

Fox's conversation is studded with quotes, paraphrases and references to her favorite writers. "I love George Eliot, James Joyce, D. H. Lawrence, and E. M. Forster. Tolstoy is another hero, and Flannery O'Connor a heroine. O'Connor gets better and better to me: as time passes she becomes more immediate. There are several Italian writers who mean a lot to me. Alberto Moravia is one. He is very hard and cold and very brilliant. His greatest work, I think, is *The Conformist*. Hard to believe, but it is out of print in this country. Cesare Pavese, too, is enormously important; his autobiography *This Business of Living* is a cornerstone for me. Elsa Morante's *History: A Novel* is a stupendous effort depicting Italy during its fascist period. The title alone expresses her ambition. In Europe, it is considered the finest novel to come out of Italy since the war—its first edition sold out within hours. Here, sales languished and reviews carped about the book's considerable length. Here, it seemed, Morante's ambition was held against her.

"It is the work of other writers and the examples of their lives that provide the deepest encouragement and the most abiding inspiration. In some ways, the work is harder now than it was. I am more conscious of craft now and much more deliberate in my efforts. And at times I'm weary of myself, tired of my own mind. Yet, to an extent we are all prisoners of ourselves, even though we write to lessen that bondage. And perhaps, on balance, the enterprise is easier. I no longer feel that people are looking over my shoulder with every sentence I write. Even the parrot who used to look over my shoulder is gone now. Early in my career, I was hungry for attention, for praise, for awards. I am less vain now. I have my work to do, and I do it. Come what may."[1]

FOOTNOTE SOURCES

[1] Based on an interview by Marguerite Feitlowitz for *Something about the Author.*

[2] Paula Fox, "A Childhood of Sermons and Sonnets," *New York Times Book Review,* July 12, 1981.

[3] Margot Hentoff, "*How Many Miles to Babylon?,*" *New York Times Book Review,* September 24, 1967.

[4] Ruth Hill Viguers, *Horn Book,* October, 1967.

[5] Irving Howe, "On *Desperate Characters,*" *New Republic,* April 19, 1980.

[6] C. S. Hannabuss, *Children's Book Review,* winter, 1974-75.

[7] Anita Moss, "Paula Fox," *Dictionary of Literary Biography,* Volume 52, Gale, 1986.

[8] Albert V. Schwartz, *Interracial Books for Children,* Volume 5, number 5, 1974.

[9] Binnie Tate, *Interracial Books for Children,* Volume 5, number 5, 1974.

[10] Julius Lester, *New York Times Book Review,* January 20, 1974.

[11] Lee Kingman, editor, *Newbery and Caldecott Medal Winners 1966-1975,* Horn Book, 1975.

[12] "Books," *Newsweek,* September 27, 1976.

FOR MORE INFORMATION SEE:

BOOKS

Sheila Egoff and others, editors, *Only Connect: Readings on Children's Literature,* Oxford University Press, 1969.

John Rowe Townsend, *A Sense of Story: Essays on Contemporary Writers for Children,* Lippincott, 1971, revised and enlarged edition published as *A Sounding of Storytellers: New and Revised Essays on Contemporary Writers for Children,* Lippincott, 1979.

Contemporary Literary Criticism, Gale, Volume II, 1974, Volume VIII, 1978.

Children's Literature Review, Volume I, Gale, 1976.

Doris de Montreville and Donna Hill, *Fourth Book of Junior Authors and Illustrators,* H. W. Wilson, 1978.

D. L. Kirkpatrick, editor, *Twentieth-Century Children's Writers,* St. Martin's, 1978, new edition, 1983.

Lina Mainiero, editor, *American Women Writers: A Critical Reference Guide from Colonial Times to the Present,* Ungar, 1980.

Alleen Pace Nilsen and Kenneth L. Donelson, *Literature for Today's Young Adults,* 2nd edition, Scott, Foresman, 1985.

PERIODICALS

Atlantic Monthly, December, 1967.

Horn Book, August, 1969, April, 1970, December, 1970 (p. 623), April 1974, August, 1974, October, 1977 (p. 514ff),

A young hawk ... bit and clawed against the confining hand. (From *The King's Falcon* by Paula Fox. Illustrated by Eros Keith.)

April, 1984 (p. 219ff), August, 1984 (p. 496ff), January/February, 1987 (p. 21ff).

New York Times Book Review, February 1, 1970, October 8, 1972, October 3, 1976, November 9, 1980, May 8, 1983 (p. 12ff), November 11, 1984, November 18, 1984.

New Leader, February 2, 1970.

New Yorker, February 7, 1970, November 1, 1976.

New York Times, February 10, 1970, September 22, 1972, September 16, 1976.

Newsweek, March 16, 1970, December 1, 1980.

Saturday Review, September 19, 1970 (p. 34), January 23, 1971, October 16, 1976.

New York Review of Books, October 5, 1972, October 28, 1976, June 27, 1985.

New Statesman, November 8, 1974, December 4, 1981.

Time, October 4, 1976.

Washington Post Book World, October 31, 1976, February 8, 1981, September 23, 1984.

New Republic, January 15, 1977.

Critique: Studies in Modern Fiction, Volume 20, number 2, 1978 (p. 33ff).

Perry Nodelman, ''How Typical Children Read Typical Books,'' *Children's Literature in Education,* number 12, winter, 1981 (p. 177ff).

Children's Literature, number 11, 1983 (p. 156ff).

Ms., October, 1984.

Nation, November 3, 1984.

Commonweal, January 11, 1985.

Times Literary Supplement, February 21, 1986.

School Library Journal, November, 1987 (p. 33ff), May, 1988 (p. 48ff).

OTHER

Jacqueline S. Weiss, ''Paula Fox'' (videocassette), Profiles in Literature Series, Temple University, 1987.

FRAME, Paul 1914-

PERSONAL: Born May 4, 1914, in Riderwood, Md.; son of Paul and Gretchen (Reiman) Frame; married Jean Fisher Welch, 1947; children: Mindy, Debbie. *Education:* Attended National Academy of Design, 1930, and Columbia University, 1931-35. *Politics:* ''Non-consistent Republican.'' *Home:* 7 Stuyvesant Oval, New York, N.Y. 10009.

CAREER: Lord and Taylor, New York, N.Y., staff artist, 1936-41; free-lance artist, 1945—; author and illustrator of children's books. *Military service:* U.S. Air Force, achieved rank of master sergeant, 1941-45. Volunteer at Odyssey House (a drug program), 1970s. *Awards, honors: The Case of the Ticklish Tooth, Rama of the Golden Age, Haunted House,* and *The Story of Corn* were each chosen one of Child Study Association of America's Children's Books of the Year, 1971, *How Did Life Get There?,* 1972, *Willie's Whizmobile,* and *Tiger up a Tree,* both 1973, and *Sports Star: Bob Griese* and *Sports Star: Walt Frazier,* both 1975.

WRITINGS:

JUVENILE; ALL SELF-ILLUSTRATED

(With wife, Jean Frame) *How to Give a Party,* F. Watts, 1972.

Drawing Dogs and Puppies, F. Watts, 1978.

Drawing Cats and Kittens, F. Watts, 1979.

Drawing the Big Cats, F. Watts, 1981.

Drawing Sharks, Whales, Dolphins, and Seals, F. Watts, 1983.

Drawing Reptiles, F. Watts, 1986.

Paul Frame with wife, Jean.

ILLUSTRATOR; ALL JUVENILE

Mark Twain (pseudonym of Samuel L. Clemens), *The Adventures of Huckleberry Finn,* A. Whitman, 1951.

M. Twain, *The Adventures of Tom Sawyer,* A. Whitman, 1955.

Mary Calhoun, *Katie John,* Harper, 1960.

Nan Gilbert (pseudonym of Mildred Geiger Gilbertson), *Champions Don't Cry,* Harper, 1960.

M. Calhoun, *Depend on Katie John,* Harper, 1961.

Frances Cavanah, *Jenny Lind and Her Listening Cat,* Vanguard, 1961.

Margaret Pope Trask, *Three for Treasure,* Crowell, 1962.

Kathryn Kenny (house pseudonym), *Trixie Belden and the Mystery at Bob-White Cave,* A. Whitman, 1963.

Charles S. Verral, *Robert Goddard: Father of the Space Age* (biography), Prentice-Hall, 1963.

M. Calhoun, *Honestly, Katie John!,* Harper, 1963.

Doris Faber, *Horace Greeley: The People's Editor* (biography), Prentice-Hall, 1964.

Patricia Miles Martin, *John Fitzgerald Kennedy* (biography), Putnam, 1964.

D. Faber, *Robert Frost: America's Poet* (biography), Prentice-Hall, 1964.

William D. Hayes, *Johnny and The Tool Chest,* Atheneum, 1964.

George Kramer, *The Left Hander,* Putnam, 1964.

Ernest L. Thayer, *Casey at the Bat,* Prentice-Hall, 1964.

Carli Laklan, *Two Girls in New York,* Doubleday, 1964.

Hal Higdon, *Heroes of the Olympics* (biography), Prentice-Hall, 1965.

Stewart Graff and Polly Anne Graff, *Helen Keller: Toward the Light* (biography), Garrard, 1965.

Martha Tolles, *Too Many Boys*, T. Nelson, 1965.

Helen D. Olds, *Lyndon Baines Johnson* (biography), Putnam, 1965.

Charles P. Graves, *John F. Kennedy: New Frontiersman* (biography), Garrard, 1965.

D. Faber, *Clarence Darrow: Defender of the People* (biography), Prentice-Hall, 1965.

Catherine Woolley, *Ginnie and the Cooking Contest*, Morrow, 1966.

Peggy Parish, *Key to the Treasure*, Macmillan, 1966.

Marian T. Place, *The First Book of the Santa Fe Trail*, F. Watts, 1966.

Bessie Holland Heck, *The Year at Boggy*, World, 1966.

Edmund O. Scholefield (pseudonym of William E. Butterworth), *Tiger Rookie*, World, 1966.

Scott Corbett, *The Case of the Gone Goose*, Little, Brown, 1966.

E. O. Scholefield, *L'il Wildcat*, World, 1967.

Jean Lee Latham, *David Glasgow Farragut: Our First Admiral* (biography), Garrard, 1967.

Burke Boyce, *The Emperor's Arrow*, Lippincott, 1967.

Miriam E. Mason, *Caroline and the Seven Little Words*, Macmillan, 1967.

Jack Newcombe, *The Game of Football* (history), Garrard, 1967.

William Wise, *Franklin Delano Roosevelt* (biography), Putnam, 1967.

C. Woolley, *Ginnie and the Wedding Bells*, Morrow, 1967.

K. Kenney, *Trixie Belden and the Marshland Mystery*, Golden Press, 1967.

James McCague, *Mississippi Steamboat Days* (history), Garrard, 1967.

E. O. Scholefield, *Maverick on the Mound*, World, 1968.

Anne Terry White, adapter, *Ali Baba [and] Abu Kir and Abu Sir: Two Arabian Tales*, Garrard, 1968.

Wyatt Blassingame, *Eleanor Roosevelt* (biography), Putnam, 1968.

Myra Clarke Crandell, *Molly and the Regicides*, Simon & Schuster, 1968.

M. E. Mason, *Sara and the Winter Gift*, Macmillan, 1968.

P. Parish, *Clues in the Woods*, Macmillan, 1968.

Adrian Paradis, *Henry Ford* (biography), Putnam, 1968.

W. D. Hayes, *Hold That Computer!*, Atheneum, 1968.

Claire Bishop, *Mozart: Music Magician* (biography), Garrard, 1968.

C. Woolley, *Chris in Trouble*, Morrow, 1968.

Sam Epstein and Beryl Epstein, *Harriet Tubman: Guide to Freedom* (biography), Garrard, 1968.

Clive Toye, *Soccer* (nonfiction), F. Watts, 1968.

W. Wise, *Booker T. Washington* (biography), Putnam, 1968.

Muriel Stanek, *I Know an Airline Pilot*, Putnam, 1969.

Willard Luce and Celia Luce, *Sutter's Fort: Empire on the Sacramento* (history), Garrard, 1969.

Elizabeth Honness, *Mystery at the Villa Caprice*, Lippincott, 1969.

P. M. Martin, *Jacqueline Kennedy Onassis* (biography), Putnam, 1969.

Catherine Owens Peare, *Mahatma Gandhi: Father of Nonviolence* (biography), Hawthorn, 1969.

Sally Glendinning, *Jimmy and Joe Catch an Elephant*, Garrard, 1969.

S. Glendinning, *Jimmy and Joe Find a Ghost*, Garrard, 1969.

Lynn Perkins, *Let's Go to a Paper Mill*, Putnam, 1969.

S. Corbett, *The Case of the Fugitive Firebug*, Little, Brown, 1969.

C. Woolley, *Ginnie and the Mystery Cat*, Morrow, 1969.

I. G. Edmonds, *Revolts and Revolutions* (history), Hawthorn, 1969.

Felix Sutton, *Getting to Know Virginia* (nonfiction), Coward, 1969.

Eric Whitehead, *Ice Hockey* (nonfiction), F. Watts, 1969.

Edward Allen, *Heroes of Texas* (biography), Messner, 1970.

S. Glendinning, *Jimmy and Joe Get a Hen's Surprise*, Garrard, 1970.

S. Glendinning, *Jimmy and Joe Fly a Kite*, Garrard, 1970.

A. T. White, reteller, *Knights of the Table Round* (legend), Garrard, 1970.

O. Henry (pseudonym of William S. Porter), *The Ransom of Red Chief*, Hawthorn, 1970.

Ann Finlayson, *Champions at Bat: Three Power Hitters* (biography), Garrard, 1970.

S. Glendinning, *Jimmy and Joe Look for a Bear*, Garrard, 1970.

Ruby L. Radford, *Dwight D. Eisenhower* (biography), Putnam, 1970.

C. Woolley, *Libby's Uninvited Guest*, Morrow, 1970.

Kurt Unkelbach, *You're a Good Dog, Joe: Knowing and Training Your Puppy*, Prentice-Hall, 1971.

Helen Stone Peterson, *Susan B. Anthony: Pioneer in Woman's Rights* (biography), Garrard, 1971.

S. Corbett, *The Case of the Ticklish Tooth*, Little, Brown, 1971.

E. Honness, *Mystery of the Maya Jade*, Lippincott, 1971.

Peter R. Limburg, *The Story of Corn* (nonfiction), Messner, 1971.

Elizabeth Gemming, *Getting to Know New England* (nonfiction), Coward, 1971.

C. Woolley, *Cathy and the Beautiful People*, Morrow, 1971.

S. Glendinning, *Jimmy and Joe Go to the Fair*, Garrard, 1971.

S. Glendinning, *Jimmy and Joe Meet a Halloween Witch*, Garrard, 1971.

Norah Smaridge, *Trailblazers in American Arts* (biography), Messner, 1971.

P. Parish, *Haunted House*, Macmillan, 1971.

(From *Sara and the Winter Gift* by M. E. Mason. Illustrated by Paul Frame.)

(From *Horses* by Ruby E. McCreight. Illustrated by Paul Frame.)

Jane Werner Watson, reteller, *Rama of the Golden Age: An Epic of India* (folklore), Garrard, 1971.

S. Corbett, *Dead before Docking,* Little, Brown, 1972.

Elizabeth Rider Montgomery, *Duke Ellington: King of Jazz* (biography), Garrard, 1972.

S. Glendinning, *Jimmy and Joe See a Monster,* Garrard, 1972.

Lorraine Henriod, *The Rock Hunters,* Putnam, 1972.

John McInnes, *The Chocolate Chip Mystery,* Garrard, 1972.

Daniel Cohen, *How Did Life Get There?* (nonfiction), Messner, 1973.

S. Glendinning, *Jimmy and Joe Save a Christmas Deer,* Garrard, 1973.

K. Unkelbach, *Tiger up a Tree: Knowing and Training Your Kitten,* Prentice-Hall, 1973.

Robert Hood, *Let's Go to a Baseball Game,* Putnam, 1973.

Dawn C. Thomas, *Pablito's New Feet,* Lippincott, 1973.

Gail Ranadive, *If You'd Been Born in India,* A. Whitman, 1973.

Irwin Shapiro, *Willie's Whizmobile,* Garrard, 1973.

Marshall Burchard and Sue Burchard, *Sports Star: Tom Seaver* (biography), Harcourt, 1974.

Olive W. Burt, *Black Woman of Valor* (biography), Messner, 1974.

Victoria Chapman, *Let's Go to a Service Station,* Putnam, 1974.

R. Hood, *Let's Go to a Stock Car Race,* Putnam, 1974.

S. Corbett, *The Case of the Silver Skull,* Little, Brown, 1974.

S. Glendinning, *Jimmy and Joe Have a Real Thanksgiving,* Garrard, 1974.

Neil Grant, *The New World Held Promise: Why England Colonized North America* (history), Messner, 1974.

Emily Hearn, *Ring around Duffy,* Garrard, 1974.

S. Corbett, *The Case of the Burgled Blessing Box,* Little, Brown, 1975.

S. H. Burchard, *Sports Star: Walt Frazier* (biography), Harcourt, 1975.

S. H. Burchard, *Sports Star: Brad Park* (biography), Harcourt, 1975.

Frame's illustration for the cover of a book published in the early '80s.

S. H. Burchard, *Sports Star: Bob Griese* (biography), Harcourt, 1975.

P. Parish, *Pirate Island Adventure,* Macmillan, 1975.

David R. Collins, *Harry S. Truman: People's President* (biography), Garrard, 1975.

S. H. Burchard, *Sports Star: Pele* (biography), Harcourt, 1976.

Grant Lyons, *Andy Jackson and the Battles for New Orleans* (history), Messner, 1976.

S. H. Burchard, *Sports Star: Jim "Catfish" Hunter* (biography), Harcourt, 1976.

O. W. Burt, *Ghost Towns of the West* (history), Messner, 1976.

R. Hood, *Let's Go to a Basketball Game,* Putnam, 1976.

Michael Chester, *Let's Go to a Recycling Center,* Putnam, 1977.

Anne Eliot Crompton, *The Rain-Cloud Pony,* Holiday House, 1977.

P. Parish, *Hermit Dan,* Macmillan, 1977.

Elizabeth Van Steenwyk, *Fly Like an Eagle and Other Stories,* Walker, 1978.

Sharon Sigmond Shebar, *Whaling for Glory!* (history), Messner, 1978.

W. E. Butterworth, *Next Stop, Earth* (science fiction), Walker, 1978.

Nancy Henderson, *Celebrate America: A Baker's Dozen of Plays,* Messner, 1978.

Judith Schoder, *Brotherhood of Pirates* (biography), Messner, 1979.

Key Soup, Dandelion Press, 1979.

Louis Phillips, *Baseball: Records, Stars, Feats, and Facts* (nonfiction), Harcourt, 1979.

Joseph Mellon, adapter, *Sleeping Beauty* (fairy tale), Dandelion Press, 1979.

Louise Gunther, *Anna's Snow Day,* Garrard, 1979.

Judi R. Kesselman and Franklynn Peterson, *Vans* (nonfiction), Dandelion Press, 1979.

L. Phillips and Arnie Markoe, *Football: Records, Stars, Feats, and Facts* (nonfiction), Harcourt, 1979.

L. Phillips and Karen Markoe, *Women in Sports: Records, Stars, Feats, and Facts* (nonfiction), Harcourt, 1979.

Alexander Williams, adapter, *Ali Baba and the Forty Thieves* (fairy tale), Dandelion Press, 1979.

Aletha Jane Lindstrom, *Sojourner Truth: Slave, Abolitionist, Fighter for Women's Rights* (biography), Messner, 1980.

(With Elliott Ivenbaum) E. Ivenbaum, *Drawing People* (nonfiction), F. Watts, 1980.

Joan Lowery Nixon, *Kidnapped on Astarr* (science fiction), Garrard, 1981.

J. L. Nixon, *Mysterious Queen of Magic* (science fiction), Garrard, 1981.

J. L. Nixon, *Mystery Dolls from Planet Urd* (science fiction), Garrard, 1981.

Ruby E. McCreight, *Horses* (nonfiction), Elsevier/Nelson, 1981.

G. Lyons, *Mustangs, Six Shooters, and Barbed Wire: How the West Was Really Won* (history), Messner, 1981.

Hilary Milton, *Space-Age Terrors!,* Wanderer Books, 1983.

H. Milton, *Horror Hotel!,* Wanderer Books, 1983.

Rhoda Blumberg and Leda Blumberg, *The Simon and Schuster Book of Facts and Fallacies* (nonfiction), Wanderer Books, 1983.

H. Milton, *Fun House Terrors!,* Wanderer Books, 1984.

H. Milton, *Escape from High Doom,* Wanderer Books, 1984.

H. Milton, *Plot It Yourself Horror Stories: Dungeon Demons,* Wanderer Books, 1985.

ALL WRITTEN BY FRANKLIN W. DIXON AND CAROLYN KEENE (BOTH COLLECTIVE PSEUDONYMS); ALL JUVENILE FICTION

Nancy Drew and the Hardy Boys, Super Sleuths! Seven New Mysteries, Wanderer Books, 1981.

"Hello! Where'd you come from?" (From *The Adventures of Huckleberry Finn* by Mark Twain. Illustrated by Paul Frame.)

Danger on Ice, Wanderer Books, 1984.

The Feathered Serpent, Wanderer Books, 1984.

Nancy Drew and the Hardy Boys, Wanderer Books, 1984.

Nancy Drew and the Hardy Boys Camp Fire Stories, Wanderer Books, 1984.

Secret Cargo, Wanderer Books, 1984.

The Secret of the Knight's Sword, Wanderer Books, 1984.

Super Sleuths, Wanderer Books, 1984.

Nancy Drew and the Hardy Boys Be a Detective Mystery Stories: Ticket to Intrigue, Wanderer Books, 1985.

Nancy Drew and the Hardy Boys Be a Detective: The Alaskan Mystery, Wanderer Books, 1985.

Nancy Drew and the Hardy Boys Be a Detective: The Missing Money Mystery, Wanderer Books, 1985.

Nancy Drew and the Hardy Boys Be a Detective: Jungle of Evil, Wanderer Books, 1985.

"NANCY DREW MYSTERY STORIES" SERIES; ALL WRITTEN BY CAROLYN KEENE (COLLECTIVE PSEUDONYM); ALL JUVENILE FICTION

The Kachina Doll Mystery, Wanderer Books, 1981.

The Swami's Ring, Wanderer Books, 1981.

Captive Witness, Wanderer Books, 1981.

The Twin Dilemma, Wanderer Books, 1981.

The Elusive Heiress, Wanderer Books, 1982.

Clue in the Ancient Disguise, Wanderer Books, 1982.

The Sinister Omen, Wanderer Books, 1982.

The Broken Anchor, Wanderer Books, 1983.

The Haunted Carousel, Wanderer Books, 1983.

Nancy Drew Ghost Stories, Wanderer Books, 1983.

The Silver Cobweb, Wanderer Books, 1983.

Enemy Match, Wanderer Books, 1984.

The Mysterious Image, Wanderer Books, 1984.
The Emerald-Eyed Cat, Wanderer Books, 1984.

Also illustrator of *Nancy Drew Ghost Stories II,* Wanderer Books. Frame was not associated with other books in the series.

*"HARDY BOYS MYSTERY STORIES" SERIES; ALL WRITTEN BY
FRANKLIN W. DIXON (COLLECTIVE PSEUDONYM); ALL
JUVENILE FICTION*

The Crimson Flame, Wanderer Books, 1983.
Cave-In, Wanderer Books, 1983.
Sky Sabotage, Wanderer Books, 1983.
The Roaring River Mystery, Wanderer Books, 1984.
The Hardy Boys Ghost Stories, Wanderer Books, 1984.
The Hardy Boys: Demon's Den, Wanderer Books, 1984.
The Hardy Boys: The Blackwing Puzzle, Wanderer Books,
1984.

Frame was not associated with other books in the series.

WORK IN PROGRESS: A series with Corinne Naden to acquaint today's youngsters with young heroines and heroes of the American Revolution; another series to introduce today's youngsters to such "American Humorists," as Mark Twain and Will Rogers; a series of special curriculum aids for grades one through six.

**The retired artist sat on a barrel in the shade close
by.** (From *The Adventures of Tom Sawyer* by Mark
Twain. Illustrated by Paul Frame.)

SIDELIGHTS: "I was born in Maryland as both my parents were. My father grew up in the small farming community of Phoenix and was primarily from an English and Irish background. My mother's family was German. They had settled in Maryland during the 1600s and made their money in shipping of various kinds, including, I'm afraid, slave trading. They were very clannish people who, up until my grandfather, only married within the Germanic community. It was a rather isolated society, very much set in its ways, that didn't show a lot of elasticity toward the outside world. My great grandfather still spoke with an accent, and my mother who was christened Margaret, was never called anything but Gretchen.

"I spent my early childhood in a suburb of Baltimore in a very country-like atmosphere untarnished by the pretense of present-day suburban living. Life in general was more gracious, devoid of the constant worry about material things. There was still time for manners, and manners meant something. We were raised to be courteous and, unlike today, we found rewards in being so.

"Nevertheless, I was spoiled more than was good for me by a mother who thought the sun rose and set on me and rarely ever punished me for anything I said or did. But my sister, six years my senior, stood for no nonsense and was pretty tough with me at times. She did more to put a little steel in my spine than anybody else and was responsible for whatever character I had until such time as my wife took over.

"My mother's life was spent running the household until my father had the bad taste to lose his money when I was six years old (unfortunately before I had time to seriously spend any of it). After that, he felt it necessary to be no less than a vice president or he wouldn't play, so needless to say it was a long time between drinks. Eventually he was put in charge of membership drives for various country clubs, and my mother had to go to work. She started a business called SOS, which was essentially an employment agency for gentile, reasonably well-educated young ladies who found themselves in embarrassed circumstances without any particular skills. They were given work as private secretaries to men of means or put to work in households that required housekeeping on a very lady-like basis."

Frame attended the Maryland State Normal School. He started drawing at the age of five, and knew from an early age that he wanted to become an illustrator. "My favorite artist was the English painter Sir Edwin Landseer. He was well-known in the early 1900s. We had reproductions of his work at home, and I had seen some of his original paintings in the Baltimore Museum. As a child I never tired of looking through his work. His horses had almost human limpid soul-searching big brown eyes that touched me deeply. The English are very anthropomorphic about animals, which appealed to me a great deal and I was set on becoming the American Landseer.

"My next great love was *King Arthur and the Roundtable* illustrated by Howard Pyle. His illustrations made a great impression on me and he influenced the beginning of my artistic endeavors more than anyone else. I spent a good deal of time copying his pen and ink drawings, and for hours on end played at being King Arthur, Sir Lancelot, Sir Galahad, or any of the legendary characters of the Round Table. Role playing provided added excitement, the kind that makes one want to express oneself in whatever medium one is talented. A lesson today's educators and editors would do well to heed. If they and others took this to heart I feel we would have far less violence in our society.

From Frame's unpublished project, *The Nonsense Book of Color.*

"My parents neither discouraged nor encouraged my drawing. They simply said, 'Oh yes, Paul likes to draw and paint.' It was a gentle acknowledgment that I spent an awful lot of time doing what they considered not terribly important.

"Miss Fitzgerald, my fourth- or fifth-grade teacher at the Maryland State Normal School, stands in my mind as one of the great people I had the privilege to be around. She was not more then five feet tall, severely hunchbacked, and very plain. However her warmth and understanding made both disappear. She used to say to me, 'Don't worry, Paul, you'll eventually learn to spell by the time you're fifty. Just keep on working with your imagination. Only remember that you have to join our world occasionally in order to survive.' She later set down my credo for life when she said, 'If you're going to deal with children, which you obviously seem to want to do, you have to tell the truth. Don't make it up. You can't fib when you draw unless it's fantasy. There is nothing worse than misinforming children, unless they know you're doing it intentionally for a set purpose.' She realized that drawing was not just a passing passion but my main interest in life.

"Throughout primary school I was a very average pupil always lost in my own dreams. It was not unusual for me to reply to a question I had been asked in class as though I was Sir Lancelot. I got a good deal of laughter out of my peers because of that nonsense. I've always said that I drew my way through four years of Latin. I filled my notebooks with drawings of Roman fortifications, soldiers, and generals. My Latin teacher was intrigued by the kind of research I put into my drawings to make

them as accurate as possible. Those drawings were quite real to me—I was there as far as I was concerned."

For some formal training Frame entered the Maryland Institute of Art where he took classes in the afternoon. "I was being trained in technique but it was pretty much a lopsided teaching. All I had really done was to copy things from whatever subject I had researched, and if there was any originality in my work it was in drawing my own version of, lets say, the Roman centurions I had researched. The school started me right off in life drawing without bothering to know whether I could draw or not. It was the wrong approach for me. I began at five years drawing horses and dogs; my largest difficulty was drawing hooves. I avoided the problem for four or five years by putting horses in tall grass. I decided, one day, it would be rather stupid to go through life not knowing how to draw the essential part of a horse, and with practice I eventually did learn to draw a horse reasonably well from the knee down. For some time, I was concerned with drawing only animals, although I occasionally made an effort at family portraits and a few landscapes, both very average. Later I changed and became interested in landscapes."

In 1926 Frame and his family moved to New York City and remained there until his mother opened a shop in Scarsdale. His desire to leave school as early as possible led him to attend summer school for two consecutive years. "I finished high school in Scarsdale when I was sixteen. I was not in the least interested in school and was anxious to get out to make my way in the world. I wanted to be independent.

"I moved back to New York City and started haunting the studios of contemporary artists. I was dying to meet some of them and I'd offer to run their errands hoping to be near a real live artist!''

In 1930 Frame attended the National Academy of Design, and in 1931 went to night school at Columbia while working at Lord and Taylor during the day. "I received a very formal and academic training at the Academy while my apprenticeship at Lord and Taylor taught me the commercial aspect of business. I worked in the production department for a year and a half, which was not very interesting because its basic function was to gather the various elements of a finished creative work and send it out to the newspapers. I was hoping for an opening in the advertising department because it was as close as I could get to drawing of any kind. I eventually learned enough about the business and made enough of a pest of myself, that the art director, Harry Rodman, a man with unending patience, gave me a chance to do an ad of a short bob satin jacket for the fall sales. I redrew the ad seventeen times and it ended up looking like an advertisement for stovepipes. Against everyone's advice Rodman ran the ad. The buyer, kept saying, 'How on earth can I sell anything from that construction.' But Rodman stood his ground, and eventually I joined ranks with the fashion staff while doing all sorts of errands none of the other artists and free-lance artists wanted to do. But it was a wonderful way to learn, and I was delighted to have my own easel, chair, and lamp. I got to the point where I did acceptable work.

"After three years on staff, I became a free-lancer until I was drafted six months after the bombing of Pearl Harbor in 1941. I was twenty-nine years old and almost the oldest man in the Air Force. They had a great deal of difficulty trying to figure out what to do with me. Since I had some knowledge of color and distortion, putting me into camouflage would have been a good way to use my abilities, but the Army didn't seem to care about logic very much. So, I did a multitude of things, none of which were terribly important. First I was tested for radio operator. It was such a monotonous job that I fell asleep during the test, and it was immediately decided that I was not needed in that area. Instead, I became an instructor in basic training until I was shipped as a tech sergeant to England for insubordination. There, I was given the responsibility of training soldiers in the glider infantry until I discovered that both my knees, particularly the right one, were quite unreliable. I spent some delightful time in North Pickingham in an unassigned pool for Air Force Personnel before being assigned to a B-17 bomb group. I flew only five missions, quite to my good fortune, because I couldn't keep an oxygen mask on. The pressure of altitude caused my sinuses to drain directly into the mask. Even though I was a fairly good instructor and managed to do well enough to oil my way into a first three-grade sergeant, that I didn't have a military turn of mind soon became obvious to all concerned.''

Released from the Army one month after V-E day in 1945, Frame returned to the States and moved to Connecticut. "A friend and I rented a place in a small town called Newton. All that time away from business meant starting all over again. I put together a whole new set of samples and decided I was not going to continue with fashion. I had learned a great deal from it, but was not the chic type and didn't really enjoy the fashion world very much. All prospects being opened, I would instead try to go into advertisement and illustration.

"A year or so later, I bought twelve acres in Newton and made plans to spend the rest of my life as a country squire. I had read all these stories about people who worked in their little studios up in the country and occasionally came into the Cliff Dwellers

Paradise, to do what they needed to do, in order to take back sufficient work to keep them happily busy for a while.

"Things didn't work out quite that way. I married Jean Welch in the meantime and we subsequently had two daughters, Mindy and Debbie. I started building my own house, leaving me little time to work on my samples and keeping me relatively empty of income. I had to go to New York to look for an agent. She got me started with work in fashion and also minor projects in advertising. A couple of years later I started book illustration with Whitman, an imprint of Western, publisher of inexpensive mass-market paperbacks and paper dolls.''

Illustrating children's books suited Frame because he had developed a great rapport with children and "I still felt like a closet romantic in the sense that I was still 'King Arthuring' and 'Robin Hooding' it. I was enjoying action stories and, may I be forgiven, highly sentimental stories involving little girls, romance, and action. I've always loved to draw action.

"My first real break in illustration came in the late fifties with the 'Katie John' series for Harper. I had as much fun reading the stories as I had illustrating them and was very disappointed when Mary Calhoun stopped writing because I thought her work was delightful. Katie John was a spunky little girl entering womanhood. Miss Calhoun wrote her stories with a particularly warm understanding of what a young lady has to go through growing up—remaining an individual and wanting to conform at the same time. Much like the kids today who try to be different by tearing holes in their jeans. They claim to be using their individuality, when in fact they are exactly alike, as if punched out by the same cookie cutter. Katie John's story dealt very well with that subject. In spirit, she reminded me very much of my own sister who had lots of sand and steel in her character. So I was predestined to be fond of Katie John.

"The Nancy Drew character was another of my favorites. I understood her. She was like the girls I knew in high school and although antiquated by today's standards, she oddly enough seemed to appeal to youngsters who at twelve were smoking pot and mouthing that phrase, 'I've got to find out who I am.'

"There was not much Nancy couldn't do: she could fly a plane, play billiards, water ski and was also a very clever amateur lawyer. She was eighteen and her beau would only kiss her on the cheek. There was very little talk about their physical relationship, instead the emphasis was on companionship. I know that's stuffy and unrealistic, but I feel strongly we should refuse to condone today's promiscuity.

"In order for me to illustrate something, I have to have understanding of the characters. I've always been this way. Even in my personal life I have to be able to feel real warmth for someone before he can become more than an acquaintance. The same principle applies to the characters I draw. If they are not my friends, it shows in the illustrations, which turn out cold and seem to only fill the pages.

"I worked with pen and ink and didn't do much color for a long time except for an occasional cover. And even those were basically pen and ink drawings with colored overlays. It wasn't until the late sixties, when I did a whole series of Trixie Belden, that I started to do color drawings and found I loved it. I was paid a flat fee and had to do them much too fast for the work to be as good as it should have been. But in those days, unless you signed a contract which included royalties, financial security was uncertain and you had to do so many books a year in order to support yourself and your family. The work sometimes suffered from that.

(Illustration by Paul Frame from *Key to the Treasure* by Peggy Parish.)

"But I have remained freelance because I like the feeling of time not running me and much prefer the fun, warmth, and rewards of being at home with my wife and children. I used both my daughters for models when they were young. They were very amenable, almost frighteningly good children, however not with very decided character.

"Freelancing can be tough, however. It takes an awful lot of time to represent yourself, and unless you are one of the half dozen leaders in the field, which I am not, you have to keep on banging on doors. I would classify myself a well-founded and competent professional who's enjoyed very good spells for several years in a row, but I've had spells which frightened me, as well.

"I've worked with and without agents. To find the right agent is the single most difficult thing to do. You need someone you can trust on a business basis, who is compatible in sensitivity and will understand what you are trying to do, knowing where to submit your work and where not to.

"If I have any advice to give young illustrators, it would be to research subjects as completely as possible, so as not to distort the truth. It means that your original research has to be checked with other sources, and you have to differentiate between 'real' and 'made up'. As good as libraries and picture galleries are, you can end up using a picture that is not accurate. Many artists are awfully good with their imagination, but are not necessarily careful about historical accuracy.

"I've illustrated a lot of biographies and always tried to be as authentic as possible. In the case of *Black Women of Valor*, for example, apart from the regular library research, I went through whatever sources I could dig out in the black community for pictures and historical information. It's also useful to consult an expert at a university or a foundation. I found that, unless extremely busy, they are quite generous with their knowledge.

"In many instances, I was lucky to be able to contact a living relative who could back up my impersonal research and say, 'that's right, that's phony, etc . . . . ' When I illustrated a children's biography of Robert Frost, I was very fortunate because his daughter, Mrs. Valentine, still lived in the village. I went to visit her and showed her my pencil drawing of Frost telling a story to a grandchild with one arm around him in the most affectionate fashion. Mrs. Valentine told me that it wasn't like her father to behave that way. He had, in fact, great difficulty showing physical affection for his children. It was invaluable for my work to be able to talk with her for an hour. So, with research you have to depend not only on the facts that you've gathered, but you also have to trust your instinct to decide what seems accurate and factual and what is tinted with prejudice. It is also essential to draw that person in the proper accoutrements and surroundings, as well.

"Research is very time consuming, but without it you cannot give a solid and totally objective view, which is, after all, the job you are paid to do when you illustrate a biography.

"I would tell children interested in drawing that they must carry a sketch pad with them at all times. It's terribly important to make sketching notes or written notes no matter what the subject, because as an illustrator you can never know for certain what you'll be asked to draw. You may learn to draw things that are very far from your center of interest, but if you develop a reputation for drawing accurately, you are likely to be asked to illustrate a variety of subjects. It is wise to make every effort not to be type cast; doing one kind of story. It becomes dull and even worse it limits your assignments and makes for slim eating.

"For many years I carried a sketchbook and took notes and made hasty sketches of what I was seeing, particularly when I went to a zoo. I also made notations about the way people dressed or handled themselves, and made sketches for characterization while riding the subway.

"Drawings have to be as convincing as words and should take you one step further. If you make sketches of poor people for instance, it's not enough to show them as shabby and unshaven. The position of the body, the way that person sits or stands is also essential to convey the impression of being really down and out and totally defeated. If the body is alert and portrayed as vital, it will be in contradiction with the impression you are trying to achieve. There must be a relationship between the attitude and the feelings you want to express.

"I'm a total believer in the actor's studio approach applied to drawing. I believe that you have to get inside the things you're drawing and to instill in yourself some understanding of the creature. You cannot do a really good job without that identification.

"And, of course, you have to keep a certain perspective. If you become too immersed or too involved in your subject you tend to be overly dramatic. Unless you are drawing a fantasy, you have to have the discipline to be as accurate and truthful as you can. Truth is very elusive—what may be true for you may not necessarily be true for someone else.

"I have also illustrated sport books, including a series on baseball, and a number of biographies of sport figures. I have filled in with illustrations when publishers couldn't get permission to use photographs of the stars, or when there were not enough photographs.

"I did a series of easy-to-read and doubled-spaced 'How to' books that I rather liked. Kids find blocks of type frightening."

With more than two hundred children's books to his credit, Frame lives in New York and continues to write and illustrate. "My agent reached an age where she retired, but during my career I built sufficient contacts with authors and other people to be able to keep on working. I would like to do a series of classics from Mark Twain to Will Rogers, people who are not noticed by youngsters and whom I would love to propagandize."[1]

FOOTNOTE SOURCES

[1]Based on an interview by Peggy Boyer for *Something about the Author*.

FOR MORE INFORMATION SEE:

Lee Kingman and others, compilers, *Illustrators of Children's Books: 1957-1966*, Horn Book, 1968.
Martha E. Ward and Dorothy A. Marquardt, *Illustrators of Books for Young People*, Scarecrow, 1975.
L. Kingman and others, compilers, *Illustrators of Children's Books: 1967-1976*, Horn Book, 1978.

GERSON, Noel B(ertram) 1914-1988 (Ann Marie Burgess, Michael Burgess, Samuel Edwards, Paul Lewis, Leon Phillips, Donald Clayton Porter, Dana Fuller Ross, Carter A. Vaughan)

OBITUARY NOTICE—See sketch in *SATA* Volume 22: Born November 6, 1914, in Chicago, Ill., died of a heart attack, November 20, 1988, in Boca Raton, Fla. Journalist, business executive, scriptwriter, and author. Gerson was an extremely prolific writer. He worked as a reporter for the *Chicago Herald-Examiner* in the early 1930s, then became an executive and writer for Chicago's WGN-Radio before the decade ended. After leaving WGN, Gerson continued writing for the medium until 1951, when he published his second book. Throughout the rest of his life, Gerson wrote numerous books in several genres—historical novels, westerns, biographies, juvenile works—and under many pseudonyms. Notable among his juvenile writings are *Nathan Hale: Espionage Agent, Rock of Freedom: The Story of the Plymouth Colony*, and *The Last Wilderness: The Saga of American's Mountain Men*. Several of his adult novels were adapted for film. Gerson's numerous works under pseudonyms include the "Wagons West" series, which he produced as Dana Fuller Ross, and the "White Indian" novels, which he wrote as Donald Clayton Porter.

FOR MORE INFORMATION SEE:

Contemporary Authors, Volumes 81-84, Gale, 1979.
Who's Who in the East, 19th edition, Marquis, 1983.
The Writer's Directory: 1984-1986, St. James Press, 1983.

OBITUARIES

Chicago Tribune, November 24, 1988.
New York Times, November 23, 1988 (p. B-8).
Washington Post, November 26, 1988.

GIVENS, Janet E(aton) 1932- (Janet Eaton)

PERSONAL: Born July 5, 1932, in New York, N.Y.; daughter of Irving D. (an investigator for the Securities Exchange Commission) and Matilda (a homemaker; maiden name, Schmelzle) Eaton; married Richard A. Givens (an attorney), August 24, 1957; children: Susan, Jane. *Education:* Queens College (now of the City University of New York), B.A., 1953; Columbia University, M.A., 1955; further graduate study at University of Maryland, University of Colorado, and Columbia University. *Home:* 147-11 68th Rd., Flushing, N.Y. 11367.

JANET E. GIVENS

CAREER: Woodside Elementary School, Silver Spring, Md., teacher, 1953-55; Bellows Elementary School, Mamaroneck, N.Y., teacher, 1955-59; Queens College (now of the City University of New York), Flushing, N.Y., supervisor of prospective teachers, 1959-60, part-time lecturer in education, 1967-68; writer, 1968—. New York City United Parents Association Delegate, 1971-72; vice-president of P.S. 219 Parent-Teachers Association, 1972-73. Literacy volunteer, 1985—.

WRITINGS:

JUVENILE NONFICTION

The Migrating Birds, Beacon Press, 1964.
Something Wonderful Happened (illustrated by Susan Elayne Dodge), Atheneum, 1982.
Just Two Wings (illustrated by S. E. Dodge), Atheneum, 1984.

OTHER

(Contributor) Dorothy T. Spoerl, editor, *Tensions Our Children Live With: Stories for Discussion,* Beacon Press, 1959.

Also author of children's plays ''Our Changing Flag,'' 1961, and ''Give Thanks for the Pilgrims,'' 1964, both published in *Instructor.* Contributor of articles to education journals (until 1957, under name Janet Eaton), including *Childhood Education.* Editor, *PS 219 News* (Queens, N.Y.), 1971-73.

WORK IN PROGRESS: *Skipper and His Zipper Coat,* a children's book about the experience of a young child who seeks help and solves problems on his own; research on science for children's books; *The First Flame,* about the discovery of fire by early peoples and its effects down to the present.

SIDELIGHTS: ''I spent most of my life in professional, volunteer, and home settings, helping young people to grow. I am an avid reader on ways to give children the best environment in which to mature.

''As a teacher and parent, I am convinced that the key to learning is the thrill and excitement of the mystery of the world, which entices rather than dragoons us to reach out for information. The attention of a young person can be caught by fiction or nonfiction if presented so as to hook into the reader's curiosity.

''In the two books published by Beacon Press, I tried to express my feelings about the natural world and the sometimes difficult struggle within one's self to understand and appreciate this world. *Tensions Our Children Live With* contains stories that can be read to children to stimulate discussion. These stories concern 'problems' children face in their daily lives that are sometimes overlooked by adults but that are real to children. They concern such challenges as handicapped children trying to adjust, broken families, and the like. Although this book was published in 1959, the same problems are present today. *The Migrating Birds* emphasizes the joy of discovering the quiet wonders that we 'see' each day but often overlook because we fail to stop and think about them.

''*Skipper and His Zipper Coat,* on which I am working, seeks to get children to want to read by hooking into their natural adversarial attitude toward adults, none of whom want to be concerned with Skipper's problem, which he solves himself.

''*The First Flame,* also in progress, seeks to instill concern for fire safety by opening the reader's eyes to the wonder and power of fire and how early peoples must have taken thousands of years to learn to control natural fire, which changed the world. Practical safety hints can then be fascinating rather than boring!

''I am also working on a concept for describing the key features of our legal system including the Constitution, Bill of Rights, Supreme Court, criminal justice, and civil suits in a way which will be exciting for grades three through eight.

''The common theme is to express the perception that we thrive on difficulty and the excitement of confronting the unknown, which kindles the latent possibilities within a young person—or an adult of any age.''

HOBBIES AND OTHER INTERESTS: Gardening, travel (England, France, Spain, Switzerland, Italy, Denmark, West Germany, Ghana).

HAWES, Louise 1943-
(Jamie Suzanne)

PERSONAL: Born June 21, 1943, in Boulder, Colo.; daughter of Maurice (an economic consultant) and Isabel (a homemaker; maiden name, Maurer) Hawes; married Stephen Jacobson, December 26, 1965 (divorced, 1978); children: Marc, Robin. *Education:* Swarthmore College, B.A., 1965; attended Lehigh University, 1971-73, and Barnes Foundation, 1977-78. *Office:* E. P. Dutton, 2 Park Ave., New York, N.Y. 10016.

CAREER: State of New Jersey, Department of Community Affairs, Division on Aging, Trenton, N.J., public information director, 1967-69; Supermarkets General Corp., Woodbridge, N.J., assistant editor, *Pathmark News,* 1970-72; Lehigh University, Bethlehem, Pa., teaching assistant in English, 1971-73; Barbizon School, Paramus, N.J., instructor in advertising and writing, 1978-79; Stanley H. Kaplan Educational Centers, New York, N.Y., advertising manager, 1980—; writer, 1985—.
Member: National Association of Children's Book Writers.
Awards, honors: New Jersey Authors Award from the New Jersey Institute of Technology, 1987, for *Nelson Malone Meets the Man from Mush-Nut.*

WRITINGS:

Nelson Malone Meets the Man from Mush-Nut (illustrated by Bert Dodson), Lodestar, 1986.
Nelson Malone Saves Flight 942 (illustrated by Jacqueline Rogers), Lodestar, 1988.

UNDER PSEUDONYM JAMIE SUZANNE; "SWEET VALLEY TWINS" SERIES

Stretching the Truth, Bantam, 1987.
Outcast, Bantam, 1987.
New Girl, Bantam, 1987.
Sneaking Out, Bantam, 1987.

FILMSTRIPS

"Birth of a Chick Embryo," Time-Life Filmstrips, 1973.

LOUISE HAWES

"This is Samantha, dear," said Mrs. Pauley. (From *Nelson Malone Meets the Man from Mush-Nut* by Louise Hawes. Illustrated by Bert Dodson.)

"Be a Fact Finder," Educational Reading Services, 1974.
"Black Americans," Educational Reading Services, 1974.

MONOGRAPHS

On Continuing Education, State of New Jersey, 1969.
Guidelines for Pre-Retirement Planning, State of New Jersey, 1975.
State Report, White House Conference on Aging, State of New Jersey, 1980.
Infoquest: A Curriculum Guide, New York City Public Schools, 1986.

Contributor of articles and stories to periodicals, including *Mademoiselle, Scholastic Voice, Extension Journal,* and *Midnight.*

WORK IN PROGRESS: Ever After, a collection of fairy tales for grownups; *Baby Face,* a novel.

SIDELIGHTS: "Before I was ten years old, I had decided to be a writer. Albert Payson Terhune, the author of countless animal stories including the famous 'Lassie' series, was largely responsible for this decision. His stories invariably involved harrowing close calls for virtuous pets and heart-wrenching conclusions that always made me determined to leave my readers crying when I grew up. The fact that my books for children aim at laughter rather than tears, doesn't disappoint me at all—as an adult, I've noticed the world is much too full of the latter and pretty short on the former!

"Perhaps the most rewarding part of writing for young readers is the mail. Even before the paperbacks came out, I received letters from all over the country, letters from girls and boys I'd never met, but who had met me! What a wonderful, life-redeeming feeling to be told that, because of a book of mine, some youngster wants to be a writer, too!

"Not that there weren't detours along the way to this happy outcome. Both my parents were gifted, bright people who enjoyed painting as well as writing. For years, I painted and drew as much as I wrote. I also tried my hand at acting and even had a sculpture studio for several years before I returned to that rock-hard place at the pit of my soul, the place where a very calm, sure voice told me, 'You can flirt with all these exciting modes of expression, you can wriggle and twist and carry on, but the way you're meant to be you is by writing. It's lonely, it's frustrating, and you can't do it at parties to the amusement and delight of your friends. But it's you.'

"*Nelson Malone Meets the Man from Mush-Nut* was written for my children when they were very close to Nelson's age, eleven. I wanted to make sure they were exposed to some stories that didn't teach or preach or serve any other nefarious, 'useful' purpose. I wanted Nelson's adventures to be what children crave most and get least—silliness and fun.

"And, yes, my son who, but for the grace of Lloyd Alexander, would be an arcade and TV *ADDICT,* is *still* crazy about video games. And, yes, my daughter and he are friendly enemies, just as Nelson and Robin are. And, gulp, yes, Nelson's preoccupied, work-at-home mother reflects my stint as an advertising manager who divides her time between Manhattan and my home office.

"*Nelson Malone Saves Flight 942* is a sixth-grade curtain call for Nelson's fifth-grade foolishness and carryings-on. He may have gained a grade in this sequel, but he's lost none of his propensity for crazy adventures—with preening rock idols, has-been magicians, newly hatched pteradactyls, not to mention pint-size ghosts and a teacher who takes her class on field trips to horror movies and amusement parks.

"Whenever anyone asks me how on earth I come up with such off-beat stories, I have a ready excuse—my mother. In fact, Nelson's wonderful teacher, Sylvia Tuckman, is patterned after the woman who used to beg my sisters and me to skip school in favor of shadow shows, talking animals, and life-size paper dolls. Because she didn't have an 'outside' job and because she was endlessly creative, lonely, and loving, she was forever bursting with exciting projects and plans. Physically, she's a small woman who lacks 'Terrible Tuckman's' imposing girth, but emotionally, she was unquestionably the largest influence in my childhood.

"Now that the paperback has increased my mail volume, I'm dividing my time between trying to answer each letter personally, continuing my job in New York, and finishing my new 'grown-up' project, a collection of fairy tales for adults called *Ever After.* This book seems a natural extension of my writing for children in that it's coming easily and with joy. I'm so glad I started writing for youngsters *first;* otherwise I'm afraid I'd be overwhelmed with MISSION and PURPOSE and other concepts generally destructive to delight. Thanks, boys and girls, for keeping me on the right track!''

HOBBIES AND OTHER INTERESTS: Drawing, sculpting, and long, renewing walks.

FOR MORE INFORMATION SEE:

Kirkus Reviews, April 1, 1986.
Ridgewood News, June 1, 1986 (p.4).
Publishers Weekly, June 27, 1986.
School Library Journal, August, 1986.
"Book Publisher Finds Lucrative Niche in Soap Opera Series for Teen-Age Girls,'' *Wall Street Journal,* February 11, 1988.
School Library Journal, May, 1988.
Reading Loft, March, 1989.
New York Times Book Review, March 12, 1989 (p. 37).

HOLMES, Peggy 1898- (Semloh)

PERSONAL: Born November 11, 1898, in Kingston-upon-Hull, England; immigrated to Canada, 1919; daughter of Fred (an interior decorator) and Rosa (a teacher; maiden name, Serool) Lewis; married Alfred Henry Holmes (a dean of court reporters), September 23, 1917 (deceased); children: Bryan Lewis. *Education:* Attended schools in England and Canada; studied singing under Victoria Nurkse. *Home:* 7720 108 St., No. 527, Edmonton, Alberta, Canada T6E 5E1. *Office:* Canadian Broadcasting Corp., 8861 75 St., Edmonton, Alberta, Canada T6C 2H3.

CAREER: Broadcaster, writer, and artist. Has worked as a bank employee, bookkeeper, and in real estate; voice placement consultant, 1935—; teacher of singing during the 1940s and 1950s; artist, and writer, beginning 1970s; Canadian Broadcasting Corporation (CBC-Radio), Alberta, Canada, writer and broadcaster for radio program "The Way It Was," 1975—; artist under pseudonym Semloh; CKUA (access radio station), Edmonton, Alberta, co-host of "Something for Seniors" program, 1981-84. Lecturer at schools, clubs, and conferences. Former board member, Canadian Cancer Society, 1940-70, Victorian Order of Nurses, Red Cross, and Young Women's Christian Association (YWCA), 1940-45; sponsor of Edmonton Light Opera Performing Ensemble (ELOPE), 1980-86, Cushion Theatre, and Senior Craft Centre. Actress in a film for ViCom, "We Care," 1986; guest appearances on radio and television programs in Canada, Great Britain, and the United States. *Member:* Association of Canadian Television and Radio Artists, Writer's Guild of Alberta, Change for Children Association, Physicians for Prevention of Nuclear War, Sherwood Park Business and Professional Women (life member), St. George's Society, Seniors' Crafts Society of Alberta, War Brides' Association (member of board).

AWARDS, HONORS: City of Edmonton Award, 1977, for outstanding services in preserving Canada's heritage; Province of Alberta Achievement Award, 1977, for excellence in arts, literature, and broadcasting; Beaver Award from Hudson's Bay Company, 1978, for unpublished manuscript "It Could Have Been Worse''; Canadian Authors Association Award, 1979, for *It Could Have Been Worse;* Alberta Culture Writer's Grant, 1980, 1982, and 1985; City of Edmonton established the Peggy Holmes Park, 1984.

WRITINGS:

(With Joy Roberts) *It Could Have Been Worse* (young adult; autobiography), Collins, 1980.
(With Andrea Spalding) *Never a Dull Moment* (autobiography), 1984.

Peggy Holmes with co-host Chris Allen.

Author of more than fifteen hundred radio scripts, mainly for Canadian Broadcasting Corp. Contributor of reviews and articles to periodicals, including *Alberta Report, Edmonton Journal,* and *Alberta Motorist.*

WORK IN PROGRESS: A third autobiographical book, *We've Made It;* a collection of her scripts and interviews; a book about her psychic experiences.

SIDELIGHTS: Known as "Canada's Oldest Broadcaster," Holmes began her career as a broadcast writer after attending a senior citizens' writing class while in her seventies. Since that time, she has written over fifteen hundred radio scripts for "The Way It Was," a Canadian Broadcasting Corporation radio show. From 1981 to 1984 she was co-hostess of her own program "Something for Seniors" on Edmonton's CKUA radio station.

At the age of seventy-seven, she began piecing together a trunkful of scribbling of a World War I war bride in the bush country of Northern Alberta. The result was *It Could Have Been Worse,* a record of her day-by-day experiences on Canada's harsh frontier during the 1920s, which became a Canadian best-seller. Holmes followed her first book with another autobiographical account, *Never a Dull Moment.* She has also completed tapes of extensive reminiscences for the Edmonton Public School Board and the Provincial Archives.

In addition to her writing, Holmes began another career while in her seventies—painting. She signs her artwork "Semloh" (Holmes spelled backwards) and has successfully sold several hundred works. A tribute to the adage "you're never too old," Holmes has made guest appearances on radio and television stations across Canada and Britain and has been featured in U.S. media.

HOBBIES AND OTHER INTERESTS: Poetry, pottery, people.

HUMBLE, Richard 1945-

PERSONAL: Born January 17, 1945, in London, England; son of Joseph Graeme (a professor of hematology) and Elsie May (Hunt) Humble. *Education:* Oriel College, Oxford, M.A. (with honors), 1966. *Politics:* Liberal. *Home and office:* Manor Mead, 2A Laureston Rd., Newton Abbot, Devon, England.

CAREER: P.B.C. Publishing Ltd., London, England, deputy executive editor, 1966-68, assistant editor, 1968-69, editor, 1969-72; Orbis Publishing Ltd., London, managing editor of military publications, 1971-73; free-lance writer. *Member:* Oriel Tortoises Boat Club, Leander Club.

WRITINGS:

Hitler's High Seas Fleet, Ballantine, 1971.

Japanese High Seas Fleet, Ballantine, 1973.
Hitler's Generals, Arthur Barker, 1973.
Napoleon's Peninsular Marshals, Macdonald & Jane's, 1973,
    Taplinger, 1975.
The Fall of Saxon England, Arthur Barker, 1975, St. Martin's,
    1976.
Marco Polo, Putnam, 1975.
Before the Dreadnought, Macdonald & Jane's, 1976.
Captain Bligh, Arthur Barker, 1976.
Tanks, Weidenfeld & Nicholson, 1977.
The Explorers, Time-Life, 1978.
Famous Land Battles: From Agincourt to the Six Day War,
    Little, Brown, 1979.
Warfare in the Ancient World, Cassell, 1980.
The Saxon Kings, Weidenfeld & Nicolson, 1980.
Undersea Warfare, Basinghall, 1981.
Aircraft-Carriers: The Illustrated History, M. Joseph, 1982.
(Editor) *Naval Warfare,* Orbis, 1983.
Fraser of North Cape, Routledge & Kegan Paul, 1983.
Battleships and Battle-Cruisers, Chartwell Press, 1983.
U.S. Fleet Carriers of World War II, Blandford, 1984.
English Castles, Weidenfeld & Nicolson, 1984.
Submarines (illustrated by Andy Farmer and Rob Shone), F.
    Watts, 1985.
U.S. Navy, Windward, 1985.
The Soldier, Roydon, 1985.
The U.S. Civil War, Admiral, 1985.
The Rise and Fall of the British Navy, Queen Anne Press, 1986.
''Crusader'': 8th Army's Forgotten Victory, Leo Cooper/Sec-
    ker, 1987.
(With Richard Hook) *The Voyage of Magellan,* F. Watts, 1989.

Contributor to *History of the Second World War, History of the
Twentieth Century, New English Encyclopedia,* and *History of
the English-Speaking Peoples.*

WORK IN PROGRESS: U.S. Carrier Sailors, for F. Watts;
*Operation Corporate: The Fleet Air Arm and the Reconquest of
the Falklands,* for Picton.

SIDELIGHTS: ''Why do I like writing about history? Well, after
all, it's the memory-bank of mankind, with an endless fund of
stories about people in all walks of life, in all ages. History is all
too often indifferently taught in schools, which makes it all the
more of a pleasure to show readers that history can be a lasting
pleasure rather than a mammoth bore.

''Then there are the armour-plated myths with which history is
encrusted. Take Captain Bligh, apparently damned to eternity by
Charles Laughton's film portrayal. I was able to prove that far
from being a sadistic orderer of non-stop floggings, no contemporary British Navy Captain ordered lighter punishments. Nor
was his career limited to the mutiny on the *Bounty.* A brilliant
seaman and navigator, he commanded in two of the toughest sea
battles of the day and was publicly thanked by Nelson himself
after the Battle of Copenhagen. And Bligh was involved in *three*
mutinies, not one.

''Again, there's the myth that Nazi Germany went to war in 1939
armed to the teeth for world conquest, bristling with tanks,
aircraft, and U-boats. In fact the German Army relied principally
on horse-drawn transport and had fewer tanks than the Allies; the
Luftwaffe relied on light bombers produced for quantity rather
than quality, and had no strategic bombing force at all; and with
only twenty-two operational submarines, U-boat supremo Do-
nitz stated bluntly that he was 'incapable of undertaking effica-
cious measures against England.'

''As long as such myths endure, I'll be happy to puncture them.
This doesn't mean that I set out deliberately to sensationalize,
defame, or debunk. The story, truly told, has it own appeal.''

FOR MORE INFORMATION SEE:

Times Literary Supplement, April 20, 1984.

IRONSIDE, Jetske 1940-
(Jetske Sybesma, Yetska)

PERSONAL: Born May 5, 1940, in The Netherlands; daughter
of Kornelis (a doctor) and Anna (Hyilkema) Sybesma; married
R. G. Ironside, May, 1972 (divorced, 1988); children: Pernille
(daughter). *Education:* Royal Academy, The Hague, Netherlands, M.O., 1961; attended University of Washington, Seattle,
exchange student, 1963-64; Maryland Institute, Baltimore,
M.F.A., 1966; graduate work at University of Illinois, Cham-
paign, 1967-68; Bryn Mawr College, Ph.D., 1973. *Home:* RR
2, Site 18, Box 8, Winterburn, Alberta, Canada T0E 2N0.
Office: University of Alberta, Department of Art and Design,
Edmonton, Alberta, Canada T6G 2C9.

CAREER: University of Alberta, Edmonton, Alberta, Canada,
associate professor of history of art, 1968—. Albert Art Foundation, board of directors, 1982-88, vice-chairman, 1987-88.
Exhibitions: ''All Alberta,'' ACA Gallery, Calgary, Alberta,
Canada, 1988; Winter Olympic Games, 1988.

ILLUSTRATOR:

Muriel Whitaker, *Pernilla in the Perilous Forest,* Oberon, 1979.

WORK IN PROGRESS: Illustrations for *Alphabet;* writing and
illustrating *Art and History of Art for Children.*

JETSKE IRONSIDE

SIDELIGHTS: "With the benefit of extensive training in fine art (M.F.A.) and in the history of art (Ph.D.), I am interested in making children aware of the delights one can find visually in the 'history' of art—or, the 'history' of our culture. This enchances the visual literacy of children at an early age because it provides them with images ('visual rhymes') other than those used in our popular culture—television, cartoons, advertising, etc.

"I am further interested in pursing a career as an artist (sculpture, painting, and drawing) and as an art historian (Hieronymus Bosch, Bruegel, landscape painting, contemporary art)."

JOHNSTON, Ginny 1946-

PERSONAL: Born May 18, 1946, in Salem, N.J.; daughter of Dewey Elton (a chemist) and Martha (a homemaker; maiden name, Roop) Waters; married Rob Johnston (a property manager), September 1, 1973. *Education:* Georgia State University, B.A., 1968, M.Ed., 1970, Ed.S., 1973. *Home:* 4615 Stonehenge Dr., Atlanta, Ga. 30360. *Office:* Fernbank Science Center, 156 Heaton Park Dr., Atlanta, Ga. 30307.

CAREER: DeKalb County School System, Atlanta, Ga., elementary school teacher, 1968-70; Fernbank Science Center, Atlanta, life sciences instructor, 1970— ; author. *Member:* Authors' Guild, Society of Children's Book Writers, Georgia Herpetological Society, Zoo Atlanta, Delta Kappa Gamma. *Awards, honors:* Outstanding Science Trade Book for Children from the National Science Teachers Association, 1984, for *Are Those Animals Real?*, 1985, for *Andy Bear*, 1986, for *The Crocodile and the Crane*, and 1988, for *Scaly Babies*.

GINNY JOHNSTON

WRITINGS:

ALL WITH JUDY CUTCHINS; ALL NONFICTION FOR CHILDREN

Are Those Animals Real? How Museums Prepare Wildlife Exhibits, Morrow, 1984.
Andy Bear: A Polar Bear Grows Up at the Zoo (illustrated with photographs by Constance Noble), Morrow, 1985.
The Crocodile and the Crane: Surviving in a Crowded World, Morrow, 1986.
Scaly Babies: Reptiles Growing Up, Morrow, 1988.
Scoots, the Bog Turtle (illustrated by Frances Smith), Atheneum, 1989.
Windows on Wildlife, Morrow, 1990.

Author of publications for the Fernbank Science Center entitled *Primarily for Understanding Science* and *Just for Understanding Science*.

SIDELIGHTS: "My writing career started as part of my job at Fernbank Science Center. In an attempt to reach the thousands of elementary students in DeKalb County, my co-author, Judy Cutchins, initiated a science newsletter to be distributed to each student and teacher. Within a short time, it was apparent that the job of writing one newsletter for grades kindergarten through seven was impossible. We decided on two newsletters: one for primary students and another for upper elementary classes. That is when Judy and I became a team. We shared a common goal of improving science education for children, and we hoped a self-contained science lesson would be useful and appreciated in the classrooms. Our newsletters are in their thirteenth year and some veteran teachers have kept every one!

"For several years, Judy and I reviewed science trade books and we felt we could, and should, contribute to an area of need— books of high interest, moderate vocabulary, accurate scientific concepts, and high quality photographs or illustrations. Judy has a strong artistic and creative background and we have been able to build a writing relationship that works very well for us. We bounce ideas off each other continuously and exchange rough drafts for editing. I doubt if we have ever published a single paragraph that does not contain contributions from both of us.

"We have concentrated on animal books because of our love for animals as well as their appeal to young readers. Through a storylike format we attempt to weave in an awareness of the value of every living thing and an awareness of the environmental concerns that affect them.

"While teaching remains my vocation, writing has been a very satisfactory sideline. The people I have met and worked with, the places I have been able to visit, and the comments from children who have enjoyed our books have given me memories to treasure."

KENNAWAY, Adrienne 1945-

PERSONAL: Born May 25, 1945, in Christchurch, New Zealand; daughter of Derek (an electrical engineer) and Beryl (an illustrator and art teacher; maiden name, Scott) Moore; married Anthony Kennaway (divorced). *Education:* Attended Ealing Art

School, and L'Academia de Belle Art, Rome. *Home:* 4 Hesketh Crescent, Meadfoot, Torquay, Devon TQ1 2LJ, England. *Agent:* Herta Ryder, Cambrian Rd., Richmond, Surrey TW10 6JQ, England.

CAREER: Worked as an illustrator in Mombasa, Kenya; has designed and illustrated commemorative stamps. *Exhibitions:* Gallery Watatu, Nairobi, Kenya, East Africa, 1975; New Stanley Gallery, Nairobi, 1983; Hyatt Regency, Kingdom of Dubai, 1985; Hilton Gallery, Royal Sheikdom of Abu Dhabi, 1986; James' Gallery, London, England, 1987; Nairobi, 1988. *Awards, honors: Hot Hippo* was selected one of Child Study Association of America's Children's Books of the Year, 1987; Kate Greenaway Medal from the British Library Association, 1988, for *Crafty Chameleon*.

ILLUSTRATOR:

JUVENILE, EXCEPT AS NOTED

Mwenye Hadithi (pseudonym of Bruce Hobson), *Greedy Zebra*, Little, Brown, 1984.
M. Hadithi, *Hot Hippo*, Little, Brown, 1986.
M. Hadithi, *Crafty Chameleon*, Little, Brown, 1987 (published in England as *Crafty Chamaeleon*, Hodder & Stoughton, 1987).
John Agard, *Lend Me Your Wings*, Hodder & Stoughton, 1987.
M. Hadithi, *Tricky Tortoise*, Little, Brown, 1988.
Mwalimu, *Awkward Aardvark*, Hodder & Stoughton, 1989.

Also illustrator of Leslie Brown's *Coral Reefs* (adult). Contributor to *Tales for a Prince*.

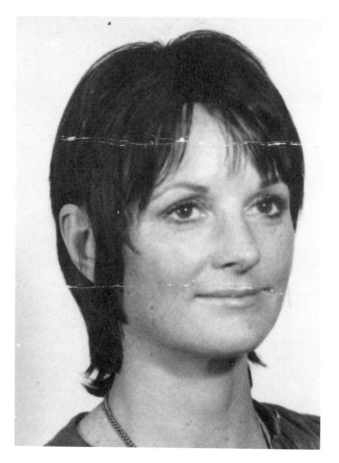

ADRIENNE KENNAWAY

ADAPTATIONS:

"Hot Hippo" (cassette; filmstrip with cassette), Weston Woods, 1989.

SIDELIGHTS: "I was born in Christchurch, New Zealand, but I never got to know the country because I was just three years old when my parents set sail for Kenya in East Africa. It is the most beautiful country in the world, with its snow-capped mountains, rain forests, lakes, savannahs, tropic Indian Ocean coast, and prolific wildlife. It is small wonder that I was captivated and spent most of my life there. Kenya's scenery, flora, and fauna have been the inspiration for many artists, and eventually I was to be no exception.

"Of course an *ayah* was employed to look after my brother and I, but I think it still came as a bit of a surprise to my parents when they realised that Swahili had become my main language! My father, an electrical engineer, was away a great deal overseeing contracts in various parts of East Africa, but my mother, an illustrator and art teacher, was determined that if I had any talent, then it was to be exposed. She has been a tremendous encouragement throughout my life, and in those early days would take me to sketch animals in the game park a few miles outside Nairobi. Later there were to be many safaris with my father throughout Kenya and East Africa.

"My Swahili stood me in good stead when, in 1951, my brother and I went to the first multi-racial school in Kenya. There, art had a high priority, and for the next three years we seemed to spend most of our time drawing and painting before going on to boarding school and high school and the more formal aspect of learning. Fortunately the boring part did not last too long, because in 1959 we moved to England, and I was enrolled at Ealing Art School in London. There I had an exceptional life class teacher, and I divided my time between fashion design and drawing, never quite sure which direction to follow. For two years I went to Italy and studied at L'Academia de Belle Arte in Rome where I was to learn a great deal about color and composition.

"In 1963 my father was working in Taiping, Malasia, and I joined him for a year, spending the whole time painting before taking a cargo ship back to Mombasa, Kenya, and went straight into illustrating for a publishing company. It was through this work that I met Leslie Brown, one of the world's greatest naturalists. He was preparing a tome on tropical marine fish, and invited me to illustrate it for him. The problem and the delight was that there was virtually no reference. I had to learn how to scuba dive and, once qualified, spent months diving on the Indian Ocean reefs to sketch and photograph the fish. In the process we discovered several previously unknown species, and the book *Coral Reefs* became a standard reference work.

"It was through the work I did with Leslie Brown that I was commissioned by the Kenya Post Office to design and illustrate a set of commemorative postage stamps 'Game Fish of East Africa.' This was followed by four more stamp issues, 'Marine Life,' two on ceremonial costumes of the Kenya tribes, and then 'Origins of Mankind' which celebrated the work of Richard Leakey, who has shown that the cradle of all human life might well have been East Africa.

"In my spare time, of course, I was painting, just for myself, mainly impressionist and abstract work. Unfortunately I have few of the paintings today. Some were sold at my first exhibition in Nairobi in 1975, but in those days my response to having my

Cover of the 1989 book illustrated by Kennaway. (From *Awkward Aardvark* by Mwalimu. Illustrated by Adrienne Kennaway.)

work admired was distinctly Arabian. I gave it to whoever liked it!

"The idea for my first children's book, *Greedy Zebra,* was the result of a conversation with an old Kenya friend, Bruce Hobson, who now writes under the name Mwenye Hadithi which, in the Kikuyu language, means story teller. Anyway, Bruce put the words together and I illustrated a full rough which another friend, Ken Martin, then a publisher's agent in Kenya, took to Hodder & Stoughton Children's Books in London. They published it in 1984 and the book was immediately taken up by Little, Brown in New York. *Greedy Zebra* is a story about how the zebra came to get its stripes. For long ago all the animals were the same dull color until called to a cave where they found skins of many colors, horns and tusks, bone needles and thread. However while all the other dull animals were making themselves look splendid by sewing new skins onto themselves, Zebra was too busy eating tasty grass. When he finally got to the cave he decided that he would have a mane like lion, a coat like leopard and horns like sable antelope. Alas, there was nothing left except for a few strips of black. He stitched these around his fat body—with some difficulty—but he was so fat that the

stitches went pop, pop, pop, and Zebra was left wearing his coat of stripes.

"In 1986 came *Hot Hippo* about how Hippopotamus lived on the land, was very uncomfortable in the African sun, and looked with envy at the fish in the river. He wanted so much to live in the water that he went to the mountain where Ngai, the God of Everything and Everywhere lived. Ngai, who had told the animals to live on the land, the fish in the rivers and sea, the birds in the air and the ants in the ground, had told Hippo to live on the land and eat grass. When he tells Ngai that he wants to live in the rivers and streams, Ngai fears that Hippo might eat the little fishes. Finally on a promise that he won't touch the fish, Hippo is allowed to live in the river by day, and to come out to eat grass at night. Now and again, when in the water he comes to the surface, opens his large mouth very wide, and says: 'Look, Ngai! No fishes!'

"*Crafty Chameleon* was published in 1987. Every morning Chameleon liked to sit in his favorite tree, rest, and catch flies. But also each morning Leopard jumped up into the tree and shook Chameleon to the ground. One morning Chameleon told

And every evening, Crocodile came swishing and slithering out of the water, snakking his teeth and laughing as all the small animals ran away.

(From *Crafty Chameleon* by Mwenye Hadithi. Illustrated by Adrienne Kennaway.)

leopard that if he did not leave him alone he would tie him up with rope like a dog. Leopard just laughed. Each evening Chameleon went to the river with the other animals, and each evening Crocodile came slithering out of the water to frighten the animals away. Crocodile only laughed when Chameleon threatened to tie him up as well. So Chameleon got the weaver birds to make a long rope of vines with a noose at each end. He threw a noose around Leopard's head and a noose around Crocodile, and told them to pull. They each pulled, thinking they were pulling Chameleon, and they pulled until they were both exhausted, and promised never to bother Chameleon again.

"The next story, *Tricky Tortoise,* is about how a small African tortoise outwits a mighty elephant. That was followed by *Awkward Aardvark* in which Aardvark, an anteater, keeps the other animals awake at night by snoring loudly in his tree. The monkeys, a lion, and a rhinoceros cannot stop his snores, but in the end he is brought down with a crash by the termites.

"Apart from the children's stories my main interest now is in painting birds of prey. My entire exhibition in Dubai was purchased by the Interior Minister and presented to the Sultan. I recently had an exhibition of original artwork of the children's books in Nairobi, this was followed by an exhibition of my paintings of birds of prey in the United States.

"I work mainly in watercolors, inks, and pencil. I use special colored inks for the children's books because they give such good depth and clarity, though they are by no means easy to use. You have to get it right the first time!"

Kennaway was one of several artists commissioned to illustrate stories for *Tales for a Prince,* dedicated to Prince Henry, and presented to Princess Diana in London. All the proceeds of the book are going to UNICEF.

KENNEDY, Richard (Pitt) 1910-1989

OBITUARY NOTICE: Born April 9, 1910, in Cambridge, England; died February 11, 1989, in England. Illustrator and author, Kennedy's first book, *A Boy at the Hogarth Press,*

describes the author's two years as an apprentice to Leonard and Virginia Woolf at England's Hogarth Press, and his second, *A Parcel in Time,* contrasts his wealthy upper-class grandmother with her lower-class maids. A free-lance artist beginning in the 1940s, Kennedy illustrated more than two hundred children's books, and in 1977 he published a series of his etchings, titled *Lovers and Friends.*

FOR MORE INFORMATION SEE:

Contemporary Authors, Volume 102, Gale, 1981.
Illustrators of Books for Young People, Scarecrow, 1975.

OBITUARIES

Times (London), February 14, 1989.

KIBBE, Pat (Hosley)

PERSONAL: Married John Kibbe (a lawyer); children: Jonathan, Kyle, Ethan, Allison, Justine. *Education:* Attended American Academy of Dramatic Arts. *Residence:* Yorktown Heights, N.Y.

CAREER: Actress and writer. *Awards, honors:* Children's Choice Award from the International Reading Association and the Children's Book Council, for *The Hocus-Pocus Dilemma.*

WRITINGS:

JUVENILE

The Hocus-Pocus Dilemma (illustrated by Dan Jones), Knopf, 1979.
My Mother, the Mayor, Maybe (illustrated by Charles Robinson) Knopf, 1981.
Mrs. Kiddy and the Moonbooms (illustrated by Jenny Rutherford), Bradbury, 1983.

LANDIS, J(ames) D(avid) 1942-

PERSONAL: Born June 30, 1942, in Springfield, Mass.; son of Edward (a lawyer) and Eve (a painter and teacher; maiden name, Saltman) Landis; married Patricia Lawrence Straus, August 15, 1964 (divorced); married Denise Evelyn Tiller (a writer), July 20, 1983; children: (first marriage) Sara Cass; (second marriage) Jacob Dean, Benjamin Nicholas. *Education:* Yale University, B.A. (magna cum laude), 1964. *Residence:* New York, N.Y. *Agent:* Kathy Robbins, The Robbins Office, 2 Dag Hammarskjold Plaza, New York, N.Y. 10017. *Office:* William Morrow and Co., Inc., 105 Madison Ave., New York, N.Y. 10025.

CAREER: Abelard-Schuman, New York, N.Y., assistant editor, 1966-67; William Morrow and Co., Inc., New York, N.Y., editor, beginning in 1967, later served as senior editor until 1980, editorial director, senior vice-president, and publisher of Quill trade paperbacks, 1980-85, senior vice-president, publisher, and editor-in-chief of Beech Tree Books, 1985—. *Member:* Phi Beta Kappa. *Awards, honors:* Roger Klein Award for Editing, 1973; named Advocate Humanitarian, 1977.

WRITINGS:

FOR YOUNG PEOPLE

The Sisters Impossible, Knopf, 1979.
Love's Detective (sequel to *The Sisters Impossible*), Bantam, 1984.
Daddy's Girl, Morrow, 1984.
Joey and the Girls, Bantam, 1987.
The Band Never Dances, Harper, 1989.

Also author of *Judy the Obscure,* Harper.

WORK IN PROGRESS: A novel, for Bantam.

Le CAIN, Errol (John) 1941-1989

OBITUARY NOTICE—See sketch in *SATA* Volume 6: Born March 5, 1941, in Singapore; died after a long illness, January 3, 1989. Film designer and animator, book illustrator, and author. Le Cain was best known for his illustrations for children's books. He began his career, however, as a designer and animator of films, working for Richard Williams Studios in the 1960s, then becoming a free-lance designer. He also designed sets for British Broadcasting Corporation (BBC) television productions, notably "The Ghost Downstairs," for which he received special mention from the Designers and Art Directors Association. Among the books Le Cain illustrated are several works by Rosemary Harris, including *The Lotus and the Grail* and *The Flying Ship;* an edition of Henry Wadsworth Longfellow's *Hiawatha's Childhood,* for which he won the British Library Association's Kate Greenaway Medal; and fairy tales such as *Cinderella,* and *Thorn Rose* which was selected for the International Board on Books for Young People Honor List in 1978. Le Cain's own picture books include *King Arthur's Sword,* and *The Cabbage Princess* which won a Kate Greenaway Honor Citation in 1969.

FOR MORE INFORMATION SEE:

Contemporary Authors New Revision Series, Volume 13, Gale, 1984.
Brigid Peppin and Lucy Mickelthwait, *Book Illustrators of the Twentieth Century,* Arco, 1984.

OBITUARIES

Times (London), January 6, 1989.

LITTLE, Lessie Jones 1906-1986

PERSONAL: Born October 1, 1906, in Parmele, N.C.; died of cancer, November 4, 1986, in Washington, D.C.; daughter of William Robert (a laborer) and Pattie (Ridley) Jones: married Weston W. Little, October 17, 1926; children: Weston, Jr., Eloise Little Greenfield, Gerald, Vedie Little Jones, Vera Little Black. *Education:* Attended North Carolina State Normal School (now Elizabeth City State University), summers, 1924-26. *Religion:* Protestant. *Home:* Washington, D.C. *Agent:* Marilyn Marlow, Curtis Brown Ltd., 575 Madison Ave., New York, N.Y. 10022.

CAREER: Elementary school teacher in rural North Carolina, 1924-29; U. S. Army, Office of the Surgeon General, Washington, D.C., clerk-typist, 1956-64, coding clerk, 1964-70; writer, 1974-86. *Awards, honors: Childtimes: A Three Generation Memoir* was selected one of Child Study Association of America's Children's Books of the Year, 1979, and *Boston Globe-Horn Book* Award Honor Book for Nonfiction, 1980; Parents' Choice Award from the Parents' Choice Foundation, 1988, for *Children of Long Ago.*

WRITINGS:

(With daughter, Eloise Greenfield) *I Can Do It by Myself* (juvenile; illustrated by Carole Byard), Crowell, 1978.
(With E. Greenfield) *Childtimes: A Three Generation Memoir* (illustrated by Jerry Pinkney), Crowell, 1979.
Children of Long Ago (poems; illustrated by Jan Spivey Gilchrist), Philomel, 1988.

SIDELIGHTS: Little was born in Parmele, a small town in North Carolina. "I'm next to the oldest in my family. My sister Roland was first, then me, then Clara, Mabel, and Lillie Mae. William Robert Jones, Jr., was the youngest. He didn't live but eight hours. Clara was seventeen months old when she died.

"The life of my town moved around the trains that came in and out all day long.

"Trains weren't air-conditioned in those days, and when the weather was warm, the windows were always open. Black people had to sit in the front car so that whites wouldn't get dirty from the smoke and soot and cinders that blew in the windows from the engine.

"About three hundred people lived in Parmele, most of them black. There were three black churches, a Baptist, a Methodist, and a Holiness, and one white church. Two black schools, one white. There wasn't even one doctor, and not many people would have had the money to pay one, if there had been. If somebody got down real bad sick, a member of the family would go by horse and buggy to a nearby town and bring the doctor back, or sometimes the doctor would ride on his own horse.

"There were stores, four or five stores, where you could buy clothes, or yard goods, or groceries, or hardware, and the post office was in the corner of one store. Stokes' Cafe, where the white railroad workers ate, was on one side of the tracks, and Powell's Restaurant for the black workers was on the other side.

LESSIE JONES LITTLE

"Most of the men and women in Parmele earned their living by farming. Some did other things like working at the tobacco factory in Robersonville, but most worked on the farms that were all around in the area, white people's farms usually. When I was a little girl, they earned fifty cents a day, a farm day, sunup to sundown, plus meals. After they got home, they had all their own work to do, cooking and cleaning, laundry, chopping wood for the woodstove, and shopping.

"'Here comes jumpin' Sally, just a-running, plaits a-flying, high forehead a-shining.' That's what my aunt, Sis Ada, used to say whenever she saw me coming. I was such a fidgety child. Unless I was reading or daydreaming, I was hardly ever still. I was always singing to the top of my voice, or jumping rope, or running so fast I thought my feet weren't touching the ground, or drawing pictures in the dirt with a long stick, or playing dolls, and paper dolls and mothers and school, hide-and-go-seek and hopscotch, and most of all, jacks.

"I could have played bobjacks all day long, but Mama wouldn't let me . . . . On school days I was supposed to come straight home. I couldn't stop and play the way I wanted to.

"Mama used to say, 'You always have to learn things the hard way, don't you, Lessie?' And I guess she was right. A lot of things I did learn the hard way.

"Mama taught us how to draw, my sisters and me. She taught us how to draw little things like boxes and houses and love knots, and she showed us how to make rag dolls, and even some funny-looking dolls out of corncobs. And Mama really knew how to tell a story.

"Mama loved to read. Sometimes she would get so wrapped up in a book, she'd stay awake all night long, reading.

"[She] worked as a cook and waitress at Stokes' Cafe, down near the Parmele train station. She had to be at work early in the morning to fix breakfast for the people who would be coming in or going out on the trains. Afternoons, mama would come home, and around four or five o'clock she had to go back and work until all the passengers and trainmen from the different trains had eaten their supper and all the trains had gone.

"I used to visit Mama sometimes at the cafe and drink a soda pop or something. I had to use the side door. The front door was for whites only, and they sat down at little tables to be served. Blacks used the side door and had to sit at a counter where we could only get snacks.

"Even when mama had been reading all night, she didn't have any trouble getting up early. And she made us get up, too, before she left for work . . . . We had to get breakfast, make beds, sweep floors. The whole house had to be clean. Roland had to comb Mabel's hair, and I had to comb Lillie Mae's, and everybody had better be dressed and tidy by the time Mama got home.

"I liked being near Mama. When she cooked, I would sit in a chair right near the stove and put my feet up on the woodbox and just talk and talk about all the different things I had been doing all day. And I especially liked being near her whenever I was scared.

"One night the Ku Klux Klan burned a wooden cross on Sugar Hill and that was one of my really scared times. I was playing on the porch when I saw the cross. I couldn't see the wood, all I could see was those yellow, quivering flames in the shape of a cross, and I ran. I ran in the house to find my mama. I wanted to crawl up in her lap, under her apron, but I sat on the floor as close to her as I could get. I felt safe there, close to Mama.

"Papa was a quiet man. He liked to read a lot, study his Bible and his Sunday School book and the newspaper.

"He gave us a lot of love.

"Papa sang bass in the church choir. He had a beautiful voice, such a beautiful voice. Everybody in his family could sing, and I think he could have been a professional singer if he had been born at a later time when there were more opportunities for black people. And he had the prettiest whistle I've heard. Everybody in Parmele knew Papa's whistle.

"Papa didn't get mad too often. Usually when I did something wrong, he would just say, 'Now daughter, you know you shouldn't have done that,' and I'd be so ashamed. But once in a while, he would get really mad. One time I talked back to Mama, and what did I do that for! Papa heard me and he yelled at me so loud it made my stomach hurt. He said, 'What did you say!' I told him what I'd said, but he kept on asking me. And my answer kept getting softer and softer. Finally Papa said, 'Your mama borned you into this world! Don't you ever talk to her like that again!' I said, 'Yes, sir.'

"It was hard for Papa to find work. Not long after Sis Clara died, we moved to Mount Herman, a black section of Portsmouth, Virginia. Papa worked on the docks there, and even though he didn't make much money, the work was steady. But when we moved back to Parmele, it was hard for him to find any work at all.

"Sometimes he worked on the railroad, cutting the grass that grew between the ties of the tracks. Sometimes he worked on white people's farms, but when they tried to treat him like a

The twentieth century was new, only six years old. (From *Childtimes: A Three-Generation Memoir* by Eloise Greenfield and Lessie Jones Little. Illustrated by Jerry Pinkney.)

child, he told them that he was a man, and they fired him. For about two years he rented a small piece of land and grew corn and cotton and a little molasses cane. Some of it we used, and some of it papa sold, but he really didn't have land to make much money, and by the time he got through paying the people he rented the land from and buying things from their store to farm with, he hardly had any money left.

"I guess most of the time I was growing up, Papa worked at the train station, taking luggage off one train and putting it on another, and unloading crates of fruit, things like that. He worried a lot about not being able to buy us things.

"When we lived in Mount Herman, Papa got paid once a week, and he would always bring groceries home on payday. But sometimes by the end of the week there'd be almost nothing in the house to eat, and Mama would try and mix up something to keep us from getting too hungry. Once, all we had was a little flour and cornmeal and sugar and lard.

"Some days I would get so hungry that it was hard for me to play. I'd try to play games, but that pulling inside my stomach made me feel so bad."[1]

When she was eight, Little's parent's separated and her father took care of the children. Two years later her parents reconciled and the family was once again a happy unit. "Whenever I really wanted something that I couldn't have, or wanted to do something I couldn't do, I would go off by myself and daydream. Only, I didn't call it daydreaming, I called it 'talking.' I didn't move my lips or say anything out loud. I was talking inside, although sometimes I did catch myself smiling.

"'Talking' was my secret. I never told *anybody* about it before now. I used to 'talk' sometimes while I was doing chores like sweeping the yard or helping Sis Ada iron our clothes, but most of the time I'd go off by myself and get still and quiet.

"When Mama was away that time she left home, I 'talked' a lot. When I did that, mama was right there with me."[1]

Little started her schooling in Mount Herman, and when the family returned to Parmele she attended Higgs Roanoke Seminary. "[Among other subjects] we studied black history every week out of a book by Carter G. Woodson, but we called it Negro history then. And we had to learn the names of all the forty-eight states and the name of every bone in the body. We had to be able to stand up and recite every single one of them. Anybody who didn't know the work had to stay after school.

"Our school parties were called socials. We had them in the chapel, in the evening, and they'd last until about ten o'clock. We weren't allowed to stay out late.

"First we'd have a program, recite poems and have skits, play the piano, sing solos and duets, things like that. After the program, we ate and played bobbing apples and fishing, and having our fortunes told. But the best part was the grand march. The boys and girls would get in line, two by two, and march. We'd march right up to the corners of the room and make sharp turns, and change partners sometimes. It was a lot of fun. But it wasn't dancing.

"We weren't supposed to dance. The church didn't allow it, and most of the people in our town were church people. But, at house parties, we used to sneak and dance anyway. Maybe it wasn't

She and Wade followed him to the door and watched him leave. "Can't you just tell me where you're going?" his mother called after him, but he didn't turn around.

Then Wade had to open his mouth and say something, too. Wade said, *"Hope that big ugly bulldog don't get you!"*

Donny felt funny in his stomach. He had forgotten all about that bulldog. He wished that he had gone the other way, the long way, but he couldn't turn around

(From *I Can Do It by Myself* by Lessie Jones Little and Eloise Greenfield. Illustrated by Carole Byard.)

really sneaking because some of our parents were always in the next room, but they pretended they didn't know we were dancing."[1]

In addition to house chores and school work, Little worked the fields in Parmele. "Sometimes I worked on Papa's little farm, but mostly my friends and I worked for white farmers, for pay. In the spring of the year, when the cotton plants had grown up just a few inches, we'd chop the weeds down with a hoe. In early summer we'd dig white potatoes out of the ground and separate them .... Later on in the summer we worked in tobacco.

"In the fall we picked cotton. We'd start in early September and work until school opened, and after we'd been in school for a few weeks, we had to stop and pick cotton again for a while. A lot of children had to do that. Our families needed the money. But the teachers seemed to understand, and they'd see that we caught up with the rest of the class when we went back.

"There was nothing that I liked about working in the fields. I mean *nothing!* Working in tobacco, the scent made me sick. Chopping weeds out of the cotton, the sun was too hot. Picking up potatoes, the buckets were too heavy and the sun was too hot. Picking cotton, you had to hang a burlap sack on your shoulder to put the cotton in, and pull it down the row as you picked, and when the sack started getting heavy, the strap cut into your shoulder. And my back would hurt so much from stooping over that sometimes I'd get on my knees and crawl. And then my knees would get sore. And the sun! The sun was so hot!

"Then too, some of the people we worked for were mean, or insulting.

"No, I didn't like field work one bit. But I did a lot of it anyway because we needed the money. The school didn't furnish our books, so I'd take my money and buy books, and if I had a few dollars left over, I'd buy a piece of pretty material so Mama could make me a dress.

"My last year at Higgs, I received a pin for having the best grades in the high school. It was a beautiful pin, fourteen-karat gold, made like an open book. Only two of us were seniors that year, 1924, and we had our graduation with the eighth graders at Olive Branch Baptist Church.

"That day was one of my hungry days, and later on, Mama told me that while she was watching me make my farewell speech, she was thinking, 'My child hasn't had a thing to eat today.' But it was a happy day for me anyway."[1]

Three summers after graduation, Little attended North Carolina State Normal School. In addition, she taught elementary school in rural North Carolina for the next six years.

In 1926 she married Weston W. Little whom she had met when she was thirteen and he fourteen. Together they raised five children.

Three years later they moved to Washington, D.C., where she worked as a clerk, for a number of years, at the Office of the Surgeon General.

At the age of sixty-seven already a great-grandmother, Little embarked on a new career—writing. With her daughter Eloise Greenfield, the distinguished children's book author, Little wrote and published two children's books, *I Can Do It by Myself* and *Childtimes: A Three Generation Memoir*. "I believe the picture book *I Can Do It by Myself* will give young children confidence in themselves; that it will let them know that they can get a job done if they try hard enough.

"*Childtimes: A Three Generation Memoir* is about three children from three generations: my mother, me, and my daughter. We hope this book gives children some historical facts and shows them the differences between things in use during the three generations: modes of transportation, schools, homes, clothing, and duties. We hope the book shows the worth of the black family; that although they had to face hard circumstances and hurdle many obstacles to keep on livng, they had love for each other which held them together.

"I am overjoyed that in my retirement years I have something to do that gives me so much satisfaction: I don't have any hard and fast rules about my working habits. I find the early morning, around five o'clock, a good, quiet time to concentrate, but I may work at midday or late evening or whenever I feel the urge."[2]

Little died of cancer shortly after her sixtieth wedding anniversary in 1986. Three years later her book of poems, *Children of Long Ago*, was published. These lyrical poems describe the life of black children around the turn of the century. "I hope children enjoy reading my books and I would like for them to learn something important to their lives."[2]

FOOTNOTE SOURCES

[1]Eloise Greenfield and Lessie Jones Little, *Childtimes: A Three-Generation Memoir*, Crowell, 1979.
[2]*Contemporary Authors*, Volume 101, Gale, 1981.

FOR MORE INFORMATION SEE:

OBITUARIES

Washington Post, November 13, 1986.

LIVELY, Penelope 1933-

PERSONAL: Born March 17, 1933, in Cairo, Egypt; daughter of Roger (a banker) and Vera (Reckitt) Low; married Jack Lively (a university professor) June 27, 1957; children: Josephine, Adam. *Education:* St. Anne's College, Oxford, B.A. (with honors), 1955. *Religion:* Agnostic. *Home and office:* Duck End, Great Rollright, Chipping Norton, Oxfordshire OX7 5SB, England. *Agent:* Murray Pollinger, 4 Garrick St., London WC2E 9BH, England.

CAREER: Free-lance writer and broadcaster. *Member:* Society of Authors, PEN, Arts Council, Royal Society of Literature (fellow).

AWARDS, HONORS: The Wild Hunt of the Ghost Hounds was selected one of Child Study Association of America's Children's Books of the Year, 1972, *The Ghost of Thomas Kempe*, 1973, *The House in Norham Gardens*, 1974, *The Whispering Knights*, 1976, and *The Revenge of Samuel Stokes*, 1985; *Book World*'s Children's Spring Book Festival Award, 1973, for *The Driftway;* Carnegie Medal from the British Library Association, and Hans Christian Andersen Honor List, both 1973, both for *The Ghost of Thomas Kempe;* Whitbread Book of the Year Award from the Booksellers Association of Great Britain and Ireland, 1976, for *A Stitch in Time; The Road to Lichfield* was shortlisted for the Booker Prize, 1977, and *According to Mark*, 1988; National Book Award from the Arts Council of Great

Britain for Adult Fiction, 1979, for *Treasures of Time;* Southern Arts Association Literature Prize for Adult Fiction, 1979, for *Nothing Missing but the Samovar and Other Stories*.

The Revenge of Samuel Stokes was selected one of *Booklist*'s Children's Reviewer's Choices, 1985; Children's Choice from the International Reading Association and the Children's Book Council, 1985, for *Fanny's Sister;* Booker Prize, and shortlisted for the Whitbread Award, both 1987, both for *Moon Tiger;* Order of the British Empire, 1989.

WRITINGS:

CHILDREN'S BOOKS

Astercote (illustrated by Antony Maitland), Heinemann, 1970, Dutton, 1971.
The Whispering Knights (illustrated by Gareth Floyd), Heinemann, 1971, Dutton, 1976.
The Wild Hunt of Hagworthy (illustrated by Juliet Mozley), Heinemann, 1971, large print edition, G. K. Hall, 1987, published in America as *The Wild Hunt of the Ghost Hounds* (Junior Literary Guild selection), Dutton, 1972.
The Driftway, Heinemann, 1972, Dutton, 1973.
The Ghost of Thomas Kempe (Junior Literary Guild selection; *Horn Book* honor list; illustrated by A. Maitland), Heinemann, 1973, Dutton, 1974, large print edition, G. K. Hall, 1986.
The House in Norham Gardens (ALA Notable Book; *Horn Book* honor list), Dutton, 1974.

PENELOPE LIVELY

(Jacket illustration by Larry Ross from *Uninvited Ghosts* by Penelope Lively.)

Boy without a Name (illustrated by Ann Dalton), Heineman, 1974, Parnassus Press, 1975.
Going Back, Dutton, 1975.
A Stitch in Time (*Horn Book* honor list), Dutton, 1976, large print edition, G. K. Hall, 1988.
The Stained Glass Window (illustrated by M. Pollard), Abelard, 1976.
"Time Out of Mind" (television play), BBC-TV, 1976.
Fanny's Sister (illustrated by John Lawrence), Heinemann, 1976, (*Horn Book* honor list; illustrated by Anita Lobel), Dutton, 1980.
Fanny and the Monsters (illustrated by J. Lawrence), Heinemann, 1978, new edition, 1983.
The Voyage of QV66 (illustrated by Harold Jones), Heinemann, 1978, Dutton, 1979.
Fanny and the Battle of Potter's Piece (illustrated by J. Lawrence), Heinemann, 1980.
The Revenge of Samuel Stokes, Dutton, 1981.
Uninvited Ghosts and Other Stories (illustrated by J. Lawrence), Heinemann, 1984, Dutton, 1985.
Dragon Trouble (illustrated by Valerie Littlewood), Heinemann, 1984, Barron, 1989.
A House Inside Out, Deutsch, 1987, (illustrated by David Parkins), Dutton, 1988.
Debbie and the Little Devil, Heinemann, 1987.

ADULT FICTION, EXCEPT AS NOTED

(Contributor) *My England* (nonfiction), Heinemann, 1973.

"Boy Dominic" (television play; three episodes), Yorkshire TV, 1974.
The Presence of the Past: An Introduction to Landscape History (nonfiction), Collins, 1976.
The Road to Lichfield, Heinemann, 1977, large print edition, G. K. Hall, 1987.
Nothing Missing but the Samovar and Other Stories, Heinemann, 1978.
Treasures of Time, Heinemann, 1979, Doubleday, 1981.
Judgement Day, Heinemann, 1980, Doubleday, 1981, large print edition, G. K. Hall, 1986.
Next to Nature, Art, Heinemann, 1982.
Perfect Happiness, Heinemann, 1983, Dial, 1984, large print edition, Thorndike Press, 1985.
Corruption and Other Stories, Heinemann, 1984.
According to Mark, Heinemann, 1984, Beaufort Books, 1985.
Pack of Cards, Stories 1978-86, Heinemann, 1986, Grove Press, 1989.
Moon Tiger, Deutsch, 1987, Grove Press, 1988, large print edition, G. K. Hall, 1988.
Passing On, Deutsch, 1989, Grove, 1990.

Many of Lively's books have been translated into several foreign languages. Contributor of short stories and articles to periodicals, including *Encounter, Quarto, Literary Review, Good Housekeeping, Vogue, Cosmopolitan, Options, Over 21, Woman's Own*. Reviewer for journals and newspapers, including *Encounter, Sunday Telegraph, Daily Telegraph, Books and Bookmen, Literary Review, Times Educational Supplement*, and *Standard*. Also author of radio and television scripts, and has presented a series of radio programs on children's books for the BBC.

ADAPTATIONS:

"House Inside Out" (cassette), Chivers Press, 1988.

WORK IN PROGRESS: A book tentatively titled *City of the Mind*.

SIDELIGHTS: Penelope Lively was born in Cairo on **March 17, 1933.** Her father worked for the National Bank of Egypt and the family lived near Cairo for the first twelve years of her life. "We lived four miles outside Cairo, out on the road that leads towards the Pyramids. Our house had been built at the turn of the century in a style of southern American colonial houses—shutters and verandahs and what, to me, was a huge garden teeming with mongooses and other creatures.

"I was an only child and my childhood was lonely but agreeable. I didn't go to school because there was none suitable in Cairo. Instead I was taught at home by the person who looked after me. To call her a governess would be too grand a word, but she became a surrogate mother.

"At that time there was a splendid organization called the Parents' National Education Union (PNEU) which had set itself up to provide a do-it-yourself educational kit for ex-patriot parents. They sent out books and timetables for adults administering the teaching.

"The system was based entirely on the idea of narrative and provided a very classical education with marvellous training in the use of language and memory. We read from the Bible, Greek and Norse mythology, Dickens and *Arabian Nights*. For a writer it was an ideal education. It neglected math: the timetable said, 'arithmetic or handicrafts,' so on Wednesday we opted for handicrafts.

"I had a passion for mythology and remember enjoying the Bible for its stories. I loved the language of the authorized version and absorbed it as literature rather than religious instruction. Although I was baptized into the Church of England I was probably a skeptical Christian even at the age of seven or eight. I enjoyed Shakespeare, but I don't think I read it in the raw. I probably only had Lamb's *Tales from Shakespeare,* which are actually insufferably boring, but again the interest lay in the stories.

"I had the stock classic repertoire of children's books—*Alice in Wonderland* and *The Wind in the Willows,* but I didn't have a hugely adventurous selection because there were no libraries. I loved Arthur Ransome. To a child born in Egypt his books were pure fantasy: about places where everything was green and it rained all the time. I was more interested in the characters than the setting and was amazed by these confident, bounding children. They were supposed to be about the same age I was, but I couldn't imagine ever behaving like that. I was rather shy and solitary.

"To my regret I had no Egyptian literature at all although I did know about Ra and Horus and some of the basic stories of Egyptian mythology. But Egypt affected me indirectly in the sense that I was exposed to it and to the visible past. I was aware of living in a very ancient land, which accounts for my lifelong obsession with the processes of time and of memory. Although we were surrounded by an extraordinary landscape, my parents,

(Jacket illustration by Richard Cuffari from *Going Back* by Penelope Lively.)

rather oddly, didn't do much to inform me. Nevertheless, we went to the Pyramids every Wednesday afternoon and I was taken to the tombs at Saqqara.

"I certainly had an internal narrative going. I told myself stories all the time and assumed that everybody else did too. At the age of seven I started writing something called *The Flora and Fauna of the Lower Nile Valley.* It was written in the language of a nineteenth-century clergyman and was all about sandvipers and geboas and that sort of thing. I imagine I must have read something of the kind on my parents' shelves and been impressed by the gravity of the style and wanted to imitate it.

"I didn't speak Arabic and the English residents in Cairo were very much a set on their own. My father knew some Egyptians because of his work, but my mother not at all. In those days Egyptian women were veiled, and it would have been impossible for them to have moved socially in European society."[1]

When she was six Lively accompanied her parents on one of their annual visits to England. During her stay, war was declared. "I came to England with my nurse and my parents in the summer of 1939. After a while my parents went back leaving us for a few weeks more at Golsoncott, the Somerset home of my maternal grandmother. I remember listening to the famous Chamberlain radio speech on the outbreak of war. My grandmother summoned everybody to hear it. The gardeners and the cook came in and everybody sat in the drawing room and listened. I felt slightly awestruck because of the atmosphere created and knew it was a portentous moment although I didn't have the foggiest idea what it was all about.

"There was a frantic exchange of telegrams between my parents and my grandmother. My grandmother wanted me to stay in England for the war and my parents wanted me to be sent back to Egypt. They won. My nurse and I travelled back with about twenty mothers, nannies, and children, journeying across France after the outbreak of war. There were interminable trains and endless businesses about visas. I didn't know what a visa was and mixed it up with geyser. I couldn't understand why people were always talking about hot water geysers."[1] Lively's observation of the war in Egypt was later to feed into her fiction.

"My mother was a very sociable person and 'had a good war' as the saying goes. I was sent for occasionally because she thought it would be nice to display me. I was always tidily dressed because of having a nurse. I felt bitterly resentful that I was made to wear socks in the boiling Egyptian climate. Mine was a tailored presence, not like children nowadays who are around all the time. I was banished to the nursery at meal times. I enjoyed being summoned because, being rather solitary, I was curious and liked to take a look at people. There's a strange way in which a child's eye is like a camera. A child makes no comment. It simply absorbs and retains what it sees without cluttering it with interpretation."[1]

The end of the war brought an abrupt change to Lively's world. Her parents divorced and she was sent to boarding school in England. "I wasn't asked if I wanted to go to boarding school. I was told. I was twelve or thirteen by then and a certain anxiety had crept in that I hadn't had much formal education. Also, there was the question of what to do with me. My father had custody of me and probably felt he couldn't cope with me at home all the time. He was a businessman going to an office every day.

"My nurse and I travelled to England just before the end of the war with about a hundred women and children. We came in a troop ship called *The Ranchi* which was carrying 7,000 soldiers returning from India and the Far East. Some of them hadn't been

Penelope Lively at age eight.

home for three or four years and were in a state of wild excitement. We were segregated from them on a separate deck but I was very interested in the roars of drunken carousal coming from theirs.

"We docked at night, at Greenock up in Glasgow. I woke up and looked out of the port hole and saw on the quay the enormous, hairy hoof of a Clydesdale horse. The Clydesdales were the workhorses on the docks then. I was astonished by it, having been used to camels and donkeys.

"I felt like a refugee when I arrived in London, far more of a foreigner than I ever did in Egypt. One of the things that seemed bizarre was that everyone was speaking English in the streets. London was incredibly bleak in 1945; although the bombing was over, there was heavy damage. We went first to my paternal grandmother's house in Harley Street. She was rather formidable, but she did her best for her unknown, rather waif-like granddaughter. It was an enormous house of six floors, and it was intensely cold. I remember snow on the stairs because the windows had been blown in during the blitz and never replaced."[1]

Lively was intensely unhappy during the three years she spent at school. "I never settled down at boarding school. I felt infinitely more a fish out of water than when I was in Egypt, and I suffered desperate homesickness. I was a very maladjusted and, probably, impossible adolescent. The first time I went to school I had a certain sense of anticipation, but I soon discovered it was awful. The head-mistress sent for me when I arrived and said, 'Now

Penelope, your parents are divorced. That's not very nice and I don't want you to talk to the other girls about it.' The divorce didn't come as a great shock to me, but I was embarrassed by it. It was far less acceptable than it is now.

"School was a sternly anti-cultural place. One of the punishments was to go to the library and read a book for an hour. You couldn't confess to enjoying literature in any sense. I was punished for reading poetry. There was very little privacy and my tiny locker, which held a few of my personal possessions, was inspected once a week by the matron. Once, the headmistress sent for me and pushed my copy of *The Oxford Book of English Verse* across her desk towards me saying, 'There's no need for you to read this kind of thing in your spare time, Penelope. You'll be taught all that.'

"I went into a decline for several years. I wrote poetry and hid it up my knickers because it was clearly a forbidden activity. I've never written poetry since, which I regret. Despite all this, I got distinctions in everything in School Certificate. The head-mistresses' letter to my father said, 'Penelope seems to have done rather well. I only wish I could say her performance in gymnastics and games equalled it.' There's something stimulating in having to fight against the stream."[1]

Lively's father returned to England when she was fifteen. School holidays were divided between his London house in Kensington and her grandmother's house in Somerset, Golsoncott. "I was doing all sorts of samizdat reading by then. I had a passion for most of the nineteenth-century, romantic poets, and for people like Rupert Brooke and James Elroy Flecker whom I haven't read since. I hadn't come across Eliot or Auden and I was probably restricted to Quiller-Couch's *Oxford Book of English Verse*. I'd read some of D. H. Lawrence's poetry and been perplexed by it. I didn't like it but it gave me a clue that there was more to discover. I read my way along the shelves of both grandmother's houses and read things I would find unreadable now. I discovered Charlotte Yonge and Rider Haggard. I also read a lot of Dickens with huge and lasting enjoyment. The Somerset grandmother wasn't a bookish person and most of her books reflected the taste of the 1930s; middlebrow stuff like Mary Webb and Charles Morton. I read anything that was there.

"I went often to stay with my grandmother in Somerset because I loved it so. She had always written to me when I was a child in Egypt so I felt as if I knew her. She was a warm, affectionate person with a strong character. She was very cosy and always tucked me up in bed at night even though I was thirteen or fourteen. She and I were very close until her death. I adored her.

"Golsoncott was a haven while I was at boarding school. I moped around the lanes in a state of agreeable boredom or pottered about with my grandmother who was a passionate gardener. Like Clare in *The House in Norham Gardens,* I tried to learn from my grandmother. She used to tell tales of her child-hood and I think my picture of an Edwardian middle-class girlhood comes from her. I was certainly conscious of the processes of memory while I was with her. When I came to write *Going Back,* which is about the process of memory, I thought I'd be able to do it better if I used something very significant to my own memory. Golsoncott is in the book in every detail."[1]

When she was sixteen, Lively's father, realizing her schooling would not prepare her for university, sent her to a crammer, which was dedicated to getting people through exams. In **1951** she entered St. Anne's College, Oxford.

"Oxford was a total liberation. I loved every moment of it. When I first arrived everyone else seemed much more sophisti-cated but the end of the first term I'd cottoned on fairly quickly and did the things that everybody did: made all the wrong friends immediately and had to shed them at once! I now realize I went through Oxford in a kind of sleep and didn't fulfill my potential. I didn't get a very good degree; I got too carried away by the relative freedom.

"I had been very good at English at school and it would have been natural for me to read it at Oxford, but I chose to do a history degree instead. I'm not too sure why. It was probably a deeply atavistic response to my own feelings about the past and feelings about continuity. It stemmed from growing up in Egypt. I'd always had a sense of needing to place myself in time and to make some sort of interpretation of continuities. I certainly couldn't have expressed it like that at the time. It was a kind of emotional response.

"When I read history at Oxford we were expected to do the long haul through English history, and I'm eternally grateful for that. My special subjects were the medieval period and late eight-eenth-century and early nineteenth-century colonial history. I was very bad at political theory—Aristotle, Rousseau and Hobbes.

"I read a lot for my degree, and I was also discovering people like Elizabeth Bowen and Ivy Compton Burnett, authors I've been passionate about ever since. I read most of the contempo-rary fiction that was coming out. Iris Murdoch was teaching at Oxford (although she didn't teach me) and I certainly read her. I still remember my amazement of meeting girls who had been to

Two words in the spidery writing . . . seemed to hit him smack between the eyes. (From *The Ghost of Thomas Kempe* by Penelope Lively. Illustrated by Ant-ony Maitland.)

completely different kinds of schools and were openly admitting to enjoying poetry. I'd learned to think of it as a furtive activity, as if there were something rather nasty and reprehensible about it.

"I made close friends at university, although, oddly, I didn't keep in touch with any of them later. It was a very happy and sociable time. Oxford was very strict then, far removed from what it's like now. At the women's colleges we had to be in by eleven fifteen every night and if we were even two minutes late we went to the principal the next day to justify ourselves. Men were allowed in your room between two in the afternoon and seven in the evening. Being caught with a man in your room out of hours usually meant being sent down.

"Nobody complained, we just accepted it. It was like living on the front line. Everybody transgressed the rules. The important thing was negotiation to see how you could break them. Every-one helped one another and we all covered up for each other. In my hostel there was a girl whom we all knew had her boyfriend in all night once or twice a week, and we helped smuggle him out in the morning.

"Not having had a brother and having been at a single sex boarding school, I had had absolutely nothing to do with boys of my own age until I went to Oxford and found myself surrounded by them. I remember thinking, 'My God, how does one cope with this?'"[1]

After she graduated in **1955**, Lively went back to London and took a secretarial course. She returned to Oxford as a research secretary and soon afterwards met her husband, Jack. "It was clear that I wasn't going to become an academic and after I came down from Oxford I had no particular plan. In those days girls were advised to take a secretarial course and I don't regret having done that. It was a six month's crash course and I learned to type well—which has been useful ever since—and to do shorthand—which was absolutely useless.

"I wanted to get out of London and was offered a job as a research secretary to a Professor of Race Relations at St. Anthony's College, Oxford."[1]

Married after eighteen months in this job, Lively became pregnant with her first child in **1958**. The family moved to Swansea, where Jack had been given an assistant lectureship at the University. Their second child, Adam, was born in **1961**. Jack's career then took them to Sussex University before his return to Oxford as Fellow in Politics at St. Peter's College in **1963**.

"Josephine was born within a year of our marriage and I gave up my job when I was six months pregnant. I was twenty-four. I'd always wanted children and, although Josephine was an accident—we hadn't intended to have a baby quite so soon—I wasn't in the least sorry. The problem was that Jack had a tiny academic income, but then Swansea University gave him his first permanent job and we moved there.

"Academic salaries were low, so we were still terribly hard up. I had Adam within three years, so I was housebound with two under five. I felt strongly that I wanted my children to be looked after by their mother, I didn't want a repetition of my own childhood. I was determined that I was going to give up five years to looking after them and there was no nonsense about nannies or *au pair* girls—not that we could have afforded them in any case.

"I was a bit lonely in Swansea but it was mitigated by having women friends with shared interests. Sometimes I was bored and fretful and felt there must be more to life than afternoon walks with the baby in the park, but I wasn't really unhappy either. It was just the restlessness of any young woman housebound with small children. Jack was a splendid and participating father, very much involved. Josephine and Adam fought their way through childhood. They're both strong characters. Adam was a delightful and wicked little boy, and he bullied his sister no end.

"I told my children stories, but I was never that good at it. I read to them inordinately and I think that's when my interest in children's books began."[1]

When her son began school, Lively gave herself six months to decide what to do next. "I can vividly remember the first day Adam went to primary school and thinking, 'Now where do I go?' By then we were living outside Oxford again and I thought I would probably drift back into teaching which seemed the obvious thing for someone with a history degree. I revelled in the new-found freedom of having space to myself and began to read a lot of history. I started to explore landscape history and, in a curious way, that led to writing. I didn't plan on it; it was haphazard. I remember thinking in a modest way, 'I wonder if I could write a children's book?' And so it all began. The household became a bit disorganized because I was trying to push domestic things into the least time possible. I was astonished

when my first book for children, *Astercote,* was published and even more astonished when my writing began to do well."[1]

Lively's first books were written for children. Her interest in history, both shared and personal, found its way into her work. "I'm a very English writer in the sense that I need to write with a very strong and close sense of topography and place, and this is very much within an English tradition."[2]

"When I started writing for children, the fantasy aspect of historical memory interested me very much—legend and folklore. People make attempts to meet the imaginative challenge of the landscape itself—the age-old response to the amazing fact that the world we live in is older than we are ourselves, that other people have been here before us.

"I do have a great sympathy with the ancient desire to pay tribute to the landscape's role as a shrine to the past, the consciousness which has been around since prehistory that we only pass through the world, make a faint mark on it, and then hand it on to someone else."[3]

"My particular preoccupation, as a writer, is with memory. Both with memory in the wide historical sense and memory in the personal sense—that it is what we are all either enriched by or encumbered with; I am never sure which. I find memory a very complicated and ambiguous thing; I don't understand its function in our lives and I try to explore this function by writing novels which are concerned in one way or another with the operation of memory. *The Ghost of Thomas Kempe,* which is intended to be, and I hope is, an entirely light-hearted book, is concerned at one level with a child's growing awareness of the layers of memory of which people are composed—that an old woman is also the child she once was. This, to us as adults, is self-evident, though I suspect not as evident as it should be; we underestimate the force of memory in our lives. I think children often are not aware of memory—they simply haven't been here long enough yet to have had time to observe its effects—but it naturally arouses their curiosity. Here is a landscape littered with objects which have been there a great deal longer than people—historical memory. Adults are always recalling the past. Why? What does it matter? Does it matter? We all need a sense of time and a sense of continuity. We all change and will change again. The moment when a child begins to realize this—begins to be able to project himself both backward and forward in time—is the beginning of maturity. And if childhood is anything, it is the process whereby we acquire maturity and, with any luck, a full and responsible maturity. Immaturity is dangerous. Childish adults are not attractive people."[4]

Already the author of sixteen children's books, Lively has firm ideas about the craft and about exactly where the writer's responsibility lies. "A child reading a satisfying book should come away feeling that there is something he can't quite put his finger on—some sense of mystery, some intangible that he can't isolate or describe. And the mystery is the presence of the adult—the way in which I have tried not to patronize but have invited the child to join me. If this is detectable, however, the book has failed. I could not have written *Thomas Kempe* if I had not been reading, in the year or two before I wrote it, a lot of important and very serious recent historical writing on the nature of popular superstition and belief in the seventeenth century; but if I had allowed that to show, the book would have been a history book instead of the entertainment that I intended it to be.

"Similarly, . . . —*A Stitch in Time*—was rooted in an interest in Darwin and the *Origin of Species* and the Victorian debate about natural selection; but all this, I hope, is well concealed underneath, a story about a girl spending a summer holiday at Lyme

Fanny dreamed that a cat was mewing outside her door. (From *Fanny's Sister* by Penelope Lively. Illustrated by Anita Lobel.)

Regis and fantasizing about what may have happened to the Victorian child who made a sampler that she sees. It's another kind of ghost story. The ghost, in one form or another, is a most useful literary device for those of us concerned with memory and illusion.

"So I am deceiving the reader, in a sense, but for the best possible motive. It is not that I am sugaring the pill or disguising instruction as something else but simply that I am refusing to abandon the things that interest me on the grounds that they may be too complex or demanding for someone of ten or twelve.

"And so my loyalty, as a writer, must be to the book before the child. I am writing books, not conforming to some kind of preconceived notion of what children like to read or of what makes a good children's book. I have no idea, frankly, about either of those things. I'm not a child, and I don't expect I remember any more distinctly than most people what it was like to be one. I can't clear my head of all the intellectual and imaginative equipment and experience of thirty years—I can't go back to childhood, but what I can do is offer the child a product of all this equipment and experience. And in this sense it seems to me that the writer for children must invite children to come to him or her rather than go to them.

"I am writing the book I want to write—the one that satisfies me creatively—but in such a way that I offer it to children or invite them to come and share the fun with me. I am not abandoning my own adult preoccupations because the book I am writing is for children."[4]

In **1977** Lively's first novel for adults, *The Road to Lichfield*, was published. She wrote it in tandem with her children's book, *The Voyage of QV66*. Gradually, she has come to concentrate solely on adult fiction.

"I got to a point with children's books when I began to feel that I was possibly going to be writing the same book over and over again. I was running out of inspiration. More importantly, the preoccupations I had couldn't be expressed any more in terms of children's books. I'd gone as far as I could and if I wanted to discuss fictionally the things I was interested in I would have to write adult books.

"By the time I wrote *The Road to Lichfield* I had built up accretions of notes, a method I'd used for my later children's books. Writing is a very deliberate and hard working process. It's certainly not a question of sitting down and waiting for the muse to strike. It's all conscious.

"I have to have the whole structure in my head before I begin to write, although I don't think I worked like that when I first started. One of the things I've learned is to have a long gestation period. Nowadays it's a year or more before I start writing. I write instructions to myself in an exercise book; fragments of dialogue, long passages which will eventually be incorporated into the book but which are at this stage acting as a sort of guide. Not everything in the exercise book will go into the novel, but a lot will."[1]

History and memory play as central a role in Lively's adult books as they do in her work for children. "We take the children to Stonehenge or wherever, but we'd probably shrink from exposing them to a candid account of Bronze Age beliefs and practices. We like the past gutted and nicely cleaned up; then we know where we are with it.

"This attitude is in some ways an extension of what we do with our own pasts. We select what pleases, to some extent, and keep it bright and shiny and in good repair. The obsessions that most people—of whatever age—have about their parents is perhaps the most interesting aspect of this combined search for, and rejection of, our own pasts. We want to get rid of them, hang on to them, blame them for all that went wrong and attribute to them all that went well. It's fascinating. I'm as perplexed as to what it's all about as anyone else; but as a novelist, I can at least try to explore the process a bit and without presuming to come up with any answers, point things out. At the moment I'm interested in pointing out the element of fantasy in our treatment of the past— that, to a great extent, we make it up.

"I am offended by the misuse and misapprehension of [history], and worried about how, in a large sense, a lot of people simply do not realize that history is true—that it has actually happened, that it's not some kind of picturesque entertainment, but that there actually is—was—a past. That unrealistic, romantic view is objectionable and insensitive because it's totally without any kind of imaginative concept of pain or distress.

"Something that preoccupies me very much, too, is the nature of evidence, the conflicting evidences there are not just about life, but about any episode. *According to Mark* is about precisely that. It concerns a biographer and his growing realization that there is no such thing as the single truth about a life. And, indeed, who is to tell this? Certainly the person least likely to tell the truth is the liver of the life himself.

"Life is governed by Fate—governed by outside forces over which one has no control. This is one of the things that most people find unacceptable about life and therefore find various

The rat was not a fussy housekeeper. (From *A House Inside Out* by Penelope Lively. Illustrated by David Perkins.)

ways of trying to camouflage. Always people have sought ways of pretending to themselves that Fate can be avoided or outwitted. The novelist actually does that by being Fate; by making a structure.''[2]

Over the years, Lively has perfected a working method. ''I've used the same one with adult books. The theme or idea comes first and I build out from that. The characters and setting will be vehicles for the idea. My characters are totally fictional, except in the sense that for any author all characters stem from observation. I've never lifted a character straight from life. I don't think that would work. If you took someone you knew and put him in a book, he would go on doing the things that the person does in real life, whereas your characters have to be your creatures and you must be able to manipulate them. Obviously aspects of myself feed into characters. There are aspects of me, for example, in Freda in *The Voyage of GV66*. Freda is me as my children saw me when I was being the most irritating and tiresome kind of mother. If any child in the children's books is me, it would be the solitary and slightly anxious little girl, Maria, in *A Stitch in Time*. There are probably bits of me in many of the characters in the adult books, but I'd be hard put to say which.

''It's fun creating disagreeable characters. For instance, Diana in *According to Mark* is the kind of person I don't like much, but I enjoyed creating her. I had a lot of fun with Laura in *Treasures of Time* as well. There's a sense in which people are not responsible for their own inadequacies. The clergyman in *Judgement Day* is inadequate, but I felt sympathy for him.''[1]

In **1987** Lively won the coveted Booker Prize for her novel *Moon Tiger*, which contains scenes set in Egypt during the Second World War. ''*Moon Tiger* was about thirty years in gestation.''[2]

''I went back to Egypt about five years before I began writing it. I knew I wanted to make use of my experience there, but I had no idea what kind of book I would write until I had been back and digested it again.

''I felt an astonishing sense of homecoming and everything seemed faintly familiar. I found that I knew more Arabic than I'd ever realized because words came to my lips that I didn't know I knew. Friends would ask the name of a tree and I'd say, 'That's a mish-mish,' without knowing I knew it was called that.

''Cairo has more than doubled its size since the 1940s and the suburb where we lived is now the middle of a teeming slum of jerry-built apartments. Amazingly, my house was still there, just surviving in a very battered condition. I knew it at once. It's now used as offices for what they call a technical college, which seems to be a place where boys learn how to mend bicycles. I felt like Rip Van Winkle going back.

''I began writing *Moon Tiger* about two years after I'd been back to Egypt. I employed a kaleidoscope of evidence. I spent a lot of time looking at film and still photographs in the Imperial War Museum, and I read war memoirs and diaries as well as the official war histories. But there's a layer of *Moon Tiger* that I couldn't possibly have put in from research, and that is what I actually remember. I couldn't have written the book unless I had been in Egypt as a child during the war.

''I have very vivid memories of the atmosphere of Cairo and the way people behaved and talked.''[1]

''It's extraordinary how much lies around in the head and how perceptive, how absorbent, children are, how much is simply mopped up without responding in any way but just simply taking it all in. And yet, I had no appreciation at the time, no recognition

of what it was all like or what exactly was going on even. What one has to do is to try to recover this and then reproduce it with the wisdom of maturity.''[2]

''I've had many letters from old soldiers and people who were out there. To my great joy none of them say it's inaccurate; they say, 'That's how it was.'''[1]

''It's sticking one's neck out quite a long way for a middle-aged lady novelist to write from the point of view of a thirty-two-year-old tank officer.''[2]

''The soldier is a completely made-up character. In fact, I've made him rather more intelligent and interesting than any of the people I remember being around. Many of the other characters are based on people I remembered. I had one letter from a woman enclosing a photograph of a war-time wedding with the bride in a silver fox fur and the groom in the uniform of the Eighth Hussars. She said, 'I think the beady-eyed little girl must be you.' It was. I'd obviously been a bridesmaid. She added, 'I think I must be one of the silk clad camp followers that you describe!' And yes, I remember her as just that!

''The Booker Prize does have a huge effect. The practical effect is that for a year afterwards you can't really do any work because you become the property of all the people who want you to do things. I don't know that it does much in terms of a writer's confidence. In a sense it makes it worse because you know that you're going to be exposed to even more scrutiny.''[1]

In **1989** Lively followed her Booker Prize winner with *Passing On*. ''Unlike *Moon Tiger, Passing On* didn't need a great deal of background work before I could begin. It's a simpler book in that it's about families. It's built round a very powerful phrase of Virginia Woolf's: That there's no position stronger than that of the dead amongst the living. I read it in one of her letters and thought it a remarkable and true observation. I wanted to find a way to discuss it fictionally so I worked out a framework that would allow me to do it.

''It's a book about what happens to a middle-aged brother and sister in the months immediately following the death of their manipulative and very domineering old mother. It explores the ways in which she continues to pervade their lives and the way in which they see that their lives have always been pervaded by her.''[1]

''In many of my books either somebody dies or a death is a central part of the novel. I can't explain this except perhaps again it's the novelist's temptation to manipulate.''[2]

''Several of the books explore the brother-sister relationship. I suppose I'm interested in it because it's one I haven't had myself.

''My father remarried and, many years after his divorce from my mother, had two sons with whom I have a close relationship. They're virtually the same age as my own children so it's rather more like having nephews than step-brothers. To all intents and purposes I was an only child.

''I'm often asked what I feel are my limitations. The larger limitation is being a part of the society that one is in. If you've been working all your writing life in a politically stable country in peacetime, you obviously haven't been exposed to the tests and pressures of someone writing in a society under stress—the Soviet Union, Northern Ireland, South Africa, or a host of other places one could name. This, I feel, is the principal constriction and, in a sense, it's a constriction to be grateful for. At the same

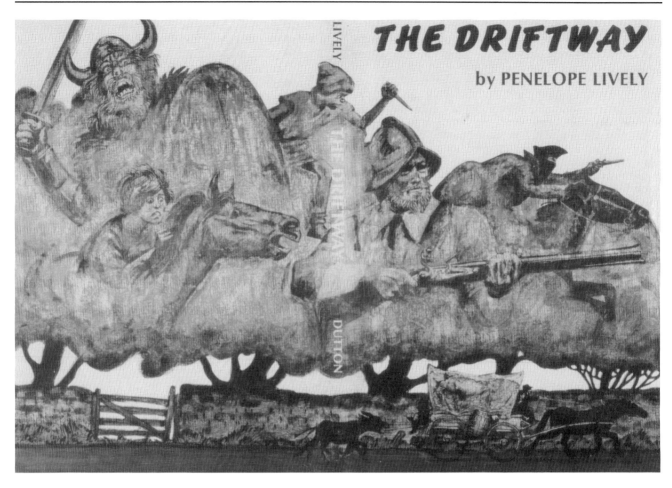

Jacket from the Dutton hardcover edition. (Jacket illustration by David K. Stone from *The Driftway* by Penelope Lively.)

time it leaves me wondering how I would have matched up to the demands of a different kind of historic circumstance?

"The other constriction I feel is not knowing enough about other people's working lives. Not knowing enough about, say, what it would be like to be a factory manager. The central character in the book I am working on at the moment is an architect. Before I can write him I need to know an awful lot about how an architect approaches his work. What is an architect's office like? What does he do when he get's there? How does he organize his day?"[1]

"I feel challenged by all the experiences that I haven't had myself. One of the novelist's great problems is that you simply haven't yourself lived enough in order to write about all the things you want to write about. You're restricted in so many different ways—by gender, by age, by social and historic circumstances. So that one of the things you're always trying to do is transcend this."[2]

Lively's collected stories (1975-86) appear in *Pack of Cards*. "I think of myself quite as much a short story writer as a novelist. I take the short story very seriously. I find it is very much a complement to writing novels. There are some ideas that I think can *only* be expressed in the short story, and there's also a curious way in which I find the short story is more autobiographical—not in the sense of telling the story of your life, but arising much more from little things, something seen, something heard, some incident that at the time appears to be quite without significance and yet will surface quite possibly years later, and you see some

way to give it a significance that transcends your own personal experience and becomes, you hope, something that has a universal resonance."[2]

"I wish I had done more short stories. When life was more spacious and I wasn't chasing my own tail as I am at the moment, I wrote them more. When I got stuck on a novel I would knock off and write a short story instead. I shall go back to them when I've cleared the decks."[1]

"Jack is always the first person to read [manuscripts]."[1] "He's the old-fashioned kind of academic in the sense that he's a man of letters. My husband is not an Eng. Lit. person in any sense, but he's very widely read in the novel and has always been my most useful critic. He's a person of compendious reading, and he often has been able to point me at just the book I've needed. All writers in their lives should have several people like that. This is very marvelous in a spouse."[2]

Lively is convinced that literature is crucial in helping us to understand ourselves and others. She is concerned that society is divided between those who read and take pleasure from books and those who don't.

"Books are divisive. Not so much in the sense of one's affinities with one kind of book or another, but they act as a huge divisive force between those who have some kind of commitment to reading and those who don't. It's a division that can be broken down. The way is through education. I feel very Jesuitical about

Once upon a time a long time ago not as long ago as all that. (From *Moon Tiger* by Penelope Lively.)

it: Give me a child until he's seven and I will make him mine forever. If you can get children to enjoy literature when they are young enough and persuade them that reading is something that will enchance life, then you're half way to creating a nation of readers."[1]

As a result of winning the Booker Prize, Lively has spent more time travelling. She is, as well, actively involved in various organizations which support literature and writers, and divides her time between the family home in Oxfordshire and a base in London.

"I've been travelling a great deal over the past year for the British Council and talking to foreign writers. Those writing in stressed countries tell me to be grateful for the constrictions of working in a more stable society. The British Council took me back to Egypt after *Moon Tiger* was published, my second return visit, and I was particularly interested to meet Egyptians my own age. I was lecturing at the Universities and many English professors there are women. The circumstances in which they grew up were so different from my own, it made me realize even more how the British kept to themselves.

"Quite apart from the backlash of the Booker Prize, I do a fair amount of work for bookish organizations. I'm on the literature

panel of the Arts Council and I've always been involved with PEN and the Society of Authors."[1]

She has also presented four series of "Treasure Islands," a BBC radio program about children's literature. "It's a BBC radio discussion programme in which I talk to people connected with children's books and it's aimed at parents, teachers, librarians, and anybody interested. We have some straight reviewing of current books but we try to make the content as wide as possible. 'Treasure Islands' is the brainchild of its producer, Sally Feldman.

"We mainly live in Oxfordshire, but I need to come to London for a night or two each week. I wear out the A40."[1]

Lively seems to have achieved a perfect balance between her professional career and a happy family life. The one element which worries her is the passing of time. "I'm a tempered optimist. I've reached the point in life when one tends to prefer optimism to pessimism. As I've grown older I've got more and more left-wing and I'm also a stern agnostic. I think my childhood gave me a taste for solitude and I rather like being alone. I need to have certain times everyday when I am alone.

"Life is good. The only part which is imperfect is the thought of time rushing past. There are lots of books I want to write and I worry that I won't be able to get them written. Days and years are not long enough. There's so much in my life—work, family, and friends—that occasionally I get panic stricken. I'm not afraid of dying, but I am irritated by the thought of old age."[1]

FOOTNOTE SOURCES

[1]Based on an interview by Cathy Courtney for *Something about the Author*.
[2]Amanda Smith, "Penelope Lively," *Publishers Weekly*, March 25, 1988. Amended by P. Lively.
[3]Penelope Lively, "Children and the Art of Memory, Part II," *Horn Book*, April, 1978.
[4]P. Lively, "Children and the Art of Memory, Part I," *Horn Book*, February, 1978.

FOR MORE INFORMATION SEE:

Times Literary Supplement, April 16, 1970 (p. 421), April 6, 1973 (p. 380), July 22, 1983 (p. 777), April 7, 1978 (p. 377), November 25, 1983 (p. 1131).
Spectator, May 9, 1970.
Books and Bookmen, May, 1970.
Horn Book, April, 1971, August, 1972 (p. 376ff), June, 1973 (p. 271ff), February, 1975 (p. 55ff), February, 1976 (p. 51), February, 1977 (p. 52ff), August, 1980 (p. 408), February, 1982 (p. 44ff).
Junior Literary Guild Catalogue, March, 1972, September, 1973.
Junior Bookshelf, June, 1974 (p. 143ff), February, 1977 (p. 22), October, 1980 (p. 241), June, 1982 (p. 106ff).
Marcus Crouch and Alec Ellis, *Chosen for Children: An Account of the Books Which Have Been Awarded the Library Association Carnegie Medal, 1936-1975*, 3rd edition, Library Association, 1977.
Children's Literature in Education, summer, 1978 (p. 59ff), autumn, 1981 (p. 24ff).
Doris de Montreville and Elizabeth D. Crawford, editors, *Fourth Book of Junior Authors and Illustrators*, H. W. Wilson, 1978.
D. L. Kirkpatrick, *Twentieth-Century Children's Writers*, St. Martin's, 1978, 2nd edition, 1983.

John Rowe Townsend, *A Sounding of Storytellers: New and Revised Essays on Contemporary Writers for Children,* Lippincott, 1979.

Sheila A. Egoff, *Thursday's Child: Trends and Patterns in Contemporary Children's Literature,* American Library Association, 1981.

COLLECTIONS

Kerlan Collection, University of Minnesota.

LORIMER, Janet 1941-

PERSONAL: Born December 31, 1941, in Los Angeles, Calif.; daughter of Chester Paine (a civil engineer) and Margaret (a poet; maiden name, Grahame) Collins; married David Scott Lorimer (a counselor), April 23, 1966; children: Kerry Kathleen, Marnie Diana. *Education:* Attended University of the Pacific, summers, 1959-60; Oceanside-Carlsbad Junior College, A.A., 1961; San Francisco State University, B.A., 1963; attended Stanislaus State University, summer, 1965. *Politics:* Democrat. *Home and office:* 91-740 Ihipehu St., Ewa Beach, Hawaii 96706. *Agent:* Laurie Harper, Sebastian Agency, 1109 Royal Lane, San Carlos, Calif. 94070.

CAREER: Elementary and junior high school teacher, 1963-66; taught educationally handicapped class, 1967-68; free-lance writer, 1974—; Leeward Community College, Pearl City, Hawaii, teacher of writing, 1989—. Guest speaker at schools and libraries; teacher of writing workshops. Member of Ewa Beach Community Association (editor of newsletter, 1972-73); President of Ewa Beach Elementary School Parents-Teachers Association, 1974-75; member of Board of Hawaii Episcopal Marriage Encounter, 1979-87; Girl Scout leader. *Member:* National Writers Club, Horror Writers of America. *Awards, honors:* Nebula Award Nomination from the Science Fiction Writers of America, and Bram Stoker Award Nomination from the Horror Writers of America, both 1987, both for adult short story, "The Natural Way."

WRITINGS:

The Biggest Bubble in the World (illustrated by Diane Paterson), F. Watts, 1982.
Tomb of Horror, Pitman, 1985.
Maze of Terror, David S. Lake, 1985.
Deadly Rose, David S. Lake, 1986.
The Night Marchers, David S. Lake, 1986.
Brannigan's Folly, David S. Lake, 1986.
Family Reunion, David S. Lake, 1986.
The Dollhouse, David S. Lake, 1986.
The Glory Girl, David S. Lake, 1986.
The Eye of Kali, David S. Lake, 1987.
Time's Reach, David S. Lake, 1987.
A Dangerous Game, David S. Lake, 1987.
Till Death Do Us Part, David S. Lake, 1987.
The Poison Pen Mystery, David S. Lake, 1987.
The Cardiff Hill Mystery, David S. Lake, 1987.
Picture of Evil, David S. Lake, 1987.
The Mystery of the Missing Treasure, Scholastic, 1987.
The Mystery of the Haunted Trail, Scholastic, 1989.
The Trouble with Buster, Scholastic, 1990.

CONTRIBUTOR TO ANTHOLOGIES

Descendants of Eve, David S. Lake, 1988.
Kathryn Ptacek, editor, *Women of Darkness II,* Tor, 1990.

Contributor of short stories and articles to periodicals, including *Highlights for Children, Beehive, 2 AM, Hawaii's Guide to Good Health, Parish Family Digest, Super Shopper, Writer's Info, Eldritch Tales, Beyond . . . Science Fiction and Fantasy,* and *Woman's World.* Author of monthly column, *Bestways,* 1983-89.

WORK IN PROGRESS: The Mystery at Gravesend, a juvenile mystery; *From the Terrible Mind of Angel Carver,* a young adult horror book; *Toby and the Bandit's Treasure,* an early chapter book; *Open Sesame: The Super-Terrific, Extra-Special Latchkey Kids Club,* a story/activity book for middle grade readers; *All You Need Is a Clean Jar,* a picture story book; *The Haunting of Harrow Hill,* a young adult novel; a series of hi/los for Wasatch Education Systems, titles include *Storm Island, The Town That Wasn't There, The Savage Solution, Spy for an Old Fox,* and *Invitation from the Grave; The Visitant,* an adult novel.

SIDELIGHTS: "When I was five years old I was desperate to learn to read. I nagged my parents to let me start school and finally they gave in, starting me in the first grade of a one-room country school house near our home in a rural part of California. Shortly after I was given my reading text book (the breath-taking adventures of 'Dick and Jane,' if memory serves), I conned my teacher into letting me take the book home one weekend. Then I conned my father into believing that the teacher had said I had to read the whole book before Monday.

"On Monday my father went to the teacher and apologized because, he said, we had not been able to finish the whole book. We had come close, but because we'd had company that weekend, he had not been able to help me as much as he wanted to complete the assignment. The teacher told my father, in horrified

JANET LORIMER

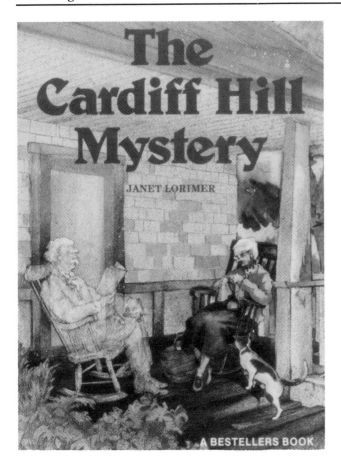

It was a sweet little place. But what was its secret?
(From *The Cardiff Hill Mystery* by Janet Lorimer. Illustrated by Sara Boore.)

tones, that learning to read the book was supposed to have taken me the rest of the semester.

"I didn't get punished for my con job. How can you punish a kid who so badly wants to learn to read? Later that year, after I had mastered reading and simple writing, I wrote my first story. It was three sentences long, with a definite beginning, middle, and end, but singularly lacking in character development and dialogue. It was, however, a sign of things to come.

"I continued to write stories as I grew up. When I was fourteen I won honorable mention for a city-wide poetry contest. At fifteen I received my first official rejection slip from *American Girl* magazine. (I was devastated.) During my senior year of high school I wrote and directed a three-act melodrama entitled 'Angel of the Mother Lode; or, The Bity Bonanza Mine' which was performed at our high school. I loved writing the play but learned the hard way that I was not cut out to be a director. Neither Hollywood nor Broadway seems to have suffered.

"I always wanted to be a writer as well as an actress, a circus performer, a nuclear physicist. My desire to see my writing published was the strongest of all my yearnings. But so many other events seemed to take precedence—college, teaching, marriage, children. After the birth of my youngest daughter, it finally sank in that I would never have enough peace and quiet in which to write and I might as well get used to writing with a toddler crawling into my lap, the sound of the neighbors fighting, and the washing machine demanding fabric softener. So I set out to become a professional writer.

"I wanted to write for adults and for two years struggled to write and sell an adult novel. It wasn't that I didn't like writing for children. I loved children's books. But for some odd reason, I was sure I couldn't succeed with children's stories.

"Then one afternoon while I was reading to my youngest daughter, I suddenly had an idea for a children's short story. I wrote it and sent it off to *Highlights for Children*. For the next two months I alternated between feeling certain I would make a sale and certain I would not. When the acceptance letter arrived, I floated on the ceiling for two days straight. My first sale!

"Although I do write for adults and now enjoy some success, my greatest accomplishments and thrills have come from writing for children and teenagers. I am particularly excited because *The Mystery of the Missing Treasure* sold over 178,000 copies in the first six months after publication.

"During the years I was a teacher, I yearned to have materials that would appeal to older elementary and junior high school students reading below grade level. I remember how frustrated I felt because I had no appropriate materials to give one of my special education students, a thirteen-year-old boy reading on a preprimer level. Today he is an adult who may very well be one of the millions of functionally illiterate adults. My concern for students who can't read led me into writing hi/los and I am especially proud of this area of my writing. At the same time, what a challenge! Adult plots, adult characters and adult dialogue written on a third-grade reading level is no easy matter, especially if the editor expects the writer to write with a specific word list of only a thousand words! I learned to appreciate my Thesaurus in a whole new way.

"A number of my stories have featured young boys as the main character. I find it very amusing that a woman writer, 'fortysomething,' can so easily slip into the mind and devious schemes of an eight- or nine- or twelve-year-old boy. To write these stories I call on my own youthful misadventures as well as those of my husband, our daughters, and their friends. The motivation for *The Biggest Bubble in the World* grew out of my desire to write a book about bubble gum as well as the frustration I, as a mother, experienced when my children got bubble gum stuck in their hair and clothes and on the pillow case. Motivation for *The Mystery of the Missing Treasure* came from my own desire to read 'buried treasure' stories as well as from living for several years in the gold rush country in northern California. My next book published by Scholastic, *The Mystery of the Haunted Trail*, was set in Hawaii and stemmed from my fascination with a local legend about the Night Marchers, ghosts of ancient Hawaiians who walk the old trails.

"Growing up with a mother who successfully published poetry helped me to appreciate everything from a writer's time constraints to SASE and rejection slips. Both my parents encouraged me to read and write, and today I'm proud to be able to send my mother copies of my books and short stories as they appear in print. It doesn't surprise me that my own daughters show considerable interest in and talent for writing.

"I refuse to pigeon-hole myself as a writer of fiction or nonfiction, of adult material or children's material. I like to think I can somehow do it all! However, writing for children and teenagers will always bring me the most fun and the greatest sense of accomplishment."

HOBBIES AND OTHER INTERESTS: Reading, making crafts, going to the beach, creating new recipes when time allows.

FOR MORE INFORMATION SEE:

Susan Yim, ''Writing Children's Books Isn't Exactly Child's Play,'' *Honolulu Star-Bulletin,* December 10, 1982.

LUPOFF, Richard A(llen) 1935-
(Ova Hamlet, Dick Lupoff, Dick
O'Donnell, Pascal Pascudniak, Addison
Steele II)

PERSONAL: Born February 21, 1935, in Brooklyn, N.Y.; son of Sol J. (an accountant) and Sylvia (a homemaker; maiden name, Feldman) Lupoff; married Patricia Loring (a bookseller), August 27, 1958; children: Kenneth Bruce, Katherine Eve, Thomas Daniel. *Education:* University of Miami, Coral Gables, Fla., B.A., 1956. *Politics:* None. *Religion:* Jewish. *Home and office:* 3208 Claremont Ave., Berkeley, Calif. 94705. *Agent:* Henry Morrison, Inc., P.O. Box 235, Bedford Hills, N.Y. 10507.

CAREER: Remington Rand Univac, New York City, technical writer, 1958-63; International Business Machines Corp., New York City, and Poughkeepsie, N.Y., writer and director of technical films, 1963-70; full-time writer, 1970-82, 1986—; various office positions, 1982-85. *Military service:* U.S. Army, 1956-58; became first lieutenant. *Member:* American Crime Writers League. *Awards, honors:* Hugo Award from the World Science Fiction Society, joint winner, with wife, Patricia Lupoff, 1962, for amateur science fiction magazine *Xero;* Hugo Award Nominee, 1975, for novelette ''After the Dreamtime,'' and 1976, for short story ''Sail the Tide of Mourning''; Nebula Award Nominee from the Science Fiction Writers of America, 1972, for novella ''With the Boomer Boys on Little Old New Alabama,'' 1975, for short story ''Sail the Tide of Mourning,'' and, 1978, for novel *Sword of the Demon.*

WRITINGS:

NONFICTION

Edgar Rice Burroughs: Master of Adventure, Canaveral, 1965, revised edition, Ace Books, 1974.
(Editor with Don Thompson) *All in Color for a Dime,* Arlington House, 1969.
(Editor with D. Thompson under real name and contributor with D. Thompson under joint pseudonym Dick O'Donnell) *The Comic-Book Book,* Arlington House, 1973.
Barsoom: Edgar Rice Burroughs and the Martian Vision, Mirage, 1976.

FICTION

One Million Centuries, Lancer Books, 1967.
Sacred Locomotive Flies, Ballantine, 1971.
Into the Aether (based on his comic strip ''The Amazing Adventures of Professor Thintwhistle and His Incredible Ether Flyer''), Dell, 1974.
The Crack in the Sky, Dell, 1976 (published in England as *Fool's Hill,* Sphere, 1976).
The Triune Man, Berkley Publishing, 1976.
Sandworld, Berkley Publishing, 1976.
Lisa Kane: A Novel of Supernatural (juvenile; illustrated by Marika), Bobbs-Merrill, 1976.
(With Robert E. Howard) *The Return of Skull-Face,* Fax, 1977.
Sword of the Demon, Harper, 1977.
Space War Blues, Dell, 1978.

The Ova Hamlet Papers (contains material originally published under pseudonym Ova Hamlet), Pennyfarthing Press, 1979.
Circumpolar!, Simon & Schuster, 1984.
Sun's End, Berkley, 1984.
Lovecraft's Book, Arkham House, 1985.
Countersolar!, Arbor House, 1987.
The Forever City (young adult), Walker, 1988.
Galaxy's End, Ace, 1988.
The Black Tower, Bantam, 1988.
The Comic Book Killer, limited edition, Offspring, 1988, Bantam, 1989.
Time's End, Ace, 1989.
Finale!, Bantam, 1990.
The Classic Car Caper, Bantam, 1990.

CHAPBOOKS

Nebogipfel at the End of Time, Underwood-Miller, 1979.
Stroka Prospekt, Toothpaste Press, 1982.
The Digital Wristwatch of Philip K. Dick, Canyon Press, 1985.

Editor of *What If?: Stories That Should Have Won the Hugo* (anthology), Pocket Books, Volume I, 1980, Volume II, 1981; also editor of five volumes of previously unpublished miscellaneous writings of Edgar Rice Burroughs, 1963-64. Contributor to anthologies, including *Again, Dangerous Visions,* edited by Harlan Ellison, Doubleday, 1972, and *New Dimensions, 4* and *5.*

Author, occasionally under pseudonym Pascal Pascudniak, with Stephen W. Stiles, of comic strips, including ''The Amazing Adventures of Professor Thintwhistle and His Incredible Ether Flyer,'' *Horib,* 1964-65, ''The Adventures of Isidore,'' *Jive Comics,* 1969, and ''Professor Thintwhistle,'' *Heavy Metal,* 1980-81.

(Jacket illustration by George Barr from *Countersolar!* by Richard A. Lupoff.)

Contributor of short stories and articles to newspapers and magazines; contributor with Michael Kurland of short story ''The Square Root of Dead'' to *Mike Shayne's Mystery Magazine;* contributor under pseudonym Addison Steele II of short story ''The Wedding of Ova Hamlet'' to *Fantastic.* Co-editor with wife, Patricia Lupoff, of *Xero,* 1960-63; book editor and reviewer, *Starship* (formerly *Algol*), 1968-79; West Coast editor, *Crawdaddy,* 1970-71, and *Changes,* 1971-72; contributing editor, *Organ,* 1972, science-fiction book reviewer, *San Francisco Chronicle,* 1979-81, editor, Canyon Press, 1986—.

WORK IN PROGRESS: Transtemporal!, Born of the Stars, Emperor of Yesterday, and *Richard Lupoff's Secret Empire* (young adult), all fiction; editor with D. Thompson and M. Thompson, *Four-Color World;* with Steve Stiles, a book version of the ''Thintwhistle'' material from *Heavy Metal,* for Fantagraphics Publishers; a five-volume compilation with others of interviews with authors, editors, and associated literary people that were broadcast on radio station KPFA in Berkeley, Calif.; compiling his essays, reviews, and miscellaneous nonfiction, for Serconia.

SIDELIGHTS: ''I've spent most of my intellectual life trying to become a 'good' writer (in the artistic sense) and a successful one (in the sense of making a living at it). I made my first sale (as a sports reporter) while still in my teens, sold my first book in 1965, and became a full-time author in 1970.

''In 1982, economic conditions caused me to abandon writing and return to office work for almost four years. This was a bitterly disappointing experience for me. I felt that I was at the peak of my skills and the debacle in my writing career was caused entirely by outside factors. However, I was able to return to writing in 1986, and while I regret the loss of those four years, the fallow period may actually have refreshed my creativity.

''Since returning to writing I have moved into areas new for me. *The Comic Book Killer* is my first formal mystery, and has won enthusiastic comments from a number of highly respected people in the field. A second mystery is in progress. A science-fiction novel for young adult readers, *The Forever City,* has also been well received.''

HOBBIES AND OTHER INTERESTS: Baseball, music, classic cinema, books.

FOR MORE INFORMATION SEE:

Analog: Science Fiction/Science Fact, July, 1977, February 2, 1981.
Magazine of Fantasy and Science Fiction, summer, 1981, January, 1986.
Science Fiction Review, November, 1981.

MacLEOD, Doug 1959-

PERSONAL: Born October 13, 1959, in Melbourne, Australia; son of Donald Frank (a Shetland pony breeder) and Marion Eva (an ethnic garment maker; maiden name, McEwan) MacLeod. *Education:* Victorian College of Arts, Diploma of Arts, 1982. *Address:* c/o Hilary Linstead and Associates, Suite 302, 9-13 Bronte Rd., Bondi Junction, New South Wales 2022.

DOUG MacLEOD

CAREER: Australian Children's Puffin Club, Melbourne, co-editor of *Puffinalia,* 1981-88; The Comedy Co., head writer, 1988. Presenter of ''RAVE,'' for Australian Broadcasting Corp., 1982-83. Member of state steering committee for International Youth Year, 1985; writer-in-residence, Playbox Theatre Co., Melbourne, 1987. *Member:* Fellowship of Australian Writers, Actors' Equity Association. *Awards, honors:* Young Australian Best Book of the Year Younger Honor, and Australian Children's Book Award Honor Book from the Children's Book Council of Australia, both 1987, both for *Sister Madge's Book of Nuns.*

WRITINGS:

JUVENILE

Hippopotabus, Outback Press, 1976.
The Story of Admiral Sneeze, Beatrice Publications, 1977.
Tales of Tuttle, Penguin, 1980.
Knees, Penguin, 1981.
In the Garden of Badthings (illustrated by Peter Thomson), Penguin, 1981.
The Fed Up Family Album (illustrated by J. Brierley), Penguin, 1983.
Frank Boulderbuster: The Last of the Great Swagmen (illustrated by M. Atchison), Puffin, 1986.
Sister Madge's Book of Nuns (illustrated by Craig Smith), Omnibus, 1986.
Ten Monster Island, Omnibus, 1987.

The Monster, Kestrel, 1988.
Bilge (play), T. Nelson, 1988.

ADULT

My Son the Lawyer Is Drowning (play), Currency Press, 1987.
(With Ian McFadyen, Glenn Robbins, Maryanne Fahey and
Peter Herbert) *The Comedy Company Holiday Book,* Pen-
guin, 1988.

Author of column in *Age.* Also author of comedy scripts and
children's stories for Australian Broadcasting Corp.

WORK IN PROGRESS: Sister Madge's Book of Nuns Part Two.

SIDELIGHTS: "I wrote a monthly column in *Age,* Melbourne's
newspaper, at the age of thirteen. My work was published in
book form when I was sixteen. This early success cemented my
desire to become a children's author. I have also performed in
numerous children's shows and have written pantomimes. I am a
keen advocate of the need to perform poetry in the classroom.

"My books are, in general, works of comic verse. I list as my
two greatest sources of inspiration the works of C. J. Dennis (an
Australian author, poet, and collector of indigenous slang) and
Ogden Nash, whose 'Custard the Dragon' was a childhood
favorite. Although a full-time writer, I do not like to consider
myself chained to the typewriter. I spend a good deal of time
performing my work at schools, libraries, and other places all
over Australia. I particularly like performing in country areas
and have used my experiences of country towns in compiling my
Frank Boulderbuster anthology. Most of the stories about Frank
the swagman are based on real events—many of the goings-on
in the Australian outback being so bizarre that no embellishment
is necessary. For example, a story featuring a race meeting
where shingleback lizards are substituted for racehorses is based
on an actual event which happens annually in the Queensland
town of Cunnamulla.

"I feel it necessary to stress that I do not write 'nonsense' verse.
The lame limericks of Edward Lear prove consistently disappointing to me. Rather, I tell stories in verse, making strong use
of wordplay and intricate rhyming patterns. I have tried to make
the 'sting in the tail' another hallmark of my style. These final
'twists' are so important to me that I frequently write my pieces
backwards; that is to say, I write the conclusion before I write the
premise.

"The reader will notice that I have been careful to avoid referring
to my work as 'poetry.' I do not consider myself to be a poet. At
the same time, I consider my work to be something better than
doggerel. 'Comic verse' is the best label I can use to describe the
form of writing which I am best at and which I find the most
enjoyable."

HOBBIES AND OTHER INTERESTS: Art and music.

MARKHAM, Marion M. 1929-

PERSONAL: Born June 12, 1929, in Chicago, Ill.; daughter of
William Joseph (a manufacturer's representative) and Marion (a
housewife; maiden name, Dammann) Bork; married R. Bailey
Markham (an executive), December 29, 1955; children: Susan
Markham Andersen, Jane Markham Madden. *Education:*
Northwestern University, B.S., 1953. *Home and office:* 2415
Newport Rd., Northbrook, Ill. 60062. *Agent:* Susan Cohen,
Writers House, Inc., 21 West 26th St., New York, N.Y. 10010.

CAREER: Station WTVP, Decatur, Ill., continuity writer, 1953-
54; Station WFTL, Fort Lauderdale, Fla., continuity writer,
1954; Earle Ludgin Advertising Co., Chicago, Ill., business
manager of television production, 1955-58; free-lance writer,
1967— . Speaker in schools. Member of the Edgar Allan Poe
Awards committees, 1983, 1985, 1986; member of board of
trustees, Northbrook Public Library, 1976-86, president, 1983-
85. *Member:* Mystery Writers of America (Midwest regional
vice-president, 1976-78), Society of Midland Authors
(chairman of general awards committee, 1987-88).

WRITINGS:

Escape from Velos (illustrated by Derek Carter), Childrens
    Press, 1981.
The Halloween Candy Mystery (illustrated by Emily Arnold
    McCully), Houghton, 1982.
The Christmas Present Mystery (illustrated by E. A. McCully),
    Houghton, 1984.
The Thanksgiving Day Parade Mystery (illustrated by Dianne
    Cassidy), Houghton, 1986.
The Birthday Party Mystery (illustrated by Pau Estrada), Hough-
    ton, 1989.

Contributor of articles and short stories to periodicals, including
Blackwood's, Coronet, London Mystery Magazine, 'Teen, and
Buffalo Spree.

MARION M. MARKHAM

WORK IN PROGRESS: The Lopsided Snowman, the first book in a new mystery series for boys and girls aged seven to ten; a young adult mystery set along the St. John's River in Florida; a fictionalized account of an actual rescue of a chimp from a research laboratory.

SIDELIGHTS: ''Although I have always written—beginning with some very bad poetry when I was nine—it was a long time before I thought of myself as a writer. Perhaps this was because I grew up in a family where books were important. I assumed that writers were very special people, and I was just someone who liked words.

''I still do like words—in stories and crossword puzzles.

''As a child I read indiscriminately: science books, particularly those about astronomy, stories about sailing, pirate stories, the 'Oz' books, and mysteries. Somehow, though, my reading skipped over the popular teen mystery series, and I began with Ellery Queen and Nero Wolfe when I was about eleven.

''I'm still indiscriminate about my reading. I read mysteries, of course, but I tend to go off on binges on certain subjects. Poisonous plants, hurricanes, viruses, plate tectonics, and the quantum theory are some that I can remember. Many of these things eventually find their way into my work. Though I no longer write nonfiction, I always enjoyed the research process that went into an article. In fact, it was because I spent so much time in the public library that I was asked to become a library trustee.

''I used to say that I was never going to live long enough to read all the books I want to read and learn about all the things that interest me. I've come to accept that, partly because I also know that I will never live long enough to write all the stories I have in my head.

''*Child Life* magazine published a short essay of mine when I was eleven. It was my first experience with being edited, and I was indignant that they took two of my paragraphs (about two separate subjects) and ran them together with an 'and.' I remember telling my mother, with some vehemence, 'That's not the way I wrote it.' I have felt that way a few times since, though never with the editor of my 'Dixon Twins' series.

''Writing mysteries, as I do now, seemed logical because I read so many. Probably, I was also influenced by stories about my police-captain grandfather. He died before I was born, but I grew up with the feeling that I knew him even though I had never met him. (I recently wrote a short story about him that I want to expand into a 'turn-of-the-century police procedural' novel.)

''My 'Dixon Twins' books reflect the two sides of my major interests. Mickey is interested in being a detective. Kate is interested in science. Both of them are me, though I confess I am a little more in tune with Kate.

''In fact, it is difficult for me to think about interests outside of writing, because I find that most things that happen to me feed into whatever I am working on at that moment. But when a book I am working on takes over my life, then things that happen in my life become part of the book.

''An appreciation of classical music (but no talent) has also always been a part of my life. And I love flowers. I plant them in my garden and cut them for my house, but my husband ends up doing the watering and weeding. I'm too busy nurturing ideas.

Which means, I guess, that I'm not really a very balanced person.''

HOBBIES AND OTHER INTERESTS: Working acrostics and crossword puzzles, book buying, listening to classical music, medicine, science, Oriental art and furniture, teaching.

FOR MORE INFORMATION SEE:

Who's Who in the Midwest, 20th edition, Marquis, 1985.

MARSHALL, Garry 1934-

PERSONAL: Born Garry Marciarelli, November 13, 1934, in New York, N.Y.; son of Anthony W. (a television producer) and Marjorie Irene (a dance instructor; maiden name, Ward) Marciarelli; married Barbara Sue Wells (a nurse), 1963. *Education:* Northwestern University, B.A., 1956. *Office:* Henderson Productions, 10067 Riverside Dr., Toluca Lake, Calif. *Publicist:* c/o Nancy Seltzer and Associates, 8845 Ashcroft Ave., Los Angeles, Calif. 90048.

CAREER: Producer, director, and writer. Drummer in Chicago, Ill., 1958; *Daily News,* New York, N.Y., reporter, 1958-59; free-lance comedy writer, New York, N.Y., 1958-60. Writer of over 100 television scripts, variety shows, and fifteen pilots, including comedy writer for ''The Jack Paar Show,'' ''The Tonight Show,'' 1960-62, ''The Joey Bishop Show,'' 1962-64, ''I Spy,'' 1966, ''Bill Dana Show,'' and ''Gomer Pyle''; writer for ''Chrysler Theatre,'' 1966; comedy writer with Jerry Belson of episodes for ''The Dick Van Dyke Show,'' 1962, ''The Lucy Show,'' 1963, and ''The Danny Thomas Show,'' 1964. Creator and executive producer of thirteen television series; writer and producer of three screenplays with partner Jerry Belson; director of thirty television shows, a music video, five feature films, two commercials, and numerous pilots. *Military service:* U. S. Army, Special Services, 1956-58. *Member:* New York Dramatists Guild, Motion Picture Academy, Television Academy, Producer's Guild, Director's Guild, Screen Actors Guild, Writer's Guild, American Federation of Television and Radio Artists, Board of Governors of the Los Angeles Music Center, Musician's Union (Local 47), Sigma Delta Chi, Alpha Tau Omega.

AWARDS, HONORS: Emmy Award from the National Academy of Television Arts and Sciences for the Best Episode of a Comedy, 1965, for ''The Dick Van Dyke Show''; Nine other Emmy Awards and four Golden Globe Awards from the Hollywood Foreign Press Association, all for television series ''Happy Days,'' ''Laverne and Shirley,'' and ''Mork and Mindy;'' Arc of Excellence Award from the National Association of Retarded Citizens, 1978; Showman of the Year from the Publicist's Guild, 1979; Man of the Year from Hollywood Radio and Television Society's Broadcasting Awards, 1980, from the Los Angeles Free Clinic, 1982, and from the National Association of Television Program Executives, 1983; Meritorious Award from the California Governor's Committee for Employment of the Handicapped, 1980; ''Star'' on the Walk of Fame, Hollywood Blvd., 1983; Member of the Year from the Caucus for Producers, Writers and Directors, 1988; Best Soft Drink Commercial ''Classic Coke'' from *Advertising Age,* 1988; Award for the Best Family Motion Picture (Drama) from the Youth in Film Awards, 1988, for ''Beaches.''

GARRY MARSHALL

WRITINGS:

TELEVISION SERIES; CREATOR AND EXECUTIVE PRODUCER

(With J. Belson) ''Hey Landlord,'' NBC-TV, 1966-67.
(With J. Belson) ''The Odd Couple,'' ABC-TV, 1970-75.
''Me and the Chimp,'' CBS-TV, 1971-72.
''The Little People'' (later named ''The Brian Keith Show''), NBC-TV, 1972-74.
''Happy Days,'' ABC-TV, 1972-83.
''Barefoot in the Park,'' ABC-TV, 1975-76.
''Laverne and Shirley,'' ABC-TV, 1976-83.
''Blansky's Beauties,'' ABC-TV, 1977-78.
''Mork and Mindy,'' ABC-TV, 1978-82.
''Angie,'' NBC-TV, 1979-81.
''Who's Watching the Kids?,'' NBC-TV, 1980-81.
''Joannie Loves Chachi,'' ABC-TV, 1982-84.
''Nothing in Common'' (based on film), NBC-TV, 1987-88.

SCREENPLAYS; WRITER AND PRODUCER

(With Jerry Belson) ''How Sweet It Is!,'' National General, 1968.
(With J. Belson) ''The Grasshopper,'' National General, 1970.
''Evil Roy Slade'' (television movie), MCA-TV, 1971.

STAGE PLAYS

''Shelves,'' first produced in Chicago, Ill. at Pheasant Run Playhouse, February, 1976.
(Adapter) Lawrence Schwab, G. G. De Sylva, and Frank Mandel, *Good News* (libretto; words and music by Lew Brown, G. G. De Sylva, and Ray Henderson), Tams Witmark Music Library, 1978. (With J. Belson) ''The Roast'' (two-act), first produced on Broadway at Winter Garden Theatre, May 8, 1980.
(With Lowell Ganz) ''Wrong Turn at Lungfish,'' staged reading November, 1988.

MOTION PICTURE DIRECTOR

(And executive producer) ''Young Doctors in Love,'' Twentieth Century-Fox, 1982.
(Also writer with Neal Marshall) ''The Flamingo Kid,'' ABC Motion Pictures, 1984.
''Nothing in Common,'' Tri-Star, 1986.
''Overboard,'' Metro-Goldwyn-Mayer/United Artists, 1987.
''Beaches,'' Touchstone, 1988.

WORK IN PROGRESS: Director of ''Three Thousand,'' a feature film for Touchstone.

SIDELIGHTS: ''I was a mediocre journalist, a mediocre musician, a mediocre actor, a mediocre athlete. I had to find something I could do well.''[1]

A surprising beginning for a man who, on the night of January 28, 1979, had created the three top-rated shows on network television. Garry Marshall had indeed found something he could do well . . . make people laugh. ''I got a degree in journalism from Northwestern University but I wasn't very good at it. I wasn't a good student. Everybody seemed to be better than me. When I got out of school, I worked in the newspaper field but not very successfully. The reason was that I was too funny! So, I got into comedy writing.

''At that time, I wrote things for comedians. I would go to different night clubs and try to sell jokes. Some bought, some threw me out, and a few took me under their wing. Phil Foster, in particular, was one of the people who helped me. He was the comedian who later became the father on 'Laverne and Shirley.'''[1]

The time was the early sixties and Marshall landed a job writing sketches for Jack Paar on ''The Tonight Show.'' He wrote funny letters from imaginary kids from camp that Paar liked so much, he put Marshall on his writing staff. To Marshall, Paar quipped, ''I like you, Garry, because you think like a four-year-old.''[2] It was during his two-year stint with Paar that Marshall met Joey Bishop. One of the hottest comedians of his time, Bishop was a regular guest host. Recognizing talent when he saw it, Bishop eventually drafted Marshall for ''The Joey Bishop Show,'' and in 1962 Garry Marshall found himself in Hollywood.

Teaming up with writer Jerry Belson, the two men proceeded to work on the hottest comedy shows of the decade, writing over one hundred episodes of shows like ''The Lucy Show,'' ''The Danny Thomas Show,'' and ''The Dick Van Dyke Show,'' for which they won an Emmy Award for Best Episode of a Comedy. To this day, Marshall enjoys the collaborative process.

In 1967, Marshall and Belson ventured into screenwriting. Their first effort was a motion picture entitled ''How Sweet It Is,'' starring Debbie Reynolds, which the team also produced. That was followed by a film entitled ''The Grasshopper,'' starring Jacqueline Bisset. While both films were well received by the film community, Marshall and Belson's careers as television writers were about to skyrocket. ''I started doing pilots in the '60s. I noticed that certain guys, like Sheldon Leonard ['The Danny Thomas Show'] and Quinn Martin ['The Fugitive']; whatever *they* did got on the air and in a good time slot, too. So I said to myself, 'How do *I* get to be one of those guys?' Well, I got to be one.''[3]

Neil Simon's comedy, ''The Odd Couple'' was the toast of Broadway in the spring of 1965. The play, about the antics of two very different best friends trying to share an apartment and cope

(The hit television series "Laverne and Shirley" starred Penny Marshall [right] and Cindy Williams.)

with divorce, features a hard-drinking sports writer, Oscar Madison and his fuss-budget roommate, Felix Unger. Marshall and Belson thought the play a perfect vehicle for television. Jack Klugman and Tony Randall were cast in the lead rolls. The series aired September 24, 1970 and ran successfully for five seasons. For the rest of the decade Marshall continued to create hit after hit.

"In the education of the American people I am Recess. I do Recess well. My shows are very positive. I still believe in love and having people love each other."[3]

"I do things that I like to see and that please me. Comedy is my tool, and how crazy the comedy or how serious the comedy or how emotional the comedy is up to me and the story. I think that my approach is not to do what everybody else is doing. In television I tried to do things that were counter to what went on . . . . Nostalgia was becoming popular in those days, but all of it was serious. So I made a comedy nostalgia program called 'Happy Days.' There hadn't been one of those on since 'I Remember Mama.' Then I also saw there was a wave of shows featuring bright young women, all of whom had wonderful jobs, lovely clothes and looked like Mary Tyler Moore, . . . there were no blue collar girls on television at all. I also noticed that there was no physical comedy . . . since Lucy left, so I gave 'Laverne and Shirley' some of that stuff. With 'Mork and Mindy,' I found somebody who *had* to be on television because nobody had ever seen a man work like this—Robin Williams. Sometimes I built a

show around a unique talent . . . . I'm just trying to do what other people are *not* doing."[4]

Marshall's brainchild "Happy Days" is a nostalgic trip back to life in the 1950s. In its early seasons the show focused on Richie Cunningham, a rosy-cheeked teen in middle-class Milwaukee. His biggest problems seemed to be how to get a date, when and if to kiss her, and what to do with his chewing gum when he did. Inevitably Richie (played by Ron Howard), at last in a romantic situation, would lean against a doorbell, awakening the girl's grumbling father, or hook his date's sweater on his cufflink, or let his car slip out of gear and into the lake beneath "Inspiration Point." As Richie grew up in the series his awkwardness with girls eased, and he confronted other conflicts usually centered around his academic endeavors. But in all situations his innocence prevailed.

A minor character at the show's inception was Arthur Fonzarelli (played by Henry Winkler). "The Fonz" or "Fonzie," as he was called, ultimately became the star of "Happy Days." The show's audience loved the tough, yet tender, high school dropout who made all the other guys squirm with fear and all the girls squeal with delight. Most of all he gave Richie and his friends lessons in being "cool," Fonzie's forte. Fonzie taught them that it's cool to cry, cool to express one's feelings, cool to be loyal to one's friends and oneself. In the meantime he decided it was uncool to be uneducated and returned to night school so he could receive his diploma with Richie and the other boys.

(Henry Winkler [near left] and Ron Howard [near right] starred in the eleven-year television series ''Happy Days.'')

Another Marshall hit sitcom ''Laverne and Shirley,'' visited ''Happy Days'' before its spin off. Laverne (characterized by Marshall's sister, Penny Marshall) was the feisty and hot-blooded, but nevertheless soft-hearted and innocent, roommate of terminally cute and pert Shirley (Cindy Williams). Both had high hopes of finding, if not rich doctors for husbands, at least dates for Saturday night. Often compared to the slapstick characters played by Lucille Ball and Vivian Vance in ''I Love Lucy,'' Laverne and Shirley frequently found themselves in precarious situations—as guinea pigs in scientific experiments, swimming in a vat of beer, or wrestling with a robot gone berserk in a toy store, for instance.

Another of Marshall's productions, ''Mork and Mindy,'' was inspired by a ''Happy Days'' episode in which Marshall, at the urging of his ten-year-old daughter, introduced an alien from another planet. Mork from Ork (played by Robin Williams) visited Milwaukee and tried to kidnap Richie. Though unsuccessful in that attempt, Mork did succeed in capturing the hearts of the ''Happy Days'' audience. Set in Denver, the series was based on Mork's cultural assimilation and his discoveries of earth customs. Mork was befriended by Mindy McConnell (Pam Dawber), and he moved in with the perky music store clerk.

They eventually married and had a son played by Jonathan Winters. (Orkans are born as adults and get younger as years go by.) The show was extremely well received in its first season, primarily due to Williams' fresh ad-libs and zany antics.

Putting together a weekly situation comedy is not for the faint of heart. Monday morning, the script goes ''to the table'' with the actors. The following two days, the show is rehearsed in a rehearsal hall while the script is constantly being perfected. On Thursday, the company moves to the sound stage where the script is ''blocked'' for three cameras. Friday is show day in front of two ''live'' audiences. ''Funny is funny. On television, in a nightclub, in the theater, movies, no matter where, funny is funny. And the key is the audience. You're funniest when you use the audience. I use the audience as a barometer. I listen to the 300 people, and I can *hear* whether they laugh or don't laugh; so I don't need subjective opinions about what's funny.

''The three-camera technique gives me the best chance to be funny, because I always have three cameras looking at *everything*. I don't have to pick the very best shot until later in the quietness of the editing room. Then I can listen to the audience,

(Pam Dawber and Robin Williams as they starred in the ABC television series ''Mork and Mindy.'')

see where they laughed, and pick the funniest shot. For me it works better than picking the shots electronically as you shoot.

''The . . . technique involves lots of rehearsal. We're often rewriting up to the very last moment. I have even rewritten lines in front of the audience. I welcome contributions from anybody in my shows, because comedy can come from any place. Many of my cameramen have given me funny lines. Gate guards have contributed. The more creative the atmosphere, the better.''[5]

Marshall draws many of his stories from a strong memory of what it was like growing up in the Bronx. But it was not always an easy life. An asthmatic child, Marshall was plagued with allergies. Still, he looks back on his childhood with fondness. ''I had a happy childhood. I was sick all the time, but I remember the happy times. If I get up in the morning and I'm not sick, I know it's going to be a heck of a day.''[6]

''In the neighborhood where we grew up in—the Bronx—you only had a few choices. You were either an athlete or a gangster, or you were funny. We all grew up surrounded by the sense of laughter . . . . I look at life with a bend so I always think I'll have comedy in my work.''[4]

The ''we'' Marshall refers to are sisters, Ronnie Hallin, now a television producer, and Penny, whose career break came when her big brother cast her as Laverne De Fazio in the hit series ''Laverne and Shirley.'' Penny has since become a motion picture director, her biggest hit being ''Big,'' starring Tom

Hanks. She cast Garry in a cameo role in her first film entitled ''Jumpin' Jack Flash'' a fifteen million dollar film starring Whoopi Goldberg.

Eventually, Marshall took a hiatus from his many years in television production. ''I was in television too long. I had done it for twenty years . . . over 1,000 situation comedies—that was the only type of show that interested me in television—and I was no longer . . . scared.''[7] ''I think you have to be a little bit scared in order to do good work—fear keeps a person alert.''

Convinced that television pigeonholes writers and knowing it's up to the writer to break free, Marshall began to direct motion pictures. His first time out, he played it safe directing a crazy comedy called ''Young Doctors in Love.'' After that, he began to choose scripts that reflected his continued interest in the family. ''I come from a pretty close family. I like to do stories about father/son, mother/daughter relationships.''[1]

''The Flamingo Kid'' is a coming-of-age story about eighteen-year-old, Brooklyn-born, Jeffrey Wells (played by Matt Dillon). From a solid, working class family, Jeffrey takes a summer job at an elite club in Far Rockaway called the El Flamingo. Early on, the boy's head is turned by the glamourous life of the club and especially by a high roller supersalesman (played by Richard Crenna), who convinces Jeffrey that the way to ''the top'' is through the school of hard knocks. Jeffrey rebels against his father's beliefs, including long-standing plans for college, in lieu of the fast track and easy money. But as the summer wanes,

(ABC's television series ''The Odd Couple'' starred Jack Klugman and Tony Randall.)

Jeffrey sees that the supersalesman is really a fraud. Disillusioned but wiser, he reconciles with his father, realizing his values are not so old-fashioned after all. ''The Flamingo Kid'' is the type of coming-of-age story that is the hallmark of Garry Marshall's work.

From Richie Cunningham and the Fonz in ''Happy Days'' to Laverne De Fazio and Shirley Feeney in ''Laverne and Shirley,'' to Jeffrey Wells in ''The Flamingo Kid,'' Marshall writes about the dilemmas and ethical choices American teenagers face when trying to grow up: how they fit into their families and how they fit into their society. ''I like to write about young people and how they grow up and what happens to them. I always feel that the three major influences on young people are their parents, their environment and their friends. So, I write about those three subjects a lot.''[1]

Marshall's next film, ''Nothing in Common,'' was a mature variation on the father/son theme. It is the story of successful, but free-spirited, David Basner (played by Tom Hanks), whose prolonged adolescence comes to an abrupt halt when his parents separate and his father, Max (played by Jackie Gleason), becomes chronically ill. ''It is a story about a son having to take care of his father—I'm 55 and my father's now 86 . . . . For the last ten years I've been into that arena of taking care of one's parents as an adult. What I thought made 'Nothing in Common' particularly my kind of story was that David wasn't just an average Joe. He was a very funny person who has to get serious. To me that was interesting because it's not what people are used

to. I think that threw a few people who saw the film. But most seemed to like that it showed a person could be serious and amusing in the same lifetime, which I think is real.''[7]

''The Flamingo Kid'' was a teen story with adult ramifications. ''Nothing in Common'' moves into somewhat meatier areas although the comedy is not far away. Marshall refers to the drama/comedy mix as emotional comedy.

In 1987, Marshall directed ''Overboard,'' a wacky comedy starring Goldie Hawn and Kurt Russell. In this film, Hawn plays the spoiled, rich wife of Edward Herrmann. Suffering from amnesia after she hits her head when she tumbles from her yacht, she is saved by a local carpenter (played by Kurt Russell). Russell happens to be a single father who needs Hawn to fill in as ''mom'' to his four children whom he is about to lose to social services. Once again, the story involves a family, but the film is a light return to traditional comedy affectionately referred to as a ''romp.'' And, it has as it's main topic Marshall's other favorite theme: the love story.

Marshall will certainly continue to direct and write comedies but will always be looking to do what the other guy ISN'T doing. He stresses, ''I would like my films to be more offbeat than anything I did in TV.''[7]

''Television can reach more people, but in film, you can use a little more poignant material. Television is also limited because

(Marshall co-wrote over 100 episodes of ''The Dick Van Dyke Show.'' Broadcast on CBS television, it starred Dick Van Dyke and Mary Tyler Moore.)

of the censorship. Also, there are a lot of actors and actresses I want to work with who don't do television.''[1]

One such film that fits these criteria was his project for 1988. Called ''Beaches,'' it's the film adaptation of the popular novel by Iris Rainer Dart. It stars Bette Midler and Barbara Hershey. ''It's a very strong story about female friendship. I've dealt with a lot of stories about male friendship but I haven't done female friendship since 'Laverne and Shirley.' This story delves into a very dramatic and realistic friendship between two women over a forty-year period of time.''[1]

In any event, whether shooting a dramatic film or a weekly ''sitcom,'' Marshall is clearly a man who is happy with his work. ''I've done . . . over a thousand situation comedies. I can't look you in the eye and say that every one of those episodes was brilliant and perfect. Some *were* perfect. Some were good. Some were pretty good. Some were a little embarrassing—but every piece I've tried to make professional. I've never been ashamed of anything I've done. However, people often don't take comedy seriously. Woody Allen said that comedy isn't better than drama, but it's harder to do. He's absolutely right. Comedy *is* hard to do. Some people will always put you down for doing a certain kind of comedy. When the reviews of 'Nothing in Common' came out, a friend of mine said, 'You know, the reviews are so good that it's now safe to mention your *television* credits.'''[4]

Marshall is leading the life he always imagined, ''I like to make people laugh. I didn't know how I would be doing it but I knew somewhere I would get a chance.''[1]

FOOTNOTE SOURCES

[1]Based on an interview by Deborah Jones for *Something about the Author*.
[2]Maureen Orth and Martin Kasindorff, ''Candy Store,'' *Newsweek*, March 7, 1977.
[3]Dwight Whitney, ''He Can Hiccough and Somebody Will Develop It into a Series,'' *TV Guide*, May 19, 1979.
[4]Michael Singer, ''From the Director's Chair,'' *1987 5th Annual International Edition of Film Directors: A Complete Guide*, Lone Eagle Publishing, 1988.
[5]*Hollywood Reporter* (advertisement), Eastman Kodak Co., 1980.
[6]''Garry Marshall: Having Fun and Happy Endings,'' ABC Motion Pictures Press Department, press release for ''Young Doctors in Love,'' 1982.
[7]Tom Hinckley, ''Garry Marshall: Television's Man with the Midas Touch Turns to Film,'' *Cable Guide*, August, 1987.

FOR MORE INFORMATION SEE:

Life, June 3, 1966.
Time, September 13, 1968, April 29, 1974, December 12, 1977, July 26, 1982.

(Erin Moran and Scott Baio as they appeared on the ABC television network series ''Joanie Loves Chachi.'')

New York Times, January 17, 1974, February 3, 1974, February 8, 1976, May 9, 1980, October 2, 1980 (p. D1ff).
Newsweek, March 29, 1976, March 7, 1977, July 26, 1982.
New West, January 31, 1977 (p. 62ff).
People Weekly, December 25, 1978-January 1, 1979 (p. 70).
New Leader, January 29, 1979.
Saturday Review, March 31, 1979.
Film Comment, July-August, 1979.
Los Angeles Times, September 4, 1979 (p. 8ff), December 13, 1981 (p. 44), December 27, 1984 (p. 1ff).
English Journal, November, 1979.
TV Guide, December 8, 1979 (p. 4ff).
New Yorker, May 19, 1980.
Los Angeles Herald-Examiner, August 28, 1980 (p. B1ff), December 29, 1984 (p. C1ff), April 1, 1987 (p. C1ff).
Contemporary Literary Criticism, Volume 17, Gale, 1981.
Joel Eisner and David Krinsky, *Television Comedy Series: An Episode Guide to 150 Sitcoms in Syndication,* McFarland, 1984.
Beverly Hills 213, August 20, 1986 (p. 6ff).
Character, February, 1988 (p. 1ff).

McCUTCHEON, Elsie 1937-

PERSONAL: Surname sounds like ''Mi-kut-chun''; born April 6, 1937, in Glasgow, Scotland; daughter of Harold (a journalist) and Pearl (a homemaker; maiden name, Jackson) Ballantyne; married James McCutcheon, July 14, 1963 (died, November 21, 1987); children: Alison. *Education:* Glasgow University, M.A. (with honours), 1960. *Politics:* Liberal. *Religion:* Agnostic. *Home:* ''Wendover,'' Sharpes Lane, Horringer, Bury St. Edmunds, Suffolk 1P29 5PS, England.

CAREER: English teacher in comprehensive schools in Glasgow, Scotland, 1961-63; writer, 1968—. Member of Norfolk Archaeology Rescue Group (publicity officer, 1975-77); Horringer Court Middle School, Suffolk, England, co-opted governor, 1988—. *Member:* Writers Guild of Great Britain, Suffolk Institute of Archaeology, Suffolk Local History Council, Friends of the Suffolk Record Office (editor of newsletter, 1985—), Bury St. Edmunds Library Users' Group (committee member, 1987—). *Awards, honors:* Guardian Award Runner-up, 1984, and selected one of Child Study Association of America's Children's Book of the Year, 1986, both for *Summer of the Zeppelin.*

WRITINGS:

JUVENILE

The Moonlight Paupers, Dobson, 1979, Farrar, Straus, 1985.
Summer of the Zeppelin, Dent, 1983, Farrar, Straus, 1985.
The Rat War, Dent, 1985, Farrar, Straus, 1986.
Smokescreen, Dent, 1986.
Storm Bird, Farrar, Straus, 1987.
Twisted Truth, Dent, 1988.

ADULT

Bury St. Edmunds: Historic Town, Alastair Press, 1987.
Norwich through the Ages, Alastair Press, 1989.

Contributor of short stories and articles to periodicals, including *She, Good Housekeeping, Ideal Home, Lady, Annabel, My Weekly, Suffolk Fair, Norfolk Fair, Scotland's Magazine, Eastern Daily Press,* and *People's Friend.*

ADAPTATIONS:

''Summer of the Zeppelin'' (record), Royal National Institute for the Blind, 1986.
''The Rat War'' (record), Royal National Institute for the Blind, 1987.

WORK IN PROGRESS: A young adult novel set in Suffolk during World War II.

SIDELIGHTS: ''I was born in Glasgow, Scotland just in time to become a very young war-evacuee. My father was whisked off to the army. My mother, granny, baby sister, and I went to live in a small holiday town in Argyilshire. Our cottage had no bathroom, an outside water closet, and gas-lamps. But there was a burn (brook) at the bottom of the long garden and a farm across the road, and I never remember being unhappy there.

''My father (who was starting his own career as a writer) used to send me books that had been thrown out of a school his regiment was billeted in. These were mainly German stories! My favourite was *Tales of the Taunus Mountains* which I have to this day. I was addicted to books by the age of five, when I 'swapped' a new pencil-case for a tattered old copy of *Hans Andersen's Fairy Tales,* to my mother's fury.

''I was very unhappy when we returned to Glasgow after the war. Books then became my escape from strange city streets and unknown faces. My father encouraged me to read all I wanted, but my mother used to force me to go out and play with the neighbourhood kids. Gradually she succeeded. I became one of the local gang. In those days there was no television, so we nearly all read a lot. We exchanged books. The boys liked the 'Dr. Dolittle' books and 'Biggles, the Pilot' and the girls went for authors like Noel Streatfeild. As my father now reviewed books for a local paper, I was in clover—being given all the children's books for my opinion.

''At school English was always my best subject. (I was a dunce at math, science, and especially needlework.) But, oddly enough, I never thought of being a writer. My father was the writer of the family. Who was I to compete with him? Besides my mother had made me too convivial in the end. I always wanted to be out and about with a gang. I was either playing cricket or tennis or (later) going off to the Highlands on long cycling holidays.

''At secondary school I became interested in modern languages—French and German. I decided to study these at university. My English teacher was furious. The angrier she got, the more stubborn I became. Later I discovered how astute she had been. Two years of intensive reading and writing foreign languages did terrible things to my own style of writing. I can remember the day when the truth hit me. I chanced on an old school essay and reread it. I knew I didn't have that fluency any more. And I also knew I wanted it back. I decided to stop reading modern languages and switch to English. The whole world was mad at me, it seemed, my French tutor, my parents, my boyfriend, my advisor of studies. But I stood out for what I wanted. Soon I was immersed in English literature.

''It was to be ten years later, though, before I had my first story published in *She* magazine, which was the beginning of my writing career. And seven years after that before an enthusiasm for local history combined with interest in my own young daughter's reading to produce *The Moonlight Paupers,* my first

McCutcheon with two young fans.

children's book. It was not until I wrote *The Summer of the Zeppelin*, though, that I knew I was 'home' at last, that I had found my niche. I love children and I love writing for them. I can think of no happier way of spending my life.

''Nowadays, I find I have more and more invitations to visit schools and talk to the readers of my novels. I cannot remember a single visit that I have not thoroughly enjoyed. The only problem I ever have is that the time flies by too quickly, and quite often I have to go back for a second visit to answer the questions that could not be fit in. The fact that I have a twelve-year-old Shetland sheepdog (who looks like a miniature 'Lassie') and that I could not bear to put him into kennels, means that my school visits have to be local. There are enough schools in my area, however, to keep me busy for quite some time! Since all of my books except *Twisted Truth* have been set in Suffolk, Suffolk youngsters are familiar with the locations. The question I am most often asked is which of my books is my own favorite. Then I have to say *Storm Bird* because it is set in a Suffolk seaside town, and I spent many happy days by the sea steeping myself in the atmosphere before I began writing it.''

HOBBIES AND OTHER INTERESTS: Local history research, gardening, theater (classical music concerts whenever possible), playing the piano, leisure country walking with friends, visiting the local middle school.

FOR MORE INFORMATION SEE:

Bury Free Press (Bury St. Edmunds, Suffolk), September, 1980.
East Anglian Daily Times, January 24, 1986.

McGUFFEY, Alexander Hamilton 1816-1896

PERSONAL: Born August 13, 1816, in Youngstown, Ohio; died at home, June 3, 1896, in Cincinnati, Ohio; son of Alexander (a farmer) and Anna (Holmes) McGuffey; married Elizabeth M. Drake, May 9, 1839 (died, September, 1864); married Caroline V. Rich, 1866; children: (first marriage) Harriet, Daniel, Charles, Edward, Anna, Helen, Alice, Frederick, William; (second marriage) Winthrop, Telford, Harold, Margaret, Kingley. *Education:* Miami University, Ohio, graduated, 1832; also attended Cincinnati Law School. *Residence:* Cincinnati, Ohio.

CAREER: Educator. Woodward College, Cincinnati, Ohio, professor, 1832-1834(?); lawyer in Cincinnati, beginning 1839.

WRITINGS:

Eclectic Progressive Spelling Book, Truman & Smith, 1837 [other editions published as *McGuffey's Newly Revised Eclectic Spelling Book: Showing the Exact Sound of Each*

Syllable, According to the Most Approved Principles of English Orthoepy, W. B. Smith & Co., 1846, American Book Co., 1896; *McGuffey's New Eclectic Spelling Book*, Sargent, Wilson & Hinkle, 1865; *McGuffey's Eclectic Spelling Book*, Van Antwerp, Bragg & Co., 1879, American Book Co., 1896; *McGuffey's Alternate Speller*, edited by William B. Watkins, Van Antwerp, Bragg & Co., 1888; *McGuffey's Speller and Definer*, edited by W. B. Watkins, American Book Co., 1901; *McGuffey's Eclectic Spelling-Book*, Gordon Press, 1976].

McGuffey's Rhetorical Guide, Clark, Austin & Co., 1844, new edition published as *Fifth Eclectic Reader*, 1844 [other editions published as *McGuffey's Newly Revised Rhetorical Guide; or, Fifth Reader of the Eclectic Series*, W. B. Smith & Co., 1853; *McGuffey's New Fifth Eclectic Reader: Selected and Original Exercises for School*, Van Antwerp, Bragg, & Co., 1879, published as *McGuffey's Fifth Eclectic Reader*, with a foreword by Henry Steele Commager, New American Library, 1962, revised edition, Gordon Press, 1974; *McGuffey's Revised Eclectic Fifth Reader*, Van Nostrand].

ALL WITH BROTHER, WILLIAM HOLMES McGUFFEY

McGuffey's Newly Revised First-Fifth Reader, W. B. Smith, 1843-44 [other editions published as *McGuffey's Newly Revised Eclectic First-Fifth Reader*, W. B. Smith, 1853; *Eclectic Readers* (contains *First Reader, Second Reader, Third Reader, Fourth Reader*, and *Fifth Reader*), Van Antwerp, Bragg & Co., 1879, *McGuffey's First-Sixth Eclectic Reader*, Van Antwerp, Bragg & Co., 1879, American Book Co., 1896, revised edition, 1970; *McGuffey's New First-Sixth Eclectic Reader*, Van Antwerp, Bragg, & Co., 1885, American Book Co., 1930; *McGuffey's Alternate First-Sixth Reader*, Van Antwerp, Bragg, & Co., 1887-89; *McGuffey's First-Fifth Eclectic Reader*, American Book Co., 1901].

Sixth Eclectic Reader, Truman & Smith, 1857 [other editions published as *McGuffey's New Sixth Eclectic Reader*, W. B. Smith & Co., 1857; *McGuffey's New Sixth Eclectic Reader: Exercises in Rhetorical Reading with Introductory Rules and Examples*, Sargent, Wilson & Hinkle, 1857, Gordon Press, 1974; *McGuffey's Sixth Eclectic Reader*, with a

flag, and Bess has a little bed for her doll.

Jip is with them. Robert will make him draw Bess and her doll in the cart.

LESSON XXV.

Jāmeṣ	Mā′rў
made	săng
mӯ	lāy
spōrt	spāde
lăp	dĭḡ
dŏll′ṣ	sănd

said (sĕd)   ӯ

"Kate, will you play with me?"

(Illustration from *McGuffey's First Eclectic Reader* by Alexander and William McGuffey.)

foreword by Henry Steele Commager, New American Library, 1962; *McGuffey Revised Eclectic Sixth Reader*, Van Nostrand].

Meddlesome Mattie and Other Selections from McGuffey's Readers, edited by Edith Dickson, Harper & Brothers, 1931.

Old Favorites from the McGuffey Readers, edited by Harvey C. Minnich, American Book Co., 1936, Singing Tree Press, 1969.

McGuffey Readers, nine volumes, Gordon Press, 1973.

McGuffey Reader Update: Homesite Edition, compiled by Milton R. Reuzin, Scott Press, 1975.

The Annotated McGuffey: Selections from the McGuffey Eclectic Readers, 1836-1920, edited by Stanley W. Lindberg, Van Nostrand, 1976.

The Original McGuffey's Eclectic Series, seven volumes (reproduction of 1837 series), Mott Media, 1982.

Also author of *McGuffey Readers Set with Belly Band*, Van Nostrand.

SIDELIGHTS: Alexander McGuffey is remembered today primarily for his collaboration with his older brother, William Holmes McGuffey, on several of the McGuffey *Readers*, by far the most popular schoolbooks of the nineteenth century.

Alexander was responsible for all or nearly all of the *Eclectic Progressive Spelling Book*, originally published in 1837, and

ALEXANDER HAMILTON McGUFFEY

32 *ECLECTIC SERIES.*　　　　　*McGUFFEY'S PRIMER.* 33

LESSON XXVII.

look	gō	John
hēre	all	whēel
mĭll	hăve	round
	ŏŏ　　j	

Look! there are John and Sue by the mill pond.

They like to see the big wheel go round.

They have come to play on the logs and in the boat.

John and Sue will play here all day.

The cows like grass.
They stand in the shade.

(From *McGuffey's Eclectic Primer* by Alexander and William McGuffey.)

McGuffey's Rhetorical Guide, originally published in 1844 and later expanded as *McGuffey's Fifth Eclectic Reader* and *McGuffey's Sixth Eclectic Reader*.

As a prominent attorney and active citizen of Cincinnati, Mc-Guffey never lived his life in the shadow of his renowned brother. Moreover, they presented quite different personalities: while William was a rather dour ecclesiastical presence—appropriate to his station of Professor of Moral Philosophy, and Presbyterian minister—Alexander was a worldly and elegant type. His granddaughter, Alice McGuffey Ruggles, explained: "Alexander was the lucky one. Somehow in an age of wood and pewter he had managed to be born with a silver spoon in his mouth. Petted by his family, tutored by William, praised by the professors at Miami, he never knew the scrabbling struggles for a living and an education that his brother William had endured. Thanks to his Pestalozzian education, he graduated from Miami at sixteen and through William's friends secured a professorship of belles-lettres at Woodward College in Cincinnati. He took up his residence in that city and remained there a pillar of polite society for the whole of his long life."[1]

Biographer Jacob D. Cox noted that: "[William] McGuffey took charge of the education of his brother, Alexander, when the latter was only nine years of age, but already a studious youth. Such indeed was his talent and strong scholarly bent that he completed his college course and graduated at the very early age of sixteen. To so brilliant a collegian it was a matter of course that he should be invited to teach, and he soon became professor of ancient languages in Woodward College, from that time making Cincinnati his home. He was admitted to the bar as soon as he reached his majority, and for nearly sixty years he was an honored member of the legal profession. His tastes led him to seek the quieter walks of business, and the greater part of his life was spent in chamber practice as a counsellor, especially in the management of trusts and the settlement of estates. He was methodical and extremely accurate, conducting business with systematic thoroughness. In arguments he was logical and keen rather than oratorical, and took pleasure in the analysis of strictly legal questions of property rights rather than in appeals to a jury.

"His scholarly training and his love of literature found employments collateral to his professional work, especially in his first year at the bar. He was the active collaborator with President [William] McGuffey in the compilation of McGuffey's *Readers*, the most popular series of school books published west of the Allegheny Mountains. It is understood that the *Fifth Reader* in the series, so well known for its exquisite selections from a very broad field in English literature, was wholly his work, as was the *Speller*, which completed the series. It alone sufficiently shows his early and wide acquaintance with the masterpieces of our language, and his solid judgment in drawing from the 'well of English undefiled.' His fondness for the classi in our own and in the ancient tongues lasted through his life and was a perennial source of pleasure to him and to his friends. He had, too, the gift of a racy humor and a skill with the pencil which, in the way of illustration and caricature, often charmed the circle of his intimates.

"Mr. McGuffey was twice married. In 1839 he married Miss Elizabeth M. Drake . . . by whom he had a large family of sons and daughters. After her death, he married Miss Caroline V. Rich . . . . His children and his children's children followed him with love and reverence, and he saw the good fruit of his own life and principles in their useful lives and honored stations. He retained remarkable physical activity nearly to the end. No acute disease prostrated him, but at the close of the winter his bodily powers gradually failed, and without much pain he slowly and peacefully faded away."[2]

In the year of his death, his fellow Trustees of Cincinnati College published a brief memorial essay. It well sums up the man, his environment and his achievements: "In the death of Alexander Hamilton McGuffey, Cincinnati has lost one of its oldest and most respected citizens. Few indeed are the survivors whose lives reach back to the pioneer period, when Ohio was almost a continuous forest, and the farms of its settlers were sparsely scattered openings in the nearly unbroken woods. What are now its great cities were then mere villages, and its thriving county seats were only hamlets at the cross-roads.

"He died at his home on Mt. Auburn on the 3d of June, 1896, when he was within a few weeks of completing his eightieth year."[2]

FOOTNOTE SOURCES

[1]Alice McGuffey Ruggles, *The Story of the McGuffeys*, American Book Co., 1950.
[2]Jacob D. Cox, *Memorial of Alexander Hamilton McGuffey*, Robert Clarke Co., 1896.

FOR MORE INFORMATION SEE:

Henry M. Vail, *A History of the McGuffey Readers*, Barrows Brothers, 1911.
William Ernest Smith, *About the McGuffeys: William Holmes McGuffey and Alexander H. McGuffey Who Compiled the McGuffey Readers of Which 125,000,000 Copies Have Been Sold*, Cullen, 1963.

McGUFFEY, William Holmes 1800-1873

PERSONAL: Born September 23, 1800, in Washington County, Pa.; died May 4, 1873, in Charlottesville, Va.; son of Alexander (a farmer) and Anna (Holmes) McGuffey; married Harriett Spinning, April 3, 1827 (died, 1853); married Laura Howard, 1857; children: (first marriage) Mary Haines, Henrietta, William Holmes, Charles Spinning, Edward Mansfield; (second marriage) Anna. *Education:* Attended Old Stone (or Greersburg) Academy, Darlington, Pa., 1818-20; Washington College, A.B. (with honors), 1826. *Residence:* Charlottesville, Va.

CAREER: Writer; educator. Taught school in Paris, Kentucky; Miami University, Oxford, Ohio, professor, 1826-36, department head, 1832-36; ordained Presbyterian minister, 1833; Cincinnati College, Ohio, president, 1836-39; Ohio University, Athens, president, 1839-43; Woodward College, Cincinnati, Ohio, professor, 1843-45; University of Virginia, Charlottesville, professor, 1845-73. *Member:* Western Literary Institute, College of Teachers. *Awards, honors:* D.D., Washington College, 1842.

WRITINGS:

The First Eclectic Reader, Truman & Smith, 1836, [other editions published as *The Eclectic First Reader*, Truman & Smith, 1838; *McGuffey's Newly Revised Eclectic First Reader*, W. B. Smith & Co., 1848; *McGuffey's New First Eclectic Reader*, Sargent, Wilson & Hinkle, 1863; *McGuffey's New First Eclectic Reader: For Young Learners*, Wilson, Hinkle & Co., 1863, Gordon Press, 1974; *McGuffey's First Eclectic Reader*, American Book Co., 1892; *McGuffey Revised Eclectic First Reader*, Van Nostrand].
The Second Eclectic Reader, Truman & Smith, 1836 [other editions published as *The Eclectic Second Reader*, Truman & Smith, 1838; *Newly Revised Eclectic Second Reader: Containing Progressive Lessons in Reading and Spelling*, Clark, Austin & Smith, 1853; *McGuffey's New Second*

46   *ECLECTIC SERIES.*

LESSON XXXV.

fĭn'ished	bŏn'net	lĕs'son
sāved		whīte
a wāy'		I've
ăm		wŏrk
seăm'per	rĕad'ў	gär'den

THE WHITE KITTEN.

Kitty, my pretty, white kitty,
Why do you scamper away?
I've finished my work and my lesson,
And now I am ready for play.

Come, kitty, my own little kitty,
I've saved you some milk come and see;
Now drink while I put on my bonnet,
And play in the garden with me.

(From *McGuffey's First Eclectic Reader* by Alexander and William McGuffey.)

WILLIAM HOLMES McGUFFEY

Reader: For Young Learners, Wilson, Hinkle & Co., 1873; *McGuffey's Second Eclectic Reader*, American Book Co., 1879, Gordon Press, 1974; *McGuffey Revised Eclectic Second Reader*, Van Nostrand].

Eclectic Primer, Truman & Smith, 1837 [other editions published as *McGuffey's Newly Revised Eclectic Primer*, W. B. Smith & Co., 1849, Pioneer Historical Society, 1965; *Leigh's McGuffey's New Primary Reader*, Wilson, Hinkle & Co., 1864; *Leigh's McGuffey's New Eclectic Primer*, Wilson, Hinkle & Co., 1864; *McGuffey's Eclectic Primer*, Van Antwerp, Bragg & Co., 1881, American Book Co., 1896, revised edition, 1974, this edition published as *McGuffey's Pictorial Eclectic Primer*, Gordon Press, 1974; *McGuffey's Practice Primer* (designed to accompany *McGuffey's Revised Primer*), Van Antwerp, Bragg & Co., 1888; *McGuffey's Alternate Primer*, American Book Co., 1894; *McGuffey's New Eclectic Primer; In Phonetic Pronouncing Orthography*, H. W. Wilson & Co., 1964; *McGuffey's Pictorial Eclectic Primer* (illustrated by Millicent McGuffey), Buck Hill, 1965; *McGuffey Revised Eclectic Readers Primer*, Van Nostrand].

Third Eclectic Reader, Truman & Smith, 1837 [other editions published as *The Eclectic Third Reader: Containing Selections in Prose and Poetry from the Best American and English Writers*, Truman & Smith, 183(?); *McGuffey's Newly Revised Eclectic Third Reader*, W. B. Smith & Co., 1848; *McGuffey's Newly Revised Eclectic Third Reader, Containing Selections in Prose and Poetry, with Rules for Reading; and Exercises in Articulation, Defining, Etc.*, Wilson, Hinkle & Co., 1853; *McGuffey's New Third Eclectic Reader: For Young Learners*, Wilson, Hinkle & Co., 1873, American Book Co., 1885, Gordon Press, 1974; *McGuffey Revised Eclectic Third Reader*, Van Nostrand].

Fourth Eclectic Reader, Truman & Smith, 1837 [other editions published as *The Eclectic Fourth Reader: Containing Elegant Extracts in Prose and Poetry from the Best American and English Writers*, Truman & Smith, 183(?); *McGuffey's Newly Revised Eclectic Fourth Reader: Containing Elegant Extracts in Prose and Poetry, with Rules for Reading, and Exercises in Articulation, Defining, Etc.*, Sargent, Wilson & Hinkle, 1853; *McGuffey's New Fourth Eclectic Reader*, Wilson, Hinkle & Co., 1857; *McGuffey's Fourth Eclectic Reader*, Van Antwerp, Bragg & Co., 1879, Gordon Press, 1974; *McGuffey Revised Electic Fourth Reader*, Van Nostrand].

The Eclectic Reader, Truman & Smith, 18(?) [other editions published as *McGuffey's Newly Revised Eclectic Reader, Containing Selections in Prose and Poetry, with Rules for Reading; and Exercises in Articulation, Defining, Etc.*, W. B. Smith & Co., 1853; *McGuffey's New Eclectic Reader*, Sargent, Wilson & Hinkle, 1857; *McGuffey's New Eclectic Reader: For Young Learners*, Wilson, Hinkle & Co., 1863; *McGuffey's New Eclectic Reader: Selected and Original Exercises for Schools*, Van Antwerp, Bragg & Co., 1866; *McGuffey's New Eclectic Reader: Instructive Lessons for the Young*, Wilson, Hinkle & Co., 1866].

High School Reader, Truman & Smith, 1857 [other editions published as *McGuffey's New High School Reader: For Advanced Classes*, Wilson, Hinkle & Co., 1857, Van Antwerp, Bragg & Co., 1885; *McGuffey's High School*

7. As soon as he got round the next corner, George stopped, because he was very sorry for what he had done.

8. He said to himself, "I have no right to spend my silver dollar, now. I ought to go back, and pay for the glass I broke with my snowball."

(Illustration from *McGuffey's Second Eclectic Reader* by Alexander and William McGuffey.)

Reader, Van Antwerp, Bragg & Co., 1889; *McGuffey's New High School Reader*, Gordon Press].

Juvenile Speaker, Truman & Smith, 1860 [another edition published as *McGuffey's New Juvenile Speaker: Containing More Than Two Hundred Exercises, Original and Selected, for Reading and Speaking*, W. B. Smith & Co., 1860].

Photographic Reduction of McGuffey's Reading Charts, Van Antwerp, Bragg & Co., 1881.

List of New Words by Lessons of the Primer and First Four McGuffey Readers, compiled by Scott H. Blewett and Benjamin Blewett, E. P. Gray, 1884.

(Editor) *Natural History Readers*, two volumes, Van Antwerp, Bragg & Co., 1887-88.

Also author of *A Treatise on Methods of Reading*, published in England, and *McGuffeys Illustrated Address Book*, and *McGuffey Display Carton Six Address Books Set*, both published by Van Nostrand.

WITH BROTHER, ALEXANDER HAMILTON McGUFFEY

McGuffey's Newly Revised First-Fifth Reader, W. B. Smith, 1843-44 [other editions published as *McGuffey's Newly Revised Eclectic First-Fifth Reader*, W. B. Smith, 1853; *Eclectic Readers* (contains *First Reader, Second Reader, Third Reader, Fourth Reader*, and *Fifth Reader*), Van Antwerp, Bragg & Co., 1879; *McGuffey's First-Sixth Eclectic Reader*, Van Antwerp, Bragg & Co., 1879, American Book Co., 1896, revised edition, 1970; *McGuffey's New First-Sixth Eclectic Reader*, Van Antwerp, Bragg & Co., 1885, American Book Co., 1930; *McGuffey's Alternate First-Sixth Reader*, Van Antwerp, Bragg & Co., 1887-89; *McGuffey's First-Fifth Eclectic Reader*, American Book Co., 1901].

Sixth Eclectic Reader, Truman & Smith, 1857 [other editions published as *McGuffey's New Sixth Eclectic Reader*, W. B. Smith & Co., 1857; *McGuffey's New Sixth Eclectic Reader: Exercises in Rhetorical Reading with Introductory Rules and Examples*, Sargent, Wilson & Hinkle, 1857, Gordon Press, 1974; *McGuffey's Sixth Eclectic Reader*, with a foreword by Henry Steele Commager, New American Library, 1962; *McGuffey Revised Eclectic Sixth Reader*, Van Nostrand].

Meddlesome Mattie and Other Selections from McGuffey's Readers, edited by Edith Dickson, Harper & Brothers, 1931.

Old Favorites from the McGuffey Readers, edited by Harvey C. Minnich, American Book Co., 1936, Singing Tree Press, 1969.

McGuffey Readers, nine volumes, Gordon Press, 1973.

McGuffey Reader Update: Homesite Edition, compiled by Milton R. Revzin, Scott Press, 1975.

The Annotated McGuffey: Selections from the McGuffey Eclectic Readers, 1836-1920, edited by Stanley W. Lindberg, Van Nostrand, 1976.

The Original McGuffey's Eclectic Series, seven volumes (reproduction of 1837 series), Mott Media, 1982.

Also author of *McGuffey Readers Set with Belly Band*, Van Nostrand.

SIDELIGHTS: William Holmes McGuffey was born, the second of eleven children, in a log cabin on his grandfather William's farm in Western Pennsylvania on **September 23, 1800.** The elder William had homesteaded the farm not long after emigrating from Scotland in 1774. McGuffey's father Alexander became an Indian fighter, serving under Generals St. Clair and Anthony Wayne during the Indian Rebellion of 1790-1794

before marrying Anna Holmes, the daughter of a well-to-do farmer who had the none-too-common ability of reading and writing.

When McGuffey was two years old, the family left the comparative comforts of Western Pennsylvania to homestead on the frontier of Ohio, then known as the Northwest Territory. They staked their 160 acres, built a cabin, and established their farm. Living in the wilderness did not afford great opportunity for formal schooling, and McGuffey's early education was largely in the hands of his mother. One story, probably apocryphal, has it that Anna McGuffey was so concerned about her children's education that she prevailed upon her husband to build a road to Youngstown, the closest village with a school. That road is known today as "McGuffey's Road."

Many years later, William McGuffey's granddaughter, Alice McGuffey Ruggles, explained: "When winter came and the road was muddy and the afternoons short and stormy, it was arranged that Jane and William should board at the minister's house, returning home for week ends.

"The clergyman confirmed all that Anna had told him about William's ability and, to the intense delight of both William and his mother, began to teach the lad Latin, in those days the hallmark of learning as distinguished from mere education. He lent William books and put him on the track of borrowing others. The lad would tramp miles to get one and sit up half the night reading, trying to commit the contents to memory before he returned it. With books so scarce, the faculty of memorizing was a help.

"William studied with Mr. Wick until he was fifteen or sixteen. Then his teacher gave him a certificate and advised him to become a roving teacher."[1]

There was no organized system of teacher certification in the subscription school system: the would-be instructor was interviewed by the district school committee to ascertain his appropriateness for the position. Often, letters of recommendation from prominent citizens and credentials from colleges and academies were sufficient guarantee. It is likely that McGuffey's certification from Mr. Wick satisfied the town fathers, for immediately upon graduation he advertised to, "hold a four-month session of school on lot 4, West Union [now Calcutta, Ohio] to tutor all pupils commencing the first day of September 1814."[2]

A subscription teacher would generally canvass a district during vacations for pupils the following winter and the instructor would set up shop only if a sufficient number of students could be located. Forty-eight students enrolled in McGuffey's school. As with other subscription schools, instruction continued for ten to fifteen weeks, eleven hours a day, six days a week. The children brought their own books, usually the *Bible*. When school was out of session, it is likely that McGuffey, like his students, returned home to help with the farm work.

In **1816** brother Alexander Hamilton was born in Youngstown, the sixth of seven McGuffey children. Alexander was later to collaborate with William on the *Readers*.

In **1818** McGuffey enrolled in Greersburg Academy. Another story has it that the Reverend Thomas E. Hughes, headmaster of Greersburg Academy in Greersburg, Pennsylvania, was traveling through the countryside in search of students. It was evening as Reverend Hughes happened to pass the McGuffey homestead where he overheard the muffled voice of McGuffey's mother appealing to her husband to provide for the further education of

140   *ECLECTIC SERIES.*   *SECOND READER.*   141

2. Softly taps the Spring, and cheerly,—
    "Darlings, are you here?"
 Till they answer, "We are nearly,
    Nearly ready, dear."

3. "Where is Winter, with his snowing?
    Tell us, Spring," they say.
 Then she answers, "He is going,
    Going on his way.

4. "Poor old Winter does not love you;
    But his time is past;
 Soon my birds shall sing above you;—
    Set you free at last."

Mary Mapes Dodge.

LESSON LXIV.

lāte	strạw	Jĕn'ny	snôrt'ed	Tĕm'plar
äunt	rō͝gue	re pōrt'	ḡrāz'ing	di rĕet'ly
dĭtch	ăet'ed	sẽrv'ĭçe	sup pōṣe'	⸱ea rĕssed'
hīred	e rĕet'	prĭcked	mō'ment	ḡrō'çer ĭeṣ

JENNY'S CALL.

1. "It's of no use, Mrs. Templar; I have been trying the greater part of an hour

to catch that rogue of a horse. She won't be caught."

2. Such was the report the hired man brought in to Mrs. Templar one pleasant May morning, when she had been planning a ride.

3. "I suppose it can not be helped, but I wanted her very much," she said, as she turned away.

4. "What was it you wanted, mother?" asked Jenny Templar, a bright, brown-haired, brown-eyed girl of twelve, who had just come into the room.

(From *McGuffey's Third Eclectic Reader* by Alexander and William McGuffey.)

their eldest son. Hughes retired to his night's lodgings but returned the next morning to inquire if any "likely lads" were among the McGuffey clan. McGuffey returned with Hughes to Greersburg, where he studied for the next two years.

When he graduated from Greersburg Academy, he attempted to return to teaching. Alice Ruggles recalled: "The town fathers of a new school at Warren, Ohio were looking for a headmaster. William decided to apply. The salary would be small but regular. But he failed to qualify. At the oral examinations, two of the examiners, graduates of Yale, propounded questions he simply could not answer. Bitterly disappointed, he made a brave resolution. He would enroll at Washington College . . . and get a thorough grounding before he attempted anything else.

"William's courses at Washington were Latin, Greek, Hebrew, ancient history, and philosophy. No modern languages, modern history, science, or mathematics. He never felt the lack. The subjects he took were those of the 'higher education,' the old scholastic curriculum that had been handed down from the days of Abelard and before.

"Whatever William studied, he attacked with characteristic thoroughness and made completely his own. His prodigious memory was useful. For years he had known entire books of the *Bible* by heart. But it was impossible to memorize all the classics in four languages. So when he had no money to buy a needed book, he copied out the contents of a borrowed volume, word for word, and bound the pages by hand. Today at Washington . . . they show a Hebrew grammar of William's, copied in this way."[1]

McGuffey's six years of study at Washington College were interrupted by his teaching in rural schools to earn money for his support and education. It was during one of these periods that he came to the attention of Robert Hamilton Bishop who was scouting for professors for his Miami University in Oxford, a tiny village in the backwoods of Ohio. Ruggles related the story: "Bishop was a Presbyterian minister . . . the most distinguished classical scholar in the West and an enterprising person. He had heard of William's attainments and his gift for teaching. He visited the primitive little school and watched the threadbare young teacher with the burning eyes and limber speech conduct his classes. He sought an interview and offered a professorship in ancient languages at Miami, salary $600.

134   *ECLECTIC SERIES.*   *THIRD READER.*   135

LESSON LII.

TRUE COURAGE.

One cold winter's day, three boys were passing by a schoolhouse. The oldest was a bad boy, always in trouble himself, and trying to get others into trouble. The youngest, whose name was George, was a very good boy.

George wished to do right, but was very much wanting in courage. The other boys were named Henry and James. As they walked along, they talked as follows:

Henry. What fun it would be to throw a snowball against the schoolroom door, and make the teacher and scholars all jump!

James. You would jump, if you should. If the teacher did not catch you and whip you, he would tell your father, and you would get a whipping then; and that would make you jump higher than the scholars, I think.

Henry. Why, we would get so far off, before the teacher could come to the door, that he could not tell who we are. Here is a snowball just as hard as ice, and George

would as soon throw it against the door as not.

James. Give it to him, and see. He would not dare to throw it.

Henry. Do you think George is a coward? You do not know him as well as I do.

Here, George, take this snowball, and show James that you are not such a coward as he thinks you are.

George. I am not afraid to throw it; but I do not want to. I do not see that it

(From *McGuffey's Third Eclectic Reader* by Alexander and William McGuffey.)

"William was dazzled. He would have to think it over. There was one 'out'—President Bishop could not wait, the place must be filled at once. If William accepted, he would have to leave Washington without a degree. Would he ever be able to go back? And what about the ministry? He would have to consult his mother.

"He arranged for a substitute to take over the Kentucky school [where he was then teaching] and went back to northern Ohio.

"He thought his mother looked ill and aged. But she greeted him as cheerfully as ever and, on the very first evening, turned over little Aleck's lessons to William while she sat by with sewing.

"Later in the evening, alone with his mother, William said, 'If I go to Miami, let me take Aleck with me.'

"He was surprised when she agreed promptly."[1]

So McGuffey arrived in Oxford in **January, 1826,** accompanied by his ten-year-old brother, Alexander. Wylie wrote to him soon after: "Upon the whole I am inclined to think that you acted wisely in going to Oxford. You had raked up all the information

to be found here, and the prospect afforded you there, of being useful, and at the same time preparing yourself for more extended usefulness in the future, while your funds may be accumulating instead of diminishing, I consider singularly felicitous. I did wish you very much to remain and graduate regularly with us, and afterward to settle in some situation within striking distance of me, and in a more civilized land of the world. But I know it must not be according to my mind and I wish you to be where you will be most useful and happy."[2]

Later that year, the trustees of Washington College voted McGuffey his A.B. degree without his completing the course work.

That same year, McGuffey met Harriett Spinning, the sister of an Oxford merchant. She was four years his junior, and was said to have been beautiful, intelligent, and deeply religious. The courtship was brief, but before he proposed McGuffey wrote to Reverend Wylie to ask his advice. Wylie answered, "I have no advice for those who contemplate matrimony for they are usually bound to commit it."[2]

He was right; they were married in **April, 1827.** Writing in 1892, their daughter Henrietta remembered: "Her maiden name was

what made me say, "Little girl, what do you want?"

5. How she stared at me, just as if nobody had spoken kindly to her before. I guess

she thought I was sorry for her, for she said, so earnestly and sorrowfully, "I was thinking how good one of those gingerbread rolls would taste. I haven't had anything to eat to-day."

(Illustration from *McGuffey's Third Eclectic Reader* by Alexander and William McGuffey.)

Harriett Eliott Spinning. She had been baptised Henrietta but her father for some reason called her Harriett and so in time she got to be called by that name altogether and the name Henrietta was in a manner forgotten until I, her second daughter was born and was called *Henrietta*.

"She was a beautiful woman always but I have been told by a gentleman who saw her when my father brought her as a bride to Oxford that she was *the most beautiful woman* he had ever seen. Her hair was dark brown, her eyes gray, a straight delicate nose and beautiful small mouth. Her hair waved in deep waves all over her head. She wore it from my earliest recollection, curled on each side of her face and kept in place with small shell side combs.

"Oxford was a very small place when my father married and took his bride there, and houses were hard to get. I suppose my father and mother boarded at first. My mother's health failing, Dr. Hughes told my father if he would go to housekeeping he thought his wife's health would be better. So my father had [built] a pretty comfortable two-story brick house painted bright red situated south of the University Campus just across the road from it.

"I have been told it was the third brick house of any built in Oxford and at that time it was considered a very fine house. It is a good house yet although over sixty-years-old. The first four years of my life were spent in this house."[3]

While McGuffey had been hired as a professor of Greek, Latin, and Hebrew, he was more interested in the courses on mental and moral philosophy, a field which encompassed theology, ethics, and metaphysics. At Miami, as at other institutions of the period, those courses were reserved for the college president, and in order to achieve appointment to the chair of moral philosophy, McGuffey is believed to have threatened his resignation. Bishop reluctantly relinquished his chair in moral philosophy to McGuffey in 1832, but soon tensions developed which were to divide the faculty at Miami. While Bishop was socially and theologically liberal, McGuffey was conservative in both areas.

One major point of disagreement was in the area of discipline, and while Bishop and much of the faculty favored giving students a role in the running of the University, McGuffey strongly dissented. The disagreement became quite strong, but McGuffey seems to have prevailed substantially because of his popularity and effectiveness as a teacher. One student's letter of support for McGuffey included this testimonial: "I do not recall that there ever occurred a single instance of unfaithfulness neither in laxity or rigidity in your department. Some severe cases of discipline have occurred . . . . I have seen severity used even to the bringing of tears and to the driving of the individual in fury from the classroom. But I cannot recollect that I have ever seen you even in the strictest moments of severity go further than my judgment approved. I have always been an advocate of strict discipline as you and the other instructors in this institution have long known."[2]

Several reminiscences of McGuffey's personal demeanor and appearance have come down to us, and none would have us suppose that he was anything but reserved in his affections and strict in his observance of discipline. One favorite student recounted: "I can, even now, very clearly recall the dress, appearance, and gait of Professor McGuffey as he entered or left the chapel or his classroom . . . or walked to and from his newly founded family-nest . . . diagonally from the southern campus gate. The fashions of clothes, as of other institutions, have often and greatly changed since those 'primitive' days. If any one now cares to know the Professor's then apparel, it was somewhat thus: A silk stove-pipe hat (these silken shams were just beginning to supplant the honest furs of high-priced Beaver); a complete suit of a certain stuff, called Bombazine, black in color, of the dress pattern; and usually a cane (as I remember), composed his everyday costume. A black broadcloth frock coat was his Sunday, or pulpit, apparel . . . . When it is added that he was most habitually and characteristically neat in his person and apparel, this class of reminiscences ought to suffice."[4]

Another, later recollection was more vivid: "He was a man so ugly as not to be readily forgotten; a huge mouth, a portentous nose, sandy reddish grey hair, worn so long that it curled up a little above his ears, a vast forehead heightened by baldness, keen eyes that snapped and twinkled at you. His dress was wonderfully neat, but the most old fashioned I ever saw outside a museum. For his Sunday morning lectures to his class in Bible Studies he would array himself in a dark blue coat with brass buttons cut somewhat like the evening dress coat of the present day and known from its shape as a 'shadbellied coat.' Around his neck was a high linen collar surrounded by a voluminous black silk stock. When Professor Francis H. Smith first saw him he wore knee breeches with black silk stockings and low shoes fastened with shining buckles. In my time he had reconciled himself to trousers, but it seemed to me that this was his only concession to modernity. When that mouth of his broadened into a smile he looked to me like some genial monster. When he scowled even the young devils in his classroom believed and trembled."[4]

Before taking up his position at Miami University, McGuffey had promised his mother that he would become a Presbyterian minister. Although she died in 1829, McGuffey did not forget his promise. He was ordained in October, **1833.**

McGuffey's skill in oratory, as teacher and cleric, was legendary. A former student recounted: ''As a preacher, lecturer, or orator, Dr. McGuffey's character was so simple and so uniform as to be easily described and understood. His manner as to attitudes and gestures was remarkable for its severe quietude and naturalness. Standing upon his feet firmly and erect, though not ungracefully stiff, he rarely moved from his first position or attitude. His few and slight gestures were so quiet as not to be consciously observed by the spectator. His voice was as moderate in pitch and compass as accorded with his modest gestures. His enunciation was distinct and deliberate; the words were not uttered too rapidly to be easily carried along and understood as utterances of thought—and often of the most profound and refined thought. And so entirely free was he from any vociferation, that this simple phrase—a conversational tone and rate—better expresses his elocution than any longer or fuller list of descriptive epithets could possibly explain it. He spoke without notes, always, and in appearance purely extempore.''[4]

Another former student described his classes in elocution: ''He was an orator, and had a remarkable mastery of language. He made the subjects of his department interesting to the students,

conveyed his thoughts with great clearness and force, and led them to the complete mastery of the subject of study. His students will never forget him in the classroom.

''Nor will they ever forget his instruction in elocution. The students assembled in his study, in the early morning before breakfast, for exercises in elocution. Each was required in turn to declaim before him and the class. The students were thus trained in the art of speaking, and were able to face an audience in the chapel on all occasions requiring public speeches.''[4]

Shortly after arriving in Oxford, McGuffey started a little school to experiment with educational methods. According to his granddaughter, Alice Ruggles: ''The pupils were the children of his friends and later his own little girls, Mary and Henrietta, born in 1830 and '32 . . . . The classroom was the yard behind his home where Harriet cultivated the inevitable flowerbeds, but where the logs lay just as they had fallen, cut from the primeval forest.

''William divided the children into groups, one group to a log. Between times they were allowed to stretch their little legs running about in the open. The scheme was a great success.

''The daily lessons William arranged for these classes gradually took shape as a book. The exercises and some of the stories were original, and other stories were selected and adapted from other books. He had already published in London *A Treatise on Methods of Reading,* which attracted some attention on this side of the water. By 1833 his *First Reader* was ready for printing, but it was several years later that he was approached by the Cincinnati publisher who was to make a fortune out of the *McGuffey Readers.*''[1]

For several years, McGuffey had been preparing the first readers by arranging his students by age and ascertaining their interests, ability, and comprehension by trying out various materials. In the final selection, most of the readings were compiled from other sources, some of them popular textbooks of the time. In fact, after the appearance of the first edition, one publisher brought suit for ''over-imitation'' and copyright infringement. After a few months, the suit was dropped and McGuffey reworked his texts by making minor changes for future editions.

The contract for the first of the *Eclectic Readers* was signed on **April 28, 1836** with the Cincinnati publishing firm of Truman & Smith. Its terms were extremely favorable to the publisher: McGuffey was to receive a royalty of ten per cent up to the receipt of one thousand dollars. After that point, the copyright became the wholly owned property of the publisher. This deal made the publisher quite wealthy, while McGuffey was to receive over the years only token payments beyond the one thousand dollars. Four *Eclectic Readers, The Eclectic Primer,* and *The Eclectic Progressive Spelling Book* appeared in 1836 and 1837. The *Speller* was, in fact, the work of Alexander McGuffey, although he was not then publically credited.

The term ''eclectic'' was first applied to the McGuffey Readers, although it was to be applied widely in later textbooks of all possible subjects.

McGuffey's publishers attempted to increase sales by pitching readers to the regional pride of the South and West. Advertisements for the *Readers* carried such statements as this one from 1838: ''The above works have been prepared by a few untiring laborers in the cause of Education (President McGuffey and others) *for the purpose of furnishing the South and West* with a complete, uniform, and improved set of school books, commencing with the alphabet; and which might obviate the constant

MᶜGUFFEY'S

FOURTH READER.

I. PERSEVERANCE.

1. ''WILL you give my kite a lift?'' said my little nephew to his sister, after trying in vain to make it fly by dragging it along the ground. Lucy very kindly took it up and threw it into the air, but, her brother neglecting to run off at the same moment, the kite fell down again.

(25)

(Page from *McGuffey's Fourth Eclectic Reader* by Alexander and William McGuffey.)

6. It was a trying moment for the poor, little, lonely boy; however, this time he did not ask Tom what he might or might not do, but dropped on his knees by his bedside, as he had done every day from his childhood, to open his heart to Him who heareth the cry and beareth the sorrows of the tender child, and the strong man in agony.

7. Tom was sitting at the bottom of his bed unlacing his boots, so that his back was towards Arthur, and he did not see what had happened, and looked up in wonder at the sudden silence. Then two or three boys laughed and sneered, and a big, brutal fellow, who was standing in the middle of the room, picked up a slipper and shied it at the kneeling boy, calling him a sniveling young shaver.

8. Then Tom saw the whole, and the next moment the boot he had just pulled off flew straight at the head of the bully, who had just time to throw up his arm and catch it on his elbow. "Confound you, Brown; what's that for?" roared he, stamping with pain. "Never mind what I mean," said Tom, stepping on to the floor, every drop of blood in his body tingling: "if any fellow wants the other boot, he knows how to get it."

9. What would have been the result is doubtful, for at this moment the sixth-form boy came in, and not another word could be said. Tom and the rest rushed into bed and finished their unrobing there, and the old janitor had put out the candle in another minute, and toddled on to the next room, shutting the door with his usual, "Good night, gen'l'm'n."

10. There were many boys in the room by whom that little scene was taken to heart before they slept. But sleep seemed to have deserted the pillow of poor

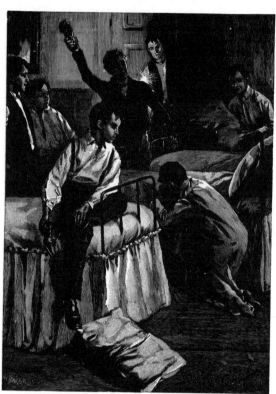

Tom. For some time his excitement and the flood of memories which chased one another through his brain, kept him from thinking or resolving. His head throbbed, his heart leapt, and he could hardly keep himself from springing out of bed and rushing about the room.

(Etching from *McGuffey's Fourth Eclectic Reader* by Alexander and William McGuffey.)

difficulties and perplexities occasioned by the too frequent changes in School Books. The effort has been successful. The fact that SIX HUNDRED THOUSAND of the Eclectic School Books have been disposed of during the short time they have been before the public, is the best evidence of their superior excellency. *They have gone into GENERAL USE and have become the Standard School Books of the West and South.*"[5]

However, as the *Readers* achieved greater success and national distribution, such appeals to local pride became less common until they were replaced with statements disclaiming regionalism. In 1844 the *Fourth Reader* promised that "NO SECTIONAL matter, reflecting upon the local institutions, customs, or habits of any portion of the United States, is to be found among their contents, and hence they are extensively used at the South and at the North, in the East as well as the West."[5]

In 1841, the firm of Truman & Smith was dissolved when the partners decided to go their separate ways. Winthrop B. Smith made Mr. Truman an offer he didn't refuse: that Truman take nearly the entire firm including the rights to most publications, all the cash and all other tangible and intangible assets, while Smith would take only the rights to the textbooks the firm had

published: the six McGuffey books and a few other works. Truman has since faded into obscurity, while Smith, under the corporate name of W. B. Smith & Co., made publishing history and became a millionaire many times over.

The long publishing history of the *McGuffey Readers* extends over 110 years of astoundingly successful sales. Even before 1850 over seven million copies were sold, and by 1890 they had become the basic readers in school systems in thirty-seven states. In all, over 122 million copies were sold from the first to the final printing in 1950, placing their sales in a class with the *Bible* and *Webster's Dictionary*. It is fair to say that no other school books have had anywhere near their impact on the American consciousness. Henry Ford, a great admirer of the *Readers*, wrote, "Most youngsters of my day were brought up on the *McGuffey Readers*. Most of those youngsters who still survive have a profound respect for the compiler of the *Readers*. The moral principles Dr. William Holmes McGuffey stressed, the solid character building qualities he emphasized, are stressed and emphasized . . . today even though the *McGuffey Readers* themselves are not 'required reading.'"[2]

Over the years there were many editions of the *Readers* which were altered to suit the sensibilities of their times. The McGuffey brothers had no role in carrying out or approving revisions of the 1857 editions or any editions after that; all changes to the texts and illustrations were the work of the publishers. And while, eventually, the *Readers* were to seem stodgy, conservative, and out-of-date, at their inception they were quite progressive for their times and far lighter in tone and method from the dour texts familiar to American students. For instance, early nineteenth-century school children might encounter such ditties as this one from *The New England Primer:*

> "There is a dreadful fiery Hell
> Where wicked ones must always dwell.
> "When wicked children mocking said
> To an old man, *Go up Bald Head,*
> God was displeased with them and sent
> Two bears which them in pieces rent."[4]

In **1836** McGuffey resigned from the faculty of Miami University to become President of the newly reorganized Cincinnati College. But the nationwide economic crash of 1837 wreaked havoc everywhere, and in particular with McGuffey's ability to attract donations and endowments from those in the community formerly able to so give. He was soon involved in the liquidation of the College's assets.

However, while at Cincinnati, McGuffey's renown as a speaker continued to grow. There is a story circulating that a group of citizens, unable to crowd themselves into the lecture hall, cut a hole in the ceiling and gathered on the floor above every Sunday to hear his sermons.

In **1838,** the retiring President of Ohio University in Athens wrote to offer McGuffey his post. At that time McGuffey's duties at Cincinnati kept him from accepting, but the following year he changed his mind in view of his altered circumstances. He arrived in Athens in 1839 and immediately sparked discord with the townspeople. Apparently the campus had become the town cow pasture and McGuffey, objecting to this particular form of community service, erected a fence to keep the cows off the grounds. To further enrage local residents, McGuffey sought to revalue rent-generating plots of University lands, as he was required to by public statute.

Whenever he appeared in public, McGuffey was pelted with mud and at least once was burned in effigy. More significantly, the townsmen petitioned the state legislature to reduce the University's appropriation. Further difficulties were caused by McGuffey's very strict discipline, so strict that in 1841 only one of sixteen seniors was able to graduate. Made miserable by these reverses, he resigned in 1843 and returned to Cincinnati to live with Alexander where he taught for a short time at Woodward College, a high school.

By **1845** McGuffey had received an appointment as Professor of Moral Philosophy at the University of Virginia in Charlottesville, a position he was to keep for the rest of his life. The initial faculty vote on his appointment was split, probably for two reasons. Although McGuffey was not an abolitionist, he was known for having emancipationist tendencies, opinions not well received in the South of the time. The other reason was expressed in a letter from a friend: "I do not think it probable that you will obtain the appointment in the University of Virginia. If I am not mistaken the power is chiefly in the hands of those who incline to Infidelity or Episcopacy; and they will not be very likely to give *such* an appointment to a Presbyterian, if they can find men of their own stripe who will be at all competent."[4]

Nonetheless, McGuffey's reputation as a distinguished preacher, educator, and lecturer persuaded the faculty to offer him the position.

Many warm remembrances of McGuffey at Virginia have come down to us. This one from a fellow member of the faculty: "It was a wonderful sight, not to be paralleled in these lazy, degenerate days. When the Rotunda clock struck nine on Sunday morning, Dr. McGuffey stalked into his lecture-room and mounted the rostrum. Every seat would be filled with an attentive, silent throng of students. The talk would begin at once—simple, informal, direct, sententious. He did not appear so much to explain things difficult, obscure, dark; rather he seemed to illuminate them, and then the clouds would lift suddenly and all would seem plain, clear, shadowless, easy. We always resented the substitution of any casual visitor for our own professor.

"McGuffey had discovered a method for himself and had learned to use it with matchless skill. His method was to illustrate every abstract proposition with some concrete example. His felicity and fertility in the application of this method were quite wonderful. He was rich in pungent anecdote, apt in citation from history and literature and life, skillful in analogy. The one phrase you would hear from all his students was, 'He makes us think.'"[4]

In **1853** McGuffey's wife Harriett died of acute appendicitis while on vacation at her family's home in Dayton, Ohio. The next year further tragedy struck him when his fifteen-year-old son Charley died of cholera while on vacation at Lake Champlain, In **1857** he married Laura Howard, the daughter of the dean of the University of Virginia. Their one child, Anna, lived only to the age of four.

McGuffey died in Charlottesville, Virginia of "congestion of the brain" on **May 4, 1873.** During his last years, he was occupied chiefly with writing a massive opus of "Mental Philosophy" in four volumes. None were published, and the work exists only in manuscript at the McGuffey Museum at Miami University.

FOOTNOTE SOURCES

[1]Alice McGuffey Ruggles, *The Story of the McGuffeys,* American Book Co., 1950.
[2]John H. Westerhoff III, *McGuffey and His Readers: Piety, Morality, and Education in Nineteenth-Century America,* Abingdon, 1978.
[3]From the journal entries of Henrietta McGuffey Hepburn, April 5, 1892, in the Walter Havighurst Collections Library, Miami University, Ohio.
[4]Harvey C. Minnich, *William Holmes McGuffey and His Readers,* American Book Company, 1936.
[5]Stanley W. Lindberg, *The Annotated McGuffey: Selections from the McGuffey Eclectic Readers, 1836-1920,* Van Nostrand, 1976.

FOR MORE INFORMATION SEE:

BOOKS

Henry M. Vail, *A History of the McGuffey Readers,* Burrows Brothers, 1911.
M. Tope, *William Holmes McGuffey and a History of the McGuffey School Books; Containing Also a Phrenological Delineation,* Phrenological Era Press, 1929.
W. J. Cameron, *The Mind of McGuffey,* Miami University (Ohio), 1937.
Stanley J. Kunitz and Howard Haycraft, editors, *American Authors, 1600-1900,* H. W. Wilson, 1938.

104 *ECLECTIC SERIES.*

3. To speak within bounds, I am chief person of the municipality, and exhibit, moreover, an admirable pattern to my brother officers by the cool, steady, upright, downright, and impartial discharge of my business, and the constancy with which I stand to my post. Summer or winter, nobody seeks me in vain; for all day long I am seen at the busiest corner, just above the market, stretching out my arms to rich and poor alike; and at night I hold a lantern over my head, to show where I am, and to keep people out of the gutters.

4. At this sultry noontide, I am cupbearer to the parched populace, for whose benefit an iron goblet is chained to my waist. Like a dramseller on the public square, on a muster day, I cry aloud to all and sundry, in my plainest accents, and at the very tiptop of my voice. "Here it is, gentlemen! Here is the good liquor! Walk up, walk up, gentlemen, walk up, walk up! Here is the superior stuff! Here is the unadulterated ale of father Adam! better than Cognac, Hollands, Jamaica, strong beer, or wine of any price; here it is, by the hogshead or the single glass, and not a cent to pay. Walk up, gentlemen, walk up and help yourselves!"

5. It were a pity if all this outcry should draw no customers. Here they come. A hot day, gentlemen. Quaff and away again, so as to keep yourselves in a nice, cool sweat. You, my friend, will need another cupful to wash the dust out of your throat, if it be as thick there as it is on your cowhide shoes. I see that you have trudged half a score of miles to-day, and, like a wise man, have passed by the taverns, and stopped at the running brooks and well curbs. Otherwise, betwixt heat without and fire within, you would have been burnt to a cinder, or melted down to nothing at all — in the fashion of a jellyfish.

6. Drink, and make room for that other fellow, who seeks my aid to quench the fiery fever of last night's potations, which he drained from no cup of mine. Welcome, most

FIFTH READER. 105

rubicund sir! You and I have been strangers hitherto; nor, to confess the truth, will my nose be anxious for a closer intimacy, till the fumes of your breath be a little less potent.

(Illustration from *McGuffey's Fifth Eclectic Reader* by Alexander and William McGuffey.)

Richard D. Mosler, *Making the American Mind: Social and Moral Ideas in the McGuffey Readers,* King's Crown Press, 1947.

Carolyn Sherwin Bailey, *Candle for Your Cake* (juvenile), Lippincott, 1952.

John A. Nietz, *Old Textbooks,* University of Pittsburg Press, 1961.

Dorothy Heiderstadt, *Frontier Leaders and Pioneers* (juvenile), McKay, 1962.

Charles Carpenter, *History of American Schoolbooks,* University of Pennsylvania Press, 1963.

Benjamin F. Crawford, *William Holmes McGuffey: The Schoolmaster to Our Nation,* Carnegie Church Press, 1963.

William Ernest Smith, *About the McGuffeys: William Holmes McGuffey and Alexander H. McGuffey, Who Compiled the McGuffey Readers of Which 125,000,000 Copies Have Been Sold,* Cullen, 1963.

Ruth Miller Elson, *Guardians of Tradition: American Schoolbooks of the Nineteenth Century,* University of Nebraska Press, 1964.

Andrew Curtin, *Gallery of Great Americans* (juvenile), F. Watts, 1965.

Barbara Williams, *William H. McGuffey: Boy Reading Genius* (juvenile), Bobbs-Merrill, 1968.

L. Edmond Leipold, *Famous American Teachers* (juvenile), Denison, 1972.

W. J. Burke and Will D. Howe, *American Authors and Books, 1640 to the Present Day,* 3rd edition, Crown, 1972.

B. F. Crawford, *Life of William Holmes McGuffey,* Carnegie Church Press, 1974.

Robert B. Downs and others, *Memorable Americans, 1750-1950,* Libraries Unlimited, 1983.

Dictionary of Literary Biography, Volume 42, Gale, 1985.

PERIODICALS

Ohio Archaeological and Historical Quarterly, April, 1927.

Christian Science Monitor, September 18, 1935.

Colophon, spring, 1936.

Time, August 3, 1936, July 28, 1952 (p. 52).

Publishers Weekly, September 19, 1936.

New York Times Book Review, January 3, 1937, May 17, 1987 (p. 46).

Journal of the National Education Association, September, 1946 (p. 300ff).

Ohio Schools, September, 1950 (p. 255ff).

112   *ECLECTIC SERIES.*

Haply some hoary-headed swain may say,
   "Oft have we seen him at the peep of dawn
Brushing, with hasty step, the dews away,
   To meet the sun upon the upland lawn:

"There, at the foot of yonder nodding beech,
   That wreathes its old, fantastic roots so high,
His listless length at noontide would he stretch,
   And pore upon the brook that babbles by.

"Hard by yon wood, now smiling as in scorn,
   Muttering his wayward fancies, he would rove;
Now, drooping, woeful-wan, like one forlorn,
   Or crazed with care, or crossed in hopeless love.

"One morn, I missed him on the customed hill,
   Along the heath, and near his favorite tree:
Another came; nor yet beside the rill,
   Nor up the lawn, nor at the wood was he:

"The next, with dirges due, in sad array
   Slow through the church-way path we saw him borne:—
Approach and read (for thou canst read) the lay
   'Graved on the stone beneath yon aged thorn."

THE EPITÁPH.

Here rests his head upon the lap of Earth,
   A youth, to Fortune and to Fame unknown:
Fair Science frowned not on his humble birth,
   And Melancholy marked him for her own.

Large was his bounty, and his soul sincere,
   Heaven did a recompense as largely send:
He gave to Misery (all he had) a tear;
   He gained from Heaven ('t was all he wished) a friend.

(From *McGuffey's Sixth Eclectic Reader* by William and Alexander McGuffey.)

Coronet, July, 1954 (p. 122ff).
Journal of Education, October, 1954 (p. 31ff).
Carnegie, January, 1955 (p. 21ff).
Saturday Evening Post, January 22, 1955 (p. 30ff), April, 1977 (p. 62ff).
American Heritage, August, 1957 (p. 11ff).
Farmers Quarterly, spring, 1959 (p. 76ff).
Nation's Schools, November, 1959 (p. 65).
New York Times Magazine, December 3, 1961 (p. 1ff).
Saturday Review, June 16, 1962 (p. 50ff).
Elementary English, November, 1963 (p. 743ff).
PTA, November, 1967 (p. 6ff).
U.S. News & World Report, May 2, 1983 (p. 76).
Smithsonian, November, 1984 (p. 182ff).

COLLECTIONS

De Grummond Collection at the University of Southern Mississippi.
Walter Havighurst Collections Library, Miami University, Ohio.

MORAN, Tom 1943-

PERSONAL: Born December 5, 1943, in Philadelphia, Pa.; son of George F. (a personnel administrator) and Alice (a social worker; maiden name, Foulk) Moran; married Marilyn Groch (an artist), June 24, 1978; children: Rachel Louise, Michael Thomas. *Education:* California State Polytechnic College (now University), San Luis Obispo, B.S., 1965; California State College (now University), Long Beach, M.S., 1968. *Residence:* Venice, Calif. *Office:* 218 Howland Canal, Venice, Calif. 90291.

CAREER: California Institute of Technology, Pasadena, research engineer at Jet Propulsion Laboratory, 1966-69; free-lance journalist, 1969-74; aide to Los Angeles city council member Pat Russell, 1974-78; *Ocean Front Weekly,* Venice, Calif., editor, 1979; free-lance journalist, 1979-82; Loral Electro Optical Systems, Pasadena, aerospace technical writer, 1982-83; North American Aircraft, Rockwell International, El Segundo, Calif., technical publications supervisor, 1983—. Member of board of advisers of Beyond Baroque Foundation; member of board of directors of Project Heavy West, 1976-78, Venice U.S.A., 1980-82, and Venice Historical Society,

Many are homemade one-of-a-kind models. (From *Kite Flying Is for Me* by Tom Moran. Illustrated with photographs by the author.)

1986—; member of Los Angeles Regional Criminal Justice Planning Board, 1976; member of Southern California Association of Governments Regional Airport Planning Board, 1976-77.

WRITINGS:

(Author of text) *The Photo Essay: Paul Fusco and Will McBride* (illustrated with photographs by P. Fusco and W. McBride), Crowell, 1974.

(With Tom Sewell) *Fantasy by the Sea,* Peace Press, 1980.

Roller Skating Is for Me (juvenile), Lerner, 1981.

BMX Is for Me (juvenile; self-illustrated with photographs), Lerner, 1982.

Frisbee Disc Flying Is for Me (juvenile; self-illustrated with photographs), Lerner, 1982.

(With Andrew David) *River Thrill Sports* (juvenile), Lerner, 1983.

Kite Flying Is for Me (juvenile; self-illustrated with photographs), Lerner, 1984.

Canoeing Is for Me (juvenile; illustrated with photographs by Robert L. Wolfe), Lerner, 1984.

Bicycle Motorcross Racing (juvenile), Lerner, 1986.

A Family in Ireland (juvenile; self-illustrated with photographs), Lerner, 1986.

A Family in Mexico (juvenile; self-illustrated with photographs), Lerner, 1987.

Contributor of articles to *California Living, Chic, Los Angeles, Swank, Canoe, Beyond Baroque, Los Angeles Times Magazine, Los Angeles Times, Los Angeles Herald Examiner, Seattle Times,* and *Washington Post.*

WORK IN PROGRESS: Juvenile novel; a book on traveling with infants and toddlers; a juvenile book on the United States Army, for Lerner.

SIDELIGHTS: ''I ran head-on into the world of books years ago during a summer reading program at the Scranton, Pennsylvania public library. Using a pirate ship theme, the librarians were awarding a certificate and colored stars for reading accomplishments. I started reading to earn a gold star and I don't think I have slowed a bit since then.

''I quickly realized that books could both entertain me and expand my range of experience far beyond the borders of that coal mining city. As my reading prowess increased so did the menu of books I devoured. I read mysteries and novels and books about baseball and boxing, foreign lands and local landmarks, American Indians, soldiers, and cowboys, cars and airplanes. The stories from these pages enriched my own fantasy play and influenced how I approached life. I knew things—knowledge brought to me by books—and thus I discovered new levels of self-confidence in myself. Sticker stars were no longer important, I was on my own voyage of discovery. I think, from those very early years it was clear that one of my goals was to write these wonderful things called books, to continue the chain that fed me.

''Books are still a most important tool. When we added a large addition to our house, doing the work ourselves, I arrived home with books on carpentry, plumbing, and electrical wiring. When our car needs maintenance, I turn to a volume of mechanic's instructions. When it is time to relax, there is deftly written fiction from around the globe. If I need to know how the video recorder, home computer, or stereo works, I am confident that there are books out there that will answer my questions.

''I began writing juvenile books as a free-lance assignment evolving from geographic coincidence. Lerner Publications' editor, Elizabeth Petersen, was in need of an author to write a book on roller skating for an introductory sports series. Roller skating was in the early stages of what would become a major boom of activity, fueled by new technology skates and the public's desire to skate outdoors near parks and beaches. The eye of this roller storm was the California coastal town of Venice, where I live and work. My name was suggested and I soon accepted the challenge.

''Southern California's year round climate proved an excellent base for writing and photographing books in Lerner's 'Sports for Me' series. The most enjoyable part of the preparation was working with the children and parents who helped me by enthusiastically demonstrating their skills for my camera, answering questions for my notebook, and making me understand how the activities were perceived by the young people themselves.

"The most enduring pleasure has been the friendships developed while preparing the two volumes for the 'Families around the World' series. In each case I walked into the life of another family, strangers—separated by culture and distance, even language. For several weeks we were together as they openly shared their daily rituals with me. I asked questions by the shipload and clicked the shutters of my cameras at a nerve-jangling pace. In each case, Ireland and Mexico, I came as an intruder and left as a friend. We continue to exchange letters, phone calls, and year end presents; these books became the catalysts for lasting friendships.''

HOBBIES AND OTHER INTERESTS: Boxing, stamp collecting, ocean swimming.

NEWMAN, Robert (Howard) 1909-1988

OBITUARY NOTICE—See sketch in *SATA* Volume 4: Born June 3, 1909, in New York, N.Y.; died of a brain tumor, December 7, l988, in Branford, Conn. Author. A full-time free-lance writer, Newman was the author of numerous books for children, both fiction and nonfiction. Titles include *The Enchanter, Corbie, The Boy Who Could Fly, Grettir the Strong, The Twelve Labors of Hercules, The Case of the Baker Street Irregular, The Case of the Watching Boy,* and *Night Spell,* a runner-up for the 1978 Edgar Allan Poe Award. Newman, who began his career as a writer for radio shows, also wrote television and movie scripts and contributed verse and short stories to periodicals.

FOR MORE INFORMATION SEE:

Contemporary Authors New Revision Series, Volume 19, Gale l987.
The Writer's Directory: 1988-1990, St. James Press, l988.

OBITUARIES

New York Times, December 9, l988 (p. D-8).

NORTON, Mary 1903-

PERSONAL: Born December 10, 1903, in London, England; daughter of Reginald Spenser (a physician) and Mary Savile (Hughes) Pearson; married Robert Charles Norton (a shipping magnate; deceased), September 4, 1926; married Lionel Bonsey, April 24, 1970; children: Ann Mary, Robert George, Guy, Caroline. *Education:* Attended convent schools in England. *Politics:* Liberal. *Religion:* Anglo-Catholic. *Home:* 102 Town's End, West St., Hartland, North Devonshire EX39 6BQ, England. *Address:* c/o Harcourt Brace Jovanovich, Inc., 757 Third Ave., New York, N.Y. 10017.

CAREER: Writer, 1941—. Old Vic Theatre Company, London, England, actress, 1925-26; actress, London, 1943-45. *Wartime service:* Served two years with the British War Office in England, and two years with the British Purchasing Commission in New York, during World War II. *Member:* P.E.N., Writers and Authors, Society of Authors. *Awards, honors:* Carnegie Medal, 1952, and Lewis Carroll Shelf Award, 1960, both for *The Borrowers; New York Herald Tribune*'s Spring Book Festival Honor Book, and Carnegie Medal Commendation, both 1959, and International Board on Books for Young People Honor List, 1960, all for *The Borrowers Afloat; Are All the Giants Dead?* was selected one of *New York Times* Outstanding Books, 1975.

WRITINGS:

JUVENILE

The Magic Bed-Knob; or, How to Become a Witch in Ten Easy Lessons, (illustrated by Waldo Peirce), Putnam, 1943, published in England as *The Magic Bed-Knob* (illustrated by Joan Kiddell-Monroe), Dent, 1945.
Bonfires and Broomsticks (illustrated by Mary Adshead), Dent, 1947.
Bed-Knob and Broomstick (revised edition of *The Magic Bed-Knob* and *Bonfires and Broomsticks*; illustrated by Erik Blegvad), Harcourt, 1957, reissued, 1975, large print edition, G. K. Hall, 1989.
Are All the Giants Dead? (illustrated by Brian Froud), Harcourt, 1975.

''THE BORROWERS'' SERIES

The Borrowers (illustrated by Diana Stanley), Dent, 1952, published in the United States (ALA Notable Book; illustrated by Beth Krush and Joe Krush), Harcourt, 1953, large print edition, G. K. Hall, 1986.
The Borrowers Afield (illustrated by D. Stanley), Dent, 1955, published in the United States (ALA Notable Book; illustrated by B. Krush and J. Krush), Harcourt, 1955, reissued, 1970, large print edition, G. K. Hall, 1987.
The Borrowers Afloat (illustrated by D. Stanley), Dent, 1959, published in the United States (ALA Notable Book; illustrated by B. Krush and J. Krush), Harcourt, 1959, reissued, 1973, large print edition, G. K. Hall, 1988.
The Borrowers Aloft (illustrated by D. Stanley), Dent, 1961, published in the United States (ALA Notable Book; illustrated by B. Krush and J. Krush), Harcourt, 1961, reissued, 1974.
The Borrowers Omnibus (illustrated by D. Stanley), Dent, 1966, published as *The Complete Adventures of the Borrowers* (illustrated by B. Krush and J. Krush), Harcourt, 1967.
Poor Stainless: A New Story about the Borrowers (illustrated by D. Stanley), Dent, 1971, published in the United States (illustrated by B. Krush and J. Krush), Harcourt, 1971.
The Adventures of the Borrowers, four volumes, Harcourt, 1975.

MARY NORTON

Arrietty snuggled down. (From *The Borrowers* by Mary Norton. Illustrated by Beth and Joe Krush.)

The Borrowers Avenged (illustrated by Pauline Baynes), Kestrel, 1982, published in the United States (ALA Notable Book; illustrated by B. Krush and J. Krush), Harcourt, 1982.

ADAPTATIONS:

''Bedknobs and Broomsticks'' (motion picture; starring Angela Lansbury, Roddy McDowall, and David Tomlinson), Walt Disney Productions, 1971.
''The Borrowers,'' (television special; starring Eddie Albert, Tammy Grimes, and Judith Anderson), NBC-TV, December 14, 1973, (record, cassette), Caedmon, 1974.
''The Magic Bed-knob'' (radio program), BBC-Radio.
''Bonfires and Broomsticks'' (radio program) BBC-Radio.

WORK IN PROGRESS: An autobiography.

SIDELIGHTS: Mary Norton is well known for her ''Borrowers'' series, the seed for which was planted in her childhood days in the countryside of Leighton Buzzard. The stories describe a family of six-inch high people who live in hiding in the houses of human beings. The idea for the books '' . . . seems to be part of an early fantasy in the life of a very short-sighted child, before it was known that she needed glasses. Detailed panorama of lake and mountain, the just-glimpsed boat on a vague horizon, the scattered constellation of a winter sky, the daylight owl—carven

and motionless against the matching tree trunk—the sight of romping hares in a distant field, the swift recognition of a rare bird on the wing, were not for her (although the pointing fingers and shouted 'look-looks' in no way passed her by: on tiptoed feet and with screwed-up searching eyes she would join in an excitement which for her held the added element of mystery).

''On the other hand, for her brothers country walks with her must have been something of a trial; she was an inveterate lingerer, a gazer into banks and hedgerows, a rapt investigator of shallow pools, a lier-down by stream-like teeming ditches. Such walks were punctuated by loud, long-suffering cries: 'Oh, come *on* . . . for goodness' sake . . . we'll never get there . . . . What on earth are you staring at *now*?'

''It might only be a small toad, with striped eyes, trying to hoist himself up—on his bulging washerwoman's arms—from the dank depths of the ditch on to a piece of floating bark; or wood violets quivering on their massed roots from the passage of some sly, desperate creature pushing its way to safety. What would it be like, this child would wonder, lying prone upon the moss, to live among such creatures—human oneself to all intents and purposes, but as small and vulnerable as they? What would one live on? Where make one's home? Which would be one's enemies and which one's friends?

''She would think of these things, as she scuffed her shoes along the sandy lane on her way to join her brothers. All three would climb the gate, jumping clear of the pocked mud and the cow pats, and stroll along the path between the coarse grass and the thistles. On this particular walk they would carry bathing suits in rolled towels because, beyond the wood ahead, lay a rocky cove with a deserted patch of beach.

'''Look, there's a buzzard! There! On that post!' But it wasn't a buzzard to her: there was a post (or something like a post) slightly thickened at the top. 'There she goes! What a beauty!' The thickened end of the post had broken off and she saw for a second a swift, dim shadow of flight, and the post seemed a great deal shorter.

''Buzzards, yes, they would be the enemies of her little people. Hawks too—and owls. She thought back to the gate which so easily the three human children had climbed. How would her small people manipulate it? They would go underneath of course—there was plenty of room—but, suddenly, she saw through their eyes the great lava-like (sometimes almost steaming) lakes of cattle dung, the pock-like craters in the mud—chasms to them, whether wet or dry. It would take them, she thought, almost half an hour of teetering on ridges, helping one another, calling out warnings, holding one another's hands before, exhausted, they reached the dry grass beyond. And then, she thought, how wickedly sharp, how dizzily high and rustling those thistle plants would seem! And suppose one of these creatures (Were they a little family? She thought perhaps they might be) called out as her brother had just done, 'Look, there's a buzzard!' What a different intonation in the voice and a different implication in the fact. How still they would lie—under perhaps a dock leaf! How deathly still, except for their beating hearts!

''Then for this child, as for all children, there were the ill days—mumps, chicken-pox, measles, flu, tonsilitis. Bored with jigsaw puzzles, coloured chalks, familiar story-books (and with hours to go before the welcome rattle of a supper tray), she would bring her small people indoors—and set them mountain climbing among the bedroom furniture. She would invent for them commando-like assault courses; from window seat to bedside table without touching the floor; from curtain-rod to picture rail; from

How cozy those winter evenings could be. (From *The Borrowers* by Mary Norton. Illustrated by Beth and Joe Krush.)

corner cupboard, via the chimney-piece to coal scuttle. To help them achieve such feats she would allow them any material assistance they could lay their hands on: work baskets were for rifling—threads and wools for climbing ropes, needles and pins for alpenstocks. She would allow them the run of any half-opened drawer or gaping toy cupboard; then, having exhausted all the horizontal climbs, she would decide to start them from the floor and send them upwards towards the ceiling. This, she found, was the hardest task of all: chair and table legs were polished and slippery and the walls (except for a large picture called 'Bubbles' and one called 'Cherry Ripe') terrifyingly stark. At this point she would encourage them to build teetering pagodas of strong-smelling throat lozenges on down-turned medicine glasses which would serve them as stairways to greater heights. Long curtains helped with this too, of course, and trailing bedclothes where they touched the carpet. Wicker-work waste-paper baskets also had their uses. After a while she began to realize that there was no place in the room they could not reach at last—given time, privacy, and patience.

"What did they live on? she began to wonder. The answer was easy: they live on human left-overs as mice do, and birds in winter. They would be as shy as mice or birds, and as fearful of the dangers surrounding them, but more discerning in their tastes and more adventurously ambitious.

"In the dull, safe routine of those nursery years, it was exciting to imagine there were others in the house, unguessed at by the adult human beings, who were living so close but so dangerously."[1]

Mary Norton was born on **December 10, 1903** in London, England. Her father, a surgeon, traced his ancestry to the sixteenth-century poet, Edmund Spenser. Her formative years

were spent in the "Manor House" which was often bustling with activity. "My mother would have people stay at the house, and as I, the only little girl, was always having to give up my room for the guests, I sometimes rebelled: 'I'll sleep with Mr. James and I'll sleep with Mr. Molinieux but I won't sleep with Izzy.' Izzy was a very brusque kitchen maid. I was never one of those children who remembered a darling old cook. But we absolutely adored our very beautiful nurse."[2]

The family moved to "The Cedars," a large Georgian house overlooking the old town market to accommodate a growing family which now included a widowed aunt and her daughter. "Around the same time, my godfather's sister, a nun, opened a little school where I was sent as a boarder. It was a terrible place. Prebendary Preedy's sister was tall and aristocratic but cold as ice, and her partner was a rich nun who looked hideously ugly—like a toad. There were only six boarders and I remember writing in my cubicle: 'I'm wretched here.' The two women found my note and told me: 'You are wretched here? Get up, pack your bags and go. We keep you here for very little.' Later I was sent to St. Margaret's Convent in East Grinstead, which was pretty awful too.

"Eventually, it was decided that sharing 'The Cedars' wasn't working out and my father bought a very large practice in Lambeth. The Old Vic and the Lambeth Palace were nearby as well as St. Thomas' hospital where my two elder brothers went to study. The Prince of Wales—husband to Mrs. Simpson—was our landlord. He was a very good landlord and very nice to my father. My brother James was at Osmond and Dartmouth with him, where they contracted chicken pox together. After my father became Mayor of Lambeth, he and the Prince used to meet many times.

(The 1970 Disney movie ''Bedknobs and Broomsticks,'' starring Angela Lansbury, mixed animation with live action.)

''My father's practice was filled with many poor patients and he loved to help them. His wealthy patients were his friends and didn't pay him. When he died, it was discovered that he had very little money left for my mother. The borough found her a flat, overlooking the Oval Cricket Ground—my whole family was mad about cricket.

''After I left my convent school, I was sent to St. James' Secretarial College, where everyone was sending their daughters in hope they would become secretary to the Prime Minister. I was absolutely hopeless and was never able to take shorthand. I made a terrific mess of my first job for McAfee, the great shoemakers. They were going into liquidation and by mistake I added a few naughts to a figure. I was sacked because of it. I sat there with tears rolling down my cheeks and McAfee asked, 'My child, is there anything else you'd like to do?' and I answered, 'I love acting.'

''My first love (and perhaps, still, my last) was the theatre. As the only girl among four brothers I was a tireless impresario, enlisting them and such friends who came to play with us into enacting scene after scene from well-loved and much-read books—or in less conventional (but more melodramatic) improvisations of our own. These performances would take place in the more remote parts of the garden or in various deserted bedrooms of the house away from the watchful eyes of the supervisors. Privacy had to be assured—we never acted our plays to adult audiences, never rehearsed them, and never

attended professional performances. Ours was the 'living theatre,' a dimension born of the moment.''[2]

1925. Entered the Old Vic Theatre to be trained as an actress under the tutelage of manager Lilian Baylis, a formidable character who earned a lasting place in the history of British theater. ''The playwright Arthur Rose ['Me and My Girl'], a friend and patient of my father, was having lunch with us one day, and I told him I'd love to go on stage. My parents remained totally silent but Arthur said: 'Mary would be perfectly all right with Lilian Baylis at the Old Vic. I'll be able to tell you in a minute if you've got any talent, and, if you have, I'll work with you on your audition.' He asked me to learn Juliet's potion soliloquy, and he used to come hear me recite it in our drawing room. I would also go to the theater where he was putting on a musical and I remember delivering Juliet's speech standing in the aisle while looking at a pile of chorus girls rehearsing their high kicks on stage. It was the most extraordinary thing but Arthur would say 'That's all right. It's very good for you.'

''The Old Vic was a big, empty place with what seemed to me a huge stage with just one chair under a light. They were auditioning for members of the company and five male and five female students they were accepting every year. After I gave my speech Lilian Baylis said: 'You've got no voice my dear. Go sit in the back of the stalls, I'll see you before you go.' I waited at the back and was left sitting in the auditorium all alone—she had forgotten I was there.

(From the 1970 Walt Disney movie ''Bedknobs and Broomsticks.'')

''I went home and called Arthur Rose to tell him what had happened. He said: 'You sit down and write one of the best letters you've ever written in your life.' So I sat on the stairs and began my letter 'You say I've no voice, but that's why I want to come and train with you.' There was no reply until weeks later when I received a typewritten note telling me when I should start rehearsals. It was marvelous.

''My two years at the Old Vic were the happiest of my life. We pinned a quotation from Sarah Bernhardt above the wash basin in our dressing room—'If the sacred fire burns in you, you will succeed.' We had a wonderful theater training; we did ballet, fencing, voice production, and had to appear on stage every night in small roles.

''We were privileged to act with great stars and to understudy them. I had to go on as Bianca in 'The Taming of the Shrew' when Edith Evans was playing Katherine. Edith upheld you and was marvelous to work with. She helped me with the first lines I ever spoke on stage. I had to come on cold and say to her, 'Mistress, your master bids you leave your books and help dress your sister's chamber up, you know tomorrow is the wedding day.' Delivering those dull lines is one of the most difficult things a young girl could be asked to do.

''There was always great excitement as to who would be cast as Beauty in 'Everyman.' When it was announced that the part was going to me, I could have died. I never felt beautiful. As a matter of fact, my parents believed children shouldn't be spoiled and

brought me up with an inferiority complex, so being chosen for Beauty was exciting.

''While I was at the Vic the Great Strike of 1926 took place, and Lilian Baylis and the company put on a free musical evening for the strikers. Five female students were turned into chorus girls and, after we finished our part, were told to sit among the strikers. Having lightly clad chorus girls sitting in their midst embarrassed these poor men. I was absolutely apolitical and didn't understand what the strike was about.

''I still lived with my parents but longed to be like the other Vic students, which didn't include having the kind of house where there was a cook and a parlor maid and where someone with a white apron opened the front door.''[2]

1926. Married Robert Charles Norton. Her husband's ancestry was a feudal family domiciled since the end of the Napoleonic Wars. They were terribly rich (shipowners and copper mines) and owned a house in Lisbon and a sizeable estate in the Portugese countryside. Bob Norton was eleven years older than me and I had known him all my life. When I was a child he used to take me to see Peter Pan and to a marvelous tea at Rumplemeyers where he'd fill me with cream cakes.

''He was six-foot-four and startlingly good looking, educated in Zurich, a student of Einstein's. He had taken his exams in three languages, fought World War One as a gunner, and was a very fine horseman and a great oarsman. When I was around eighteen

She rode on a high bicycle with a basket in front, and she visited the sick and taught the piano. (From *Bed-Knob and Broomstick* by Mary Norton. Illustrated by Erik Blegvad.)

Bob became too shy to ring me up, and would send his cousin instead to ask me to a very glamorous lunch. We never had any money other than our pocket money at the Vic, and lunching off a ripe tomato, a boiled egg, and some toasts was marvelous for me. But Bob was a great gourmet and took me to very grand restaurants. I loved good food but wasn't too keen on these gorgeous meals with too much pate de foie and caviar.

"One day Bob asked me if I would like to go to Portugal. 'You know, if you came I wouldn't like to let you go.' I realized I'd had a proposal. Instead of saying 'yes,' I said, 'It's awfully sweet of you,' and he suggested I come to see if I like Portugal. I realized that I would have to accept him in London or not accept him at all. Bob returned to Portugal for three months to install electricity in his seventy-room country house which until then had been lit by oil lamps.

"We were married in September by Prebendary Preedy and the vicar at St. Mary-at-Lambeth, the Lambeth Palace Church. It was a big wedding, all the people from the Old Vic came and remembering the difficulty I had with my lines from 'The Taming of the Shrew,' they inscribed 'You know tomorrow is the wedding day,' on my wedding present.

"We drove to Bob's country estate, 'Quinta das Aguas Livres' ['Estate of the Free Waters']. He left the next morning at the crack of dawn and I was left alone in a large house full of Portuguese servants I couldn't speak to.

"'Quinta das Aguas Livres' had been built around 1870 (the original house had been burnt down). You could see your shadow in the transparencies of the stucco wall. The drawing room was decorated in a Moorish style and the dining room of pear wood could seat forty people. All the linen was embroidered to match. I was waited on by Conceicao Domingos who was very deaf. Whenever there was a question about how to eat something like a dish called Percebos [barnacles], I shot imploring glances at Conceicao Domingos who, with many bows, came and showed me how you twist the little hoof off the barnacles to find the tender bit inside. They're actually delicious.

"The Nortons were an enormous family of very mixed nationalities. On Sundays I would sit at the head of a table of twenty to thirty related guests, and would try to be a good hostess, 'What would you like to do after lunch?' But they all knew the house better than I and were going to do what they had been accustomed to doing—tea on enormous silver trays in the garden, while they embroidered little tray cloths. I felt as though I was on stage again, playing another part. Portugal was about seventy years behind England in its ways.

"I went back to England for each of my children to be born in order that they retain their British nationality. Going back was always a holiday for me. I remember sailing on a ship with Margaret Rutherford when Rudyard Kipling was on board. I was pregnant at the time, and Margaret and I spent the voyage below

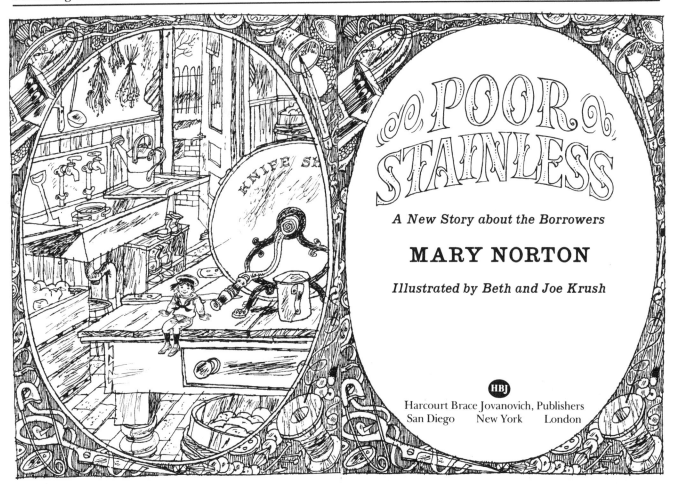

Title page for the 1971 American edition. (From *Poor Stainless* by Mary Norton. Illustrated by Beth and Joe Krush.)

deck living on champagne and dry biscuits while Bob watched Kipling playing bridge.''[2]

Portugal was squarely hit by the Great Depression and Bob Norton's fortune began to disappear. ''A millionaire named Hornung had put a big injection of money into the Norton's business. I had to sign a document stating that my husband had the right to sell the house, if necessary, and I remember Mr. Hornung saying to me just as I was ready to take up the pen, 'My child, you know that you could be signing away everything you own in the world?' My previous life had done nothing to prepare me for this kind of occasion. I signed but I had the sword of Damocles hanging over me the whole time.

''Banks were folding and Mr. Hornung put more and more money into the business, but it was hopeless, and we had to sell the contents of both the Lisbon house and the Quinta estate. We nearly furnished the American Embassy and all the English colony came and bought carpets and eiderdowns.

''My husband had terrible luck. He used to say, 'If I invented a new hat people would have their heads cut off.' He invented brine freezing so that the fish caught on the coast could be taken inland. He borrowed money to build a brine-freezing plant and for the first time in remembered history the fish left the famous sardine port at Setubal. It was a national disaster.

''After that Bob realized that charcoal was very much cheaper in Spain than in Portugal, so he organized trains and rolling stock to import it. On the very evening of transport the Portuguese government put an embargo on the importing of charcoal. I remember Bob's dear proud aunt saying to me, 'My dear, these are the sort of times we can show what we are made of.'

''When World War II broke out, Bob went to the embassy to do his war job while he was waiting to be called up into his regiment. The Norton boys were frightfully patriotic as exiles usually are. I came home to England with two of the children while Guy stayed in Portugal with his aunt and uncle.''[2]

Caroline, Norton's youngest child was born in England in 1939. Shortly thereafter Mary Norton began to work. ''Somebody lent me a studio in London with a balcony where the children could sleep. There were bombings all the time and the air-raid warden used to come around to tell me I was showing a bit of light. Finding a school for the children was a terrific struggle as well. I had to write sixteen letters before I could find a place for my eldest son, but he finally got into Christ's Hospital and Anne went to a Catholic school. I got a job working in Wormwood Scrubbs in a department called MC4D. It was a very hush-hush job tracing cables from all over the world. When Dunkirk happened we were sent to Dover, and I discovered I was working for the Royal Navy under a Commander Bickley. We were there when France fell and witnessed our men coming home absolutely exhausted with their faces all blackened. We visited them in hospital, bought them cigarettes with what little money we had, and put a little piece of orange between their lips.

''After Dover we were posted to Maidstone, Kent to do the same kind of work. The woman who ran the inn thought we were enemy agents and denounced us to the police. At last word came from London that we were Senior Service people and were to be looked after.''[2]

In **1941** Norton was told that there was a war job for her in America. ''As France had now fallen, there was talk of the British government moving to Canada if the same fate overtook England. I landed in New York with three children and forty pounds. Guy was still in Portugal, and I took steps for him to join us because Spain was very Nazi and we didn't know whether they would overrun Portugal.''

''Eventually I was vetted for a MI5 job in America connected with the work I had been doing in England with MC4D. It was based at the British Purchasing Commission.''

''I was put at a desk and had to record the sailings of all boats that came back and forth or had been sunk, and all the factories in America which had been blown up by the Germans and the Gestapo.''

''I was getting more and more fed up with my out-of-date shipping lists and started to write. I had only written one short story for *Strand* magazine, but my new effort was a true story about a mother and her son who were shipwrecked during the war. They tied themselves to what they believed to be a buoy but

"I'll help you," she said. (From *The Borrowers Avenged* by Mary Norton. Illustrated by Beth and Joe Krush.)

was in fact a mine. I sold it to a magazine. The editors were very pleased and encouraged me to write.

''Apart from being in the doghouse at work, I was trying to run the house. I used to have to leave at the crack of dawn for Wall Street, and by the time I got back the children would all be in bed—I hardly saw them. There'd be a sweet letter from Anne, who was about twelve and very responsible, saying something like, 'Good night, sleep tight, and mind the little fleas don't bite.' Anne's school was terribly anti-British and some of the children used to stamp on the union jack. It wasn't an easy time and I decided to leave my job, trust to writing, and lead a much more domestic life.

''I made up *Bonfires and Broomsticks* for my children as a bedtime story. I adored Lolly Willows in Sylvia Townsend Warner's books and liked the idea of an amateur witch. Every editor in New York turned down *Bonfires and Broomsticks* and I threw the manuscript into a drawer. I thought, 'This might come out one day; it might be all right,' but I didn't do anything about it.

''It was brought forth again when a famous American painter, Waldo Peirce, wanted an imaginative vehicle to illustrate. He got seven percent of the profit and I got three percent for my little amateurish piece of writing. Then the *New York Times* praised the writing and not his pictures. Even after that I didn't think of myself as a writer. I was just a lady with four children who had a little house and who had at last published a story.''[2]

In **1942** Norton returned to London with her children. ''In America, my children went to relatively good schools but American education was a lot behind ours in those days and I realized that they must finish their education in England. It was the middle of the war and there seemed to be no way of crossing the Atlantic. One of our sponsors found a Portuguese boat that could take us. Foreign journalists, a few English countesses with their offsprings, two writers, nicknamed Scoop and Extra, were among the passengers.

''We reached Horta in the Azores and the island of Pico which rises into a peak. It was springtime and Horta was beautiful. It was lovely seeing the old burial grounds full of English gravestones. I've always remembered one epitaph which ended with 'Our Jimmy, we thought him dying when he slept and sleeping when he died.' Then we went from island to island collecting torpedoed men who were stranded. Our ship soon became overcrowded. We had three Captains with us and were always afraid that a German submarine would come up. They were said to come up to ask for cigarettes and for any British captains of mercantile marines. Three Portuguese boats had already been sunk; we were told not to discuss the war because there were so many nationalities on board.''[2]

The boat reached its destination safely. Norton with her four children continued her journey by plane from Lisbon to London. There she found schools for her children and went to live in Chelsea. ''I was staying in my mother's little flat when a V2 fell and the force of it detached my retina. I went to the cinema, discovered that I could only see half the screen, and walked over to St. Thomas Hospital. I had difficulty saying it was a war injury because I wasn't actually hit by anything. The doctors told me that I had a fifty-fifty chance of saving my eye if I had an operation.

''I accepted that I might go blind because the doctors were very frank with me. I even started to think of some of the advantages it would have. Other blind people from the ward came to talk with

There was something strangely unreal about this room. (From *The Borrowers Afield* by Mary Norton. Illustrated by Beth and Joe Krush.)

me and I think I was doing my actress bit, playing the brave patient knitting a washing-up cloth.

"I came out of the hospital wearing black-out glasses. My sight improved, but it took five more operations."[2]

In **1947** Mary Norton found an English publisher for *Bonfires and Broomsticks*. "I also started writing short stories for the American market. Had I ever published my short stories as a collection in a book, I would have called them *Bread and Butter Stories* because we needed money badly, yet I would sometimes have to spend three months on one story to get it right."[2]

Norton also had an opportunity to revive her acting career. "It allowed me to pay for my children's school fees. I thought I was back in my old profession and stopped writing."[2]

After Bob Norton's death, Mary Norton married Lionel Bonsey in **1970.** The couple lived on the Essex coast and in Ireland before settling in Devonshire in 1980. Norton now lives in a cottage in Devon. She is a member of P.E.N., is writing short stories, and has been commissioned to write her autobiography. "I work terribly hard and sometimes rewrite a sentence six times over until the emphasis is on the right words and it falls in an interesting way. As long as one word sticks out like a sore thumb, I work on it until it reads so easily that nobody thinks I've worked so hard."[2]

FOOTNOTE SOURCES

[1]Mary Norton, "Introduction," *The Complete Adventures of the Borrowers,* Puffin, 1983.
[2]Based on an interview by Cathy Courtney for *Something about the Author.*

FOR MORE INFORMATION SEE:

New York Times, March 12, 1944, October 18, 1953, November 13, 1955, October 27, 1957, February 22, 1959.
Book Week, March 26, 1944.
Weekly Book Review, June 4, 1944.
New York Herald Tribune Book Review, October 18, 1953, November 13, 1955 (p. 5), October 20, 1957 (p. 10), May 10, 1959 (p. 3).
Saturday Review, November 14, 1953, May 9, 1959 (p. 44), May 15, 1971.
Chicago Sunday Tribune, November 15, 1953, November 17, 1957.
Times Literary Supplement, November 4, 1955, November 15, 1957, December 4, 1959, December 1, 1961, September 19, 1975 (p. 1053), November 26, 1982 (p. 1307).
Christian Science Monitor, October 24, 1957, November 16, 1961.
Ontario Library Review, November, 1958 (p. 207ff).
Manchester Guardian, October 16, 1959.
New York Times Book Review, November 12, 1961 (p. 38), May 2, 1971 (p. 34ff), November 16, 1975 (p. 29ff).

(From the 1973 NBC television special "The Borrowers," starring Judith Anderson.)

Margery Fisher, *Intent upon Reading: A Critical Appraisal of Modern Fiction for Children,* Brockhampton Press, 1961.

Roger Lancelyn Green, *Tellers of Tales,* F. Watts, 1965.

Brian Doyle, editor, *Who's Who of Children's Literature,* Schocken, 1968.

Cornelia Meigs and others, *A Critical History of Children's Literature,* revised edition, Macmillan, 1969.

Eleanor Cameron, *The Green and Burning Tree: On the Writing and Enjoyment of Children's Books,* Atlantic-Little, Brown, 1969.

Norah Smaridge, *Famous Modern Storytellers for Young People,* Dodd, 1969.

Elementary English, February, 1970 (p. 185ff).

Edna Johnson, *Anthology of Children's Literature,* 4th edition, Houghton Mifflin, 1970.

Doris de Montreville and Donna Hill, editors, *Third Book of Junior Authors,* H. W. Wilson, 1972.

"Mary Norton and the Borrowers," *Children's Literature in Education,* Volume 7, 1972.

Marcus Crouch, *The Nesbit Tradition: The Children's Novel in England 1945-1970,* Benn, 1972.

Cricket, January, 1976 (p. 41).

Children's Literature Abstracts, March, 1976.

Language Arts, May, 1976 (p. 538ff).

M. Crouch and Alec Ellis, editors, *Chosen for Children: An Account of the Books Which Have Been Awarded the Library Association Carnegie Medal, 1936-1975,* 3rd edition, Library Association, 1977.

D. L. Kirkpatrick, *Twentieth-Century Children's Writers,* St. Martin's, 1978, 2nd edition, 1983.

Zena Sutherland and others, *Children and Books,* 6th edition, Scott, Foresman, 1981.

Growing Point, November, 1982 (p. 3970ff).

Children's Literature Review, Gale, 1984.

NOVAK, Matt 1962-

PERSONAL: Born October 23, 1962, in Trenton, N.J.; son of Theresa (a factory worker; maiden name, Belfiore) Novak. *Education:* Attended Kutztown State University, 1980-81; School of Visual Arts, B.F.A., 1985. *Home and office:* P.O. Box 686, Hoboken, N.J. 07030.

CAREER: Pegasus Players, Sheppton, Pa., puppeteer, 1979-83; Walt Disney World, Orlando, Fla., animator, 1983; St. Benedict's Preparatory School, Newark, N.J., art teacher, 1986—; Parsons School of Design, New York, N.Y., instructor, 1986—; author and illustrator of children's books. *Member:* Society of Children's Book Writers.

WRITINGS:

JUVENILE; SELF-ILLUSTRATED

Rolling, Bradbury Press, 1986.
Claude and Sun, Bradbury Press, 1987.
Mr. Floop's Lunch, F. Watts, 1990.

MATT NOVAK

AWARDS, HONORS: Rupert Hughes Award, 1960, John Newbery Medal from the American Library Association, Lewis Carroll Shelf Award, and Southern California Council on Literature for Children and Young People Notable Book Award, all 1961, Hans Christian Andersen Award of Merit from the International Board on Books for Young People, 1962, William Allen White Award, and German Juvenile International Award, both 1963, Nene Award from the Hawaii Library Association, 1964, and OMAR Award, 1985, all for *Island of the Blue Dolphins;* Newbery Honor Book, 1967, and German Juvenile International Award, 1968, both for *The King's Fifth;* Newbery Honor Book, 1968, for *The Black Pearl,* and 1971, for *Sing Down the Moon;* Hans Christian Andersen Medal, 1972, for his body of work.

Sing Down the Moon was selected one of Child Study Association of America's Children's Books of the Year, 1970, *The Treasure of Topo-el-Bampo,* 1972, *Child of Fire,* 1974, *The Hawk That Dare Not Hunt by Day,* 1975, and *Zia,* and *The 290,* both 1976; Freedoms Foundation Award, 1973, for *Sing Down the Moon; Child of Fire* was selected one of *New York Times* Outstanding Books, 1974; University of Southern Mississippi Medallion, 1976; Regina Medal from the Catholic Library Association, 1978, for his body of work; *Focal* Award from the Los Angeles Public Library, 1981, for excellence in creative work that enriches a child's understanding of California; Parents Choice Award for Literature from the Parents Choice Foundation, 1984, for *Alexandra,* and 1986, for *Streams to the River, River to the Sea;* Scott O'Dell Award for Historical Fiction, 1986, and one of Child Study Association of America's Children's Books of the Year, 1987, both for *Streams to the River, River to the Sea.*

SIDELIGHTS: ''My work deals primarily with nature. I want to impart my amazement of nature's beauty to children, so that they may gain a sense of the importance of all of it. I grew up in a small town, surrounded by fields and woodland, so these things are important to me. A lot of children don't have the opportunity to experience living in such an environment. I write and illustrate books I would want to buy myself. That's how I judge my own work.''

O'DELL, Scott 1898-1989

PERSONAL: Born May 23, 1898, in Los Angeles, Calif; died of prostate cancer, October 15, 1989, in Mount Kisco, N.Y.; son of Bennett Mason (an official of the Union Pacific Railroad) and May Elizabeth (Gabriel) O'Dell. *Education:* Attended Occidental College, 1919, University of Wisconsin, 1920, Stanford University, 1920-21, and University of Rome, 1925. *Home:* Westchester County, N.Y. *Agent:* Harriet Wasserman, 137 East 36th St., New York, N.Y. 10016. *Office:* c/o Houghton Mifflin Co., 2 Park St., Boston, Mass. 02108.

CAREER: Formerly worked as a technical director for Paramount, and as a cameraman for Metro-Goldwyn-Mayer, a citrus rancher, taught a mail-order course in photoplay writing, book columnist for the *Los Angeles Mirror,* and book editor for the *Los Angeles Daily News,* 1947-55; full-time writer, beginning 1934. *Military service:* U.S. Air Force, 1942-43. *Member:* Authors Guild.

SCOTT O'DELL

WRITINGS:

FOR YOUNG PEOPLE

Island of the Blue Dolphins (ALA Notable Book), Houghton, 1960, large print edition, Isis, 1987.

The King's Fifth (*Horn Book* honor list; illustrated by Samuel Bryant), Houghton, 1966.

The Black Pearl (ALA Notable Book; *Horn Book* honor list; illustrated by Milton Johnson), Houghton, 1967.

The Dark Canoe (illustrated by M. Johnson), Houghton, 1968.

Journey to Jericho (illustrated by Leonard Weisgard), Houghton, 1969.

Sing Down the Moon (ALA Notable Book; *Horn Book* honor list), Houghton, 1970, large print edition, ABC-CLIO, 1989.

The Treasure of Topo-el-Bampo, (illustrated by Lynd Ward), Houghton, 1972.

The Cruise of the Arctic Star (illustrated by S. Bryant), Houghton, 1973, large print edition, G. K. Hall, 1976.

Child of Fire (ALA Notable Book), Houghton, 1974.

The Hawk That Dare Not Hunt by Day, Houghton, 1975.

Zia (ALA Notable Book; illustrated by Ted Lewin), Houghton, 1976, British edition (illustrated by S. Reynolds), Oxford University Press, 1977.

The 290, Houghton, 1976.

Carlota, Houghton, 1977, British edition published as *The Daughter of Don Saturnino*, Oxford University Press, 1979.

Kathleen, Please Come Home, Houghton, 1978.

The Captive, Houghton, 1979.

Sarah Bishop, Houghton, 1980.

The Feathered Serpent, Houghton, 1981.

The Spanish Smile, Houghton, 1982.

The Castle in the Sea, Houghton, 1983.

The Amethyst Ring, Houghton, 1983.

Alexandra, Houghton, 1984.

The Road to Damietta, Houghton, 1985.

Streams to the River, River to the Sea: A Novel of Sacagawea, Houghton, 1986, large print edition, G. K. Hall, 1989.

The Serpent Never Sleeps: A Novel of Jamestown and Pocahontas (illustrated by T. Lewin), Houghton, 1987.

Black Star, Bright Dawn, Houghton, 1988.

My Name Is Not Angelica, Houghton, 1989.

OTHER

Representative Photoplays Analyzed: Modern Authorship, Palmer Institute of Authorship, 1924.

Woman of Spain: A Story of Old California (novel), Houghton, 1934.

Hill of the Hawk (novel), Bobbs-Merill, 1947.

(With William Doyle) *Man Alone*, Bobbs-Merrill, 1953, published in England as *Lifer*, Longmans, 1954.

Country of the Sun, Southern California: An Informal History and Guide, Crowell, 1957.

The Sea Is Red: A Novel, Holt, 1958.

(With Rhoda Kellogg) *The Psychology of Children's Art*, Communications Research Machines, 1967.

Contributor to periodicals, including *Mirror News* (Los Angeles), *Fortnight, Independent* (San Diego), and *Saturday Review*.

ADAPTATIONS:

MOTION PICTURES

''Island of the Blue Dolphins,'' Universal, 1964.

''The Black Pearl,'' Diamond Films, 1976.

CASSETTES; RECORDS; FILMSTRIPS WITH CASSETTES

''Island of the Blue Dolphins'' (cassette; filmstrip with cassette), Pied Piper Productions.

''Island of the Blue Dolphins: An Introduction'' (filmstrip), Teaching Films, 1965.

''The Black Pearl'' (record; cassette; filmstrip with cassette), Miller-Brody, 1974.

''Sing Down the Moon'' (record; cassette; filmstrip with cassette), Miller-Brody, 1975.

''The King's Fifth'' (record; cassette; filmstrip with cassette), Miller-Brody, 1976.

''Child of Fire'' (cassette; record), Miller-Brody, 1976, (filmstrip with cassette), Random House, 1979.

''Zia'' (cassette; record), Miller-Brody, 1977, (filmstrip with cassette), Random House, 1982.

I opened the safe and removed the pearl and held it out to my father. (From *The Black Pearl* by Scott O'Dell. Illustrated by Milton Johnson.)

Island of the Blue Dolphins, The Black Pearl, The Dark Canoe, and *The King's Fifth* are available in Braille. *Island of the Blue Dolphins, The King's Fifth, Child of Fire, The Cruise of the Arctic Star, Sing Down the Moon,* and *Zia* are available as talking books.

I remember the day the Aleut ship came to our island. (Jacket illustration by Evaline Ness from *Island of the Blue Dolphins* by Scott O'Dell.)

WORK IN PROGRESS: Paradise Cove, a contemporary story about dolphins at a training center.

SIDELIGHTS: **May 23, 1898.** Born on Terminal Island, Los Angeles, California, to May Elizabeth Gabriel and Bennett Mason O'Dell, an official of the Union Pacific Railroad, O'Dell's great-grandmother was a first cousin of the Scottish novelist Sir Walter Scott (1771-1832). "Los Angeles was a frontier town when I was born there around the turn of the century. It had more horses than automobiles, more jack rabbits than people. The very first sound I remember was a wildcat scratching on the roof as I lay in bed.

"My father was a railroad man so we moved a lot, but never far. Wherever we went, it was into frontier country like Los Angeles. There was San Pedro, which is a part of Los Angeles. And Rattlesnake Island, across the bay from San Pedro, where we lived in a house on stilts and the waves came up and washed under us every day. And sailing ships went by.

"That is why, I suppose, the feel of the frontier and the sound of the sea are in my books."[1]

"[We also moved] to Claremont, just east of Los Angeles, to the foot of Mount Baldy—sagebrush country where descendants of the first Spanish settlers lived. And to Julian, an old gold-mining town southeast of Los Angeles on the Mexican border, in the heart of the Oriflamme Mountains, the ancestral home of the Diegueno Indians.

"That is why . . . many of the people I have written about are Indians, Spaniards and Mexicans."[2]

"I was four years old and I had awakened out of a long sleep. The room was dark. The sea made faint sounds among the eaves, like mice stirring. From far off came the sound of waves breaking upon the beach. Though I listened, I heard nothing else.

"Lying there in my small bed, in the deep night, it suddenly came to me that the house was deserted, that I was alone. Quickly I slid to the floor and groped along the hall to my mother's room. I felt the bed. It was empty.

"At that instant I heard from a distance the sound of music. By some strange alchemy of love and fear and memory, standing there in the empty room, music and my mother became one. I would find her where the music was. They would be together.

"I tried to open the front door, but it was locked and the back door was locked too. Then I noticed that the window above the kitchen sink was open. I found a chair and climbed upon it and thus reached the window . . . . I grasped the window sill, squirmed outside, hung for a moment, fell sprawling on the sand, and picked myself up.

"Now the music was clear on the summer air. Against the sky I could see the glow of colored lights. I ran toward it, falling in the deep sand and getting up, running again, shirttails dragging at my ankles.

"I came to a boardwalk. The walk led to a pavilion, to the source of the glowing lights, where clusters of people moved about. But the music was still farther, beyond them; and I went toward it, feeling my way through a forest of legs and a sea of dresses, to a place where couples drifted about.

"There on a platform above them was the music and below the platform, the lights shining on her, was my mother. Her back was toward me but I knew well the golden hair. With my last breath I ran across the floor, unaware of the eyes that must have been turned upon me. I stretched out my arms and clutched her dress and though she was whirling, held on. As she turned and stared down at this apparition in a nightshirt, at her son, I am forced to say that she was not so glad to see me as I was to see her.

"The human heart, lonely and in need of love, is a vessel which needs replenishing."[3]

"A boy of eight," O'Dell recalled he was "towheaded and restless, who with other boys of his age went out on Saturday mornings in sun or rain in search of the world.

"This was a small world, but a world in microcosm. It was bounded by the deep water and wharves and mud flats of San Pedro Harbor. By the cliffs and reefs of Point Firmin and Portuguese Bend. By the hills of Palos Verdes, aflame with wild mustard in spring, lion-colored in summer.

"Many summer days we left the landlocked world and went to sea. How? Each of us on a separate log. The logs had been towed into the harbor in great rafts—from Oregon. They were twelve feet long or longer, rough with splinters and covered with tar. But to each of us young Magellans, they were proud canoes, dugouts fashioned by ax and fire. Graceful, fierce-prowed, the equal of any storm.

(From the 1964 Universal film ''Island of the Blue Dolphins.'')

''We freed them from the deep-water slips where they waited for the saw mill. Astride, paddling with our hands, we set to sea, to the breakwater and beyond. We returned hours later, the watery world encompassed.

''Many mornings we went into the Palos Verdes Hills. There we turned over every likely rock, looking for small monsters. We thrust our hands down every squirrel and coyote hole in our path. Commonly we found an owl. This was the prize of all prizes. It was twice the size of your fist, soft-feathered, with great yellow eyes that blinked in the sudden sun.

''What did we do with this creature of the nocturnal air? We killed it, of course. We wrung its neck. We cut off its legs. For the exposed tendons of an owl's legs, when pulled in a certain way, made the tiny claws open and retract in a ghastly simulation of life.

''To this day, indeed to this very minute, I remember these depredations with horror.''[3]

O'Dell was educated at Long Beach Polytechnic High School, then attended Occidental College in Los Angeles, University of Wisconsin, and Stanford University. ''Grammar and high school fascinated me, too. But not college . . . . By this time I had my heart set upon writing. However, most of the courses I was forced to take to graduate had little to do with learning to write. So I forgot graduation and took only the courses I wanted—psychology, philosophy, history, and English.

''I therefore have a sense of comradeship with the students of today. I agree with those who say that they feel like prisoners marching in lockstep toward some unknown goal. I agree that classes are often too large, for I remember a Stanford class in Shakespeare which numbered seventy-six, seventy-five of whom were girls. What can you learn about Shakespeare in such surroundings, even if you're a girl?''[1]

''I had never learned to study—I hadn't the patience, ability or motivation to remember a textbook.''[4]

After college O'Dell moved on to Hollywood and taught a mail-order course in photoplay writing. During **1924** and **1925** he published *Representative Photoplays Analyzed* and worked as a technical director with Paramount Motion Picture Studio. He then attended the University of Rome while working with Metro-Goldwyn-Mayer. ''I was a cameraman on the second company of the original motion picture of 'Ben Hur,' carrying the first Technicolor camera, made by hand at M.I.T., around the Roman countryside.''[1]

After returning to Hollywood O'Dell worked as a book editor for the *Los Angeles Daily News* and as a book columnist for the *Los Angeles Mirror*.

In **1934** he published his first novel, *Woman of Spain: A Story of Old California*. It was inspired by the stories he had heard in the Spanish settlements in the Pomona Valley while working in his father's orange grove near Claremont. With its variegated geography and history, California became a major source of inspiration. ''From the north where the Klamath winds seaward through blue forests south to the sand and rocks and mesquite of the Mexican border, live the Californians. Here among productive orange groves is Riverside, originally a Spanish grant, the town itself founded and flavored by English remittance men and retired Colonial officers. A few miles away on a desert Indian reservation are the pagan sun-worshippers of Palm Springs. A few miles in the other direction is Claremont, home of the eager, thoughtful, and reverent, lush with Eastern greenery planted by missionaries home from Africa and China and the far seas. Here is a town eight thousand feet up in the mountains where the leading citizens are an ex-barmaid from Newcastle and her husband, a feudist from Tennessee. In the Pacific cove is a colony of Portuguese fishermen. In this sunny valley Italians who raise grapes and make wine. And the men of the oil fields. The lumbermen in a hundred camps. The miners who tunnel the Sierras, the Mojave, the Santa Rosas. The Mexicans who live on the fringes of most towns and cities. Hollywood. San Pedro and its tuna fleets. And, of course, the cities of Los Angeles and San Francisco.''[5]

In **1960** *Island of the Blue Dolphins*, his first novel for young adults, was published. ''Places I have known, creatures I have loved are in *Island of the Blue Dolphins*. The islands—San Nicolas, Santa Cruz, San Miguel, Catalina, Anacapa, Todos Santos, San Martin, the Coronados—seen at dawn and at sunset, in all weathers over many years. Dolphin and otter playing. A mother gull pushing her grown brood from the nest,

She had been left behind on the Island of the Blue Dolphins. (Jacket illustration from *Zia* by Scott O'Dell.)

watching them plummet a hundred feet into the sea, then flying down to herd them onto their new home, a rock safe from the tide.

''And finally there is Carolina, the Tarascan girl of sixteen, who lived on the shores of Lake Patzcuaro in central Mexico. She was one of nine children, the oldest daughter of Pedro Flores who took care of the small quinta my wife and I had rented for the summer.

''Carolina, when she first came to work for us, wore a long red skirt of closely woven wool. As a bride her mother had received the gift of sixty yards of this red cloth from her betrothed, a custom of the Tarascans. With it, by winding it around and around her waist, she made a skirt. At night she used it as a blanket for herself and her husband, and later for their children, against the fierce cold of the mountains. For each girl child she cut lengths of the cloth and this in turn became a skirt. The red skirt, the *falda roja* which Carolina wore, came to her in this fashion. She wore it proudly, as a shield against the world, in the way Karana [the heroine of *Island of the Blue Dolphins*] wore the skirt of cormorant feathers. The two girls are much alike.''[3]

''*Island of the Blue Dolphins* began in anger, anger at the hunters who invade the mountains where I live and who slaughter everything that creeps or walks or flies. This anger also was directed at myself, at the young man of many years ago, who thoughtlessly committed the same crimes against nature.

''This horror, muted but nonetheless real, colours the latter part of the book and the latter part only, because my Indian girl began her life, as most children do, in the closed world of selfishness where everything—whether clothed in fur or feathers—was an object of indifferent cruelty.

''Through her I wished to say to the young and to all who wish to listen that we have a chance to come into a new relationship to the things around us. Once, in Defoe's day, we were cunning, manipulative children, living in a palace of nature. In her brief lifetime, she made the change from that world, where everything lived only to be exploited, into a humane and meaningful world.''[6]

Island of the Blue Dolphins was adapted into a film by Universal in 1964.

In **1966** he published *The King's Fifth*, a tale of Conquistadors and Indians pitted against each other throughout much of Mexico and what is now the southwestern part of the United States during 1540 and 1541. Several Spaniards, infected by the lust for gold, set out with a Zuni girl as their guide and interpreter. Yet the treasure, once found, brings them nothing but grief. Finally, Esteban, the young narrator, is sentenced to three years for having thrown the gold into a sulphur pit without having given the king his fifth as required by law. ''Certainly a lot [of research went into] . . . *The King's Fifth*. That was an overly ambitious book when I first started it. All the cities were allegorical cities. I woke up one morning and found that I was competing with Dante. So I quit that and started over.''[7]

In **1967** *The King's Fifth* was a Newbery Honor Book and also received the German Juvenile International Award.

The Black Pearl, his third novel for young readers was based on a legend from Baja, California. It is the story of young Ramon, who finds the Pearl of Heaven in a lagoon believed to be the home of the great Devilfish. After the pearl has failed to buy divine protection from the Madonna for the fleet of Ramon's

Sometimes after winter was over, no corn was left in the bins and everyone went hungry. (From *The Treasure of Topo-el-Bampo* by Scott O'Dell. Illustrated by Lynd Ward.)

father, Ramon finally returns it to her as a gift of love. The book was a Newbery Honor Book and later adapted into a film.

1968. "Some years ago I wrote a story called *The Dark Canoe*. These three provocative words, as you remember, were spoken by Captain Ahab on board the whaler *Pequod* as he pursued through Pacific seas the monstrous White Whale, his implacable enemy, Moby Dick.

"I liked Melville's *Moby Dick* when I first read it as a boy, for its story of a strange captain and crew and their adventurous fate. I liked it when I read it again as a young man, for the same reasons and for others as well—for one thing, the glimpse it gave me into the depths of the human heart. And later, reading it in maturity, these two readings of *Moby Dick* came to mind, but for the first time I began to see Melville's masterpiece for what it is—a fleshed-out symbol, a myth. It is a myth in the tradition of Pygmalion and Galatea, of stone-burdened Sisyphus, of Tantalus, of the ill-starred lovers Orpheus and Eurydice, in which man's feelings of terror at the mysteries of life—its lurking demonisms and its delights, man's most fervent hopes and secret desires—are given substance.

"Having read and thought about *Moby Dick* over many years, aware by returning to it from time to time with refreshed interest and new insights, which to me is the hallmark of a book's greatness, I was moved to write a story about Ahab's dark canoe.

"I was convinced, thinking of the story I wished to write, of the canoe's immortality. It lived in my mind. It therefore must live in the minds of others. And living, having floated Ishmael to safety, not yet finished with its appointed mission, where was it now? On what shores or ocean seas would I find it?

"I imagined it floating into Magdalena Bay in Baja, California, still bearing the marks of the thirty life lines ending in thirty Turk's-head knots, put there by Ahab's carpenter.

"The plot of my story is conventional, but suspenseful enough, I hope, to hold a child's attention, to hold it long enough for the young reader to see and above all to feel what the story attempts to say.

"What I wished to say was both simple and many-leveled. It was this: The stories which have been written by great writers possess lives of their own. They live through the years and through the centuries. They are as substantial as mountains, more lasting than habitations. We know the odes of Sappho, for instance, but under what dust heap lies the place of her birth?"[8]

1969. O'Dell published *Journey to Jericho*, his first book for middle graders. "One of those summers my mother and I traveled across the country to visit an aunt and uncle who lived in a small coal-mining town in West Virginia. The miners with lamps on their caps, the blind mules that shoved the carts back and forth in the mine, the electric dolly that hauled the coal out of the mine, and the small steam engine that pulled it away to the railroad tipple—all these things fascinated me. Remembering them and that long-ago summer, I wrote *Journey to Jericho*."[1]

1971-1972. *Sing Down the Moon* was designated a Newbery Award Honor Book. "In 1961 I spent part of the summer in Navaho country, where the states of Arizona and New Mexico, Colorado and Utah meet. This story about Bright Morning and her flock of sheep is the result of those days among the Navahos. I think of it as a modest tribute not only to this Indian girl but also to the courage of the human spirit."[1]

"The fact that this spirit happened to be in an Indian girl is really incidental. I'm not interested in the Navajos particularly—they're not my favorite tribe even. They were marauders—they rode in and took the crops of other Indians, after the harvest sometimes. But there was this thing that happened [in 1864] at the Canyon de Chelly. Carson and the government rounded up the Indians and drove them to Fort Sumner. The important thing was the story. If the story is a good story children will read it for the suspense, and you can use suspense to do things. In *Sing Down the Moon* I wanted to call children's attention to the fact that there are such things as endurance, as loyalty to your family, loyalty to the place where you live. Nowadays people are dispersed, can live anywhere they want to. That's the trouble here in California—we're just a bunch of uprooted people. You don't know your neighbor and he never speaks to you. But this Navajo girl—she did want to go back to where her family had lived and have a child and live in a cave on the side of the Canyon. Even though she knows her people were driven out, she still goes back and starts over again. I hope there's a lesson in this, an inspiration for children. It's very strong in me, this didactic, inspiration thing."[7]

The Treasure of Topo-el-Bampo was also published. Set during the late eighteenth century in Mexico's poorest mountain village near the country's richest silver mine, the story concerns two small donkeys who save the villagers from starvation when they return loaded with silver bars.

1973. *The Cruise of the Arctic Star* interweaves the author's experiences on a small-craft voyage from San Diego to Portland, episodes from California history, excerpts from books he loves, and information on marine ecology and seamanship.

1974. "[*Child of Fire*] concerns five Chicano gangs and presents a problem that the ancestors of these boys met 400 years ago. Young Spaniards of the sixteenth-century, yearning for adventure, came to the Americas in search of gold. Their descendants, living in modern America, have the same desire for adventure, but no place to find it except in the world of drugs and pointless warfare. The Chicano, for all his proud heritage, is a prisoner of the *barrio*, a second-class citizen. *Child of Fire* deals with his problem, both realistically and symbolically and, I hope, with some understanding.

"Though I don't think you'd find any evidence of it in my present writing, I have been influenced by [Joseph] Conrad. I was a great admirer of his for many years. What he did was more complex than I am able to handle . . . . In *Child of Fire* I have a device which goes back to the Marlow situation in Conrad. I use a parole officer, in charge of fifty children, who tells the story of one particular boy. It has drawbacks of course, because you can only report what you have seen. I have a situation in which the boy leaves San Diego and goes on a tuna clipper to Ecuador, where there's a mutiny and where he's thrown in prison. In the end he escapes and gets back to San Diego. Well, he has to tell this story; there's no other way of getting it. It's not as dramatic as it would have been if the parole officer had gone with him, and so had been able to tell the story himself, like an omnipotent observer. But that was obviously impossible. So there are penalties."[7]

1975. *The Hawk That Dare Not Hunt by Day*, set in England and western Europe in the first half of the sixteenth century, tells about the tribulations of William Tyndale, the first Englishman to translate the *Bible* from Greek into the English vernacular. "I'm terribly interested in his story. He wanted every ploughboy to read the *Bible* as it came from the original Greek and Hebrew, not as it came from the Vulgate, and not as the priest read it in the pulpit. This is what Tyndale wanted to do, and this is what

Gusts of wind swept the ship's bare masts and frayed rigging. (Jacket illustration by Arvis Stewart from *The Hawk That Dare Not Hunt by Day* by Scott O'Dell.)

Tyndale did—and he did it so beautifully that when the King James version came along they used seventy to seventy-five per cent of Tyndale in it. Today we speak Tyndale. It's extraordinary if you compare the passages he translated from the Greek with the same passages in the Latin. If you are really concerned with something it gets into the fabric of the story and is transmitted to the reader. That was D. H. Lawrence's feeling, and it's certainly one I share.

"I have only done things that I've been really enthusiastic about, stories that have stirred me. With Tyndale, and with this messianic quirk of mine, I feel that I am performing a mission; it may be a little grandiloquent to call it that, yet that is my feeling. Children speak the language, but they don't know where the hell it came from. They don't know whom to credit for it, and they certainly don't know Tyndale's story, how the man lived in attics and burrows and was pursued by spies all over Germany, Holland, and Belgium, attempting to seize him and take him back to England. His *Bible* was smuggled into England. It had to be, because it was against the law to own it or read it. He very calmly gave up his life for this purpose. He was a hero.''[7]

1976. *Zia*, a sequel to *Island of the Blue Dolphins* is set in 1853 at the Santa Barbara Mission in California. Fourteen-year-old Zia sets out on an adventurous journey to rescue her aunt, Karana, with whom she then spends a few happy weeks. Throughout the novel various episodes center around the mistreatment of Indians by Spaniards and Americans.

1979. To write *The Captive,* the first volume of a trilogy on Mayan, Aztec, and Incan civilizations, O'Dell had traveled to Central and South America. "I always visit a place I am going to write about. That gives me the true feeling of the locale, the weather, the land, the sky, the people who once lived there.''[9]

From **1980** on, O'Dell lived in Waccabuc, New York, with his second wife, Elizabeth Hall, an author of college textbooks and former editor-in-chief of *Human Nature* magazine. "There's a cave at the head of this lake. A small place where a young woman named Sarah Bishop lived during the Revolutionary War. I became interested in this girl. I began my research, but the only information was one short paragraph about her in a newspaper of the time when she died. I took that sparse information and created *Sarah Bishop.* I put fiction and fact together to create her. Sarah Bishop lives through me and my words.''[9]

1981. The annual Scott O'Dell Award for Historical Fiction was founded; it carries a $5,000 prize. "This award is to encourage writers to write historical fiction, children to read historical fiction, and publishers to publish historical fiction.

"History has a very valid connection with what we are now. Many of my books are set in the past but the problems of isolation, moral decisions, greed, need for love and affection are problems of today as well. I am didactic; I do want to teach through books. Not heavy handedly but to provide a moral backdrop for readers to make their own decisions. After all, I come from a line of teachers and circuit riders going back two hundred years.

"Historical fiction has extreme value for children. Children have a strong feeling that they sprang full-grown from the forehead of Jove. Anything of the past is old hat. But no educated person, however, can live a complete life without a knowledge of where we come from. History has a direct bearing on children's lives.''[9]

Published *The Feathered Serpent,* the second installment and *The Amethyst Ring,* the concluding volume in the trilogy on ancient America and its conquest by Spain.

1984. *Alexandra* is a contemporary novel set in Florida. It features a young woman who joins her grandfather's boat as a sponge diver. As before, O'Dell portrays a woman in an unconventional role. "I have been appalled by the status of women. Women have been treated as second-class citizens. I am didactically in favor of the women's movement. The main character . . . is a typical young woman who does things men usually do. I am trying to show that women and men *do* have the same potential.''[9]

1985. In *The Road to Damietta* sixteen-year-old Ricca tells the story of St. Francis of Assisi, whom she loves. The main historical event is the Fifth Crusade. "I can usually finish a book in six months or so, but I'm going to take a full year for St. Francis. I want to get it right, it's an important book. In it I'm going to make the strongest statement I can against war. It's simply dreadful the way the world is going. It's stupid!

"This book will deal with the futility of war, the immorality of war, and I'm going to make it as strong as I possibly can.''[2]

"Writing is hard work. The only part of it I really enjoy is the research, which takes three or four months.

"I write, when I do write, which is about half my time, from seven in the morning until noon, every day of the week. I use an electric typewriter, because when you turn it on it has a little purr that invites you to start writing instead of looking out the window. I sometimes use a pen and work very slowly. But I can write with anything and anywhere and have—in Spain and Italy, Germany and France, and England and Mexico, in Rancho Santa Fe, a beautiful place in Southern California.

"When I am not writing I like to read and to work in the sun. I like to garden, to plant trees of all kinds, to be on the sea, fishing some, watching the weather, the sea birds, the whales moving north and south with the seasons, the dolphins, and all the life of the changing waters."[1]

According to his publisher, Houghton Mifflin, O'Dell receives over 2,000 letters a year from readers. "There are, of course, a few letters that you would never miss. The letter, for example, from the girl in Minnesota who wrote, asking a dozen or more questions. To have answered them all would have taken two hours, which I didn't have. After a week or so, when she failed to hear from me, she wrote again. She said among other things: 'If I don't get a reply from you in five days I will send a letter to another author I know. Anyway, I like her books better than yours.'

"In their letters children ask dozens of questions. Some are personal, like 'How much money do you make?' but mostly they want to know how you work, how stories are put together, how long it takes to write a story, and what is the most important thing a writer should have."[1]

The day dawned clear and quiet, but now a wind was rising. (Jacket illustration by Ted Lewin from *Alexandra* by Scott O'Dell.)

(Jacket illustration by Ted Lewin from *Sarah Bishop* by Scott O'Dell.)

O'Dell reflected about old age: "I look over the lake and realize I'm living on borrowed time. I tell myself this is a wonderful place to live, and then I sometimes realize it may be the last time I'll see the seasons change; this may be my last winter. It's quite sobering.

"Also, at this age I seem to have nagging memories. I try to fight them, I try not to live in the past. I try not to dwell on them. It's a bottomless pit, living in the past. I'll remember things I did that I shouldn't have done, or things I should have done that I didn't do. I think of some of the relationships that would be very simple for me now, I'd understand them better. My father and I were not very close, for whatever reason. He would never confide in me, he was interested in me only superficially. And yet, if he were here today I believe we'd have a lot in common.

"It isn't self-pity that overcomes me. It's a sense of deep regret. It's not a depression, more of an aggravated melancholy. I get over it as fast as I can!

"Older people lose their rough spots. They've seen so many instances of petty quarrels. For example, I'm now more careful about what I say. I try to understand people better, and as a rule end up understanding them more than I want to."[2]

October 15, 1989. Died of prostate cancer at the age of ninety-one in Mount Kisco, New York. O'Dell wrote right up to the time of his death. He had been working on a novel with an American Indian theme, according to his editor at Houghton

Mifflin, but put it aside to write *My Name Is Not Angelica*. The narrator of the novel about an eighteenth-century slave revolt in the West Indies is the daughter of a Senegalese sub-chief who is captured and sold to Danish slavers. *Publishers Weekly* described the novel as " . . . a moving tribute to the dignity of the human spirit . . . superbly told by a grand master of historical fiction."

"To say that my books were written *for* children is not exactly true. In one sense they were written for myself, out of happy and unhappy memories and a personal need. But all of them lie in the emotional area that children share with adults.

"Writing for children is more fun than writing for adults and more rewarding. Children have the ability, which most adults have lost, the knack to be someone else, of living through stories the lives of other people. Six months after the publication of an adult book, there's a big silence. Or so it is with me. But with a book for children it's just the opposite. If children like your book they respond for a long time, by thousands of letters. It is this response, this concern and act of friendship, that for me makes the task of writing worth the doing."[1]

FOOTNOTE SOURCES

[1]Scott O'Dell, publicity from Houghton.
[2]Allen Raymond, "A Visit with Scott O'Dell, Master Storyteller," *Early Years*, March, 1984.
[3]S. O'Dell, "Newbery Award Acceptance," *Horn Book*, August, 1961.
[4]Conrad Wesselhoeft, "*Blue Dolphins* Author Tells Why He Writes for Children," *New York Times*, April 15, 1984.
[5]S. O'Dell, "An Embarrassing Plenty," *Saturday Review*, October 30, 1943.
[6]S. O'Dell, *Psychology Today*, January, 1968.
[7]Justin Wintle and Emma Fisher, *The Pied Pipers: Interviews with the Influential Creators of Children's Literature*, Paddington Press, 1974.
[8]S. O'Dell, "Acceptance Speech: Hans Christian Andersen Award," *Horn Book*, October, 1972.
[9]Peter Roop, "Profile: Scott O'Dell," *Language Arts*, November, 1984.

FOR MORE INFORMATION SEE:

New York Times Book Review, October, 1947 (p. 8), March 25, 1973 (p. 8), February 22, 1976 (p. 18), February 24, 1980 (p. 33), May 4, 1980 (p. 26), January 10, 1986 (p. 26).
Harry Warfel, *American Novelists of Today*, American Book, 1951.
Horn Book, April, 1960, December, 1974 (p. 695ff), June, 1976 (p. 291ff), April, 1977 (p. 160ff), April, 1982 (p. 137ff), June, 1983 (p. 315), February, 1984 (p. 94ff), September-October, 1986 (p. 599).
Chicago Sunday Tribune, May 8, 1960.
New York Herald Tribune Book Review, May 8, 1960.
San Francisco Chronicle, May 8, 1960.
Scott O'Dell, "Author's Note," *Island of the Blue Dolphins*, Houghton, 1960.
Library Journal, March 15, 1961 (p. 116ff).
Publishers Weekly, March 20, 1961 (p. 28ff), November 15, 1971 (p. 21), September 11, 1981 (p. 29).
American Library Association Bulletin, April, 1961 (p. 359).
Elementary English, October, 1961 (p. 373ff), April, 1975 (p. 442ff).
Wilson Library Bulletin, December, 1961 (p. 325).
Muriel Fuller, editor, *More Junior Authors*, H. W. Wilson, 1961.

John Rowe Townsend, *Written for Children: An Outline of English Language Children's Literature*, Lippincott, 1965.
Lee Kingman, editor, *Newbery and Caldecott Medal Books 1956-1965*, Horn Book, 1965.
Cornelia Meigs, editor, *A Critical History of Children's Literature*, Macmillan, 1969.
Constantine Georgiou, *Children and Their Literature*, Prentice-Hall, 1969.
J. R. Townsend, *A Sense of Story: Essays on Contemporary Writers for Children*, Lippincott, 1971.
Martha E. Ward and Dorothy A. Marquardt, *Authors of Books for Young People*, 2nd edition, Scarecrow, 1971.
Miriam Hoffman and Eva Samuels, *Authors and Illustrators of Children's Books*, Bowker, 1972.
American Libraries, June, 1973 (p. 356ff).
Author's Choice 2, Crowell, 1974.
"Meet the Newbery Author: Scott O'Dell" (filmstrip with record or cassette), Miller-Brody, 1974.
"Scott O'Dell" (videotape), Profiles in Literature, Temple University, 1976.
Children's Literature Review, Gale, Volume 1, 1976, Volume 16, 1989.
Catholic Library World, March, 1978 (p. 340ff).
D. L. Kirkpatrick, editor, *Twentieth-Century Children's Writers*, St. Martin's, 1978, 2nd edition, 1983.
Washington Post Book World, March 9, 1980 (p. 7), January 9, 1983 (p. 11ff).
Jim Roginski, compiler, *Newbery and Caldecott Medalists and Honor Book Winners*, Libraries Unlimited, 1982.
Linda Kauffman Peterson and Marilyn Leathers Solt, *Newbery and Caldecott Medal and Honor Books, an Annotated Bibliography*, G. K. Hall, 1982.

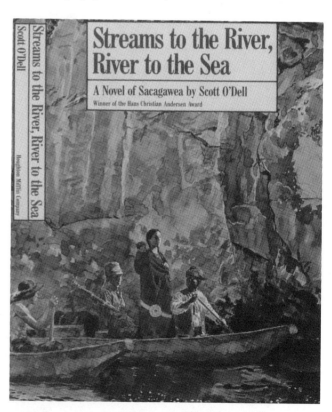

We rode all night toward the star that shines in the north, the one that never moves. (Jacket illustration by Ted Lewin from *Streams to the River, River to the Sea* by Scott O'Dell.)

Contemporary Authors, New Revision Series, Volume 12, Gale, 1984.
Contemporary Literary Criticism, Volume 30, Gale, 1984.
English Journal, April, 1984 (p. 69ff).
"A Visit with Scott O'Dell" (videotape), Houghton, 1986.
Dictionary of Literary Biography, Volume 52, Gale, 1986.

COLLECTIONS

De Grummond Collection at the University of Southern Mississippi.
Free Library of Philadelphia, Pennsylvania.
University of Oregon Library, Eugene.

OZ, Frank (Richard) 1944-

PERSONAL: Born May 24, 1944, in Hereford, England; son of Isidore (a window trimmer) and Frances Oznowicz; married Robin Garsen (a painter), December, 1979. *Education:* Attended Oakland City College, 1962. *Office:* Henson Associates, 117 East 69th St., New York, N.Y. 10024.

CAREER: Puppeteer, began with Jim Henson in 1963, characters include Fozzie Bear, Animal, Sam Eagle, Cookie Monster, Bert, Grover, and Miss Piggy; puppets have appeared on the television shows "The Muppets," "Sesame Street," and "Don't Eat the Pictures: Sesame Street at the Metropolitan Museum of Art," and in films; Henson Associates, New York, N.Y., vice-president and producer; creator and performer of Yoda in film "Empire Strikes Back"; creator and performer of characters Aughra and Chamberlain of the Skeksis in the film "The Dark Crystal"; co-director and director of films. *Member:* American Federation of Television and Radio Artists, Screen Actors Guild, Academy of Television Arts and Sciences. *Awards, honors:* Emmy Award from the Academy of Television Arts and Sciences for Outstanding Variety Series, 1977, for "The Muppet Show," and for Outstanding Performance.

WRITINGS:

(And director) "The Muppets Take Manhattan" (motion picture), Tri-Star, 1984.
(With Howard Ashman; and director) "The Little Shop of Horrors" (motion picture based on Ashman's play), Warner Bros., 1986.

DIRECTOR

(With Jim Henson) "The Muppet Movie," Associated Film, 1979.
(With J. Henson) "The Dark Crystal," Universal Pictures and Associated Film, 1982.
"Dirty Rotten Scoundrels" (motion picture), starring Michael Caine and Steve Martin, Orion Pictures, 1988.

PRODUCER

(With David Lazer) "The Great Muppet Caper," Associated Film, 1981.

RECORDINGS

"A Christmas Together," sung by John Denver, Oz, Jim Henson, and others performing as various Muppet characters, RCA Victor, 1979.

WORK IN PROGRESS: Directing "Mermaids," starring Cher and Winona Ryder, for Orion.

SIDELIGHTS: Born Frank Oznowicz in England in **1944,** Oz was only five when his parents emigrated to Northern California. "I remember very little before coming to the States, but Europe is very important to me. Unfortunately, most of my relatives died during the war in concentration camps, so that part of me is slowly ebbing away.

"By the time I was sixteen, I was six feet two inches and skinny. And shy. But when I went to Oakland Technical High School, I just decided to change personalities. When you're a kid going from school to school, there's a great potential for change. With new teachers, new environments, you're not bound by the old restrictions you placed upon yourself. I got into student government and on committees, became more popular."[1]

Both his mother and father worked many years as amateur puppeteers and provided Oz with support when he, too, began puppeteering at an early age. "Puppetry is my parents' hobby. They didn't perform, but my father [by profession, a window-trimmer for women's apparel stores] used to make puppets, and my mother would costume them. They belong to the Puppeteers of America, which holds a yearly convention. I never intended to become a puppeteer. It was only a small part of my life, but it seemed a way to express myself and make some money, playing birthday parties, supermarket openings, fairs, and bazaars. I worked marionettes—string puppets—a skeleton, a roller-skating bear. Most of the kids in school thought it was silly—they called me the 'puppet man,' although I was interested in playing ball and dating girls."[1]

"I really looked up to the most popular kid in my grammar school, and I remember one day when I was doing a puppet show that he came up to me and said, 'What the heck are you doing this stuff for? Puppets are stupid. You'll never make any money doing that.'"[2]

A few years later Oz's performing led him to the National Puppetry Festival where he met Jim Henson, creator of the Muppets. "I met Jim when I was seventeen, but I was going to be a journalist. About two years later, when I was in my first year at Oakland City College, Jim asked me to come to New York to try out performing.

"My parents were supportive but cautious about my move from school to working for Jim. 'Is this more important than school?' they wanted to know. 'What's important for you right now? Do you *want* to finish school?' They were concerned that I felt good about what I was doing."[3]

Unable to resist Henson's offer, Oz moved to New York to join the Muppet performers. It was not long before he proved to be an integral part of the ever-growing Henson Empire. "Jim started it all with his wife Jean. What I do with the Muppets, and what other people do, we've learned from Jim. His is just a rare talent. I don't consider myself involved with puppets when I think of the Muppets—they transcend that. When Jim came on the scene, it was a brand new thing."[4]

"Jim had only a small group then. We made our money in commercials and industrial shows, doing television appearances on the Ed Sullivan and Perry Como shows. Gradually, we started getting bigger."[1]

"Now the Muppets have become like Kleenex and Coca-Cola. They're part of the culture."[4]

Over the years Oz developed many famous Muppet characters: Fozzie Bear, Animal, Sam Eagle, Cookie Monster, Bert, and Grover, but the inimitable Miss Piggy is the character he made

FRANK OZ

legendary. Judging from his reputation among both fellow puppeteers and the public, she has indeed done the same for him. Evidently neither Piggy's complex character nor her star appeal were the result of advance planning. "It was an accident. It's always an accident. You can't make a huge success by design. It starts with fun with the crew between takes. In this case, it started with a karate chop. We had several pig characters and a scene called for Miss Piggy to slap Kermit the Frog. Instead of a slap, it turned into a karate chop and everybody broke up."[5]

"Somehow, that hit crystallized her character for me—the coyness hiding the aggression; the conflict of that love with her desire for a career; her hunger for a glamour image; her tremendous out-and-out ego—all those things are great fun to explore in a character."[6]

"I do have [Miss Piggy's] whole history in my mind. I think her mother mistreated her, and her father died in an accident on the farm. She left home after her mother noticed that Miss Piggy was getting more attention from people than she was.

"So Miss Piggy left home, began fending for herself, and entered a lot of beauty contests. She tried to threaten the judges beforehand, but she wouldn't sleep with them. She's a lady.

"She won second or third place a lot. She survived on the prize money for a while. When that ran out she really had to struggle. She did some modeling. She's deeply ashamed about this part of her life. She doesn't want to talk about it.

"It wasn't nude modeling. She did some ads for bacon and for footballs. It's part of her past. She needed the money.

"Then she went to charm school. But basically she's gone through a lot of pain and rejection. A *lot* of pain and rejection."[7]

"She's a character to me, not a caricature. She's full of complexities. She's a character that evolves and changes as society evolves and changes. She wants to have children, but at the same time she doesn't want to give up her career. Let's face it. She's a woman alone. She's not very attractive. She has an obsession with this frog. And she wants to have children."[8]

"She loves that little frog. She wants her frog and her career. She's torn, like everyone else."[9]

"As a star she gets adoration without risk—it's hard to give up. And then, too, like many women today, she's had independence and she enjoys it. She also enjoys wealth and power. She's had her consciousness raised, but she still likes diamonds."[10]

"When Piggy's really ripe, when all her qualities come out, it doesn't come from the intellect. It comes from inside me. I have ego and I have jealousies and I have fears and hates and loves and passions and gentleness and aggressiveness and loathesomeness. I have all those things, but it's not socially acceptable for me to bring them out. Piggy wears her heart on her sleeve."[11]

(Oz's alter-ego, Miss Piggy, starred in the 1984 movie "The Muppets Take Manhattan.")

"I can't tell where Miss Piggy is going. She changes depending on how I feel that day. Some days, I only want to be hugged. Other days, I feel more ambitious."[12]

Oz regards all the puppets he has brought to life as reflections of his own personality. "Miss Piggy is the neurotic, emotional, high-strung aspect of myself. Bert is the boring aspect of myself. Animal is the insane aspect of myself."[8]

The Muppet's first feature film, "The Muppet Movie," was the story of how the Muppets met and made it to Hollywood. Oz regarded his first experience with film production as a pleasurable departure from television. "Here you have all the time to do all the things that get compromised out of existence on the TV show. It's slower here, but it's so much more gratifying. You can take the time to set up a shot three different ways. You can stop after a take if something is bothering you. The results are infinitely more pleasing."[13]

His next film appearance came in 1980 when he brought Yoda to life in "The Empire Strikes Back," the "Star Wars" sequel. "Sometimes when you look at a design, you have no reaction whatsoever and you have to work very hard to get that character. When I saw Stuart Freeborn's design for Yoda, it was an instant gut reaction. He had a lot of wisdom, strength, warmth, and humor."[2]

"I went through the script of 'Star Wars' and 'Empire,' writing down all the things that Yoda knew about Luke, what Luke knew about Yoda, what Yoda knew about Darth Vader, the Force, and

Obi-Wan. Then, I assembled all of these pages into a biography of Yoda. I did this research to help me become comfortable with him. I did all the things that *any* actor does when creating a character. It may sound stupid, but many little things can come together, adding color and depth to a character. You want to know about a character's pet peeves, what he likes to eat, what he knows about this person or doesn't know about that person.

"The more you *know* about a character, the more comfortable you can be when you are actually shooting, since there are so many technical things to think about then, that you *can't* be working on character—you must have that already locked away inside."[3]

"My main concern during the two weeks of filming Yoda's scenes was getting the complex mechanics of the character to work right, and then I could do the acting. It took me and [three] other people to work [him]."[2] "One person operated the right hand, one person did the eyes, one person did the ears and I did the rest."[14]

"We [had] to rehearse over and over and over and over again to get a shot right. It's *not* just yourself.

"With Yoda, you can't perform spontaneously, [when you're dragging] three other people along with you. If I tried spontaneity, they wouldn't know when to do the eyes when I do the ears. In this kind of situation, the satisfaction you get working with two or three other people occurs after you rehearse and rehearse and suddenly the role opens up to you. It's a living organism. It just

(From the television special ''Don't Eat the Pictures: Sesame Street at the Metropolitan Museum of Art.'' First broadcast on PBS-TV, November 16, 1983.)

happens. It unfolds like a flower, because you are so in tune with each other. It's a wonderful moment.''[3]

''First your body knows, next your mind knows, and then you start work. It was one of the hardest things I've ever done in twenty years of performing.''[15]

Oz married painter Robin Garsen in December, 1979. His honeymoon was interrupted when he was asked to loop Yoda's dialogue. ''The 'Star Wars' people tried out several actors doing Yoda's voice but I gather the results weren't quite what they wanted. So, months after filming, they asked me to do the voice. Unfortunately, they called me the day before my wedding in Oakland, California, and they said they wanted me to go down the following week. So what finally happened was we cut our honeymoon short. We flew into Los Angeles and looped for two very long days. It's good to have a bride who is so understanding.''[14]

Oz co-directed ''The Dark Crystal'' with Jim Henson in 1982. The film was set in a fantasy world which had fallen prey to an evil group of reptilian creatures called the Skeksis. Unlike the Muppet films, ''The Dark Crystal'' did not include a single human; consequently, the technical considerations were greater. Oz was a principle performer in the film as both Aughra the sorceress and the Chamberlain of the Skeksis.

''Basically, it's like any movie: making the scenes work, getting the characters to come alive, all that stuff. But there's also an enormous number of technical problems. You have stars here that you *made*, and you have a lot of people trying to make them work. As for directing and performing, when Jim was working in a character, I'd usually be outside with the cinematographer and the assistant director, and vice versa. When we were both inside—that was harder. We had ear pieces and an audio loop so we could talk to each other and the other performers. We had monitors inside the characters so we could see what was going on. We had a whole communications network. The real difficulty in both directing and doing the performing is the frustration of wanting to do everything at once. You've got to think about your character first, and you really can't think as much about the lighting or the shot.''[16]

By the conclusion of the shooting of ''The Dark Crystal,'' Oz expressed the desire to move away from puppets and begin working more with people. ''I've been doing this for almost twenty years, and puppets have been good to me. I'm still excited about doing my characters, but puppets are limiting. For instance, doing 'Sesame Street,' you're working for kids, and your sophistication has to be held in check, because your job is to do it for that audience. One reason I like Miss Piggy is because there are so many levels—like a layer cake—so much complexity to her. There is even more to Yoda. But at the same time, we're still not talking Chekhov, we're not talking about the delicacy of a Noel Coward, the dialogue of Shaw, the absurdity

("Animal," operated by Oz, starred in "The Muppet Movie" in 1979.)

of Ionesco, the vast depth of Shakespeare, the simplicity of Thornton Wilder . . . that's what I'm excited about right now. I'd love to direct more . . . . I will never stop with Muppets and puppets, but I've been doing a lot of it for many years, and I've gotten into about seven layers of work. I'm really dying to get into seventy-eight layers."[16]

After having co-directed two films with Henson, Oz stepped out on his own as the director and principle writer of the third Muppet movie, "The Muppets Take Manhattan." "When I'm scripting, I'm looking for the characters to tell me where to go with the story, as opposed to looking for poignant moments or places for special effects. There are about six or seven songs in the movie, but those songs are part of the show, they grow out of the plot.

"Jeff Moss wrote the songs, both music and lyrics. At first, we decided where the songs had to be. Then, we decided it was too expensive and took them out, making this movie a straight comedy instead of a musical. But as we worked on the story, we kept finding perfect places for songs, so we put them all back in the movie. Sometimes, the songs are there because the character is bursting with emotion and just has to sing. In other places, they're there because it's fun."[3]

"New York is a rough city and the Muppets have a hard time. It's highfalutin to talk about messages, but this movie is about relationships. And that sticking together is most important."[17]

"My sole intention [was] to make a warm, funny movie. I'm like anybody else who goes to see a movie. You know, hundreds of people work . . . days and nights for a year or more from pre-production, through production, and into post-production in *every* department. And then suddenly, it's finished and people go see it. You watch people walk out of the theater and what do they say?

"'So. Uh, what? You wanna go to dinner?'

"I'm exactly like that. Oh, I'll talk about the movie a little, but, essentially, you forget about it. That's all I want to do. I want people to enjoy themselves for an hour-and-a-half, say, 'That was fun,' and then go have dinner. That's all.

"I'm not making art. I think that's too highfalutin. I'm just doing my best. Someone else can tell me whether it's art or not. In the meantime I just want everyone else to enjoy it."[3]

In Oz's next film, "The Little Shop of Horrors," he had the opportunity to work with people as well as with a man-eating plant. "Little Shop" is the story of Seymour, a young man from Skid Row who sells his soul to a blood-thirsty plant. The film, directed by Oz, was based on Howard Ashman's play. Oz and Ashman collaborated on the screenplay. "I looked at the script and said: 'No, I can't do this movie.' I didn't think I could get my hands around it. There were too many elements. It was a period piece, it was horror, it was comedy, there were fourteen songs, and a puppet that was going to weigh a ton."[18]

Audrey II, the blood-sucking plant, was the masterful creation of Lyle Conway. "We couldn't use the simpler technology for the

Oz readies Fozzie Bear for action on "The Muppet Show."

movie that they used for the play. We needed something bigger and more subtle for the movie. Something different.''[19]

''The key to this movie is the plant; and there is a whole new skill grown up in Britain since 'Star Wars' called animatronics. Basically, it is the art of making creatures that have a life of their own; and the skill has been developed here by an American expatriate Lyle Conway who is our plant designer. What he is making is the plant you love to hate: it sings, eats people, and thrives on blood.''[20]

''By the time Audrey II reaches her full growth, about twelve feet, it took about fifty people to operate the body and all the tentacles. And it's all puppet. We used no animation, no miniaturization, no special effects. Whenever you see Audrey, it's all Audrey.

''And as Audrey II grew, so did the complexity of the shoot. Scenes with her necessitated many takes, because some little thing was continually going wrong. The human actors were very patient.''[21]

Oz first filmed the movie with the original ending in which the plant kills everyone, but, after seeing the reaction of the preview audience, he reshot the last scenes with a happier ending. ''We had some sneaks for general audiences in California, and I sat in the theater with them. They were terribly saddened, and they left the theater in a depressed mood.

''And I did, too. It pointed up one of the big differences between stage and screen. On stage, thirty seconds after they've been eaten, Audrey and Seymour are taking curtain calls, and everyone knows they're alive. On the screen, it just doesn't come off that way. I knew they were alive—but I just didn't want them to die.

''So we went back to England for two more weeks of shooting, but it was worth it.

''I wanted to make a movie that would immediately tell people that they were in for a fantasy. That's why we shot the opening sequence the way we did with the rain falling everywhere except on the three girls. Their actions, and costumes, in such dramatic contrast to the set and the other people—and even the rain itself—were a bold stroke, an attempt to grab the audience and tell them that something different was going on.

''Don't forget that the very act of singing is unnatural. When you meet someone, you don't sing a conversation. So by taking the unnatural act of singing, and putting it in an unnatural setting, we have created our own reality.''[21]

''We did maybe thirty takes for every ten seconds that's in the film. The last number took five weeks to shoot. I don't know if the film would have been any less if I had done only twenty takes instead of thirty. But you can't underestimate audiences these days. They expect effects to look real. If one little thing is off,

Oz, together with obscured assistant Wendy Midener, operated the puppet Yoda in the movie "The Empire Strikes Back."

you can lose the whole scene. You have to be sure you've got it while you're there because you can't go back."[22]

"'Little Shop' is deceptive. It looks simple, but it's not. If it's played too campy, then the audience won't care about the characters. But if it's not campy enough, it becomes a drama and people will care too much. It's a very difficult line to tread."[23]

Oz sees comedy not only as entertainment but as a way to explore the seriousness of life. "You can always get a laugh. Anybody can get a laugh. Humor's not that difficult. Comedy is difficult, but humor is not, because you can always drop your pants and get a laugh. Throw a pie in the face and get a laugh. 'Police Academy' is a perfect example of a situation where you talk back to authority, and do something where authority sits on a pie. That's an easy laugh, but it's not very satisfying. It's not a laugh that touches you, that you can see yourself in. But I feel very strongly about the quality of laugh that you get, I'm not interested in just getting laughs. I want the *quality* of the laughs to be right.

"I believe strongly that an hour-and-a-half movie is a long time for an audience to sit there. You have to touch emotions. You don't have to be serious about it, but you must touch emotion, or else there's just a distance. That's what movies are all about, energy and emotion.

"One thing I'm pleased about with this movie is that it's not only entertainment. My main job—and if I didn't achieve this, I

would have been disappointed—is to translate the vitality and energy from the stage play to the movie. But, at the same time, I enjoyed delving into darkness. I would love to do that in my next film, even more. We're not talking 'Blue Velvet' here, but I do want to get into dark areas."[4]

Oz's wish to direct a puppetless film came true with "Dirty Rotten Scoundrels" which opened to mixed reviews in 1988.

He plans to continue to expand the range of his abilities. "I'd like to do more acting, I'd like to do a lot of other things . . . . I believe that the exciting part of life is growing in your art or craft.

"I am having the opportunity to direct and produce these days, which makes me feel good. I would also like to find time to do some writing. I like to sail and ski and travel, but all that will come in its own good time.

"I believe to become successful you don't think about being a success. Instead, you just work at doing good stuff which excites you. I never learned in any way except through trial and error and watching and learning from other people."[14]

FOOTNOTE SOURCES

[1]Edwin Miller, "There's More to Miss Piggy Than Meets the Eye!," *Seventeen,* November, 1980.
[2]Jim Wright, "The Modest Wizard Called Oz," *San Francisco Chronicle,* November 16, 1980.

"The Birth of You Know Who." (From *Miss Piggy's Treasury of Art Masterpieces from the Kermitage Collection*, edited by Henry Beard.)

[3] David Hutchison, "Frank Oz: The Man beneath Yoda, behind Miss Piggy, and Slightly to the Left of Fozzie Bear," *Starlog,* July, 1984.

[4] Randy Lofficier and Jean-Marc Lofficier, "Frank Oz: 'Little Shop of Horrors,'" *Starlog,* April, 1987.

[5] Leo Seligsohn, "A Triumph of Muppet," *Newsday,* July 8, 1984.

[6] John Culhane, "Muppets," *New York Times Magazine,* June 10, 1979.

[7] Gene Siskel, "Miss Piggy's Sordid Past Is Finally Revealed," *Chicago Tribune,* July 15, 1979.

[8] Michael Janusonis, "Henson and Moi," *Detroit News,* July 23, 1984.

[9] John Skow, "Those Marvelous Muppets," *Time,* December 25, 1978.

[10] Brad Darrach, "The Sex Goddess of the '80s? Miss Piggy Makes Her Mark on Showbiz in Indelible Oink," *People Weekly,* September 3, 1979.

[11] Aimee Lee Ball, "The Moi Nobody Knows," *Redbook,* September, 1980.

[12] Debra Wishik, "Frank Oz: The Man behind Miss Piggy," *USA Today,* July 17, 1984.

[13] David Colker and Jack Viertel, "On the Set with the Muppets," *Take One,* March, 1979.

[14] Ted Salter, "Caricature: Frank Oz," *Puppetry Journal,* March/April, 1981.

[15] Fred Hauptfuhrer and Karen Peterson, "Up Front," *People Weekly,* June 9, 1980.

[16] Paul Scanlon, "Of Puppets and People," *Rolling Stone,* February 3, 1983.

[17] "Muppet Crew Celebrates a Film and a Birthday," *New York Times,* September 26, 1983.

[18] Jack Mathews, "Frank Oz' Little Chop of Horrors," *New York Post,* January 2, 1987.

[19] Michael Blowen, "The Rent's Gone Way Up at 'The Little Shop of Horrors,'" *Boston Globe,* December 21, 1986.

[20] Michael Billington, "New Life for 'Little Shop,'" *New York Times,* December 8, 1985.

[21] Joe Pollack, "Muppets' Frank Oz Takes on 'Horrors,'" *St. Louis Post Dispatch,* December 19, 1986.

[22] J. Mathews, "Director Frank Oz Goes for the Comedy of 'Horrors,'" *Los Angeles Times,* December 19, 1986.

[23] Nancy Mills, "Just When You Thought It Was Safe to Go Back into the Greenhouse . . . ," *Los Angeles Times,* February 2, 1986.

FOR MORE INFORMATION SEE:

TV Guide, August 6, 1977 (p. 4ff), May 29, 1982 (p. 30).

New York Times, January 8, 1978 (p. 29ff), June 26, 1981 (section III, p. 8), July 13, 1984 (section III, p. 6).

Time, August 28, 1978 (p. 64).

Christian Science Monitor, November 21, 1978 (p. B3).

Hank Whittemore, "The Magical Hands of TV's Muppet Zoo," *Houston Post,* December 24, 1978.

New York Post, June 21, 1979 (p. 33ff), July 12, 1984 (p. 25).

New York Times Biographical Service, June, 1979 (p. 784ff).

Daily News (New York), July 2, 1979 (p. 49), January 21, 1986 (p. 60).

Maclean's, July 9, 1979 (p. 45ff).

Millimeter, August, 1979 (p. 148ff).

Us, July 22, 1980 (p. 53).

TV Week, October 4, 1980.

St. Louis Post Dispatch, November 26, 1980 (p. 61).

Aughra, the puppet created and performed by Oz in the movie "The Dark Crystal."

Saturday Evening Post, December, 1980 (p. 66).
The Art of the Muppets, Bantam, 1980.
Patricia Dendtler Frevert, *Muppet Magic*, Creative Education, 1980.
USA Today, October 21, 1982 (p. D1).
Newsweek, December 27, 1982, January 5, 1987 (p. 56).
Cinefantastique, April/May, 1983 (p. 25ff), January, 1987 (p. 16ff), September, 1987 (p. 24ff).
Los Angeles Times, July 11, 1984 (p. J1), December 20, 1986.
San Francisco Chronicle, December 19, 1986 (p. 79), December 20, 1986 (p. 38).
Chicago Tribune, December 24, 1986 (section 4, p. 5)
Houston Post, December 28, 1986 (p. F9).
Fangoria, number 62, 1986 (p. 42ff).

PAYNE, Bernal C., Jr. 1941-

PERSONAL: Born July 11, 1941, in St. Louis, Mo.; son of Bernal C. (a business owner in radio and TV) and Myrna (a homemaker; maiden name, Petrey) Payne; married Margaret Wieberg (an elementary school teacher), June 23, 1973. *Education:* San Diego State University, B.A. 1970; Webster University, M.A.T., 1976; Washington University, M.A.Ed., 1982. *Office:* Parkway School District, St. Louis, Mo.

CAREER: Parkway School District, St. Louis, Mo., elementary school teacher, 1973—; writer, 1983—. *Military service:* U.S. Navy, 1961-65; achieved rank of yeoman, third class. *Member:* National Education Association. *Awards, honors:* Children's

BERNAL C. PAYNE, JR.

Choice Award from the International Reading Association and the Children's Book Council, 1985, for *It's About Time*.

WRITINGS:

NOVELS

It's About Time (young adult), Macmillan, 1984, published as *Trapped in Time,* Archway, 1986.
The Late, Great Dick Hart (juvenile), Houghton, 1986.
Experiment in Terror (young adult), Houghton, 1987.

WORK IN PROGRESS: Year of the Angels, Food of the Gods, and *The Snapper,* all young adult novels.

SIDELIGHTS: "I have to confess, I wasn't a very good student in my younger days. But it wasn't entirely my fault. I lay most of the blame on Hollywood and the atomic bomb. It was all those science-fiction movies during the 1950s that warped and shaped my impressionable mind. How was an innocent kid back then supposed to see movies like 'Invasion of the Body Snatchers,' 'War of the Worlds,' and 'The Thing,' and expect to walk away unchanged? Or gobble buttered popcorn while witnessing the horrors of those atomic bomb tests in such films as 'The Incredible Shrinking Man,' 'Tarantula,' and 'Them!' What with the dread of being taken over by aliens and monsters, plus the ever-present Russians, was it any wonder that I couldn't concentrate on school? There was never any doubt in my mind that we would be invaded; it was only a question of who would get us first.

"I spent most of my formative years staring out the classroom windows of Christ the King Elementary School, conjuring up science-fiction scenes of epic proportions, while the background voices of my teachers murmured on. While Sister Mary Regis was diligently teaching us how to divide fractions by fractions, I was running through the dark streets of my town in blind panic, being chased by bug-eyed creatures bent on my destruction! Or while the good sister was demonstrating the incomprehensible methods of diagramming sentences, I was being kidnapped by Martians and whisked away in their sleek silvery saucers, never to see my family or friends again! Consequently, even though my teachers did their best to educate me and keep my attention on earthly matters, I was always staring off into space while stretching my mind out to the stars.

"And, of course, there were all those wonderful stories of time machines in magazines and comic books, cluttering up my head. Of all the inventions science-fiction writers conceived, this was the one that gave me the most pleasure and brought about my academic downfall. Throughout my grade school days I gazed out the window while making thousands of trips into the past, all of them completely beyond my control. In my fantasies, I was always the hero who knew the fate of the world, trying to act as its savior. I warned the captain of the *Titanic* just in time that he was going to run into an iceberg. I ran up and down the streets of San Francisco warning everyone about the coming earthquake. I even found Hitler when he was a little kid so I could kidnap him and prevent World War II. It wasn't so much that I graduated from my school as it was that my exhausted teachers pointed to the door and ordered me out.

Imagine waking up Christmas morning without your parents because they're far away from you— not in miles, but in years. (Jacket illustration by Linda Benson from *It's About Time* by Bernal C. Payne, Jr.)

"When I walked into Hanley Junior High, I underwent a swift and remarkable change. I gave up my aliens and flying saucers and time machines for more important things like fad clothes, rock 'n' roll, and girls. It was there that I met Dick Bernhardt, one of the best friends I ever had. He was older and wiser than I, and he drove a motorscooter that elevated him to a position among the gods. We did everything together: hunting, fishing, horseback riding; and I remember the time we explored a cave full of bats and got the devil scared out of us. Dick went on to high school before me, but he ended up dropping out to join the Navy. How I envied him making that daring move. I went on to high school a year later and built a customized '55 Chevy, enjoying driving around with a car full of kids, top down, and Elvis turned all the way up. Oh, those were the days. But even though I appeared happy-go-lucky on the outside, I now sat in school, staring out the window, wishing I was on a Navy ship, like Dick, having adventures and seeing the world. Finally, when I couldn't stand it any longer, I signed up for four years and got a destroyer in Pearl Harbor. It seemed like I was always trying to catch up with Dick—him always running faster, and me always a little bit behind.

"I started writing when I became an elementary school teacher. (It's one of life's little ironies that I'm now the one who is teaching while a few of my dreamy-eyed students are staring off into space.) I guess it was being around my fifth grade students that woke up that little boy inside me. Only now, that boy found himself with the power to turn all his daydreams into written stories. So I wrote a short story about a friendly alien who came to Earth being pursued by monster aliens who were out to kill him. I let my students read it and, to my relief and joy, they liked it, and asked for more. I willingly obliged, writing a dozen short stories, enjoying the pleasure of making all my childhood daydreams come to life. My students would gather around my desk as I read them my strange and fantastic tales. I showed them what went into the labors of writing, while they, in turn, told me what kids like to read. We taught each other a lot.

"It was just before my fortieth birthday that I finally decided I was ready to write a novel. The problem was, what kind of story would take up an entire book? My old fascination with time machines began dancing in my head. So I asked myself—or, rather, that little boy inside of me—where would I like to go in my story and what would I like to see? It suddenly struck me that instead of the usual famous people and historical events most time-travel stories deal with, I wanted to simply go back and see what my parents looked like when they were teenagers. Not a bad beginning. And what if I stood there watching at that moment when my teenage parents first met? The idea intrigued me. I took it one step further. What if I accidentally got in their way and prevented them from meeting? That would mean my parents would never get married and have me for their son. I'd have to somehow get them to meet because I'd be fighting for my future existence! The whole idea caught my imagination on fire and gave birth to my first novel, *It's About Time*.

"Ecstatic over my first book being published, I wasted no time in tackling another. Let me pause here to say that I really enjoy writing young adult science fiction. It's always the kid inside me who dictates the story while the adult part of me writes it down. Also, it allows me to do the impossible. And that's what I like doing most: taking average young people, leading ordinary humdrum lives, and putting them in incredible situations that are seemingly impossible to escape from. I always start an idea by asking myself—'What if?' For example, I was gazing out the window of my study when a boy's familiar voice inside me asked: 'What would you do if you turned sixteen and found out that all this time you really weren't human; that you were actually made by aliens from another world? More than that, you

discovered that you're a small part of a world-wide experiment using thousands of human children to help these aliens colonize the Earth. And what if one day you started slowly changing shape, transforming into one of THEM!' I grabbed my pencil and started outlining the story as fast as I could. And even though it took me a year to write, *Experiment in Terror* kept me excited right up to the very end.

"I couldn't believe it when I found out that my childhood friend Dick Bernhardt died of a brain tumor. I was shocked and I felt a small part of me die, too. I was going to miss Dick a lot, but the hero-worshipping kid inside me was going to miss him more. And neither one of us wanted to let Dick go without a final literary farewell. So I wrote a children's novel dedicated to Dick's memory, entitled *The Late, Great Dick Hart*. Only in a fantasy story could I make Dick come back to life. In mine, I have Dick come from heaven to take his friend back with him to show him what heaven is really like. When I finished the book, I fully realized what an amazing power a writer has: to be able to bring his dead friend back to life and allow him to live on, as long as someone, somewhere, was reading his story.

"For me, creating a novel is ninety per cent daydreaming and ten per cent writing. I have a big comfortable leather chair in my study, and a beautiful bay window overlooking the trees and tall old houses on my street. People see me gazing out my window, wondering why I'm not doing something more constructive like painting the shutters or mowing the lawn. What they don't know is that I'm seeing a strange new tree that sprang up over night on my front lawn. The trunk is made of smooth blue glass, and the leaves are thin transparent crystal. And hanging from its strange twisted branches is a fruit in the shape of white cubes. And I'm wondering what would happen to me if I picked one of those cube apples off the tree and took a bite . . . . "

HOBBIES AND OTHER INTERESTS: Bike riding, going for walks, watching old science-fiction movies, playing with my dog, Ashley, and my cat, Pip.

PERRY, Phyllis J. 1933-

PERSONAL: Born October 23, 1933, in Nevada City, Calif.; daughter of William H. (a miner) and Winifred (a homemaker; maiden name, Elliott) Penaluna; married David Louis Perry (retired), February 8, 1953; children: Janet Marie Perry Miller, Jill Louise Perry Fernandez. *Education:* University of California, Berkeley, A.B., 1955; San Francisco State College, M.A., 1960; University of Colorado, Ed.D., 1980. *Politics:* Democrat. *Religion:* Methodist. *Home:* 3190 Endicott Dr., Boulder, Colo. 80303. *Agent:* Norma-Lewis Agency, 521 Fifth Ave., New York, N.Y. 10175. *Office:* 3740 Martin Dr., Boulder, Colo. 80303.

CAREER: Boulder Valley Public Schools, Boulder, Colo., teacher, curriculum specialist, educational programs specialist, instructional design specialist, director of talented and gifted education, principal, 1968—. Board of directors, Nomad Community Theatre. *Member:* International Reading Association, National Association for Gifted Children, Association for Supervision and Curriculum Development, Colorado Language Arts Society, Phi Delta Kappa (Boulder chapter). *Awards, honors:* Governor's Award for Excellence in Education given by Governor Lamm, 1986; Phi Beta Kappa.

PHYLLIS J. PERRY

WRITINGS:

Spiders (illustrated by Lawrence M. Spiegel), Denison, 1964.

Let's Look at the Birds (illustrated by L. M. Spiegel), Denison, 1965.

A Trip through the Zoo (illustrated by Barbara Furan), Denison, 1968.

One Dozen Swimmers (illustrated by June Talarczyk), Denison, 1968.

Let's Look at Moths and Butterflies (illustrated by J. Talarczyk), Denison, 1969.

Let's Look at Frogs (illustrated by J. Talarczyk), Denison, 1969.

Let's Look at Snails (illustrated by Celeste K. Foster), Denison, 1969.

Let's Look at Seashells (illustrated by C. K. Foster), Denison, 1971.

Let's Learn about Mushrooms (illustrated by Haris Petie), Harvey House, 1974.

Mexican American Sketches, BVSP, 1976.

A Look at Colorado (illustrated by Dian Diggs and with photographs by David L. Perry), Pruett Publishing, 1976, 2nd edition, 1986.

Full Flowering: A Parent and Teacher Guide to Programs for the Gifted, Ohio Psychology Publishing, 1985.

Contributor to periodicals, including *Educational Leadership, Middle School Journal, G/C/T, Statement, Instructor, Challenge, Wee Wisdom, High Adventure, Story Friends, Day Care and Early Education*, and *Illinois Council for the Gifted Journal*.

WORK IN PROGRESS: A mystery novel for middle-grade children; nature series for ages seven to eleven; a fantasy/adventure novel for middle level; a Native American legend picture book.

SIDELIGHTS: "Much of my writing for adults has been in the field of public education and particularly in the area of talented and gifted education. As I work with colleagues to develop innovative approaches or to create solid foundations for educational programs, I seek to share these with others. Children are precious, and they deserve the best possible education in settings that respect their worth and dignity and promote their happiness and success.

"A second field of interest is writing for children. Hiking in the beautiful mountains of Colorado is inspiration for sharing some of the simple beauties in nature with young readers. Some of this wonder and beauty I've tried to capture in poetry, and some of my observations have been set down in prose.

"A third interest is in fiction writing. This is the newest field for me and over the past few years I have tried writing two children's novels, several plays and short stories, and some poetry for both children and adults. My hope is to concentrate on writing exciting novels for readers seven to eleven."

HOBBIES AND OTHER INTERESTS: Hiking in the mountains, acting in community theater, attending concerts, playing bridge. "I enjoy reading to my grandchildren, Casey, Clare, and Julia, and listening to their adventures. Casey often helps supply ideas for stories and is my best critic."

REESE, Robert A. 1938-
(Bob Reese)

PERSONAL: Born August 15, 1938, in Hollywood, Calif.; son of Cleo Jack (a singer), and Isabelle (an English teacher; maiden name, Ament) Reese; married Nancy Willoughby (an interior decorator), August 22, 1971; children: Natalie G., Brittany Raquel. *Education:* Attended Los Angeles Pacific College, 1958-59; Brigham Young University, B.S., 1963. *Politics:* Democrat. *Religion:* Unitarian. *Home:* 2376 East Dimple Dell Rd., Sandy, Utah 84093. *Office:* ARO Publishing, 398 South 1100 West, Provo, Utah 84601.

CAREER: Walt Disney Studios, Burbank, Calif., artist, 1956-59; Brigham Young University, Provo, Utah, supervisor of the graphic arts department, 1963-65; free-lance artist, 1965-72; ARO Publishing, Provo, Utah, founder, president, author, illustrator, 1973—.

WRITINGS:

"HOLIDAY" SERIES; SELF-ILLUSTRATED; UNDER NAME BOB REESE

Easter, ARO, 1977.

Arbor Day, ARO, 1977.

Saint Patrick's Day, ARO, 1977.

Halloween, ARO, 1977.

"TEN WORD BOOKS" SERIES; SELF-ILLUSTRATED; UNDER NAME BOB REESE

Crab Apple, ARO, 1979.

Little Dinosaur, ARO, 1979.

Sunshine, ARO, 1979.

ROBERT A. REESE

"DESERT CRITTERLANDS" SERIES; SELF-ILLUSTRATED; UNDER NAME BOB REESE

Lactus Cactus, Childrens Press, 1981.
Tweedle-De-Dee Tumbleweed, Childrens Press, 1981.
Rapid Robert Road-Runner, Childrens Press, 1981.
The Critter Race, Childrens Press, 1981.
Scarry Larry the Very, Very, Hairy Tarantula, Childrens Press, 1981.
Huzzard Buzzard, Childrens Press, 1981.

"OCEAN CRITTERLAND" SERIES; SELF-ILLUSTRATED; UNDER NAME BOB REESE

Dale the Whale, Childrens Press, 1983.
Spongee Sponge, Childrens Press, 1983.
Ocean Fish School, Childrens Press, 1983.
Oola Oyster, Childrens Press, 1983.
Wellington Pelican, Childrens Press, 1983.
Coral Reef, Childrens Press, 1983.

"CRITTERLAND READERS" SERIES; SELF-ILLUSTRATED; UNDER NAME BOB REESE

Scarry Larry Meets Big Willie, Childrens Press, 1983.
Calico Jack and the Desert Critters, Childrens Press, 1983.
Rapid Robert and Hiss the Snake, Childrens Press, 1983.

"GOING APE" SERIES; SELF-ILLUSTRATED; UNDER NAME BOB REESE

Apricot Ape, ARO, 1984.

Ape Escape, ARO, 1984.
Honest Ape, ARO, 1984.
The Ape Team, ARO, 1984.
Going Bananas, ARO, 1984.
The Jungle Train, ARO, 1984.

"YELLOWSTONE CRITTER" SERIES; SELF-ILLUSTRATED; UNDER NAME BOB REESE

Bugle Elk and Little Toot, ARO, 1986.
Buffa Buffalo, ARO, 1986.
Bubba Bear, ARO, 1986.
Mickey Moose, ARO, 1986.
Old Faithful, ARO, 1986.
Camper Critters, ARO, 1986.

"GRAND CANYON" SERIES; SELF-ILLUSTRATED; UNDER NAME BOB REESE

Abert and Kaibab Squirrels, ARO, 1987.
Wild Turkey Run, ARO, 1987.
Coco's Berry Party, ARO, 1987.
Slitherfoot, ARO, 1987.
Ravens Roost, ARO, 1987.
Surefoot, ARO, 1987.

OTHER; SELF-ILLUSTRATED; UNDER NAME BOB REESE

The Pamba and the Bink, ARO, 1984.

ILLUSTRATOR; "I CAN READ UNDERWATER" SERIES; UNDER NAME BOB REESE

Ron Reese, *Sammy Skunk*, ARO, 1974.
Alana Willoughby, *The Little Mouse*, ARO, 1974.
A. Willoughby, *Rain*, ARO, 1974.
Darrell Stoddard, *The Hero*, ARO, 1974.
Nancy Reese, *The Bee*, ARO, 1974.
R. Reese, *Crazy Cat*, ARO, 1974.
Jack Winder, *Your Face*, ARO, 1974.
N. Reese, *Smiley Snake*, ARO, 1974.
N. Reese, *Silly Egg*, ARO, 1974.
A. Willoughby, *Boots*, ARO, 1974.

ILLUSTRATOR; "I CAN EAT AN ELEPHANT" SERIES; UNDER NAME BOB REESE

R. Reese, *Toy Bear*, ARO, 1975.
Suzanne Burke, *Ollie Owl*, ARO, 1975.
R. Reese, *Mosquito*, ARO, 1975.
N. Reese, *Purple Bear*, ARO, 1975.

ILLUSTRATOR; "THE HOLIDAY" SERIES; UNDER NAME BOB REESE

A. Willoughby, *Thanksgiving*, ARO, 1977.
A. Willoughby, *Christmas*, ARO, 1977.
Judy Schoder and Sharon Shebar, *Groundhog Day*, ARO, 1977.
J. Winder, *Presidents Day*, ARO, 1977.
N. Reese, *Valentine's Day*, ARO, 1977.
N. Reese, *New Year's*, ARO, 1977.

ILLUSTRATOR; "TEN WORD BOOKS" SERIES; UNDER NAME BOB REESE

J. Schoder, *Funny Bunny*, ARO, 1979.
A. Willoughby, *My Dolly*, ARO, 1979.
S. Shebar, *Night Monsters*, ARO, 1979.
J. Winder, *Who's New at the Zoo!*, ARO, 1979.
Mike Cox, Kris Cox, and Stan Cox, *Fire Drill*, ARO, 1979.
S. Shebar, *Milk*, ARO, 1979.
M. Cox and K. Cox, *Flowers*, ARO, 1979.

ILLUSTRATOR; "BUPPET BOOK" SERIES; UNDER NAME BOB REESE

LaRue Selman, *The Hero 2*, ARO, 1980.
R. Reese, *Crazy Cat's Bad Day*, ARO, 1980.
L. Selman, *Rain Frog*, ARO, 1980.
B. Reese, *Who's a Silly Egg?*, ARO, 1980.
L. Selman, *J. D. and the Bee*, ARO, 1980.
L. Selman, *Boots 2*, ARO, 1980.
J. Winder, *What Are Faces For?*, ARO, 1980.
L. Selman, *Sammy Skunk Plays the Clown*, ARO, 1980.
Phyllis Barber, *Smiley Snakes Adventure*, ARO, 1980.

ILLUSTRATOR; "ADVENTURES OF FREDDIE FREIGHTLINER" SERIES; UNDER NAME BOB REESE

David Lester George, *Freddie Freightliner Goes to Kennedy Space Center*, ARO, 1983.
D. L. George, *Freddie Freightliner Learns to Talk!*, ARO, 1983.
D. L. George, *Freddie Freightliner to the Rescue*, ARO, 1983.

ILLUSTRATOR; "FUNNY FARM" SERIES; UNDER NAME BOB REESE; ALL WRITTEN BY WENDY KANNO

Holey Moley Cow, ARO, 1984.
Waldo Duck, ARO, 1984.
Bags the Lamb, ARO, 1984.
Elmo the Pig, ARO, 1984.
Sampson the Horse, ARO, 1984.
The Funny Farm House, ARO, 1984.

ILLUSTRATOR; "MY FIRST" SERIES; UNDER NAME BOB REESE; ALL WRITTEN BY JULIA ALLEN

My First Dentist Visit, ARO, 1987.
My First Doctor Visit, ARO, 1987.
My First Phone Call, ARO, 1987.
My First Animal Ride, ARO, 1987.
My First Camping Trip, ARO, 1987.
My First Job, ARO, 1987.

SIDELIGHTS: "My first interest in drawing began at the early age of two; always drawing my adventures and dreams. I describe myself as a dreamer, a somewhat distracted student, doodling, even in high school. With my strong interest in art, and the help of a special art teacher, Mrs. Tupper, of Bellmont High in Los Angeles, I was able to reach my potential. After high school, I was lucky enough to land my first job at Walt Disney Studios, as an in-between animation cartoonist.

"College days were mixed with playing basketball for Los Angeles Pacific College, working for Disney, and squeezing in my own art work whenever possible. Basketball was again a priority at Brigham Young University, and a move to Utah for that reason netted a college bride.

"Romance blossomed, and so did my accomplishments, including two wonderful daughters; Natalie, who is studying Special Education at the University of Utah, and Brittany, who is a student of ballet, tap, and jazz.

"Soon after graduation, I worked as the supervisor of the graphic arts department at Brigham Young University, where I became more interested in publishing my own children's books. Through a friend I learned how to market my ideas to the public schools. Around this time, in 1973, I launched ARO Publishing."

Sunshine, a book with only ten words, shows the interest Reese has in his family. The book takes place in the house they lived in at the time, and features his wife, his two daughters, himself, the van they drove, and the now famous family dog, Sunshine. It was a family trip to Yellowstone that inspired Reese to write and illustrate the "Yellowstone Critters" series, all about the adventures of the animals in Yellowstone Park. He did the same thing after a family trip to the Grand Canyon.

His books are most generally marketed to schools and libraries. Grolier Educational and Childrens Press carry the ARO line and feature Reese's books in their catalogs.

Reese still finds time to visit the gym. He continues his interest in sports and spends time with his family, in their new favorite pastime, boating. During a recent trip to Lake Powell, Reese was brainstorming on an idea of a mascot to tie his more recent "Yellowstone Critters" and "Grand Canyon Critters" together with a future series on the animals of the Niagara Falls area. It was two friends, Roy and Jonathan Spahr, that gave him the title of "Captain Critter." Captain Critter is now a red fox, who will be featured in upcoming adventures as the captain of "The Good Ship Niagara."

Further expansion of ARO Publishing includes enlarging more of his titles into "11 X 17" books, or as they are called, "Big Books." One of Reese's more popular creations is the "Buppets." A "Buppet" is an ARO Publishing book/puppet, which holds in a front pocket a storybook about the puppet character.

I like geysers a lot,   if they are not tooooo hot!

(From *Bubba Bear* by Bob Reese. Illustrated by the author.)

HOBBIES AND OTHER INTERESTS: Sports and boating.

RICHARDSON, Willis 1889-1977

PERSONAL: Born November 5, 1889, in Wilmington, North Carolina; died November 8, 1977; son of Willis Wilder and Agnes Ann (Harper) Richardson; married Mary Ellen Jones, September 1 (one source says September 3), 1914; children: Jean Paula, Shirley Antonella, Noel Justine. *Education:* Graduated from high school in Washington, D.C.

CAREER: U.S. Bureau of Engraving and Printing, Washington, D.C., clerk, 1911-54; playwright, 1920-77. Director, drama historian, teacher at institutions including Morgan College (now Morgan State University), and director of Little Theatre Group in Washington, D.C. *Member:* National Association for the Advancement of Colored People, Dramatists Guild, Harlem Cultural Council. *Awards, honors:* First prize in *Crisis* Contest Awards, 1925, for "The Broken Banjo," and 1926, for "The Bootblack Lover"; *Opportunity* Contest Awards honorable mention, 1925, for "Fall of the Conjurer"; Amy Spingarn Prize for Drama, 1925 and 1926; Public School Prize, 1926, for "The King's Dilemma"; Edith Schwarb Cup from Yale University Theatre, 1928.

WRITINGS:

PLAYS

"The Deacon's Awakening: A Play in One Act" (first produced in St. Paul, Minn., 1921), published in *Crisis*, November, 1920.
"The King's Dilemma" (one-act for children; first produced in Washington, D.C., May, 1926), published in *Brownies' Book*, December, 1920.

WILLIS RICHARDSON

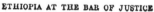
ETHIOPIA AT THE BAR OF JUSTICE

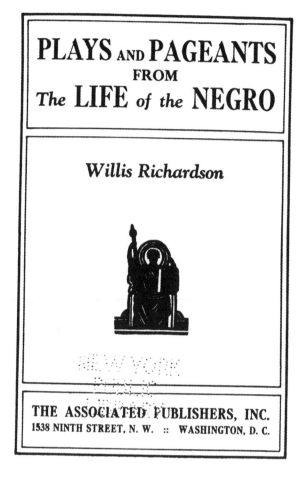

Frontispiece and title page for Richardson's 1930 anthology. (From *Plays and Pageants from the Life of the Negro* by Willis Richardson. Courtesy of the Schomburg Center for Research in Black Culture, The New York Public Library, and the Astor, Lenox, and Tilden Foundations.)

"The Gypsy's Finger Ring" (one-act for children), published in *Brownies' Book,* March, 1921.

"The Children's Treasure" (one-act for children), published in *Brownies' Book,* June, 1921.

"The Dragon's Tooth" (one-act for children), published in *Brownies' Book,* October, 1921.

"The Chip Woman's Fortune" (one-act), first produced in Chicago, January 29, 1923; produced on Broadway at Frazee Theatre, May 15, 1923.

"Mortgaged," first produced in Washington, D.C. at Howard University, March 29, 1924.

"Compromise" (one-act), first produced in Cleveland at Karamu House, February 26, 1925; produced in New York City, May 3, 1926.

"The Broken Banjo" (first produced in New York City, August 1, 1925), published in *Crisis,* February, 1926, and March, 1926.

"The Idle Head" (one-act), published in *Carolina,* April, 1927.

"The Flight of the Natives" (one-act; first produced in Washington, D.C., May 7, 1927), published in *Carolina,* April, 1929.

(Editor and contributor) *Plays and Pageants from the Life of the Negro* (twelve plays, including Richardson's "The Black Horseman," "The House of Sham," and "The King's Dilemma"), Associated Publishers, 1930, reissued, Roth Publishing, 1980.

"The Black Horseman," first produced in Baltimore, October 12, 1931.

(Editor with May Miller, and contributor) *Negro History in Thirteen Plays* (includes Richardson's one-act plays "Antonio Maceo," "Attucks, the Martyr," "The Elder Dumas," "In Menelik's Court," and "Near Calvary"), Associated Publishers, 1935.

"Miss or Mrs.," first produced in Washington, D.C., May 5, 1941.

The King's Dilemma and Other Plays for Children: Episodes of Hope and Dream (includes "The Dragon's Tooth," "The Gypsy's Finger Ring," "The King's Dilemma," "Man of Magic," "Near Calvary," and "The New Santa Claus"), Exposition Press, 1956.

The Dixwell Players

(Second Season)

PRESENT THREE ONE-ACT PLAYS

Dixwell Community House

Monday Evening, April 23rd, 1928
at 8.15 o'clock

(Program cover for an evening of three Black plays that included Richardson's "The Broken Banjo.")

Also author of one-act plays *Alimony Rastus*, Willis N. Bugbee, early 1920s, *A Ghost of the Past*, Paine Publishing, early 1920s, "Rooms for Rent," 1926, "Bold Lover," "The Brown Boy," "The Curse of the Shell Road Witch," and "The Dark Haven"; of three-act plays "Fall of the Conjurer," "The Bootblack Lover," and a version of "The Chip Woman's Fortune"; and of plays "The Peacock's Feather," 1928, "The Amateur Prostitute," "Chase," "The Danse Calinda," "Hope of the Lonely," "Imp of the Devil," "The Jail Bird," "Joy Rider," "The Man Who Married a Young Wife," "The New Generation," "The Nude Siren," "A Pillar of the Church," "The Rider of the Dream," "Attucks, the Martyr," "The House of Sham," "Antonio Maceo," "The Elder Dumas," "In Menelik's Court," "Near Calvary," "The Man of Magic," "The New Santa Claus," and "The Visiting Lady."

OTHER

Echoes from the Negro Soul (poetry), Alamo Printing, 1926.

WORK IN ANTHOLOGIES

Alain Locke, editor, *The New Negro: An Interpretation*, Boni, 1925.

A. Locke and Montgomery Gregory, editors, *Plays of Negro Life: A Source-book of Native American Drama*, Harper, 1927.

Frank Shay, editor, *Fifty More Contemporary One-Act Plays*, Appleton, 1928.

Otelia Cromwell, Eva B. Dykes, and Lorenzo D. Turner, editors, *Readings from Negro Authors*, Harcourt, 1931.

Herman Dreer, editor, *American Literature by Negro Authors*, Macmillan, 1950.

Lindsay Patterson, editor, *Anthology of the American Negro in the Theatre: A Critical Approach*, Publishers Company, 1967.

Darwin T. Turner, editor, *Black Drama in America: An Anthology*, Fawcett, 1971.

Richard Barksdale and Keneth Kinnamon, editors, *Black Writers of America*, Macmillan, 1972.

James V. Hatch and Ted Shine, editors, *Black Theatre, U.S.A.: Forty-five Plays by Black Americans 1847-1974*, Free Press, 1974.

Arthur P. Davis and Michael Peplow, editors, *The New Negro Renaissance*, Holt, 1975.

Contributor to peridicals, including *Carolinia*, *Crisis*, and *Opportunity*.

SIDELIGHTS: Richardson, the first black playwright to have a nonmusical play produced on Broadway, is remembered for his contributions to Black theater. Widely considered a pioneer, he dared to write serious plays about all levels of Black life at a time when white playwrights wrote about stereotypical "darkies" and other Black playwrights confined themselves to propaganda plays showing how Blacks were victimized by whites. According to Bernard L. Peterson, Jr., writing in *Black World*, Richardson was "the first to make a significant contribution to both the quantity and the quality of serious Black American drama."

Among Richardson's first writings were his plays for children, which often dramatize lives of Black heroes or use fairy-tale techniques to promote charity, equality, and brotherhood. Several were published in the monthly magazine *Brownies' Book* or later appeared in his collection *The King's Dilemma and Other Plays for Children: Episodes of Hope and Dream*. "The King's Dilemma," a one-act play, traces the beginnings of democracy in a kingdom whose prince chooses to befriend a Black boy despite the king's opposition. Popular among school children, the play won the Public School Prize in 1926. "The Children's Treasure" takes a contemporary subject, a poor person facing eviction, and shows how five children help by contributing their own savings toward their neighbor's rent. In other plays Richardson tells of heroic and prominent Blacks in history such as former slave Crispus Attucks, who was among the first to die in the American Revolution, Emperor Menelik of Abyssinia, and King Massinissa of East Numidia.

"The Chip Woman's Fortune," one of Richardson's best known works for adults, is famous as the first serious black play to appear on Broadway. Noted Peterson, "Black playwrights had previously been represented on The Great White Way by musical comedies and revues, but never before by a serious drama, albeit a one-act play." Presented on the same bill as Oscar Wilde's "Salome," Richardson's play portrays Aunt Nancy, an old woman who supports herself by tending a man's invalid wife and collecting chips of wood and coal for fuel. When the man, Silas, faces losing his job and the victrola he has not yet paid off, he asks Nancy to use her money to help him, but she has saved it for her son, Jim. Claiming the money Nancy has saved, Jim ultimately gives some of it to Silas for having provided for his mother.

Observed Peterson, ''Most of [Richardson's] plays were attempts at realistic treatment of Black life (both contemporary and historical) on such a variety of themes as manhood and bravery; suffering under white tyranny . . . ; the problems of the urban family; . . . the social strivings of the middle class; Black exploitation of other Blacks, and many other relevant subjects.'' The playwright worked to preserve for history an image of blacks more comprehensive than that portrayed by white writers, capturing the ''richness, diversity, and beauty of his race,'' described Patsy B. Perry in the *Dictionary of Literary Biography*. Through his plays and critical writings, his advocacy of Black theater, and his conviction that Black drama should excel on the same merits as any other drama, Richardson did much to bring Black artistry forward and promote the best characteristics of his, and all, people. Concluded Peterson, ''Willis Richardson has tried to show us 'the soul of a people, and the soul of this people is truly worth showing.'''

FOR MORE INFORMATION SEE:

Mary Anthony Scally, *Negro Catholic Writers, 1900-1943: A Bio-Bibliography*, Romig, 1945.
Black World, April, 1975 (p. 40ff).
James V. Hatch and Omarii Abdullah, editors, *Black Playwrights, 1823-1977: An Annotated Bibliography of Plays*, Bowker, 1977.
Dictionary of Literary Biography, Volume 51: *Afro-American Writers from the Harlem Renaissance to 1940*, Gale, 1987.

RILEY, Jocelyn (Carol) 1949-

PERSONAL: Born March 6, 1949, in Minneapolis, Minn.; daughter of G. D. (a sales engineer) and D. J. (a secretary; maiden name, Berg) Riley; married Jeffrey Allen Steele (a college professor), September 4, 1971; children: Doran, Brendan. *Education:* Attended Harvard University, summer, 1970; Carleton College, B.A., 1971. *Religion:* Lutheran. *Agent:* Jane Gelfman, John Farquharson Ltd., 250 West 57th St., New York, N.Y. 10107. *Office:* Box 5264—Hilldale, Madison, Wis. 53705.

CAREER: Carleton Miscellany, Northfield, Minn., managing editor, 1971; Beacon Press (publisher), Boston, Mass., marketing assistant, 1971-73; free-lance writer and editor, 1973—. Media scriptwriter for American Family Insurance, Madison, Wis., 1983-85. Independent audio-visual producer, 1986—. *Member:* Women in Communications (vice-president of Madison chapter, 1983-84; president, 1984-85), Authors Guild, PEN, National Book Critics Circle, Society of Children's Book Writers, Association for Multi-Image (vice-president of Madison chapter, 1985-86; president, 1986-87), Council for Wisconsin Writers.

AWARDS, HONORS: Carleton Huntington Poetry Prize, 1970, for ''The Winter Poems''; *Only My Mouth Is Smiling* was selected one of American Library Association's Best Books for Young Adults, and received the Arthur Tofte Memorial Award from the Council for Wisconsin Writers, both 1982; Writer's Cup from Women in Communications, Inc., 1985; Art Award from the Dane County Cultural Affairs Commission, 1986-89; Madison Arts Grant, 1986, 1987, 1989; Wisconsin Arts Board Grant, 1986, 1988, 1989; Finalist Award from the International Film and Television Festival of New York, Outstanding Achievement Award from the Association for Multi-Image International, both 1987, and Bronze Apple from the National Educational Film and Video Festival, 1988, all for ''Her Own

Words''; Certificate of Commendation from the American Association for State and Local History, 1988, for ''Belle,'' and ''Her Own Words''; Gold Medal Award from the International Film and Television Festival of New York, 1988, for ''Belle.''

WRITINGS:

Only My Mouth Is Smiling (juvenile), Morrow, 1982.
Crazy Quilt (juvenile), Morrow, 1984.
Page Proof (essays), Windigo Press, in press.

VIDEOS; WRITER AND PRODUCER

''Her Own Words,'' Jocelyn Riley Productions, 1986.
''Belle,'' Jocelyn Riley Productions, 1987.
''Zona Gale,'' Jocelyn Riley Productions, 1988.
''Patchwork: Quilts,'' Jocelyn Riley Productions, 1989.
''Votes for Women,'' Jocelyn Riley Productions, in production.
''To Be a Writer,'' Jocelyn Riley Productions, in production.

Author of newsletter, ''Her Own Words,'' 1987—. Contributor of articles and reviews to periodicals, including *Aspect, Boston, Publishers Weekly,* and *Writer*.

ADAPTATIONS:

''The Brass Ring'' (television film based on *Only My Mouth Is Smiling*), Showtime-TV, February 2, 1985.

WORK IN PROGRESS: A novel for children titled *Another Daughter;* a novella titled *Near Middle;* three biographies of women writers for children.

SIDELIGHTS: ''A major concern of both my fiction and nonfiction is women's lives and women's work. My first two novels focused on very young women protagonists growing up in a

JOCELYN RILEY

I looked up. Jennifer Normandale—better known as Jinx—was standing in front of me. (Jacket illustration by Michael and Peggy Garland from *Crazy Quilt* by Jocelyn Riley.)

predominantly female world that was nevertheless dominated by men in terms of actual (though unseen) power.

"My audio-visual work is geared for both children and adults. I am intrigued with women writers; I am currently producing and writing a series of short videos on women writers, with the scripts told entirely in their own words. Women who have been 'silenced' or forgotten for many years live again through their own words and the liveliness of audio-visual techniques.

"A second major theme of my fiction has been the effect of a severely mentally disturbed person on a whole family, particularly the children involved. I chose to concentrate on children because they are stuck in a situation in a way that a spouse, for instance, is not."

HOBBIES AND OTHER INTERESTS: Fishing, swimming, diary keeping, collecting woman's suffrage materials, gardening, cross-country skiing.

FOR MORE INFORMATION SEE:

School Library Journal, February, 1982, April, 1985, November, 1987, June-July, 1988.

Wisconsin State Journal, February 28, 1982, December 2, 1984, February 15, 1987, November 1, 1987, October 30, 1988.
Milwaukee Journal, April 11, 1982, February 1, 1985, March 1, 1987.
San Diego Union, May 2, 1982.
Houston Post, June 13, 1982.
Madison Sunshine, June 16, 1982.
Voice of Youth Advocates, August, 1982.
Boston Equal Times, August 22, 1982.
Minneapolis Star and Tribune, September 9, 1982, February 21, 1985.
Cambridge Sojourner, October, 1982.
St. Paul Pioneer Press/Dispatch, January 8, 1983, February 17, 1985.
Capital Times (Madison, Wis.), January 24, 1983, February 1, 1985.
Wisconsin Academy Review, December, 1983.
Horn Book, March, 1985.
Carleton Voice, spring, 1985.
Columbus Dispatch (Ohio), July 17, 1985.
Watertown Daily Times (Wis.), October 18, 1985.
Multi-Images Journal, November-December, 1987, May-June, 1988, March-April, 1989.
E. Fuller Torrey, M.D., *Surviving Schizophrenia: A Family Manual,* Harper, 1988.

RISKIND, Mary (Julia Longenberger) 1944-

PERSONAL: Born August 2, 1944, in Elmira, N.Y.; daughter of Harry R. (a carpenter) and Janet (Runkle) Longenberger; married Steven J. Riskind (a computer consultant), August 3, 1968; children: Paul. *Education:* Elmira College, B.A., 1966; doctoral study in social psychology at University of Michigan, 1966-73; Rutgers University, M.L.S., 1989. *Home:* 223 Brookside Ave., Ridgewood, N.J. 07450.

CAREER: Writer. Lee Memorial Library, Allendale, N.J., children's librarian, 1985-89; Montclair Public Library, Montclair, N.J., youth services specialist, 1989— . *Member:* American Library Association, Society of Children's Book Writers, Elmira College Club of New Jersey. *Awards, honors: Apple Is My Sign* was named a Notable Children's Trade Book in the Field of Social Studies by the National Council for Social Studies and the Children's Book Council, 1982.

WRITINGS:

FOR CHILDREN

Apple Is My Sign (ALA Notable Children's Book), Houghton, 1981.
Wildcat Summer, Houghton, 1985.
Follow That Mom!, Houghton, 1987.

SIDELIGHTS: "I grew up in Elmira, New York. I am the eldest of three hearing children, but both my parents were deaf. My father was born deaf (in a family of deaf parents and siblings); my mother lost her hearing as a result of scarlet fever when she was about three years old. We grew up using sign language exclusively at home. My mother tells me that I learned to sign before I could talk, so signing in a real sense is my first language.

"Many people think sign is just another form of English; it is not. American Sign Language is truly another language, though great efforts are being made—where sign is taught at all to the deaf— to teach signed English. Though there were many other hearing

MARY RISKIND

people around, on my street, etc., my earliest years were spent among the deaf community, and much as children from various ethnic groups grow up 'hyphenated,' we were always somewhat isolated from 'mainstream' America.

"There were both freedoms and responsibilities attached to being an outsider. I acted as interpreter for my parents from a very young age; I can remember, for instance, going to work with my father, who was a carpenter, to help explain to him what a particular customer wanted done. On the other hand, there was a tremendously uninhibited sense of play in my family, including my parents, that I think you seldom see in hearing adults. As a child we were the only family I knew that had an operating board-and-rope swing suspended from the living room ceiling!

"I learned to read before I went to school and was always a voracious reader, and as a child had a persistent fantasy life. (I specialized in disaster fantasies; I was always the heroine, of course.) I have strong recollections of hours spent in my father's lap waiting for him to finish reading a Grimm tale, or a chapter from *Thumper the Rabbit,* so that he could sign it to me. I also remember vividly the worn marble stairs leading to the second floor children's room of our Carnegie Library. Do I dare say it? The first book I can remember reading independently was *Little Black Sambo.* I remember a story about a milk wagon horse. I wish I could find it again. And as I got older, I loved books such as *Cheaper by the Dozen* and anything by Daphne du Maurier. I can recall an autobiography by Lillian Roth (titled *I'll Cry Tomorrow,* I believe), which had a tremendous impact on me as a teenager; I yearned for that sort of strength.

"Though, when I began writing I was struck by the rightness of it, the goodness-of-fit between me as a person and the demands of writing, I never at any time dreamed I would become a published author, I had always believed I would be a high school English teacher, and later when I went to college I set my sights on teaching psychology. I first started writing fiction when my son was small: the academic job market was very poor and I was having trouble finding what I felt was adequate child-care. Besides, I was having a wonderful time reading children's books with my son.

"My father had died long before my son was born. When Paul began to ask about him, I decided to write up a favorite anecdote that my father used to tell over and over, part of the folklore of our family, about how he had tricked his own dad, who could not hear, by calling out to the horse and stopping it as they rode into town one day. Looking back, I think the implicit meaning of that story was that it was important to maintain a sense of humor, even about something like deafness, or maybe particularly if you are deaf. As with any story that is retold, I had to make it my own, so in my hands it inevitably changed shape. Eventually I expanded and developed Harry's story to make it into a full-length book and the original anecdote is now one chapter.

"About the time I first started work on Harry, I came across a book about the deaf, but the emphasis was on body-aids and amplification. There was nothing about sign and the deaf community I knew. Frankly, I was angered that such a limited view of the deaf was being presented.

"Many of the details of *Apple Is My Sign* come from my own experience or from stories my father told. The face-blackening trick Harry plays in the study hall was actually one my father played on his schoolmates, except that by then he was shaving and he had shaved one side of his face and not the other and provoked an argument between the boys on either side of him. The traveling preacher comes from my childhood; there used to be a traveling minister who visited our town about every six weeks and deaf from miles around would come for services, no matter what their religious background. The pillow fight is based on a fight I once had with an elder half-brother. *I* was the one who came out with the blackened eye. I didn't tattle, but neither did I forget! The football chapter grew out of research into early forms of the game. My father had played at school as a young man and often talked about how hazardous a sport it was. He was not exaggerating, I discovered.

Mom was bobbing along in her orange life preserver. (Jacket illustration by Julie Downing from *Follow That Mom!* by Mary Riskind.)

''I could go on about the similarities between my background and my first book for children. Probably what was most significant for me in writing this book, however, was the extent to which I rediscovered, and reclaimed, my own deaf heritage.

''*Wildcat Summer* came out of my son's and my affection for cats. My son became especially interested in bobcats after we saw an injured one that was being housed at a nearby wildlife center. We started researching them in nature magazines and learning that their survival was increasingly in peril because of the growing demand for domestic fur. I started out with a straight nature story on bobcats for beginning readers and somehow ended up with a full-length novel. This particular story went through many iterations and as it evolved I could see it was becoming a record of my own personal struggle with myself about how to relate to a growing child, wanting to control the person my son would be, but learning in the end that I had to give him growing space and help him to grow into himself, not just someone that suited my needs. It was a tough lesson to learn but a valuable one that taught me respect for him *and* for me.

''I chose New Hampshire as the setting for *Wildcat* because we had spent a couple of summer vacations there with friends and it seemed the right place, one that I knew. I'm not certain where Grammer comes from. Aside from the cats she is my favorite character in the book. She may be drawn in part from an elderly woman who used to live next door and was almost a surrogate grandmother for our family, though our neighbor was not nearly

so ornery. We met a very sharp-tongued man on one of our visits to New Hampshire. He is part of Grammer; I guess I never believed he was really as nasty as he wanted us to think.

''*Follow That Mom!* was my attempt to write a funny story for children. I had had so many children ask me about writing a humorous book that I set it as a goal for myself. I was terrified at the prospect, since I am not a funny person and I always botch telling a joke, but once I got started I had a wonderful time. I was a Girl Scout for many years; the camping episodes in particular come out of my experience. I once had the misfortune of having to share a very small pup tent with a claustrophobic camper. I got very cold. I HATED selling Girl Scout cookies, by the way, and I buy a lot from any poor Scout who shows up at my door.

''My husband and my son say there is a lot of our family in *Follow That Mom!* I only know that we spent many a dinner time conversation discussing and free-associating to situations that came up in the story. And laughing. My son was the one who created the title.

''I had had fond dreams that being a children's writer would be lucrative enough to help support our family. Unfortunately, it has not worked out that way, so a few years ago I took a job as a children's librarian in a public library. I love what I do: it keeps me close to both children and books, but it also siphons off a lot of energy that might otherwise go into writing. I continue to write but more erratically now. Writing time is whenever I can snatch some time over a weekend or on a free evening. My next goal is to try to write a picture book, perhaps because I spend so much time these days working with them in storytimes.

''Just a word or two about the way I write. I use a journal extensively, both to warm-up before a writing session and as a way of giving an idea more substance until it has a chance to evolve. It is wonderful fun to trace my books through my journals. I used to handwrite everything, but I've become a part of the computer age and do only initial drafts by hand. I try to get to the word processor as soon as possible with a story, though the early idea stages seem to work best in pen or pencil. I suppose I am not a very disciplined writer. I prefer just to write and let happen what will, to find out what I am thinking, then to cut, cut, cut and rewrite, rewrite, rewrite!

''Books gave me so much as a child—joy, humor, courage, and I hope, wisdom. I would like to pass on those gifts to my readers.''

HOBBIES AND OTHER INTERESTS: Reading, running, baking bread, theater.

SADLER, Catherine Edwards 1952-

PERSONAL: Born December 3, 1952, in Los Angeles, Calif.; daughter of Anne (Josephson) Edwards; married Alan Sadler (an executive producer), June 20, 1976; children: Maxwell, Casey. *Education:* Attended American College of Switzerland, 1969-70, and United States International University, 1970-71; Windham College, B.A., 1974. *Agent:* Toni Mendez, Inc., 140 East 56th St., New York, N.Y. 10022.

CAREER: G. P. Putnam's Sons, New York, N.Y., editorial assistant, 1974-75, editor, 1975-77; free-lance writer and journalist, 1977-82; author of children's books, 1978—; Conran's Stores, Inc., New York, N.Y., vice-president of marketing and creative director, 1982-89; Koala Blue, Inc., Van Nuys, Calif.,

Some summer this was going to be. (Jacket illustration by James Shefcik from *Wildcat Summer* by Mary Riskind.)

Catherine and Alan Sadler with the children from *Two Chinese Families*.

vice-president of marketing, 1989—. *Member:* Author's Guild, Direct Marketing Association, Catalog Council. *Awards, honors: A Duckling Is Born* was selected an Outstanding Science and Trade Book for Children by the National Science Teachers Association and the Children's Book Council, 1981; *Two Chinese Families* was selected a Notable Children's Trade Book in the Field of Social Studies by the National Council for Social Studies and the Children's Book Council, 1982, and *Heaven's Reward,* 1985; American Catalog Silver Award from *Conran's Catalogue,* 1986, 1987, and 1989.

WRITINGS:

(Translator) Hans-Heinrich Isenbart, *A Foal Is Born* (illustrated with photographs by Hanns-Jorg Anders), Putnam, 1976.

(Translator) Max Alfred Zoll, *A Flamingo Is Born* (illustrated with photographs by Winifred Noack), Putnam, 1978.

(Translator) H. Isenbart, *A Duckling Is Born* (illustrated with photographs by Othmar Baumli), Putnam, 1981.

Two Chinese Families (illustrated with photographs by husband, Alan Sadler), Atheneum, 1981.

(Adapter) Sir Arthur Conan Doyle, *The Adventures of Sherlock Holmes,* Volumes I-IV, Avon, 1981.

Sasha: The Life of Alexandra Tolstoy (young adult), Putnam, 1982.

(Reteller) *Treasure Mountain: Folktales from Southern China* (illustrated by Cheng Mung Yun), Atheneum, 1982.

(Reteller) *Heaven's Reward: Fairy Tales from China* (illustrated by C. M. Yun), Atheneum, 1985.

WORK IN PROGRESS: The Adventures of Sherlock Holmes, Volumes V-VIII; sixteen additional stories.

SIDELIGHTS: "Being the child of an author, I have always loved to read. I was brought up in Europe and so was exposed to a great many countries and adventures at an early age. A love of travel and of cultures developed.

"My books for children have all featured families and legends or tales from other parts of the world: England, Russia, China. In each I have tried to evoke the spirit and mystery of that land. *Two Chinese Families* took my husband and me to Mainland China where we spent time with two families, seeing first-hand how they lived and worked. *Treasure Mountain* and *Heaven's Reward* both developed out of that remarkable trip—one a collection of folk tales celebrating the oral tradition of the many Chinese national minorities, the other, a collection of classic Chinese fairy tales.

"*Sasha* focuses on the life of Alexandra Tolstoy, Leo Tolstoy's daughter—first in her homeland during her father's life and then in the United States, where her work with the Tolstoy Foundation helped relocate refugees throughout the world. *The Adventures of Sherlock Holmes* takes us all back to Baker Street and the ultimate mystery tale, retold so that children can enjoy Conan Doyle and participate in a little deductive reasoning without the barriers that archaic language and references can pose.

A great tiger, sent by the Emperor of Heaven, carried her off to an island in the Southern Sea. (From *Heaven's Reward* by Catherine Edwards Sadler. Illustrated by Cheng Mung Yun.)

"Throughout my life as a writer I have worked professionally in a related field. My first job out of school was as an editorial assistant for a publisher in New York. Eventually this became an editorship in which I was responsible for acquiring books, working with the author, finding an illustrator, overseeing production and editorial direction, and so on. In my recent business positions these same skills have allowed me to function in the business world as a vice-president, responsible for all aspects of marketing—from concept through completion of graphics, catalogs, advertising, and public relations.

"I have learned that the skill of writing—not just the facility for words, but also the capacity to look at a project conceptually from beginning to end and to communicate it clearly to an audience is as vital in the business world as it is in writing a book."

HOBBIES AND OTHER INTERESTS: Spending time with her children, traveling.

SENN, Steve 1950-

PERSONAL: Born August 4, 1950, in Americus, Ga.; son of Homer Will (a grocer) and Angelyn (a nurse; maiden name, Gay) Senn; married Linda Harris (a teacher), September 18, 1978 (divorced); children: David, William Blake. *Education:* Attended Ringling School of Art, 1968-71. *Agent:* Dorothy Markinko, McIntosh & Otis, Inc., 475 Fifth Ave., New York, N.Y. 10017.

CAREER: Miami Herald, Miami, Fla., editorial artist, 1978; *Florida Times-Union,* Jacksonville, editorial artist and illustrator, 1978-81; William Cook Advertising, Jacksonville, staff writer and senior art director, beginning 1981; author and illustrator.

WRITINGS:

JUVENILE

The Double Disappearance of Walter Fozbek (self-illustrated), Hastings House, 1980.
Spacebread (self-illustrated), Atheneum, 1981.
A Circle in the Sea, Atheneum, 1981.
Born of Flame: A Spacebread Story (sequel to *Spacebread;* self-illustrated), Atheneum, 1982.
In the Castle of the Bear, Atheneum, 1985.
Ralph Fozbek and the Amazing Black Hole Patrol, Avon, 1986.
The Sand Witch, Avon, 1987.

A Circle in the Sea and *In the Castle of the Bear* have been translated into Danish.

ADAPTATIONS:

An animated version of *The Double Disappearance of Walter Fozbek* appeared on "Storybreak," CBS-TV, 1985.

WORK IN PROGRESS: Odin's Hostage, a historical novel about Vikings, gods, and hostage princes; *Three Hungers Touch the Moon,* a contemporary juvenile book about deformity; a juvenile book entitled *Fat Chance,* about a genie who becomes separated from his bottle; adult stories of horror and fantasy.

SIDELIGHTS: "Storytelling is the parent of civilization, and imagination is the reason we do not live in trees. That sounds grandiose, perhaps, because we are usually dwarfed uncomfor-

STEVE SENN

tably by anything that is distinctly true, but it may help explain why so many people, including me, write. Creating fiction is like calling God on the telephone. When I first tried constructing sentences, around age ten, it amazed me that another world could be created so instantly and so completely by written language. It is still exhilarating.

"I wanted to write stories from a very early age. I think when I was about eleven or twelve I decided I wanted to write books. Big, thick ones. At the time I was really excited about the Iliad and the Odyssey and everything about Greece, so I made up an epic about a young Greek slave who earns his freedom, becomes the King of an Aegean island, and fights at Marathon. I picked an island from a map, and made up the story. This may sound a little high-brow. The books were simple things with lots of illustrations, but I learned all the gods and legends with relish. No one taught them to me. I guess that is why I feel it is unnecessary to taper information for what adults consider to be the interests and capabilities of children.

"I was raised in the South. I know I am supposed to be the heir of a great storytelling tradition, but the only stories I can remember were sort of family gossip. True, the gossip was endless, and wove in and out of many tellings and footnotes and embellishments, but I remember no fascinating yarnspinner in my childhood. The only tradition I am heir to might be in my blood, however, because the easiest part of writing to me is the tale. The plot, the story, how you get the situations you want to tell about to happen, that's the dreamy part to me. The idea of a story is just the kernel of sand around which you spin a pearl, although most people think that's the hard part. The idea is the easy thing. Then comes the plot, the second easiest. Then you have to write it. That takes courage and arrogance. And, if you are any good at all, it takes going on even though you know the story is more ambitious than your talent. The only way to finish a book is to ignore how inadequate you feel to the task.

''All I want to do is tell good stories that bring new feelings, fears, loves, ideas, and insights to the reader. It would be nice to be paid for them. My success so far has been with children's stories, which are really stories made up by an adult and then streamlined to the limit of leanness, with a kid as protagonist. I like having my protagonist be able to react to things from a totally fresh viewpoint. Besides, children will go places with you that adults will not. I feel very lucky in finding editors, chiefly Jean Karl, who will let me take them where I want to go (usually).

''Eventually, I would like to draw on my childhood in smalltown Georgia for some children's books. Perhaps it was the place itself that made me want to invent other places and people. The place I came from was haunted. The lives of the people were bent in odd, Southern ways. Life there was contorted around several blatant but invisible lies, and in such an atmosphere it is easy to believe in witches and vampires and serpents and gods, and vital to believe in good and evil. There was an old colonial mansion on my street, and two of its columns were gone and had been replaced by timber frames. An aging heiress, in an alcoholic fog, lived inside with millions of old magazines. Never coming

There was a clumpiness and ruffle to her fur that bespoke toughness. (From *Spacebread* by Steve Senn. Jacket illustration by the author.)

outside, she was companioned only by a black maid who brought boxes of groceries and booze balanced on her head back to the mansion. Chandeliers watched this woman die. Perhaps that sounds like a cliche from a Williams play, but it is a part of my personal myth. There are stories inside me which draw on that myth and whisper secrets about the land, about chains of both steel and of lies, and some beauty that is tied up in all of it. Someday I will tell them.''

STEVENSON, Drew 1947-

PERSONAL: Born December 25, 1947, in Washington, Pa.; son of Andrew Kenneth (a mason) and Elizabeth Wells (a secretary; maiden name, Smith) Stevenson; married Gale Spates, August 28, 1988. *Education:* Bethany College, B.A., 1969; University of Pittsburgh, M.L.S., 1971. *Religion:* Presbyterian. *Home:* 82 President St., Brooklyn, N.Y. 11231. *Agent:* McIntosh & Otis, 310 Madison Ave., New York, N.Y. 10017. *Office:* Brooklyn Public Library, Grand Army Plaza, Brooklyn, N.Y. 11238.

CAREER: Tompkins County Public Library, Ithaca, N.Y., children's librarian, 1971-76, reference librarian, 1976-77, adult services librarian, 1977-88; Brooklyn Public Library, Brooklyn, N.Y., telephone reference librarian, 1988— . Member of board of directors, Literacy Volunteers of Tompkins County, and Tompkins County Senior Citizens Council; member of advisory board, Retired Senior Volunteer Program (R.S.V.P.). *Member:* American Library Association. *Awards, honors:* Margaret Mc-Namara Award from the Trinity Area School District (Washington, Pa.) and Reading Is Fundamental, Inc., 1986, for his contributions to children and reading.

WRITINGS:

The Ballad of Penelope Lou . . . and Me (illustrated by Marcia Sewell), Crossing Press, 1978.
The Case of the Horrible Swamp Monster (illustrated by Susan Swan), Dodd, 1984.
The Case of the Visiting Vampire (illustrated by S. Swan), Dodd, 1986.
The Case of the Wandering Werewolf (illustrated by Linda Winchester), Dodd, 1987.

Contributor of articles and short stories to periodicals, including *Fiction Writers* and *Grapevine Weekly*. Also contributor of mystery and suspense book reviews, *School Library Journal,* 1974-85.

WORK IN PROGRESS: A Mystery at Maplewood Manor, the first of a new mystery series for elementary school-age children, for Cobblehill Books.

SIDELIGHTS: ''I have always loved books and music. When I was a child, a corner of our apartment in Washington, Pennsylvania was set aside for my picture book collection and record player. My mother said that I would sit for hours looking through my books while listening to a scratchy seventy-eight rpm recording of 'Little Brown Jug' over and over again. I guess it drove everybody crazy.

''I wrote my first story when I was in grade school. At the time I was beginning a lifelong fascination with monsters and the supernatural. The story was about a group of kids who have a terrifying encounter with a dinosaur. My grandmother read it and then took it to the high school where she taught algebra. She told me that she read it to her classes and they all loved it. I believed

DREW STEVENSON

her and was quite thrilled that 'big kids' had enjoyed something I had done. It wasn't until I was older that I realized it wouldn't have been very smart for her students *not* to act enthusiastic about her adored grandson's story. It didn't matter though. By then I was hooked on writing.

"In grade school I also became addicted to the 'Hardy Boys' mysteries. I loved the action and the cliffhangers and would stay up as late as I could devouring them. When mom would come into the bedroom to tell me it was time to turn out the lights, I would beg her to let me read just one more chapter. She usually did because she was a lover of books, too.

"The 'Hardys' turned me into an avid mystery fan. In high school I graduated to Agatha Christie, Erle Stanley Gardner, Rex Stout, Mickey Spillane, and others. I especially liked authors who wrote a series. When I found a detective I liked I didn't want their cases to end.

"I don't know exactly when I decided to become a librarian. Because of my love of books, it was probably always somewhere in my mind. I also had an uncle who was a librarian and he encouraged me. After I graduated from Bethany College I went to the University of Pittsburgh to work on my master's degree in library science.

"While I was at Pitt, Professor Margaret Hodges became my mentor. Mrs. Hodges is a prolific author of children's books. Her *St. George and the Dragon* won the coveted Caldecott Award. It was this enthusiastic advocate of children who re-

introduced me to the joys of children's books and inspired me to become a children's librarian.

"In 1971 I graduated from Pitt and became assistant children's librarian at the Tompkins County Public Library in Ithaca, New York. During the five years I spent in the children's room I worked very hard to build up a rapport and trust with the children. I had a small army of children who regularly asked me to recommend a 'good' book for them to read. What a responsibility! And what a joy when they would return to tell me how much they had enjoyed a particular book that I had recommended and to ask me for another. With my reputation constantly on the line I had to learn what books were liked, what were not, and why. What I learned from the children during those years was a tremendous help when I later began writing books for them.

"During this period I became friends with John and Elaine Gill who own and operate the Crossing Press. They were interested in starting a line of children's books and began coming into the children's room to get a feel for the market. They began asking my advice and soon I was reading manuscripts for them and making recommendations.

"Cut!" she finally hollered. "O.K., Raymond, into the monster costume." (Illustration by Susan Swan from *The Case of the Horrible Swamp Monster* by Drew Stevenson.)

''After Elaine found out that I had written my own original story for an appearance I made on a local television show called 'TV Storyhour' she asked to read it. Although she liked it, she asked me if I would write a new story in rhyme. I did, and it was called *The Ballad of Penelope Lou . . . and Me*. The story was about a young man who is deathly afraid of water but falls in love with a young woman who is a fearless sailor. The young man tries to trick his love into believing he too is a brave sea traveller. The trick backfires and our hero ends up on a terrifying trip on the back of a huge whale. Of course, everything ends happily for all concerned.

''The Gills liked the story and decided to publish it. We were lucky to get the talented Marcia Sewell to draw the illustrations. *The Ballad of Penelope Lou . . . and Me* was published in 1978.

''Now that I had done a picture book I decided to try some novels for older children. By then I had left the children's room to become head of adult services. Even so, my experiences as a children's librarian remained vivid in my mind and influenced the direction my writing would take.

''Mysteries, monsters, and a series. I had loved them as a child, and I had found that the children of today shared the same passion. I decided to combine all three elements in the hope that, if they were ever published, my books would never gather dust in the presence of children.

''I started from the monster angle. My main character, J. Huntley English, is a boy who believes that monsters do exist and is desperate to have a close encounter with one. Unfortunately for him, he lives in a small Pennsylvania town, hardly a hotbed of monster activity. This doesn't dissuade Huntley from constantly looking for and seeing monsters where none exist.

''Early on, I had to decide whether to have Huntley and his friends actually deal with real monsters or not. I decided against it. Real monsters would have placed these books in the realm of fantasy and/or horror stories. I wanted them to be mysteries in the classic mold of *The Hound of the Baskervilles*. Therefore, each book begins with Huntley on the trail of a particular type of monster, like a vampire or a werewolf. Strong evidence is accumulated that, amazingly enough, there is indeed a monster on the loose in Huntley's hometown. However, as Huntley and company delve deeper into each case, they eventually discover that there is a very human crime behind each of their monster investigations. If he can't capture monsters, Huntley will definitely settle for criminals.

''I aim for a lot of suspense and cliffhangers in my stories, but I haven't forgotten that children love to laugh as much as they love to be scared. While suspense is at the core of each of Huntley's mysteries, I always include plenty of humor to keep the chuckles coming. Much of the humor is centered around Huntley's best friend, Raymond Almond, who narrates the books. Raymond is one of those people best described as a 'disaster magnet.' He freely admits he's a coward, but he always keeps his wry sense of humor and, one way or another, he always comes through for his buddies in the end. I find that children love to laugh along with Raymond. Maybe it's because there's a lot of Raymond in each of us.

''Over the past twenty years there have been more and more 'issue' books appearing for children. These are books, both fiction and nonfiction, which deal with the serious issues facing children. Death, drugs, adoption, sex, sexual abuse, racism, sexism, ageism, and divorce are a few of them. We always need authors willing and able to deal with these difficult topics to help children understand and come to terms with them.

''But I want to make a case for those of us in the 'light brigade.' I honestly believe that what we do is every bit as important. We make reading fun for children. A child who learns early on that reading is enjoyable has the best chance of being a lifelong reader. Once they are hooked on reading, children can be guided in other directions and into more challenging material. But we have to hook them first.

''I love visiting schools to talk with the children about reading and writing. I have stood outside a classroom door, waiting to go in to speak to the students, listening while the teacher finished reading a chapter in one of my books. I heard the children gasp and I heard them laugh and I heard them begging for just one more chapter. Everyone was having fun. Especially me!''

HOBBIES AND OTHER INTERESTS: Cooking, reading mysteries, watching horror films, travelling, listening to music.

STOWE, Leland 1899-

PERSONAL: Born November 10, 1899, in Southbury, Conn.; son of Frank Philip (in the lumber business) and Eva Sarah (Noe) Stowe; married Ruth F. Bernot (divorced); married Theodora F. Calauz, June 17, 1952; children: (first marriage) Bruce B., Alan A. *Education:* Wesleyan University, Middletown, Conn., B.A., 1921. *Politics:* Independent. *Religion:* Protestant. *Home:* 801 Greenhills Dr., Ann Arbor, Mich. 48105.

CAREER: Worcester Telegram, Worcester, Mass. reporter, 1921-22; *New York Herald,* New York City, staff reporter, 1923-24; news editor for *Pathe News,* 1924-26; *New York Herald Tribune,* New York City, staff reporter, 1924, 1926, Paris correspondent, 1926-35, political correspondent in North and South America, 1936-39; *Chicago Daily News,* Chicago, Ill., war correspondent in England, Finland, Norway, Hungary, Yugoslavia, Bulgaria, Romania, Turkey, Albania, and Greece, 1939-40, and in China, Burma, India, Thailand, Malaya, Indo-China, Iran, the Soviet Union, and Libya, 1941-43; American Broadcasting Co., New York City, radio commentator, 1944-46; lecturer and free-lance writer, 1947—; University of Michigan, Ann Arbor, professor of journalism, 1956-69. Free-lance war correspondent in France, Belgium, and Germany, 1944, and Italy and Greece, 1945; radio commentator for Mutual Broadcasting System, 1945-46; director of news and information service of Radio Free Europe, 1952-54.

AWARDS, HONORS: Pulitzer Prize for Foreign Correspondence, 1930, for covering events in Paris in 1929; Legion of Honor (France), 1931; M.A. from Wesleyan University, 1936, and Harvard University, 1945; Distinguished Service Award from Sigma Delta Chi, Overseas Press Club of America, and University of Missiouri's School of Journalism, all 1941, for war reporting from Finland and Norway; LL.D. from Wesleyan University, 1944, and Hobart College, 1946; Military Cross (Greece), 1945; James L. McConaughty Award from Wesleyan University, 1963.

WRITINGS:

Nazi Means War, Faber, 1933, Whittlesey House, 1934.
No Other Road to Freedom, Knopf, 1941.
They Shall Not Sleep, Knopf, 1943.
While Time Remains, Knopf, 1946.
Target: You, Random House, 1949.

LELAND STOWE

Conquest by Terror: The Story of Satellite Europe, Random House, 1951.

Crusoe of Lonesome Lake, Random House, 1957.

The Last Great Frontiersman: The Remarkable Adventures of Tom Lamb, Paperjacks, 1982.

Contributor of about a hundred articles to national magazines, including *Life, Look, Nation, New Republic,* and *Harper's.* Foreign editor, *Reporter,* 1949-50; roving editor, *Reader's Digest,* 1955-76.

SIDELIGHTS: Stowe writes that his chief motivation is "to inform the public in the United States and other countries of important political and social developments directly affecting their lives." His writings and lectures (totaling over three hundred in the United States) included major forewarnings of the coming of World War II (1933-39), the assured ultimate victory of Britain and her allies over Nazi Germany (1941-43), the spread of Communist regimes and controls in Europe and China as a result of World War II (1941-45), and the inevitable Soviet nuclear menace to the United States (1946-57).

"I am certain that the Soviet-American proliferation of nuclear missiles and other related weapons . . . constitutes the greatest, almost inestimable peril not only to our people but to most of mankind. Next to this the energy crisis . . . threatens to undermine, if not destroy, democratic governments, including our own and much or most of free enterprise systems as we now know them."

FOR MORE INFORMATION SEE:

Joseph J. Mathews, *Reporting the Wars,* University of Minnesota Press, 1957.

John Hohenberg, *Foreign Correspondence,* Columbia University Press, 1964.

Phillip Knightley, *The First Casualty,* Harcourt, 1975.

COLLECTIONS

Mass Communications History Center, Madison, Wisconsin.

SZEKERES, Cyndy 1933-

PERSONAL: Surname is pronounced *Zeck*-er-es; born October 31, 1933, in Bridgeport, Conn.; daughter of Stephen Paul (a toolmaker) and Anna (Ceplousky) Szekeres; married Gennaro Prozzo (an artist), September 20, 1958; children: Marc, Christopher. *Education:* Pratt Institute, Certificate, 1954. *Home:* Box 280, RFD 3, Putney, Vt. 05346.

CAREER: Illustrator of children's books.

WRITINGS:

My Workbook Diary, 1973, McGraw, 1972.
Cyndy's Animal Calendar, 1973, McGraw, 1973.
Cyndy's Animal Calendar, 1975, McGraw, 1974.
My Workbook Diary, 1975, McGraw, 1974.
Long Ago (calendar), McGraw, 1976.
Long Ago, McGraw, 1977.
A Child's First Book of Poems, Golden Books, 1981, published as *Cyndy Szekeres' Book of Poems,* Golden Books, 1987.
Cyndy Szekeres' ABC, Golden Books, 1983.
Puppy Too Small, Golden Books, 1984.
Scaredy Cat, Golden Books, 1984.
Thumpity Thump Gets Dressed, Golden Books, 1984.
Baby Bear's Surprise, Golden Books, 1984.
Cyndy Szekeres' Counting Book 1 to 10, Golden Books, 1984.
Suppertime for Frieda Fuzzypaws, Golden Books, 1985.
Hide-and-Seek Duck, Golden Books, 1985.
Nothing-to-Do Puppy, Golden Books, 1985.
Good Night, Sammy, Golden Books, 1985.
Puppy Lost, Golden Books, 1986.
Sammy's Special Day, Golden Books, 1986.
Little Bear Counts His Favorite Things, Golden Books, 1986.
Melanie Mouse's Moving Day, Golden Books, 1986.
Cyndy Szekeres' Mother Goose Rhymes, Golden Books, 1987.
Cyndy Szekeres' Book of Fairy Tales, Golden Books, 1988.
Good Night, Sweet Mouse, Golden Books, 1988.
Cyndy Szekeres' Favorite Two-Minute Stories, Golden Books, 1989.

"THE TINY PAW LIBRARY" SERIES

A Busy Day, Golden Books, 1989.
The New Baby, Golden Books, 1989.
Moving Day, Golden Books, 1989.
A Fine Mouse Band, Golden Books, 1989.

ILLUSTRATOR

Sam Vaughan, *New Shoes,* Doubleday, 1961.
Jean Latham and Bee Lewi, *When Homer Honked,* Macmillan, 1961.
Majorie Flack, *Walter, the Lazy Mouse,* Doubleday, 1963.
Evelyn Sibley Lampman, *Mrs. Updaisy,* Doubleday, 1963.
Phyllis Krasilovsky, *Girl Who Was a Cowboy,* Doubleday, 1965.

CYNDY SZEKERES

(With others) Alvin Tresselt, editor, *Humpty Dumpty's Story-book*, Parents Magazine Press, 1966.
Edward Ormondroyd, *Michael, the Upstairs Dog*, Dial, 1967.
Nancy Faulkner, *Small Clown and Tiger*, Doubleday, 1968.
Kathleen Lombardo, *Macaroni*, Random House, 1968.
Peggy Parrish, *Jumper Goes to School*, Simon & Schuster, 1969.
Adelaide Holl, *Moon Mouse*, Random House, 1969.
Barbara Robinson, *Fattest Bear in the First Grade*, Random House, 1969.
John Peterson, *Mystery in the Night Woods*, Scholastic Book Services, 1969.
Joy Lonergan, *Brian's Secret Errand*, Doubleday, 1969.
Patsy Scarry, *Little Richard*, McGraw, 1970.
P. Scarry, *Waggy and His Friends*, McGraw, 1970.
Kathryn Hitte, *What Can You Do without a Place to Play?*, Parents Magazine Press, 1971.
Lois Myller, *No! No!*, Simon & Schuster, 1971.
P. Scarry, *Little Richard and Prickles*, McGraw, 1971.
Betty Jean Lifton, *Good Night, Orange Monster*, Atheneum, 1972.
Mary Lystad, *James, the Jaguar*, Putnam, 1972.
Betty Boegehold, *Pippa Mouse*, Knopf, 1973.
A. Holl, *Bedtime for Bears*, Garrard, 1973.
P. Scarry, *More about Waggy*, American Heritage Press, 1973.
Miriam Anne Bourne, *Four-Ring Three*, Coward, 1973.
Albert Bigelow Paine, "Hollow Tree" series, three books, Avon, 1973.
M. Lystad, *The Halloween Parade*, Putnam, 1973.

Kathy Darling, *Little Bat's Secret*, Garrard, 1974.
Robert Welber, *Goodbye, Hello*, Pantheon, 1974.
Julia Cunningham, *Maybe, a Mole*, Pantheon, 1974.
Albert B. Paine, *Snowed-In Book*, Avon, 1974.
Jan Wahl, *The Muffletumps' Christmas Party*, Follett, 1975.
J. Wahl, *The Muffletumps' Storybook*, Follett, 1975.
Carolyn S. Bailey, *A Christmas Party*, Pantheon, 1975.
B. Boegehold, *Here's Pippa Again*, Knopf, 1975.
J. Wahl, *The Clumpets Go Sailing*, Parents Magazine Press, 1975.
Andrew Bronin, *Gus and Buster Work Things Out*, Coward, 1975.
Marjorie W. Sharmat, *Edgemont*, Coward, 1976.
J. Wahl, *Great-Grandmother Cat Tales*, Pantheon, 1976.
J. Wahl, *The Muffletumps' Halloween Scare*, Follett, 1977.
J. Wahl, *Doctor Rabbit's Foundling*, Pantheon, 1977.
Tony Johnston, *Night Noises and Other Mole and Troll Stories*, Putnam, 1977.
T. Johnston, *Five Little Foxes and the Snow*, Putnam, 1977.
Mary D. Kwitz, *Little Chick's Story*, Harper, 1978.
J. Wahl, *Who Will Believe Tim Kitten? A Read Aloud-Read Alone Book*, Pantheon, 1978.
A. Holl, *Small Bear Builds a Playhouse*, Garrard, 1978.
Judy Delton, *Brimhall Comes to Stay*, Lothrop, 1978.
M. W. Sharmat, *The 329th Friend*, Four Winds Press, 1979.
T. Johnston, *Happy Birthday, Mole and Troll*, Putnam, 1979.
Catherine Hiller, *Argentaybee and the Boonie*, Coward, 1979.
J. Wahl, *Doctor Rabbit's Lost Scout*, Pantheon, 1979.
B. Boegehold, *Pippa Pops Out!*, Knopf, 1979.

(Illustration by Cyndy Szekeres from *The Night before Christmas* by Clement C. Moore.)

B. Boegehold, *Hurray for Pippa!*, Knopf, 1980.

P. Scarry, *Patsy Scarry's Big Bedtime Storybook*, Random House, 1980.

Polly B. Berends, *Ladybug and Dog and the Night Walk*, Random House, 1980.

Marci Ridlon, *Woodsey Log Library*, four volumes, Random House, 1981.

Margo Hopkins, *Honey Rabbit*, Golden Books, 1982.

Marci McGill, *The Six Little Possums: A Birthday ABC*, Golden Press, 1982.

M. McGill, *The Six Little Possums and the Baby Sitter*, Golden Press, 1982.

M. McGill, *The Six Little Possums at Home*, Golden Press, 1982.

M. McGill, *The Six Little Possums: Pepper's Good and Bad Day*, Golden Press, 1982.

Clement C. Moore, *The Night before Christmas*, Golden Books, 1982.

Selma Lanes, selector, *A Child's First Book of Nursery Tales*, Golden Books, 1983, published as *Cyndy Szekeres' Book of Nursery Tales*, 1987.

S. Lanes, selector, *Cyndy Szekeres' Book of Nursery Tales*, Golden Books, 1988.

B. Boegehold, *Here's Pippa*, Knopf, 1989.

ADAPTATIONS:

"Moon Mouse" (filmstrip), Random House.

WORK IN PROGRESS: "The Tiny Paw Library" series centering on a mouse family—mother, father, brother, sister, younger sister and a new baby. "The series brings attention to the problems that arise in any family with a new baby. Of course, many of the 'problems' are quite hilarious and sweet. I didn't intend for these books to have a moral, but as I finish each one, it seems to be saying 'I'm okay; you're okay.'"

SIDELIGHTS: "I grew up in Fairfield, Connecticut, in an area that originally had been farmland. Nature played a big part in my life. We were exposed to fruit and nut trees, and every so often a crop would sprout in the middle of a field, reseeding itself even though it was no longer being cultivated.

"I was a child toward the end of the Depression and our treasures were not things that could be bought—they were made from things that ignited our imagination. Making 'secrets' meant going out in the woods, pulling up a tuft of grass and laying out flowers in a pattern, covering it with broken glass, making a picture, and then covering it up again with the grass. A 'best friend's gift' was to let her know your 'secret.' This was our most solemn token of friendship. Of course if we wanted to break a friendship, we'd say, 'Want to see so-and-so's secret?' Going into the woods was for us better than a trip to Tiffany's. The colors put jewels to shame—the bright orange of a mushroom, for example, or hidden, shade-loving blossoms. Walking in the woods is like turning pages in a book—there's so much to see and ponder over.

"I can't remember a time when I didn't draw. I was the artist in the family, an aptitude inherited from my father who never had a chance to develop his talent."[1]

"The first artistic efforts of mine that I can remember were pencil sketches done on paper bags that my father had flattened and cut up to serve as my drawing paper. I was always encouraged by my family to draw, and later by my friends, to illustrate. Why did I draw at all? . . . It was a fascination with what I saw—simple things—flowers, grass, fog—the variety of details and differences in animals and people. I loved to read books as a kid and there were never enough illustrations in them. Then, sometimes, I didn't agree at all with what the illustrator chose to do!"[2]

"In my family, we learned early to be independent. This meant not only doing housework and cooking, but emotional self-reliance, as well. I was left to solve my own problems which I did through writing poetry, talking it out. I was well-equipped for life as an artist, and the things that were traumatic for some of my peers—finding jobs, managing time and money—pretty much rolled off my back.

"I never dreamed I would go to college. I assumed that I was headed for a job in a factory and probably marriage. But my

"Blah! The thought of spending another day with myself makes me want to go back to bed!" (From *The 329th Friend* by Marjorie Weinman Sharmat. Illustrated by Cyndy Szekeres.)

father learned of the money that could be made doing advertising art and decided that I should go to art school. A week before high school graduation, I applied to Pratt. Suprisingly, I was accepted. I had no intention of embarking on a career in advertising. I had my heart set on becoming an illustrator. I remembered how strongly I reacted to books when I was a kid. The illustrations usually disappointed me, because they contradicted the text or served as reproductions of text without adding anything original. N. C. Wyeth and Arthur Rackham were exceptions and established a standard for me.

''Being a student at Pratt meant very hard work. During the first year the demands are particularly gruelling. I couldn't get into freshman housing because I applied so late. This turned out to be a blessing, because I had to move into a house with upperclassmen who were extremely supportive of my 'freshman agony.' In the best sense of the word, Pratt was a melting pot, combining kids from privileged families exposed to travel and art with kids of factory workers. The school was highly selective of talent and not concerned with the particulars of your life and your background. What mattered was your work and your commitment. I learned as much from my fellow students as I did in the classroom, and I learned a tremendous amount in class.

''After graduation came the cruel realization that there simply weren't any jobs which encouraged creativity. My first employment was with a display house, painting mechanized statues of Santa Claus and his elves. For two years I did children's fashion

illustration for Saks Fifth Avenue. This called for a slick, commercial style, which soon began to get in the way of my real work—anthropomorphic illustrations—which I was doing on the side to please myself.

''At about this time, I met my husband, a painter and etcher, who worked at night in a post office. Our dates usually took us to the zoo where we'd spend hours sketching. My husband is a gifted teacher and gave me wonderful criticism on my drawings. After we married, Jerry taught art in the parochial school system creating a most productive turmoil in the process, and I was able to concentrate on drawing.

''I was pregnant with the first of our two sons when I got that first book. It was 1959. Careers for women were something one did whilst waiting for marriage and homemaking duties to intercede. I was a threat, I guess, to our friends also newly married and parenting. My combining that with a career was constantly under attack. I learned to call myself a homemaker and shut up about the illustrating. While illustrating and family life began simultaneously, priorities went to *family*, and illustrating, growing with each experience, developing a style, moved *very* slowly. Redoing an illustration was a luxury; time was so precious. Developing a character through hundreds of sketches, researching details in dozens of books—this was impossible. My peers were moving faster, most of them male (fellow students at Pratt were Tomie de Paola, Arnold and Anita Lobel). I needed more growing, much more time in my efforts to feel satisfied with

(Frontispiece and title page from *Hide-and-Seek Duck* by Cyndy Szekeres. Illustrated by the author.)

those early books. Still, in them I see the glimmer of what has finally started to develop. As the boys needed less of me, more time went into work. I was able to give more attention to my intentions! Personality, emotion, individuality, convincing living details—all requiring much research, sketching and rejecting and redoing.

"Another important factor influencing my art was our move to Putney, Vermont, where we bought a house a quarter of a mile into the woods on eleven acres. The woods are vital to my work. There I sketch and collect details for backgrounds. In the winter, I bring inside frozen patches of leaves and bark. It thaws in the house, then the small creatures hibernating gradually awaken all over the studio. In warmer weather I lie down on the ground to see things from the vantage point of a small animal. My eyes can only take in parts of twigs, blades of grass, and stones appear to be enormous. The range of colors in the woods is also astonishing—thousands of shades of green, brown and gray as well as the more vivid, conventionally dramatic hues."[1]

A look into Szekeres' studio: "It's my own place to work, goof off, go mad! It's small, bright and warm—and in Vermont, warmth is a plus! For the tools I work with (watercolors, gouache, inks, pencils, brushes) good storage, and lots of it, is important. I use old furniture like a dentist's cabinet, a grocer's desk, and printer's-type drawers—they have the shallow multidrawers I need. Besides, old worn wood is nice to live with. And these pieces have character. I like that!

"For research, our good libraries are indispensable. But I supplement them with my own personal library. And I have my collection of happy clutter: plants and flowers from nearby woods, hats from just about everywhere and toys (animal-type toys, of course). They're informative, inspiring . . . and fun to play with.

"Along with his own work, my husband manages the financial arrangements, research and mechanical tasks (dummies and paste-ups), leaving me free to draw. He continues to be my stalwart critic and teacher. I'll be drawing a rabbit, say, and he'll stop, peer over my shoulder and then quietly place a photograph of a rabbit on my desk, which means, 'Look again, you haven't seen it closely enough.'

"All of my illustrations are anthropomorphic. I know this arouses objection in certain circles, but I know that animals have emotions and that the connections between humans and animals are strong and deep. This has nothing to do with sentimentalizing animals so often seen on greeting cards done by artists with no apparent feelings about animals. Anthropomorphizing is more than just putting a dress on a rabbit.

"I don't draw animals exclusively. I carry a sketchbook with me, and whenever I have the time, I sketch. When I have a good sketch of a person, I develop it into an animal character. The work becomes an interesting marriage of human and animal qualities, since anthropomorphized animals do things that regular animals don't.

"There is a delight and magic about the anthropomorphic animal world. No such place exists to inform you. Your imagination, which is mostly unused and unexercised, must take you there and give it form and detail. While a story about a specific child is just that, his or her story, when you do a story about a rabbit in pants and a vest, even bear who wears only his own fur, these characters are everybody and anybody . . . you and me.

(From ''The Emperor's New Clothes'' in *Book of Fairy Tales,* adapted by Cyndy Szekeres. Illustrated by Cyndy Szekeres.)

''Each picture may take from eight to fourteen hours a day, depending on how effective I am at working—we're all uneven on different days—but it's about two and a half months by the time I've got all the sketches prepared and start work on the finishes.''

Szekeres developed her own techniques for maintaining perspective. ''Most people who do stories with mice will do the whole tree and make it look as though the mice are six feet tall. I usually go out in the garden with a tray and pick up objects and then try to keep them in the right perspective.

''After sixteen years of illustrating, I wrote my first book. I had the idea to do a bicentennial calendar concentrating on family life

in 1776 to show kids what eating, sleeping, playing, etc. was like two hundred years ago. It occurred to me that this would make a wonderful book and suggested it to my editors, assuming that they would bring in a writer. Instead they asked me to do the text in addition to the pictures. I was at once thrilled and terrified. Luckily, I have an old friend who is also an editor. She basically taught me how to put a text together. I consider myself extremely lucky that my editors have liked what I've done.

''I've written steadily since, starting with the story, the words inspire the images. I write an outline, rehash and revise, then do the initial drawings on tracing paper. I make doodles rather than full drawings on the dummy because I don't like to repeat myself. I always worked to scale until recently when I found that

(From *Long Ago* by Cyndy Szekeres. Illustrated by the author.)

my drawings are tighter and better textured when reduced, so I work on a larger scale now.''[1]

''The hardest thing about becoming an illustrator is developing oneself. The learning never stops. It is so easy to be influenced by technical tricks or accomplishments or others' appealing styles. We leave school well trained in anatomy, composition, layout, and color—all mediums and techniques. To sort out these 'tools' and to use them to define the particular and unique point of view each artist is privileged to have—that is what it is all about, an endless fascinating task.''[2]

''Whether it's to decorate, to inform or to entertain, illustrating requires good training, a vivid imagination, special talent and hard and demanding work. It also takes a dedication to see out— beyond all influences and limitations—a very individual, personal perspective that can connect with the viewer in an understanding, enriching way. Each idea and each picture is best served by a particular type of art and when the pictures suit the story, it's a joy to see.

''Besides illustrating, if I can find time, I would like to paint. Recently I jessoed some masonite and hope to start soon. The

paintings I see in my mind's eye are abstract, concerned primarily with color. Helen Frankenthal is an artist whose work I find very exciting. Thoughts of what I will do, don't resemble her work, but I find it inspiring.''[1]

Szekeres is a busy illustrator and is given work constantly. ''I've got a schedule worked out for the next two to five years. There's always a book that's at the printer's and a book that's on the drawing board.''[1]

Of her work in progress, ''The Tiny Paw Library'' series, Szekeres admits that the whole experience ''has been a delight. It seems that the characters come to life and perform before me. I can barely sketch fast enough to keep up with them. If you create something that has substance, it takes on a life of its own. It's hard to imagine a bigger thrill.

''Illustrating is communicating. To communicate, one must have something to say and know one's audience. Achieving this end is about as complicated and difficult as qualifying for the cutting end of brain surgery, at least for me it is, and I'm still working at it.

"Illustrating is a serious profession. It requires good space, equipment, research, and reference materials. And it's hard work. But it's fun for me because it's what I want to do. I hope I help make reading fun for children.

"To be an artist or an illustrator, I have some very simple advice: know yourself, and draw, draw, draw."[1]

FOOTNOTE SOURCES

[1]Based on an interview for *Something about the Author* by Marguerite Feitlowitz.
[2]Lee Kingman and others, compilers, *Illustrators of Children's Books, 1967-1976*, Horn Book, 1978.

FOR MORE INFORMATION SEE:

Martha E. Ward and Dorothy A. Marquardt, *Illustrators of Books for Young People*, Scarecrow, 1975.

COLLECTIONS

Kerlan Collection at the University of Minnesota.

TERRELL, John Upton 1900-1988

OBITUARY NOTICE: Born December 9, 1900, in Chicago, Ill.; died of a heart attack, December 1, 1988, near Los Angeles, Calif. Cowboy, historian, journalist, and author, Terrell, who became an award-winning historian of the Old West ran away from home in the eighth grade to become a cowboy. Although he wrote more than forty works, including children's books and novels, he is best remembered for his histories, such as *Life among the Apaches*, and *The Arrow and the Cross: A History of the American Indian and the Missionaries*. Among his other works was *Plume Rouge: A Novel of the Pathfinders*, which became a best-seller prior to World War II. His books for young readers include *The United States Department of the Interior: A Story of Rangeland, Wildlife, and Dams* and *Search for the Seven Cities: The Opening of the American Southwest*, for which he earned a Western Writers of America Award in 1970. In addition, Terrell worked as a reporter for the *San Francisco Chronicle*, as West Coast editor for the United Press, and war correspondent for *Newsweek*.

FOR MORE INFORMATION SEE:

Contemporary Authors, Volume 29-32R, Gale, 1972.

OBITUARIES

Los Angeles Times, December 4, 1988.
Washington Post, December 5, 1988.
Chicago Tribune, December 7, 1988.

THAYER, Ernest Lawrence 1863-1940
(Phin)

PERSONAL: Born August 14, 1863, in Lawrence, Mass.; died of a cerebral hemorrhage, August 21, 1940, in Santa Barbara, Calif.; son of Edward Davis (a woolen manufacturer) and Ellen (Darling) Thayer; married Rosalind Buel Hammett, September 9, 1913; children: (stepson) Buel Hammett. *Education:* Harvard University, A.B. (magna cum laude), 1885. *Religion:* Episcopalian. *Residence:* Santa Barbara, Calif.

CAREER: Journalist and poet. *San Francisco Examiner*, Calif., writer and author of column under pseudonym, Phin, beginning 1886, "Casey at the Bat" first appeared here in 1888 and was first read on stage by De Wolf Hopper in "Prince Methusalem," at Wallack's Theater, New York City, August 14, 1888; worked in his father's woolen mills, 1887-88; wrote ballads for New York *Journal*, beginning 1896. Thayer travelled for several years throughout Europe until 1912 when he settled in Santa Barbara, California and engaged in philosophical study and in writing, but not for publication. *Military service:* Active in various home service campaigns during World War I. *Member:* Phi Beta Kappa, Delta Kappa Epsilon. *Awards, honors: Casey at the Bat*, edition illustrated by Leonard Everett Fisher was selected one of *New York Times* Best Illustrated Books of the Year, 1964, edition illustrated by Wallace Tripp was selected a Children's Choice by the International Reading Association and the Children's Book Council, 1979, and edition illustrated by Ken Bachaus was selected one of Child Study Association of America's Children's Books of the Year, 1986.

WRITINGS:

Casey at the Bat (first appeared in *San Francisco Examiner*, June 3, 1888), Amsterdam Book, 1901 [other editions illustrated by Paul Frame, Prentice-Hall, 1964, Jim Hull, Dover, 1977, Ken Bachaus, Raintree, 1984, and Patricia Polacco, Putnam, 1988].
The First Book Edition of Casey at the Bat (illustrated by Leonard Everett Fisher), introduction by Casey Stengel, F. Watts, 1964.
Casey at the Bat: A Ballad of the Republic, Sung in the Year 1888 (illustrated by Wallace Tripp), Coward, 1978.
The Illustrated Casey at the Bat: The Immortal Baseball Ballad (illustrated by Keith Bendis), Workman, 1987.

Ernest L. Thayer's graduation portrait, 1885.
(Courtesy of the Harvard University Archives.)

(From the animated movie ''Casey at the Bat.'' Copyright 1942 by Walt Disney Productions.)

Casey at the Bat: A Centennial Edition (illustrated by Barry Moser), Godine, 1988.

COLLECTIONS

Martin Gardner, *The Annotated Casey at the Bat: A Collection of Ballads about the Mighty Casey,* Potter, 1967, 2nd edition, University of Chicago Press, 1984.

Editor of Harvard *Lampoon.*

ADAPTATIONS:

MOTION PICTURES

''Casey at the Bat,'' starring De Wolf Hopper, 1916, starring Wallace Beery, Paramount, 1927, Walt Disney Productions, 1941, Lumin Films, 1967.
''Reading Poetry: Casey at the Bat,'' Oxford Films, 1972.

RECORDINGS

''Casey at the Bat,'' Victor Talking Machine, 1909, Library of Congress.

CASSETTES

''Casey at the Bat,'' Raintree, 1984.

FILMSTRIPS

''Casey at the Bat,'' Encyclopaedia Britannica Films, 1960, Weston Woods, 1967, Cooper Films and Records, 1969, Listening Library, 1983.

TELEVISION

''Shelley Duvall's Tall Tales and Legends: Casey at the Bat,'' Think Entertainment, Showtime, March, 1986.

OPERA

''The Mighty Casey,'' music by William Schuman, libretto by Jeremy Gury, ''Omnibus,'' CBS-TV, March 6, 1955.

SIDELIGHTS: Ernest Lawrence Thayer was born August 14, 1863 to Edward Davis and Ellen Thayer in Lawrence, Massachusetts. By the time he entered Harvard, the family had moved to Worcester, Massachusetts where his well-to-do father ran one of several of his textile mills.

At Harvard University, where Thayer made a brilliant record as a philosophy major, he met fellow student William Randolph Hearst. ''It was through [him] that I came to write the now famous baseball poem, 'Casey at the Bat.' I came to know Mr. Hearst through association with him on the *Lampoon,* Harvard's humorous publication. For a term [he] was business manager of that organ, while I did creative work. During the years 1883, 1884, and 1885 I wrote jokes, composed editorials, and designed

(From the animated filmstrip ''Casey at the Bat.'' Produced by Weston Woods, 1967.)

drawings, putting in much faithful time. During my junior year I was president of the *Lampoon*.''[1]

One of Thayer's colleagues, poet and philosopher George Santanya wrote: ''The man who gave tone to the *Lampoon* was Ernest Thayer . . . . He seemed a man apart: his wit was not so much jocular as Mercutio-like, curious and whimsical, as if he saw the broken edges of things that appear whole. There was some obscurity in his play with words and a feeling (which I shared) that the absurd side of things is pathetic.''[2]

In 1885 Thayer graduated Phi Beta Kappa and the Ivy orator of his class. ''I went abroad for a year, and on returning had nothing special to do. Meanwhile Hearst had gone back to San Francisco and taken charge of the *Examiner,* and was making things pretty lively, for he was just beginning to display his marvelous ability. At his request I went to that city and became a member of the staff . . . . To me was assigned the task of doing editorials, specials, and reporting. I fear that my work was more varied than I was versatile.

''But still I did not have any intention of taking up newspaper work seriously. I had gone to the coast with a view of seeing the country, and for a change rather than learning the newspaper business.

''In the fall of 1887 I began to read W. S. Gilbert's 'Bab Ballads,' and decided that I could do something in that line. I wrote a poem for each Sunday issue [often under the nickname 'Phin'].

''I evolved 'Casey' from the situation I had seen so often in baseball—a crack batsman coming to the bat with the bases filled, and then fallen down. Every one well knows what immense excitement there is when that situation occurs in baseball, especially when one of the best batsmen of the team comes up.

The enthusiasm is at fever heat and if the batsman makes good the crowd goes wild; while, if the batsman strikes out as 'Casey' did, the reverse is the case and the silence that prevails is almost appalling—and very often the army of the disappointed cannot refrain from giving vent to their feelings.

''I was never a baseball fan, and never was even interested in any degree in the game and it was only on account of my friend, classmate, and associate on the *Lampoon,* Sam Winslow, that I became interested. Naturally, as Sam was captain of the nine,—one of the best nines that Harvard ever had,—one that went through a season without a defeat—that I felt stirred. I scribbled 'Casey' during May, 1888, and it was printed in the *Examiner* on June 3, 1888.

''For a year and six months I wrote voluminously for the *San Francisco Examiner,* turning off everything from editorials to obituaries. The demand was heavy, and the competition *nil.* What impression I may have had on the Pacific Slope I have never been able to gauge. The great, luminous and unforgettable fact in connection with it was that it paid me five dollars a column. However, at the end of a year and six months my health broke and I had to return East.''[1]

''Casey at the Bat'' might have suffered the fate of Thayer's other ballads and fallen into obscurity if not for the renowned actor De Wolf Hopper. Hopper was preparing for his performance of the musical comedy ''Prince Methusalem'' at Wallack's Theatre in New York City in the late 1880s when his wife telegraphed, saying that their twenty-month-old son was critically ill.

It was baseball night at Wallack's, the audience filled with members of the Chicago White Sox and New York Giants. A friend of Hopper's, literary light Archibald Clavering Gunter, had clipped ''Casey'' from the paper and given it to Hopper, suggesting he recite the ballad between acts of the performance. Hopper was in such a state over his son's condition that he told the theater manager he could not memorize anything.

Then while the writhing pitcher ground the ball into his hip . . . . (Illustration by Wallace Tripp from *Casey at the Bat: A Ballad of the Republic, Sung in the Year 1888* by Ernest Lawrence Thayer.)

But one scornful look from Casey, and the multitude was awed. (Illustration by Leonard Everett Fisher from *Casey at the Bat* by Ernest Lawrence Thayer.)

A second telegraph arrived to say that the child was out of danger, and the actor celebrated his joy by memorizing ''Casey'' in an hour.

In one historic night, Hopper launched his own career, and immortalized Thayer's great ballad with his rendition. ''[It] scored an enormous hit. [It] lifted this audience . . . out of their seats.''[3]

''When I dropped my voice to B flat, below low C, at 'the multitude was awed,''' recalled Hopper, ''I remember seeing Buck Ewing's gallant mustachios give a single nervous twitch. And as the house, after a moment of startled silence, grasped the anticlimactic denouement, it shouted its glee.

''They had expected, as any one does on hearing Casey for the first time, that the mighty batsman would slam the ball out of the lot, and a lesser bard would have had him do so, and thereby written merely a good sporting-page filler. The crowds do not flock into the American league parks around the circuit when the Yankees play, solely in anticipation of seeing Babe Ruth whale the ball over the centerfield fence. That is a spectacle to be enjoyed even at the expense of the home team, but there always is a chance that the Babe will strike out, a sight even more healing to sore eyes, for the Sultan of Swat can miss the third strike just as furiously as he can meet it, and the contrast between the terrible threat of his swing and the futility of the result is a banquet for the malicious, which includes us all. There is no more completely satisfactory drama in literature than the fall of Humpty Dumpty.''[4]

In his memoirs Hopper recalled reciting the ballad on stage and at parties over 10,000 times during the following forty-seven years.

Following the success of his first rendition, Hopper sought out Gunter to discover who had penned the ballad. Gunter had only one clue: the initials ''E.L.T.'' signed to the work. Although by 1900 almost everyone in America had read or heard the poem, no one knew who had written it, and many came forward declaring themselves the author.

Hopper continued his search. ''I tried for four years to find the man responsible for that thing.''[3]

One night after delivering the poem in a Worcester theatre, Hopper received a note inviting him to a local club to meet the author of ''Casey.'' ''A well-to-do manufacturer . . . [who] had no idea until I reached Worcester that the poem had scored a huge success.''[3]

''He was the most charming of men, but was slight of build and inclined to deafness and, like most persons so afflicted, very soft-spoken. He had, too, at that time a decided Harvard accent.''[5]

Thayer was persuaded to recite the ballad, and Hopper later commented: ''I have heard many another give 'Casey.' Fond mamas have brought their sons to me to hear their childish voices lisp the poem, but Thayer's was the worst of all. In a sweet, dulcet . . . whisper he implored 'Casey' to murder the umpire, and gave this cry of mass animal rage all the emphasis of a caterpillar wearing rubbers crawling on a velvet carpet. He was rotten.''[5]

Thayer soon became frustrated by the constant battle to prove his authorship. ''The publicity of the poem, made through its recitation by Hopper and the declaration of the author, caused me to receive many requests for the original and correct text. For years

I never went anywhere that I was not requested to recite 'Casey.' This was continued to such an extent that it seemed very much like taking a rise out of me. All my classmates were aware of the fact that I wrote 'Casey' and they scouted the idea that any one else should claim the authorship.''[1]

Thayer even went so far to track down some of the imposters. ''The claimants to the authorship of 'Casey' multiply through the years, and I am getting a little tired of the subject. I have heard of as many as three in as many weeks. Some years ago the supporters of a man named Valentine had a long and very circumstantial account about when and where he wrote the verses, in a Los Angeles paper. Valentine was dead at the time, but the story of his career interested me so much that I employed a Pinkerton detective to look into the matter. It is simply impossible to stop this kind of thievery, but I would cheerfully give up a little money for the pleasure of scorching one of the thieves. I started on the trail of two other claimants, only to find that they had found refuge in the grave. If I can get hold of a live one, who is a person of any consideration, I should like to make the beggar ashamed of himself.''[6]

So too, many baseball players claimed to have *been* the famous Casey. ''The verses owe their existence to my enthusiasm for college baseball, not as a player, but as a fan . . . . The poem has no basis in fact. The only Casey actually involved—I am sure about him—was not a ball player. He was a big, dour Irish lad of my high school days. While in high school, I composed and printed myself a very tiny sheet, less than two inches by three. In one issue, I ventured to gag, as we say, this Casey boy. He didn't like it and he told me so, and, as he discoursed, his big, clenched, red hands were white at the knuckles. This Casey's name never again appeared in the *Monohippic Gazette*. But I suspect the incident, many years after, suggested the title for the poem. It was a taunt thrown to the winds. God grant he never catches me.''[4]

Despite the tremendous popularity of ''Casey,'' Thayer's opinion of his own work remained modest. ''During my brief connection with the *Examiner,* I put out large quantities of nonsense, both prose and verse, sounding the whole newspaper gamut from advertisements to editorials. In general quality 'Casey' (at least in my judgment) is neither better nor worse than much of the other stuff. Its persistent vogue is simply unaccountable, and it would be hard to say, all things considered, if it has given me more pleasure than annoyance. The constant wrangling about the authorship, from which I have tried to keep aloof, has certainly filled me with disgust.''[4]

In 1895 he recited ''Casey'' for his Harvard decennial class reunion. ''We give today a wider and larger application to that happy phrase of the jury box, 'extenuating circumstances.' We have found that playing the game is very different from watching it played, and that splendid theories, even when accepted by the combatants, are apt to be lost sight of in the confusion of active battle. We have reached an age, those of us to whom fortune has assigned a post in life's struggle, when, beaten and smashed and biffed by the lashings of the dragon's tail, we begin to appreciate that the old man was not such a damned fool after all. We saw our parents wrestling with the same dragon, and we thought, though we never spoke the thought aloud, 'Why don't he hit him on the head?' Alas, comrades, we know now. We have hit the dragon on the head and we have seen the dragon smile.''[4]

Thayer did no more literary work after ''Casey'' until 1896. ''Then I received an urgent call to go to San Francisco which I did not accept. I did go to New York for a short while and wrote four ballads for the *Journal.* The best was 'Murphy's Pig,' a story of the New York political leader of that day. But these did

The outlook wasn't brilliant for the Mudville nine that day. (Illustration by Barry Moser from *Casey at the Bat* by Ernest Lawrence Thayer.)

(Elliott Gould starred as Casey on ''Shelley Duvall's Tall Tales and Legends,'' Showtime Television, 1986.)

not catch on, and were doomed to the quick oblivion that meets newspaper verse.''[1]

Thayer worked for his family's mills and traveled abroad for a few years until he retired in Santa Barbara, California in 1912. He married Mrs. Rosalind Buel Hammett a year later. Friends urged him to write, but for years he responded simply, ''I have nothing to say.''[4]

It was not until shortly before his death on August 21, 1940 that he attempted to write again, but by then it was too late. ''*Now* I have something to say, and I am too weak to say it.''[4]

By the time of his death, ''Casey'' had been established as an authentic American masterpiece. William Lyon Phelps of Yale commented, ''The psychology of the hero and the psychology of the crowd leave nothing to be desired. There is more knowledge of human nature displayed in this poem than in many of the works of the psychiatrist. Furthermore, it is a tragedy of Destiny. There is nothing so stupid as Destiny. It is a centrifugal tragedy, by which our minds are turned from the fate of Casey to the universal. For this is the curse that hangs over humanity—our ability to accomplish any feat is in inverse ratio to the intensity of our desire.''[7]

FOOTNOTE SOURCES

[1]Homer Croy, ''Casey at the Bat,'' *Baseball*, October, 1908.
[2]*The National Cyclopaedia of American Biography*, Volume XXXIII, James T. White, 1947.
[3]Anthony Austin, ''75 Years Ago—,'' *New York Times*, June 9, 1963.
[4]Martin Gardner, *The Annotated Casey at the Bat: A Collection of Ballads about the Mighty Casey*, 2nd edition, University of Chicago Press, 1984.
[5]''E. L. Thayer Dead; Author of 'Casey,''' *New York Times*, August 22, 1940.
[6]John W. Glenister, ''Who Wrote 'Casey at the Bat,''' *Baseball*, June, 1908.
[7]William Lyon Phelps, *What I Like in Poetry*, Scribner, 1934.

FOR MORE INFORMATION SEE:

New York Times, March 13, 1932 (section III, p. 2), August 31, 1940 (p. 8).
Current Biography 1940, H. W. Wilson, 1941.
Martha E. Ward and Dorothy A. Marquardt, *Authors of Books for Young People*, 2nd edition, Scarecrow, 1971.
Hartford Courant, August 8, 1976 (p. 12F).

OBITUARIES

New York Herald Tribune, August 22, 1940.
Time, September 2, 1940.
Newsweek, September 2, 1940 (p. 55).

THOMAS, Dylan (Marlais) 1914-1953

PERSONAL: Born October 27, 1914, in Swansea, Carmarthenshire (now Glamorganshire), Wales; died of pneumonia caused by acute alcoholism (some sources list cause of death as a cerebral ailment), November 9, 1953, in New York, N.Y.; buried at St. Martin's Churchyard, Laugharne, Wales; son of D. J. (a grammar school master) and Florence (Williams) Thomas; married Caitlin Macnamara, July 11, 1937; children: Llewelyn

DYLAN THOMAS

(son), Colm (son), Aeronwy (daughter). *Education:* Attended grammar school in Swansea, Wales.

CAREER: Poet and prose writer. Began career as a reporter for the *South Wales Daily Post*, a reviewer for the *Herald of Wales*, and an actor; wrote film and radio scripts for the British Ministry of Information during the mid-1930s; worked for the British Broadcasting Corporation (BBC) during the 1940s as a documentary scriptwriter and a radio commentator on poetry; gave public poetry readings, including extensive lecture tours in the United States, 1950-53; made sound recordings of his own work and the work of other writers, including William Shakespeare, William Butler Yeats, Dame Edith Sitwell, Walter de la Mare, Thomas Hardy, and Djuna Barnes.

AWARDS, HONORS: ''Poets' Corner'' Prize from the *Sunday Referee*, 1934; Blumenthal Poetry Prize, 1938; Levinson Poetry Prize, 1945; Traveling Scholarship from the Society of Authors, 1947; Foyle's Poetry Prize for *Collected Poems: 1934-1952*, 1952; Italia Prize, 1954, for an abridged radio recording of ''Under Milk Wood;'' *A Child's Christmas in Wales* (edition illustrated by Edward Ardizzone) was selected one of *New York Times* Best Illustrated Books of the Year, 1980; Notable Children's Trade Book in the Field of Social Studies from the National Council for Social Studies and the Children's Book Council, and one of Child Study Association of America's Children's Books of the Year, both 1986, both for *A Child's Christmas in Wales* (edition illustrated by Trina Schart Hyman).

One Christmas was so much like another,
in those years around the sea-town corner now
and out of all sound except the distant speaking
of the voices I sometimes hear a moment before sleep,
that I can never remember whether it snowed
for six days and six nights when I was twelve
or whether it snowed for twelve days and
twelve nights when I was six.

(From *A Child's Christmas in Wales* by Dylan Thomas. Illustrated by Ellen Raskin.)

WRITINGS:

POEMS

Eighteen Poems, Sunday Referee/Parton Bookshop, 1934.
Twenty-Five Poems, Dent, 1936.
New Poems, New Directions, 1943.
Deaths and Entrances, Dent, 1946, revised edition edited with notes by Walford Davies (illustrated by John Piper), Gwasg Gregynog, 1984.
Selected Writings of Dylan Thomas, New Directions, 1946.
Twenty-Six Poems, Dent, 1950.
In Country Sleep and Other Poems, Dent, 1952.
Collected Poems: 1934-1952, Dent, 1952, reissued, 1984, published as *The Collected Poems of Dylan Thomas,* New Directions, 1953.
The Colour of Saying: An Anthology of Verse Spoken by Dylan Thomas, edited by Ralph Maud and Aneirin Talfan Davies,

Dent, 1963, published as *Dylan Thomas's Choice,* New Directions, 1964.
Collected Poems, Dutton, 1966.
Poem in October, Coach House Press, 1970.
The Poems of Dylan Thomas, edited by D. Jones, New Directions, 1971, revised edition, Dent, 1978.
Poems, edited by Daniel Jones, Dent, 1974.
Dylan Thomas: Selected Poems, edited by Walford Davies, Dent, 1974.

POEMS IN ANTHOLOGIES

Poems of Tomorrow, edited by Janet Adam Smith, Chatto & Windus, 1935.
Viking Book of Poetry of the English Speaking World, Viking, 1941.
Poetry in War Time, edited by M. J. Tambimutu, Faber, 1942.
Modern British Poetry, edited by Louis Untermeyer, Harcourt, 1942.

The Penguin Book of Contemporary Verse, Penguin Books, 1950.

The Faber Book of Twentieth-Century Verse, Faber, 1953.

The Major Poets: English and American, edited by Charles M. Coffin, Harcourt, 1954.

The Atlantic Book of British and American Poetry, edited by Edith Sitwell, Atlantic/Little, Brown, 1958.

The Penguin Book of Religious Verse, Penguin Books, 1963.

Poetry of the Thirties, edited by Robin Skelton, 1964.

Poetry of the Forties, edited by R. Skelton, 1968.

Contributor of poems to periodicals, including *Living Age*, *Poetry, New English Weekly*, and *New Verse*.

SHORT STORIES AND ESSAYS

Portrait of the Artist as a Young Dog (autobiographical short stories; contains "The Peaches," "A Visit to Grandpa's," "Patricia, Edith, and Arnold," "The Fight," "Extraordinary Little Cough," "Just Like Little Dogs," "Where Tawe Flows," "Who Do You Wish Was with Us?," "Old Garbo," and "One Warm Saturday"), New Directions, 1940, reissued, 1956.

Quite Early One Morning (contains "Reminiscences of Childhood," "Quite Early One Morning," "Memories of Christmas," "Holiday Memory," "The Crumbs of One Man's Year," "Laugharne," "Return Journey," "Welsh Poets," "Wilfred Owen," "Sir Philip Sidney," "Wales and the Artist," "Walter de la Mare as a Prose Writer," "A Dearth of Comic Writers," "On Reading One's Own Poems," "Three Poems," "On Poetry," "How to Begin a Story," "The Festival Exhibition, 1951," "The International Eisteddfod," and "A Visit to America"), preface and notes by A. T. Davies, Dent, 1954, enlarged edition (also includes "A Child's Christmas in Wales," "A Story," "Our Country," "Artists of Wales," "Replies to an Enquiry," and "How to Be a Poet"), New Directions, 1954.

A Child's Christmas in Wales, New Directions, 1955, (other editions illustrated with woodcuts by Ellen Raskin, New Directions, 1959, and illustrated by Edward Ardizzone, Dent, 1979, [*Horn Book* honor list], Godine, 1980, and Trina Schart Hyman, Holiday House, 1985).

A Prospect of the Sea and Other Stories and Prose Writings (contains "A Prospect of the Sea," "The Lemon," "After the Fair," "The Visitor," "The Enemies," "The Tree," "The Map of Love," "The Mouse and the Woman," "The Dress," "The Orchards," "In the Direction of the Beginning," "Conversation about Christmas," "How to Be a Poet," "The Followers," and "A Story"), edited by Daniel Jones, Dent, 1955.

Adventures in the Skin Trade and Other Stories (contains "Adventures in the Skin Trade" [unfinished novel], "After the Fair," "The Tree," "The Enemies," "The Visitor," "The Lemon," "The Burning Baby," "The Orchards," "The Mouse and the Woman," "The Horse's Ha," "A Prospect of the Sea," "The Holy Six," "Prologue to an Adventure," "The Map of Love," "In the Direction of the Beginning," "An Adventure from a Work in Progress," "The School for Witches," "The Dress," "The Vest," "The True Story," and "The Followers"), New Directions, 1955 (published in England as *Adventures in the Skin Trade*, with a foreword by Vernon Watkins, Putnam, 1955, new edition with drawings by Ceri Richards, 1982).

The Collected Prose of Dylan Thomas, New Directions, 1969.

Early Prose Writings of Dylan Thomas, edited by Walford Davies, Dent, 1971, reissued, 1983, New Directions, 1972.

The Collected Stories, Dent, 1983, New Directions, 1984.

A Visit to Grandpa's (illustrated by Robin Jacques), 1984.

SHORT STORIES IN ANTHOLOGIES

Welsh Short Stories, Faber, 1937.

Short Story Study: A Critical Anthology, edited by A. J. Smith and W. H. Mason, Edward Arnold, 1961.

Contributor of short stories and essays to periodicals, including *New English Weekly, New World Writing, Life and Letters Today, Janus, Contemporary Poetry and Prose, Delta*, and *Mademoiselle*.

POETRY AND PROSE COLLECTIONS

The World I Breathe, New Directions, 1939.

The Map of Love, Dent, 1939.

Selected Writings of Dylan Thomas, New Directions, 1946, revised edition edited by J. P. Harries, Heinemann, 1970.

Miscellany: Poems, Stories, Broadcasts, Dent, 1963, reissued as *Miscellany One: Poems, Stories, Broadcasts*, 1974.

Miscellany Two: A Visit to Grandpa's and Other Stories and Poems, Dent, 1966.

Miscellany Three: Poems and Stories, Dent, 1978.

LETTERS AND NOTEBOOKS

Selected Letters of Dylan Thomas, edited by Constantine Fitz-Gibbon, Dent, 1956, published as *Selected Letters*, New Directions, 1967.

Letters to Vernon Watkins, edited with introduction by Vernon Watkins, New Directions, 1957.

The Notebooks of Dylan Thomas, edited by Ralph Maud, New Directions, 1967 (published in England as *Poet in the Making: The Notebooks of Dylan Thomas*, Dent, 1968).

Twelve More Letters, Daedalus Press, 1969.

Collected Letters of Dylan Thomas, edited by Paul Ferris, Macmillan, 1985.

RADIO SCRIPTS

"Quite Early One Morning," BBC, 1944.

"The Londoner," BBC, 1946.

"Return Journey," BBC, 1947.

FILM SCRIPTS

(With Louise Birt) "Three Weird Sisters," British National Pictures, 1948.

The Doctor and the Devils (based on a short story by Donald Taylor), New Directions, 1953, published with an introduction by John Ormond, Time, 1964.

The Beach of Falesa (based on a short story by Robert Louis Stevenson), Stein & Day, 1963, 2nd edition, 1983.

Twenty Years A-Growing (based on a short story by Maurice O'Sullivan), Dent, 1964.

Me and My Bike (unfinished screenplay; introduction by Sydney Box, illustrated by Leonora Box), McGraw, 1965.

The Doctor and the Devils and Other Scripts (contains "The Doctor and the Devils," "Twenty Years A-Growing," "A Dream of Winter," and "The Londoner" [with an introduction by R. Maud]), New Directions, 1966.

Also author or co-author of numerous educational film scripts for the British Ministry of Information.

OTHER

(Author of introduction) *An Exhibition of Work by Mervyn Levy*, Arts Center, 1948.

Under Milk Wood: A Play for Voices (first produced in New York City at the Young Men's/Young Women's Hebrew Association, May 14, 1953), New Directions, 1954, new edition, with preface and musical settings by Daniel Jones, published as *Under Milk Wood: A Play in Two Acts*, 1958, new edition, Dent, 1962.

Suddenly he . . . blew so stridently, so high, so exquisitely loud . . . . (Illustration by Fritz Eichenberg from *A Child's Christmas in Wales* by Dylan Thomas.)

Conversation about Christmas, privately printed, 1954.

Quite Early One Morning: Broadcasts by Dylan Thomas, with preface and notes by Ichiro Nishizaki and Hobutko Suto, Hokuseido Press (Tokyo), 1956.

Rebecca's Daughters, Little, Brown, 1965.

Two Tales: Me and My Bike [and] *Rebecca's Daughters* (illustrated by Leonora Box), Sphere, 1968.

(With John Davenport) *The Death of the King's Canary* (novel), introduction by C. FitzGibbon, Viking, 1977.

ADAPTATIONS:

"Under Milk Wood" (play), first produced on BBC-Radio, 1954, produced in California at American Conservatory Theater, 1966, (motion picture), starring Peter O'Toole, Elizabeth Taylor, and Richard Burton, Timon/Altura Films, 1971.

"A Boy Growing Up" (play), first produced in London, 1955.

"The Doctor and the Devils" (play), Vanbrugh Theatre, Royal Academy of Dramatic Arts, 1961, (motion picture), Twentieth Century-Fox, 1985.

"Adventures in the Skin Trade" (play), 1966.

"A Child's Christmas in Wales," PBS-TV, December 23, 1987.

SOUND RECORDINGS

"Selections from the Writings of Dylan Thomas" (includes "Fern Hill," "Do Not Go Gentle," "A Child's Christmas in Wales," "And Death Shall Have No Dominion," "In Country Sleep," and works by other authors), Caedmon, 1952-60.

"Under Milk Wood" (record; cassette) Caedmon, 1954.

"Under Milk Wood: A Play for Voices" (record), Argo, 1954.

"A Child's Christmas in Wales" (cassette), Library of Congress, 1954.

"Dylan Thomas Reading a Visit to America" (cassette), Caedmon.

"Dylan Thomas Reading Quite Early One Morning" (record; cassette), Caedmon.

"Dylan Thomas Reading from His Work and the Works of Sean O'Casey and Djuna Barnes" (cassette), Caedmon.

"Dylan Thomas Reading Over Sir John's Hill and Other Poems" (cassette), Caedmon.

"Dylan Thomas Reading And Death Shall Have No Dominion and Other Poems" (cassette), Caedmon.

"Dylan Thomas: In Country Heaven—The Evolution of a Poem" (cassette), Caedmon.

"An Evening with Dylan Thomas Reading His Own and Other Poems," Caedmon, 1963.

"Dylan Thomas Reading His Complete Recorded Poetry" (record), Caedmon, 1963.

"Dylan Thomas Reading His Poetry" (record; cassette), Caedmon.

"The force that through the green fuse drives the flower" (record), University Microfilms, 1968.

Dylan Thomas and wife, Caitlin.

"Dylan Thomas Reading from His Own Work," Caedmon, 1971.

"In Country Heaven: The Evolution of a Poem," Caedmon, 1971.

"The Complete Recorded Stories and Humorous Essays" (contains "A Child's Christmas in Wales," "Quite Early One Morning," "Reminiscences of Childhood," "Return to Swansea," "A Few Words of That Kind," "A Visit to America," "An Irreverent Introduction," "A Visit to Grandpa's," "Holiday Memory," "A Story," and "Laugharne"), Caedmon, 1972.

"Return Journey to Swansea" (radio play; performed by Thomas and a supporting cast), Caedmon, 1972.

"Dylan Thomas Reads from His Adventures in the Skin Trade and Two Poems" (cassette), Caedmon, 1975.

"Dylan Thomas Reading A Child's Christmas in Wales" (cassette; compact disk), Caedmon.

"Dylan Thomas Soundbook" (record; cassette), Caedmon.

SIDELIGHTS: Born **October 27, 1914,** in Swansea, Wales, Thomas' real education came from the freedom to read anything in his father's library which was well stocked with all the classics and more. "It was when I was very young, and just at school, that, in my father's study, before homework that was never done, I began to know one kind of writing from another, one kind of goodness, one kind of badness. My first, and greatest, liberty was that of being able to read everything and anything I cared to. I read indiscriminately, and with my eyes hanging out. I could never have dreamt that there were such goings-on in the world between the covers of books . . . all of which were words, words, words, and each of which was alive forever in its own delight and glory and oddity and light."[1]

1925. Attended Swansea Grammar School where he did not excel in his studies and was quite rambunctious. Years later he reminisced about his school days. "He looked like most boys, no better, brighter, or more respectful; he cribbed, mitched, spilt ink, rattled his desk and garbled his lessons with the worst of them; he could smudge, hedge, smirk, wriggle, wince, whimper, blarney, badger, blush, deceive, be devious, stammer, improvise, assume offended dignity or righteous indignation as though to the manner born; sullenly and reluctantly he drilled, for some small crime, under Sergeant Bird, so wittily nicknamed Oiseau, on Wednesday half-holidays, appeared regularly in detention classes, hid in the cloakroom during algebra, was, when a newcomer, thrown into the bushes of the lower playground by bigger boys, and threw newcomers into the bushes of the lower playground when *he* was a bigger boy; he scuffled at prayers, he interpolated, smugly, the time-honoured wrong irreverent words into the morning hymns, he helped to damage the headmaster's rhubarb, was thirty-third in trigonometry, and, as might be expected, edited the school magazine."[2]

"I wrote endless imitations, though I never thought them to be imitations but, rather, wonderfully original things, like eggs laid by tigers. They were imitations of anything I happened to be reading at the time . . . . I tried my callow hand at almost every poetical form.

"I wanted to write poetry in the beginning because I had fallen in love with words. The first poems I knew were nursery rhymes, and before I could read them for myself I had come to love just the words of them, the words alone. What the words stood for, symbolised, or meant, was of very secondary importance; what mattered was the *sound* of them as I heard them for the first time on the lips of the remote and incomprehensible grown-ups who seemed, for some reason, to be living in my world. And these

words were, to me . . . [like what] might be to someone, deaf from birth, who has miraculously found his hearing.

"The things that first made me love language and want to work *in* it and *for* it were nursery rhymes and folk tales, the Scottish Ballads, a few lines of hymns, the most famous Bible stories and the rhythms of the Bible, Blake's *Songs of Innocence,* and the quite incomprehensible magical majesty and nonsense of Shakespeare heard, read, and near-murdered in the first forms of my school.

"And as I read more and more, and it was not all verse, by any means, my love for the real life of words increased until I knew that I must live *with* them and *in* them, always. I knew, in fact, that I must be a writer of words, and nothing else. The first thing was to feel and know their sound and substance; what I was going to do with those words, what use I was going to make of them, what I was going to *say* through them, would come later. I knew I had to know them most intimately in all their forms and moods, their ups and downs, their chops and changes, their needs and demands."[1]

1931. Left school having failed all his exams but English, and worked for a year and a half as a reporter for the *South Wales Daily Post.* From all accounts, he was a terrible reporter: he got the facts wrong, and rarely showed up to cover the events, preferring instead to hang out in the local bars and pool halls. "The sixteen months or less I was on the staff were already showing signs of a reporter's decadence. Another two years I'd have been done for. Not that I was afraid of the Mermaid's grip. I still sedulously pluck the flowers of alcohol, and, occasionally, but not as often as I wish, am pricked by the drunken thorn (an atrocious image!). No, what I feared was the slow but sure stamping out of individuality, the gradual contentment with life as it was, so much per week, so much for this, for that, so much left over for drink and cigarettes. That be no loife for such as Oi!"[3]

As a self-affected bohemian, he began developing a public persona as a prankster and storyteller which became his trademark later during the London years. He also acquired the reputation of a great drinker, and alcohol became a disease that plagued him to his death. "[Drinking] is only frightening when I am whirlingly perplexed, when my ordinary troubles are magnified into monsters and I fall weak down before them, when I do not know what to do or where to turn. When I am . . . anywhere I like, and am busy, then drink's no fear at all and I'm well, terribly well, and gay, and unafraid, and full of other, nicer nonsenses, and altogether a dull, happy fellow only wanting to put into words, never into useless, haphazard, ugly and unhappy action, the ordered turbulence, the ubiquitous and rinsing grief, the unreasonable glory, of the world I know and don't know."[3]

1932. Began acting with the Swansea Little Theatre, meanwhile writing drafts of poems in the notebooks he had been keeping since the late twenties. Thomas' notebooks mostly contained the bulk of his first two published volumes of poetry, and charted the development of his famous early style which he called his "wombtomb" period. He was firmly committed as a poet by now, and started submitting his writings to various publications. "There must be no compromise, there is always only the one right word . . . despite its foul or merely ludicrous associations . . . . It is part of a poet's job to take a debauched and prostituted word, like the beautiful word, 'blond,' and to smooth away the lines of its dissipation, and to put it on the market again, fresh and virgin.

"[The poet] has only one limitation, and that is the widest of all: the limitation of form. Poetry finds its own form; form should never be superimposed; the structure should rise out of the words and the expression of them. I do not want to express only what other people have felt; I want to rip something away and show what they have never seen. Because of the twist in myself I will never be a very good poet; only treading the first waves, putting my hands in deeper and then taking them out again.''[3]

Thomas began to see poetry in physical terms. ''I fail to see how the emphasising of the body can, in any way, be regarded as hideous. The body, its appearance, death, and diseases, is a fact, sure as the fact of a tree. It has its roots in the same earth as the tree . . . . All thoughts and actions emanate from the body. Therefore the description of a thought or action—however abstruse it may be—can be beaten home by bringing it onto a physical level. Every idea, intuitive or intellectual, can be imaged and translated in terms of the body, its flesh, skin, blood, sinews, veins, glands, organs, cells, or senses.

''Through my small, bonebound island I have learnt all I know, experienced all, and sensed all. All I write is inseparable from the island. As much as possible, therefore, I employ the scenery of the island to describe the scenery of my thoughts, the earthquakes of the body to describe the earthquakes of the heart.

''I can't help what I write. It is part of me, however unpleasant a part it may be, and however necessary it should be to cauterize and castrate that part.''[3]

Always on Christmas night there was music. An uncle played the fiddle, a cousin sang "Cherry Ripe," and another uncle sang "Drake's Drum." It was very warm in the little house. Auntie Hannah, who had got on to the parsnip wine, sang a song about Bleeding Hearts and Death, and then another in which she said her heart was like a Bird's Nest; and then everybody laughed again; and then I went to bed.

(From *A Child's Christmas in Wales* by Dylan Thomas. Illustrated by Trina Schart Hyman.)

May, 1933. ''And Death Shall Have No Dominion,'' first poem published outside of Wales. ''I write a poem on innumerable sheets of scrap paper, write it on both sides of the paper, often upside down and criss cross ways, unpunctuated, surrounded by drawings of lamp posts and boiled eggs, in a very dirty mess; bit by bit I copy out the slowly developing poem into an exercise book; and, when it is completed, I type it out. The scrap sheets I burn, for there are such a lot of them that they clutter up my room and get mixed in the beer and butter.''[3]

His youth and artistic longings made Thomas restless to leave Wales. ''It's impossible for me to tell you how much I want to get out of it all, out of narrowness and dirtiness, out of the eternal ugliness of the Welsh people, and all that belongs to them, out of the pettinesses of a mother I don't care for and the giggling batch of relatives. What are you doing. I'm writing. Writing? You're always writing. What do you know? You're too young to write. (I admit that I very often look even younger than I am.) And I *will* get out . . . . I shall have to get out soon . . . . I'm sick, and this bloody country's killing me.''[3] In **November, 1934** he moved to London.

In London, Thomas shared a room with artist friends from Swansea. Soon, however, he was living a bohemian life, relishing the image of the pet-in-the-gutter, and moving from place to place as girls and friends came and went. His squalid domestic habits earning him nicknames such as ''Ditch'' and ''The Ugly Duckling.'' ''I wouldn't be at home if I were at home. Everywhere I find myself seems to be nothing but a resting place between places that become resting places themselves . . . . It may be a primary loneliness that makes me out-of-home. It may be this or that, and this and that is enough for to-day. Poor Dylan, poor him, poor me.

''The city goes on, myself now a very insignificant part of it . . . . This is the quarter [the Chelsea area] of the pseudo-artists, of the beards, the naughty expressions of an entirely outmoded period of artistic importance, and of the most boring Bohemian parties I have ever thought possible. Slightly drunk, slightly dirty, slightly wicked, slightly crazed, we repeat our platitudes on Gauguin and Van Gogh as though they were the most original things in the world. There are, of course, scores of better people that I do meet, but these little maggots are my companions for most of the time.''[3]

Wife Caitlin would later recall: ''Dylan spent every day in London going round the pubs. It was his life. He would start when they opened at eleven o'clock, always with the same routine. He would head for the nearest bar and then set up a line of light ales along the counter, which he would down one by one. If he was with a group of friends, they would all do that, each setting up their own line of drinks. They all believed that if they had hangovers from the night before this was what they had to do to clear their heads before starting all over again. Every morning Dylan went through this routine; it was his sort of recovery-drink.

''As the day went on, he might move from one pub to another, telling stories, cracking jokes, playing pub games, meeting other writers, and drinking endless pints of beer.

''Dylan would start performing in the bars, and the others would stand back and listen. He didn't appear to monopolise the conversation deliberately but once Dylan had started he soon had an audience helpless with laughter. People loved listening to him. Dylan loved telling stories that never ended: that was Dylan.''[4]

(From the television special "A Child's Christmas in Wales," starring Denholm Elliott [right] and Mathonwy Reeves. Presented December 23, 1987 on PBS-TV.)

But Thomas was never completely happy in London, and he established a longlife pattern of travel between the city and some rural retreat, usually in Wales. "London, city of the restless dead. It really is an insane city, and filled me with terror. Every pavement drills through your soles to your scalp, and out pops a lamp-post covered with hair. I'm not going to London again for years; its intelligentsia is so hurried in the head that nothing stays there; its glamour smells of goat; there's no difference between good and bad."[3]

December 18, 1934. The publication of his first book, *Eighteen Poems*, was well received and earned him a name in literary circles. It was suggested that Thomas' poetry was influenced by surrealism. This would not be the last time, and he always objected to that assertion. "I am not, never have been, never will be, or could be for that matter, a surrealist . . . . I think I do know what some of the main faults of my writing are: immature violence, rhythmic monotony, frequent muddleheadedness, and a very much overweighted imagery that leads too often to incoherence. But every line *is* meant to be understood; the reader *is* meant to understand every poem by thinking and feeling about it, not by sucking it in through his pores, or whatever he is meant to do with surrealist writing."[3]

"I do not mind from where the images of a poem are dragged up: drag them up, if you like, from the nethermost sea of the hidden self; but before they reach paper, they must go through all the rational processes of the intellect. The Surrealists, on the other hand, put their words down together on paper exactly as they emerge from chaos; they do not shape these words or put them in order; to them, chaos is the shape and order. This seems to me to be exceedingly presumptuous; the Surrealists imagine that whatever they dredge from their subconscious selves and put down in paint or in words must, essentially, be of some interest or value. I deny this."[1]

April 12, 1936. Fell in love with Catlin Macnamara whom he met at the Wheatsheaf, a London pub where the artists and the writers of the thirties used to hang out. They were married in Cornwall during the summer of 1937.

April, 1937. Did his first radio broadcast on BBC, "Life and the Modern Poet." Broadcasting eventually became an active part of his career and monetary survival. Thomas was very gifted at recitation and became well known for it. "When I read aloud the poems of modern poets I like very much, I try to make them alive from inside. I try to get across what I feel, however wrongly, to be the original impetus of the poem. I am a practicing interpreter, however much of a flannel-tongued one-night-stander.

"But in my own poems I've had my say, and when I read them aloud I can only repeat it. When I read, for instance, my earliest poems aloud, my interpretation of them—though that's far too weighty a word just for reading them aloud—can't be considered as the final or original interpretation, performance, or blare. I do not remember now the first impulse that pumped and drove those lines along . . . ."[5]

During the next few years, Thomas and his wife moved back and forth between his parents and her mother—London, England and Laugharne, Wales. Money was a constant worry for them, and poverty became a practical problem for the rest of Thomas' life. "[A writer] needs as much money as he wants to spend. It is after his housing, his feeding, his warming, his clothing, the nursing of his children, etc., have been seen to—and these should be seen to by the State—that he really needs money to spend on all the luxurious necessities. Or, it is then that he doesn't need money because he can do without those necessary luxuries. How much money depends, quite obviously, on how much he wants to buy. I *want* a lot, but whether I *need* what I want is another question . . . . A serious writer (I suppose by this you mean a good writer, who might be comic) can earn enough money by writing seriously, or comically, if his appetites, social and sensual, are very small. If those appetites are big or biggish, he cannot earn, by writing what he wishes to write, enough to satisfy them. So he has to earn money in another way: by writing what he doesn't want to write, or by having quite another job.

"I myself get about a quarter of the money I want by writing what I don't want to write and at the same time trying to, and often succeeding in, enjoying it. Shadily living by one's literary wits is as good a way of making too little money as any other, so long as, all the time you are writing BBC and film scripts, reviews, etc., you aren't thinking, sincerely, that this work is depriving the world of a great poem or a great story. Great, or at any rate very good, poems and stories do get written in spite of the fact that the writers of them spend much of their waking time doing entirely different things . . . . The State should do no more for writers than it should do for any other person who lives in it. The State should give shelter, food, warmth, etc., whether the person works for the State or not. Choice of work, and the money that comes from it, should then be free for that man; what work, what money, is his own bother.

"My advice to young people who wish to earn their living by writing is: DO."[1]

1939. Their first child, Llewelyn Edouard, was born. Thomas was not present for the birth and did not see his son until after Caitlin came home from the hospital. He repeated this behaviour for the births of their next two children, Aeronwy Bryn and Colm Garan Hart. According to Caitlin: "Dylan's reaction to the birth of Llewelyn didn't surprise me very much because I had already come to realise that in many ways he was immature, acting like a child without thinking of the consequences.

"Colm was definitely Dylan's favourite because he used to play and laugh, and this was Dylan's idea of how a baby ought to be. He didn't cuddle him much, though. Dylan was never very physical towards the children, . . . but I think he must have been proud of them because he used to carry their photographs around with him all the time in his wallet, and he would often show them to friends, particularly when he was a long way from home and feeling depressed; Dylan was very sentimental about them when he was far away.

"He was sentimental about the children on paper, but he couldn't stand much of their company. (Whenever we travelled anywhere by train I would have to sit with the children in one compartment, while he made his journey in another. Usually he would sit in the restaurant car, eating and drinking, while I was left alone with them . . . .)"[4]

Published *The World I Breathe*, in the United States, and in England *The Map of Love*, which did not do well, partly because of the change of atmosphere brought on by World War II. There also survived from that period, an unfinished novel about a young provincial poet's move to London, *Adventures in the Skin Trade*, and *The Death of the King's Canary*, a detective story whose suspects are caricatures of famous writers and poets of the day. Both books were published posthumously. In addition, publishers backed out from a collection of short stories to be called *The Burning Baby*, because they feared obscenity charges might arise.

1940. *Portrait of the Artist as a Young Dog*, a collection of short stories based on his childhood in Wales, published. Caitlin noted that "Dylan was pleased when [it] came out, but he didn't show much excitement. He looked upon it as a lesser work than the poetry; he didn't regard his prose as being as important."[4]

With his literary reputation now well established, Thomas was approached to sign literary manifestos and join societies. "I wouldn't sign any manifesto unless I had written every word of it, and then I might be too ashamed.

"I still don't like the idea of societies, groups, manifestos. I don't think it does any harm to the artist to be lonely *as* an artist. (Let's all 'get together,' if we must, and go to the pictures.) If he feels personally unimportant, it may be that he is. Will an artistic milieu make his writing any better? I doubt it, I'm afraid. God, inspiration, concentration (cool, hot, or camp), John O'London's, opium, living, thinking and loving, hard work, anything you like, may or may not do that. It—the milieu, the organisation for responsibility, though that's an unfair phrase I admit, may make him realise—perhaps, in an extremely lonely case, for the first time—that there are others like himself, other perplexed people who are trying to write as well as possible and to attach an importance to writing.

"The English poets now are such a pinlegged, nibcocked, paperhearted crowd you could blow them down with one bellow out of a done lung."[3]

England entered World War II and Thomas worked desperately to avoid the draft. "I am trying to get a job before conscription, because my one-and-only body I will not give. I know that all the shysters in London are grovelling about the Ministry of Information, all the half-poets, the boiled newspapermen, submen from the islands of crabs, dismissed advertisers, old mercuries, mass-snoopers, and all I have managed to do is to have my name on the crook list and a vague word of hope.

"What I'm doing is writing urgent and bad-tempered letters to everybody who has ever said publicly that I am a better poet than Alfred Noyes, and telling them that, unless someone does something soon, there'll be one better-than-Alfred poet less, that the Armed Forces are not conducive to the creation of contemplative verse, and that all my few sources of income are drying up as quickly as blood on the Western Front. Though it will probably leave my correspondents unmoved, there is nothing else that I can think of to do. The Army Medical Corps is presumably admirable, but I don't want to help—even in a most inefficient way—to patch poor buggers up to send them out again into quick insanity and bullets."[3]

Caitlin recalled the night before Thomas was to submit to a medical exam. "He drank himself silly in Brown's Hotel, mixing beer with sherry, whisky and gin, deliberately trying to give himself a hangover. The next morning he came out in spots, and was shaking and coughing his guts up. At one stage, he even fainted. They classified him C3, right down at the bottom of the list.

"Dylan was delighted: 'I've done it; I've done it; I've got away with it,' he said excitedly when he got back to Laugharne, and he

The Boat House, Thomas' home from 1949 until his death. (Photograph courtesy of BBC Hulton.)

got drunk again that night to celebrate it . . . . And for years afterwards that was one of his pub stories.''[4]

Began writing war propaganda films for Strand Films and continued throughout the war effort. ''I'm working, for the first time since I sold my immortal soul, very very hard, doing three months' work in a week. I hate film studios. I hate film workers. I hate films. There is nothing but glibly naive insincerity in this huge tinroofed box of tricks. I do not care a bugger about the Problems of Wartime Transport.''[3]

September, 1944. Moved to Majoda, New Quay, where he wrote several major poems, and a film script, *Twenty Years A-Growing.* Although Thomas felt and wrote better in the country, he often suffered bouts of depression. ''I have found, increasingly as time goes on, or around, or backwards, or stays quite still as the brain races, the heart absorbs and expels, and the arteries harden, that the problems of physical life, of social contact, of daily posture and armour, of the choice between dissipations, of the abhorred needs enforced by a reluctance to 'miss anything,' that old fear of death, are as insoluble to me as those of the spirit. In few and fewer poems I can despair and, at rare moments, exult with the big last, but they first force me every moment to make quick decisions and thus to plunge me into little hells and rubbishes at which I rebel with a kind of truculent acceptance. The ordinary moments of walking up village streets, opening doors or letters, speaking good-days to friends or strangers, looking out of windows, making telephone calls, are so inexplicably (to me) dangerous that I am trembling all over before I get out of bed in the mornings to meet them. Waking to remember an appointment at X that coming evening is to see, before X, galleries of menacing commonplaces, chambers of errors of the day's conventions, pits of platitudes and customary gestures, all beckoning, spurning; and through, over and out of these I must somehow move before the appointment, the appointment that has now become a shining grail in a dentist's surgery, an almost impossible consummation of illegal pleasure to be achieved in a room like a big gut in a subterranean concentration-camp. And especially, of course, in London.''[3]

February 7, 1946. Published *Deaths and Entrances,* a collection of poems. The book was such a success that Thomas became a public figure, and remained one until the end of his life. By the time the war ended, his whole attitude toward his earlier work had changed, and he had acquired a new confidence. However, his obsession with his craft remained relentless. ''I am a painstaking, conscientious, involved and devious craftsman in words, however unsuccessful the result so often appears, and to whatever wrong uses I may apply my technical paraphernalia, I use everything and anything to make my poems work and move in the directions I want them to: old tricks, new tricks, puns, portmanteau-words, paradox, allusion, paranomasia, paragram, catachresis, slang, assonantal rhymes, vowel rhymes, sprung rhythm. Every device there is in language is there to be used if you will. Poets have got to enjoy themselves sometimes, and the twistings and convolutions of words, the inventions and contrivances, are all part of the joy that is part of the painful, voluntary work.''[1]

From 1946 to 1948, Thomas wrote only one poem, complaining that debts and anxiety stood in the way of his writing. In search of inspiration, he visited Italy with his family during the summer of 1947 on a Travelling Scholarship from the Society of Authors. ''I am awfully sick of it here, on the beautiful hills above Florence, drinking chianti in our marble shanty, sick of vini and contadini and bambini, and sicker still when I go, bumpy with mosquito bites, to Florence itself, which is a gruelling museum. I loved it in Rome, felt like Oppenheim on the Riviera, but . . . in this villa, . . . I can write only early in the morning, when I don't get up, and in the evening, when I go out.

''We have got to know lots of the young intellectuals of Florence, and a damp lot they are. They visit us on Sundays. To overcome the language, I have to stand on my head, fall in the pool, crack nuts with my teeth, and Tarzan in the cypresses. I am very witty in Italian, though a little violent; and I need space.''[3]

Soon after their return, the Thomas' moved to South Leigh, Oxfordshire, into a house bought for them by their friend and patroness, Margaret Taylor. Thomas' parents, now invalids, moved in with the couple who by now were having violent quarrels often stimulated by Thomas' consumption of alcohol. These always ended by passionate letters from Thomas to his wife in an attempt to reconcile. ''My darling, I love you. I love you, if that is possible, more than ever in my life, and I have always loved you. When you left, going upstairs in the restaurant with that old horror, I sat for a long time lost lost lost, oh Caitlin sweetheart I love you. I don't understand how I can behave to you senselessly, foully, brutally, as though you were not the most beautiful person on the earth and the one I love forever . . . . Oh Cat Cat please, my dear, don't let me lose you. Let me come back to you. Come back to me. I can't live without you. There's nothing left then. I can't ask you to forgive me, but I can say that I will never again be a senseless, horrible, dulled beast like that. I love you.''[3]

1949. Visited Prague as a guest of the Czechoslovak Writers' Union. Started to write routinely again, and completed a couple of poems, but self-doubt about his writing set in again. ''I do not, now, read any of my poems with much pleasure, because they tell me I should be writing other poems *now*, because they say I should work on poems every day; because, when I see all their faults, I think that in the new poems I should be writing, *those* kind of faults, at least, would not occur again; because, falling so short of the heights I had wished them, they are cruel and not-to-be-gainsaid reminders of the fact that only through unceasingly devoted and patiently passionate work at the words of *always* new poems can I ever hope to gain even an inch or a hairslength. I do not like reading my old poems; because I *am* not working on new poems; because I must earn my living by bits and pieces of forced prose, by exhibitionist broadcasts, by journalistic snippets, because, nowadays, I can never spare the time to begin, work through, and complete a poem *regardless* of time; because my room is littered with beginnings, each staring me accusingly in the eyes.''[3]

He accepted writing commissions for their advance payments then stalled anxious publishers with profusely apologetic letters that contained more or less, fabricated excuses.

February 20, 1950. Went to New York to begin a three-month poetry reading and lecture tour of the United States. He was a great success and spent a good deal of time drinking and partying in the light of adulation. ''When he returned to Laugharne, he was tremendously excited, enormously stimulated,'' recalled Caitlin. ''He had had one hell of a good time, as well as giving all those lectures and readings. He had also done some rather scandalous things . . . and he had been forgiven because he was a genius . . . . That new life got right under his skin.

''He came back to Laugharne dead to the world; he was so tired he could barely talk or walk . . . . [But] he felt that all the things he had been working for over the years had now been recognized, and that his beloved poetry was now being understood.''[4]

A few months later, Caitlin learned that Thomas had a mistress while in America, and that she had arrived in London. This provoked the first major crisis in their marriage. According to Caitlin: ''We had so many rows after that that I can't pin down what they were about or separate the occasions. They were always late at night after we'd walked back from Brown's, always caused by 'The Affair.' When we had those rows I would throw myself at him, push him to the floor, grab him by the hair and keep banging his head against it, beating the Jesus out of him. He did mildly respond but in no way hurt me. He would struggle for a bit while I was punching and kicking him . . . . Sometimes he would pass out and I'd be quite nervous in case I'd banged his head too hard and killed him. Then, after the rows, we would end up in each other's arms.''[4]

1951. Visited Persia to write a documentary for the Anglo-Iranian Oil Company. Caitlin wrote to him suggesting that their marriage was over. After Thomas' return to Langhorne in February, they reconciled.

January 20, 1952. Arrived in New York for his second U.S. tour, this time with Caitlin. They toured for three months. Caitlin recounted that: ''Most mornings Dylan would whip out of the Chelsea Hotel very early and into the bar next door to get his usual light ales, and then either return there or go round to the White Horse Tavern, which was the nearest thing to an English pub he had found in New York.

''Dylan's money went on drink, but I believe quite a lot was pinched as well—he was always a soft touch. He was always careful, though, not to drink too much before his readings—all he would take were a few light ales—but once they were over he would move on to the shorts and start drinking heavily.''[4]

By **1953** Thomas was in his blackest period. At that time Caitlin wrote: ''He has, as good as, given up writing, for the actor's ranting boom, and lisping mimicry, anything he sells is either a rehashed bubble and squeak of adolescence, or a never to be fulfilled promise in the future. Which obviously, when the future comes, and it always does in the end, makes things very difficult. And the only way out is to run, which we are just about, on the verge, of doing again.''[3]

Thomas himself lamented, ''For a whole year I have been able to write nothing, nothing, nothing at all but one tangled, sentimental poem as preface to a collection of poems written years ago *[Collected Poems]*.

''[During my last U.S. tour] I began to feel nervous about the job in front of me, the job of writing, making things in words, by myself, again. The more I used words, the more frightened I became of using them in my own work once more. Endless booming of poems didn't sour or stale words for me, but made me more conscious of my obsessive interest in them and my horror that I would never again be innocent enough to touch and use them. I came home fearful and jangled. There was my hut on a cliff, full of pencil and paper, things to stare at, room to breathe and feel and think. But I couldn't write a word. I tried then to write a poem, dreading it beforehand, a few obscure lines every dumb day, and the printed result shook and battered me in any faith in myself and workman's pride left to me. I couldn't write a word after that. These are the most words I have written for a year.

''And then, because I wouldn't write at all, I got broke—I'd brought little or no money back from the States—and kept the wolf just a hairy inch from my door and my sleep by croaking poems, and such, on the air: an appalling retrogression to an American habit that had gone bad on me. I didn't croak enough to keep me going, and lectured, then, to English women: less intimidating, maybe, but less profitable, too, than American. And all the time I couldn't, I really couldn't do the one thing I had to do: write words, my own words, down on paper.''[3]

March 31, 1953. *Collected Poems* published in the U.S. One month later against Caitlin's strong objections, Dylan arrived in New York for his third American tour. It lasted six weeks.

In May of that year, the first reading of *Under Milkwood* was staged in New York. Thomas had begun working on it in 1949 and was adding material to it up until the last moment. But the play was never completely finished. The piece, inspired by Laugharne and it's people, was in the style Thomas described as ''prose with high blood pressure.'' Thomas wanted it to be '' . . . a play, an impression for voices, an entertainment out of the darkness, of the town I live in, and to write it simply and warmly and comically with lots of movement and varieties of moods, so that, at many levels, through sight and speech, description and dialogue, evocation and parody, you come to know the town as an inhabitant of it. That is an awkward and highfalutin way of speaking: I only wanted to make the town alive through a raw medium . . . the piece will develop . . . through all the activities of the morning town—seen from a number of eyes, heard from a number of voices—through the long lazy lyrical afternoon, through the multifariously busy little town evening of meals and drinks and loves and quarrels and dreams and wishes, into the night and the slowing-down lull again and the repetition of the first word: Silence. And by that time, I hope to make you utterly familiar with the places and the people; the pieces of the town will fit together; the reasons for all these behaviours.''[3] The

Auntie Hannah, who had got on to the parsnip wine, sang a song about Bleeding Hearts and Death. (Illustration by Edward Ardizzone from *A Child's Christmas in Wales* by Dylan Thomas.)

performance was a success. In the years to come it was staged hundreds of times and eventually adapted to the screen.

May, 1953. *The Doctor and the Devils,* a film script published. After his death a number of other film scripts were published, but only "Three Weird Sisters" was produced in 1948.

Upon his return to Laugharne, Caitlin remembered "Dylan was almost too shattered to work. He looked miserable, and though he soon slipped back into his old routine, he didn't seem happy to be home with me and the children . . . . He didn't really become his old self again, though he still didn't think of going to see a doctor, of course."[4]

August 10, 1953. Thomas made his first and only television appearance for BBC, reading one of his short stories.

Left for New York in a deep state of depression to begin his fourth American tour. "Isn't life awful? Last week I hit Caitlin with a plate of beetroot, and I'm still bleeding. I can't finish a poem, or begin a story, I chew my nails down to my shoulders, pick three-legged horses with beautiful names, take my feet for grey walks, moulder in Brown's, go to bed as though to an office, read with envy of old lonely women who swig disinfectant by the pint, think about money, dismiss it as dirt, think about dirt."[3]

November 5, 1953. Thomas collapsed into a coma from alcohol, sedative and other drug abuse. Four days later, on November 9, he died. "Poetry, to a poet, is the most rewarding work in

(Richard Burton as he appeared in the movie "Under Milk Wood," the tale of a Welsh village by the sea.)

the world. A good poem is a contribution to reality. The world is never the same once a good poem has been added to it. A good poem helps to change the shape and significance of the universe, helps to extend everyone's knowledge of himself and the world round him."[6]

A Child's Christmas in Wales, published posthumously in 1954, is a detailed recollection of Christmas—its weather, sights, sounds, food, presents—as perceived by Dylan as a child. Since its first publication, it has been regarded as a classic. In 1987 it gained new attention when a film version was broadcast on PBS television.

FOOTNOTE SOURCES

[1]Andrew Sinclair, *Dylan Thomas: Poet of His People,* M. Joseph, 1975.
[2]Dylan Thomas, *Quite Early One Morning,* New Directions, 1954.
[3]Paul Ferris, editor, *The Collected Letters of Dylan Thomas,* Dent, 1985.
[4]Caitlin Thomas with George Tremlett, *Caitlin: Life with Dylan Thomas,* Holt, 1986.
[5]D. Thomas, "Dylan Thomas . . . On Reading His Poetry," *Mademoiselle,* July, 1956.
[6]D. Thomas, James Stephens, and Gerald Bullett, "On Poetry: A Discussion," *Encounter,* November, 1954.

FOR MORE INFORMATION SEE:

BOOKS

Henry Treece, *How I See Apocalypse,* Lindsay Drummond, 1946.
Elder Olson, *The Poetry of Dylan Thomas,* University of Chicago Press, 1954.
John Malcolm Brinnin, *Dylan Thomas in America,* Atlantic/ Little, Brown, 1955.
H. Treece, *Dylan Thomas: "Dog among the Fairies,"* Benn, 1956.
J. Alexander Rolph, *Dylan Thomas: A Bibliography,* New Directions, 1956, Greenwood Press, 1974.
Caitlin Thomas, *Leftover Life to Kill,* Atlantic/Little, Brown, 1957.
G. S. Fraser, *Dylan Thomas,* Longman, 1957, revised edition, 1972.
John Wain, *Preliminary Essays,* St. Martin's, 1957.
John Bayley, *The Romantic Survival,* Constable, 1957.
G. S. Fraser, *Vision and Rhetoric,* Faber, 1959.
J. M. Brinnin, editor, *A Casebook on Dylan Thomas,* Crowell, 1960.
E. W. Tedlock, editor, *Dylan Thomas: The Legend and the Poet; A Collection of Biographical and Critical Essays,* Heinemann, 1960.
William York Tindall, *A Reader's Guide to Dylan Thomas,* Farrar, Straus, 1962.

Clark Emery, *The World of Dylan Thomas*, University of Miami Press, 1962.

David Holbrook, *Llareggub Revisited: Dylan Thomas and the State of Modern Poetry*, Bowes, 1962.

H. H. Kleinman, *The Religious Sonnets of Dylan Thomas*, University of California Press, 1963.

T. H. Jones, *Dylan Thomas*, Barnes & Noble, 1963.

Ralph Maud, *Entrances to Dylan Thomas' Poetry*, University of Pittsburgh Press, 1963.

D. Holbrook, *Dylan Thomas and Poetic Dissociation*, Southern Illinois University Press, 1964.

John Ackerman, *Dylan Thomas: His Life and Work*, Oxford University Press, 1964.

Aneirin Talfan Davies, *Dylan: Druid of the Broken Body*, Dent, 1964.

Bill Read, *The Days of Dylan Thomas*, McGraw, 1964.

J. S. Dugdale, *Dylan Thomas: Under Milk Wood*, James Brodie, 1964.

Constantine FitzGibbon, *The Life of Dylan Thomas*, Little, Brown, 1965.

Jacob Korg, *Dylan Thomas*, Twayne, 1965.

C. B. Cox, editor, *Dylan Thomas: A Collection of Critical Essays*, Prentice-Hall, 1966.

William T. Moynihan, *The Craft and Art of Dylan Thomas*, Cornell University Press, 1966.

R. Maud, editor, *The Notebooks of Dylan Thomas*, New Directions, 1967.

Min Lewis, *Laugharne and Dylan Thomas*, Dobson, 1967.

C. FitzGibbon, editor, *Selected Letters of Dylan Thomas*, New Directions, 1967.

Robert Coleman Williams, editor, *A Concordance to the Collected Poems of Dylan Thomas*, University of Nebraska Press, 1967.

Nicolette Devas, *Two Flamboyant Fathers*, Morrow, 1967.

Alphonsus M. Reddington, *Dylan Thomas: A Journey from Darkness to Light*, Paulist Press, 1968.

Douglas Cleverdon, *The Growth of Milk Wood*, New Directions, 1969.

R. Maud and Albert Glover, *Dylan Thomas in Print: A Bibliographical History*, University of Pittsburgh Press, 1970.

Richard Morton, *An Outline of the Works of Dylan Thomas*, Forum House, 1970.

Annis Pratt, *Dylan Thomas's Early Prose: A Study in Creative Mythology*, University of Pittsburgh Press, 1970.

Paul West, *Doubt and Dylan Thomas*, University of Toronto Press, 1970.

Daniel Jones, editor, *Dylan Thomas: The Poems*, New Directions, 1971.

Tryntje Van Ness Seymour, *Dylan Thomas's New York*, Lime Rock Press, 1971.

Walford Davies, editor, *Dylan Thomas: New Critical Essays*, Dent, 1972.

D. Holbrook, *Dylan Thomas: The Code of Night*, Athlone Press, 1972.

Robert K. Burdette, *The Saga of Prayer: The Poetry of Dylan Thomas*, Mouton, 1973.

Rushworth M. Kidder, *Dylan Thomas: The Country of the Spirit*, Princeton University Press, 1973.

Dan Davin, *Closing Times*, Oxford University Press, 1975.

Andrew Sinclair, *Dylan Thomas: No Man More Magical*, Holt, 1975.

R. B. Kershner, Jr., *Dylan Thomas: The Poet and His Critics*, American Library Association, 1976.

Paul Ferris, *Dylan Thomas*, Dial, 1977.

David Daiches, *Two Studies*, Folcroft, 1977.

D. Jones, *My Friend Dylan Thomas*, Dent, 1977.

Donald Hall, *Remembering Poets: Reminiscences and Reflections; Thomas, Frost, Eliot, Pound*, Harper, 1978.

J. Ackerman, *Welsh Dylan*, John Jones, 1979.

Rayner Heppenstall, *Four Absentees: Brendan Gill, George Orwell, Dylan Thomas, and J. Middleton Murray*, Arden Press, 1979.

Margaret A. Hardesty, *That Momentary Peace: The Poem*, University Press of America, 1982.

Rollie McKenna, *Portrait of Dylan: A Photographer's Memoir*, State Mutual Book, 1982.

PERIODICALS

Atlantic Monthly, February, 1954, December, 1954, June, 1957, October, 1965 (p. 63ff), November, 1965.

Critical Quarterly, spring, 1962, spring, 1974 (p. 57ff).

PMLA, September, 1963, December, 1964.

Queen's Quarterly, autumn, 1964.

English Journal, January, 1966, December, 1966.

McCall's, February, 1966 (p. 78ff).

Bucknell Review, March, 1966.

Texas Quarterly, summer, 1966.

Wall Street Journal, June 8, 1967.

New Republic, June 10, 1967.

Southern Review, October, 1967.

National Library of Wales Journal, summer, 1968.

English Language Notes, March, 1969.

Studies in Short Fiction, fall, 1969, winter, 1969.

TV Guide, December 19, 1987 (p. 32ff).

OBITUARIES

New York Times, November 10, 1953.

Times (London), November 10, 1953.

Spectator (London), November 13, 1953.

Observer (London), November 15, 1953.

Time, November 16, 1953.

Poetry, January, 1954.

Wilson Library Bulletin, January, 1954.

COLLECTIONS

Lockwood Memorial Library of the State University of New York at Buffalo.

Humanities Research Center of the University of Texas.

British Broadcasting Company Archives and Script Libraries.

British Library at the British Museum.

Massachussetts Institute of Technology.

Harvard University.

TINBERGEN, Niko(laas) 1907-1988

OBITUARY NOTICE: Some sources spell given name Nikolas; born April 15, 1907, in The Hague, Netherlands; immigrated to England, naturalized citizen, about 1955; died after an apparent stroke, December 21, 1988, in Oxford, England. Ethologist, scientist, educator, documentary filmmaker, illustrator, and author. Tinbergen was co-recipient of the Nobel Prize for medicine and physiology in 1973 for his work in ethology, the branch of zoology that studies animal behavior, which he pioneered in the late 1930s. Noted for his insightful, thorough, and sometimes pedantic studies of animal behavior, Tinbergen examined such subjects as the homing habits of sand wasps and the mating drives of seagulls. He also wrote and illustrated childrens's books on zoological topics, including *Curious Naturalists*.

During World War II, Tinbergen protested the dismissal of Jewish teachers and was held by the Nazis in a detention camp in the Netherlands; the letters he wrote home to his children were published in two volumes for young readers, *Kleew* and *The Tale of John Stickle*. In 1949 he joined the faculty of Oxford University, retiring as emeritus professor of animal behavior. While at Oxford, he wrote the first handbook on ethology, *The Study of*

Instinct. After his retirement Tinbergen and his wife Elisabeth Amelie Rutten used ethology to advance the treatment of autistic children. They published the results of their findings in *Autistic Children: New Hope for a Cure.* Tinbergen's other works include *Social Behavior in Animals, The Herring Gull's World, Bird Life,* and several award-winning nature documentaries. In addition, he and W. H. Thorpe founded the journal *Behavior.*

FOR MORE INFORMATION SEE:

Contemporary Authors, Volume 108, Gale, 1983.
Who's Who, 141st edition, St. Martin's, 1989.

OBITUARIES

Chicago Tribune, December 24, l988.
Globe and Mail (Toronto), December 24, 1988.
Los Angeles Times, December 24, 1988.
New York Times, December 24, 1988.
Times (London), December 24, 1988.
Washington Post, December 24, l988.

TREASE, (Robert) Geoffrey 1909-

PERSONAL: Born August 11, 1909, in Nottingham, England; son of George Albert (a wine merchant) and Florence (Dale) Trease; married Marian Boyer (a teacher), August 11, 1933; children: Jocelyn Heather (Mrs. Norman Payne). *Education:* Scholar at Queen's College, Oxford, 1928-29. *Politics:* ''Nonpartisan, but keenly interested.'' *Religion:* Church of England. *Home:* 1 Yomede Park, Newbridge Rd., Bath BA1 3LS, England. *Agent:* Murray Pollinger, 4 Garrick St., London WC2E 9BH, England.

CAREER: Journalist in London, England, 1930-32; Clacton-on-Sea, Essex, England, teacher, 1933; full-time writer, 1933—. Lecturer on children's literature. *Military service:* British Army, 1942-46; served in India. *Member:* Royal Society of Literature (fellow), Society of Authors (chairman, 1972-73; member of council, 1974—; chairman of children's writers' group, 1963-64, 1968-70), PEN, National Book League. *Awards, honors:* New York Herald Tribune's Spring Book Festival Award for Nonfiction, 1966, for *This Is Your Century.*

WRITINGS:

JUVENILE FICTION

Bows against the Barons (illustrated by Michael Boland), International Publishers, 1934, revised edition, Meredith, 1966, reissued, Hodder & Stoughton, 1983.
Comrades for the Charter (illustrated by M. Boland), Lawrence, 1934.
Call to Arms, International Publishers, 1935.
Missing from Home (illustrated by Scott), Lawrence & Wishart, 1936.
Red Comet (illustrated by Fred Ellis), Cooperative Publishing Society of Foreign Workers (Moscow), 1936, published as *Red Comet: A Tale of Travel in the U.S.S.R.,* Lawrence & Wishart, 1937.
The Christmas Holiday Mystery (illustrated by Alfred Sindall), A. & C. Black, 1937, published as *The Lakeland Mystery,* A. & C. Black, 1942.
Mystery on the Moors (illustrated by A. Sindall), A. & C. Black, 1937.
Detectives of the Dales (illustrated by A. C. H. Gorham), A. & C. Black, 1938.

In the Land of the Mogul: A Story of the East India Company's First Venture in India (illustrated by J. C. B. Knight), Basil Blackwell, 1938.
A Cue for Treason (illustrated by Beatrice Goldsmith), Basil Blackwell, 1940, U.S. edition (illustrated by L. F. Grant), Vanguard, 1941.
Running Deer (illustrated by W. Lindsay Cable), Harrap, 1941.
The Grey Adventurer (illustrated by B. Goldsmith), Basil Blackwell, 1942.
Black Night, Red Morning (illustrated by Donia Nachsen), Basil Blackwell, 1944.
Trumpets in the West (illustrated by Alan Blyth), Basil Blackwell, 1947, U.S. edition (illustrated by Joe Krush), Harcourt, 1947.
Silver Guard (illustrated by A. Blyth), Basil Blackwell, 1948.
The Hills of Varna (illustrated by Treyer Evans), Macmillan (London), 1948, published as *Shadow of the Hawk* (illustrated by J. Krush), Harcourt, 1949.
The Mystery of Moorside Farm (illustrated by A. Blyth), Basil Blackwell, 1949.
No Boats on Bannermere (illustrated by Richard Kennedy), Heinemann, 1949, Norton, 1965.
The Secret Fiord (illustrated by H. M. Brock), Macmillan (London) 1949, U.S. edition (illustrated by J. Krush), Harcourt, 1950.
Under Black Banner (illustrated by R. Kennedy), Heinemann, 1950.
Web of Traitors: An Adventure Story of Ancient Athens, Vanguard, 1952 (published in England as *The Crown of Violet* [illustrated by C. Walter Hodges], Macmillan, 1952).

Trease at eighty. (Photograph © T. Bailey. Courtesy of the Nottingham *Evening Post.*)

The tale of Troy is one of the oldest in the world. (Illustration by Chris Molan from *Hidden Treasures* by Geoffrey Trease.)

The Barons' Hostage: A Story of Simon de Montfort (illustrated by Alan Jessett), Phoenix House, 1952, revised edition, Brockhampton Press, 1973, T. Nelson, 1975.

Black Banner Players (illustrated by R. Kennedy), Heinemann, 1952.

The New House at Hardale, Lutterworth, 1953.

The Silken Secret (illustrated by A. Jessett), Basil Blackwell, 1953, Vanguard, 1954.

Black Banner Abroad, Heinemann, 1954, Warne, 1955.

(Editor) *Six of the Best: Stories*, Basil Blackwell, 1955.

The Fair Flower of Danger, Basil Blackwell, 1955.

Message to Hadrian, Vanguard, 1955 (published in England as *Word to Caesar* [illustrated by Geoffrey Whittam], Macmillan, 1956).

The Gates of Bannerdale, Heinemann, 1956, Warne, 1957.

Escape to King Alfred, Vanguard, 1958 (published in England as *Mist over Athelney* [illustrated by R. S. Sherriffs and J. L. Stockle], Macmillan, 1958).

The Maythorn Story (illustrated by Robert Hodgson), Heinemann, 1960.

Thunder of Valmy (illustrated by John S. Goodall), Macmillan (London), 1960, published as *Victory at Valmy*, Vanguard, 1961.

Change at Maythorn (illustrated by R. Hodgson), Heinemann, 1962.

Follow My Black Plume (illustrated by Brian Wildsmith), Vanguard, 1963.

A Thousand for Sicily (illustrated by B. Wildsmith), Macmillan (London), 1964, Vanguard, 1966.

The Dutch Are Coming (illustrated by Lynette Hemmant), Hamish Hamilton, 1965.

Bent Is the Bow (illustrated by Charles Keeping), T. Nelson, 1965.

The Red Towers of Granada (illustrated by C. Keeping), Macmillan (London), 1966, Vanguard, 1967.

The White Nights of St. Petersburg (illustrated by William Stobbs), Macmillan (London), 1967, Vanguard, 1968.

The Runaway Serf (illustrated by Mary Russon), Hamish Hamilton, 1968.

A Masque for the Queen (illustrated by Krystyna Turska), Hamish Hamilton, 1970.

Horsemen on the Hills, Macmillan (London), 1971.

A Ship to Rome (illustrated by Leslie Atkinson), Heinemann, 1972.

A Voice in the Night (illustrated by Sara Silcock), Heinemann, 1973.

Popinjay Stairs, Macmillan (London), 1973, Vanguard, 1982.

The Chocolate Boy (illustrated by David Walker), Heinemann, 1975.

The Iron Tsar, Macmillan (London), 1975.

When the Drums Beat (illustrated by Janet Marsh), Heinemann, 1976, revised edition published as *When the Drums Beat and Other Stories*, Pan Books, 1979.

Violet for Bonaparte, Macmillan (London), 1976.

The Seas of Morning (illustrated by David Smee), Penguin, 1976.

The Spy Catchers (illustrated by Geoffrey Bargery), Hamish Hamilton, 1976.

The Field of the Forty Footsteps, Macmillan (London), 1977.

The Claws of the Eagle (illustrated by Ionicus), Heinemann, 1977.

Mandeville, Macmillan (London), 1980.

A Wood by Moonlight and Other Stories, Chatto & Windus, 1981.

The Running of the Deer (illustrated by Maureen Bradley), Hamish Hamilton, 1982.

Saraband for Shadows, Macmillan (London), 1984.

The Cormorant Venture, Macmillan (London), 1984.

Tomorrow Is a Stranger, Heinemann, 1987.

The Arpino Assignment (illustrated by Paul Leith), Walker, 1988.

Hidden Treasure (illustrated by Chris Molan), Lodestar, 1989.

A Flight of Angels (illustrated by Eric Stemp), Lerner, 1989.

Shadow under the Sea, Walker, 1990.

JUVENILE NONFICTION

Fortune, My Foe: The Story of Sir Walter Raleigh (illustrated by Norman Meredith), Methuen, 1949, published as *Sir Walter Raleigh: Captain and Adventurer*, Vanguard, 1950.

The Young Traveller in India and Pakistan, Phoenix House, 1949, Dutton, 1956.

Enjoying Books, Phoenix House, 1950, revised edition, 1963.

There *was* danger in what we had decided to do.
(Cover illustration by Val Biro from *A Cue for Treason*
by Geoffrey Trease.)

(Translator) Rene Guillot, *Companions of Fortune* (illustrated
by Pierre Collot), Oxford University Press, 1952.

(Translator) R. Guillot, *The King's Corsair* (illustrated by Pierre
Rousseau), Oxford University Press, 1953.

The Young Traveller in England and Wales, Dutton, 1953.

The Seven Queens of England, Vanguard, 1953, revised edition,
Heinemann, 1968.

Seven Kings of England (illustrated by Leslie Atkinson), Vanguard, 1955.

The Young Traveller in Greece, Phoenix House, 1956, published as *The Young Traveler in Greece,* Dutton, 1956.

Edward Elgar: Maker of Music, Macmillan (London), 1959.

Wolfgang Mozart: The Young Composer, Macmillan (London),
1961, St. Martin's, 1962.

The Young Writer: A Practical Handbook (illustrated by Carl
Hollander), T. Nelson, 1961.

Seven Stages, Heinemann, 1964, Vanguard, 1965.

This Is Your Century, Harcourt, 1965.

Seven Sovereign Queens, Heinemann, 1968, Vanguard, 1969.

Byron: A Poet Dangerous to Know, Holt, 1969.

The Phoenix and the Flame: D. H. Lawrence, a Biography,
Viking, 1973 (published in England as *D. H. Lawrence:
The Phoenix and the Flame,* Macmillan, 1973).

Days to Remember: A Garland of Historic Anniversaries
(illustrated by Joanna Troughton), Heinemann, 1973.

Britain Yesterday (illustrated by R. Hodgson), Basil Blackwell,
1975.

Timechanges: The Evolution of Everyday Life, Kingfisher,
1985, F. Watts, 1986.

Living through History: The Edwardian Era, Batsford, 1986.

ADULT

Walking in England, Fenland, 1935.

Such Divinity (novel), Chapman & Hall, 1939.

Only Natural (novel), Chapman & Hall, 1940.

Tales Out of School: A Survey of Children's Fiction, Heinemann, 1949, revised edition, Heinemann Educational,
1964.

Snared Nightingale (novel), Macmillan (London), 1957, Vanguard, 1958.

So Wild the Heart (novel), Macmillan (London), 1958, Vanguard, 1959.

The Italian Story: From the Earliest Times to 1946, Macmillan
(London), 1963, Vanguard, 1964.

The Grand Tour, Holt, 1967.

(Editor) *Matthew Todd's Journal: A Gentleman's Gentleman in
Europe, 1814-1820,* Heinemann, 1968.

The Condottieri: Soldiers of Fortune, Thames & Hudson, 1970,
Holt, 1971.

Nottingham: A Biography, Macmillan, 1970.

A Whiff of Burnt Boats: An Early Autobiography, Macmillan
(London), 1970, St. Martin's, 1971.

Samuel Pepys and His World, Putnam, 1972.

Laughter at the Door: A Continued Autobiography, St. Martin's, 1974.

London: A Concise History, Scribner, 1975.

*Portrait of a Cavalier: William Cavendish, First Duke of
Newcastle,* Taplinger, 1979.

PLAYS

The Dragon Who Was Different and Other Plays (juvenile;
includes "The Dragon Who Was Different," "The Mighty
Mandarin," "Fairyland Limited," and "The New Bird"),
Muller, 1938.

"After the Tempest" (one-act), first produced in Welwyn,
Hertfordshire, 1938, produced in London, 1939, published
in *Best One-Act Plays of 1938,* edited by J. W. Marriott,
Harrap, 1939.

"Colony," first produced in London at Unity Theatre, 1939.

The Shadow of Spain and Other Plays (juvenile; includes "The
Shadow of Spain," "The Unquiet Cloister," and "Letters
of Gold"), Basil Blackwell, 1953.

"Time Out of Mind," first produced on BBC television, January
1, 1959, produced in London at Comedy Theatre, London,
1967.

Also author of teleplay "Into Thin Air," 1973, and of radio
plays, "Mr. Engels of Manchester 'Change," 1947, "Henry
Irving," 1947, "Lady Anne," 1949, "The Real Mr.
Ryecroft," 1949, and "Elgar of England," 1957. Trease's
books have been published in more than twenty countries,
including France, Germany, Russia, Estonia, Poland, Romania,
Spain, Portugal, Italy, Greece, Israel, Norway, Sweden, Denmark, Iceland, Holland, and Japan. Contributor to periodicals,
including *Times Literary Supplement, Times Educational Supplement, Horn Book, Junior Bookshelf,* and *Author.*

ADAPTATIONS:

"Popinjay Stairs" (radio play), BBC, 1973.

He felt close to the common people of Russia for the first time. (Illustration by William Stobbs from *The White Nights of St. Petersburg* by Geoffrey Trease.)

WORK IN PROGRESS: A junior novel set in modern Italy (Calabria), for Walker Books.

SIDELIGHTS: For a span of over fifty years, Geoffrey Trease has established himself as a prolific writer, largely of historical fiction. ''I've always refused to accept the title of 'historian.' I am a writer of historical fiction. Historians are people with specialist academic qualifications in their chosen field.''[1]

The youngest of three brothers, Trease was born to a family of wine and spirit merchants in Nottingham, England. ''My brothers were great athletes. Since I wasn't, I was driven into a false contempt for games. I became more intellectual.''[1]

''My writing began before I knew one letter from another. I sat at an oblong table, its top chequered for chess . . . . Before me lay a voluminous and virginal desk diary . . . . What mattered was the delectable acreage of plain white pages . . . unsullied by anything save the printed days of the week. It was for this that the diaries were passed on to me, to scribble in. And scribble I did, the pencil clenched, the small fist moving ceaselessly across the paper, covering line after line and page after page with squiggly 'pretend writing' meaningless to anyone but myself. I was making up stories, muttering the words I did not yet know how to represent, mouthing them silently . . . . Somehow I had already acquired the notion that a story did not really exist until it was written down. I could not write in that sense, but I did what I could. I had got the idea. I was infected for life.''[2]

''I can't remember much about the stories I made up, except that desert islands were a prevailing feature because I'd seen 'Swiss Family Robinson' and 'Robinson Crusoe.' I was very much influenced by whatever book or film I'd seen last. I never finished a story because every time I'd go to the pictures, I'd start another.''[1]

One of his stories, however, Trease did recall. '''Crash! The captain's head struck the deck.' These are the very first words I can remember of any story I ever wrote. I do not know how the story went on. I have no idea *why* the captain's head struck the

deck. Had the ship hit a coral reef? Or had the poor man been clubbed by a mutineer? Or a pirate? Or a cannibal? As a small boy I loved stories crammed with such dramatic happenings, and the tales I made up myself were full of similar ingredients.

''But the opening words I shall never forget, because I heard them recited, with a devilish chuckle of ridicule, by my brother Bill, who had just discovered my notebook hidden behind the sofa, and was disclaiming its contents to my infinite humiliation and fury.

''So, at a tender age, I had already experienced the thrill of literary creation. And it was followed almost immediately by the less exhilarating experience of hostile criticism. Just as well, really. I knew from the start what I was in for. If you don't like the heat, they say, stay out of the kitchen. If you want to write, you must learn to bear the criticism of editors and reviewers— everything from trivial nit-picking to devastating ridicule and demolition. I can thank Bill for that little baptism of fire . . . . I've been remarkably lucky in my critics since then.''[3]

Trease spent his boyhood in Nottingham. ''I was lucky enough to grow up in a very happy home. My father ran the wine business for my widowed grandmother. It was an old-fashioned place in the centre of the city . . . whose Sheriff had once hunted Robin Hood and his outlaws in the neighboring forest of Sherwood. Modern Nottingham is a big industrial city, and its ancient royal castle, perched on a precipitious rock, was rebuilt as a duke's mansion in the seventeenth century and is now used as a public art gallery and museum. Dad's wine business lay just down the street from the castle gateway, and had deep cellars, filled with bottles and casks of wine, cellars that were almost caves hewn out of the sandstone. As a little boy I caught the romance of the place, peering down the breakneck steps into those shadowy depths, hearing the names of distant regions in France and Spain and Portugal from which the wines were shipped.''[3]

World War I provided many boyhood memories for Trease. ''I remember my father coming in on the very day war broke out. I was nearly four. He said, 'All the police and firemen have gone off to enlist and they've commandeered all the horses. I've been to the ironmongers and ordered a brand new dustbin. It's to go upstairs in the attic and we shall buy a sack of flour to put in it because the Germans will try to starve us out.'

"I was nearer to the air-raids during the First World War than during the Second, but I wasn't afraid. I was precociously interested. The bombs dropped on Nottingham, indeed, one on my father's business. The police came in the middle of the night to take my father to identify bodies—the flat over the shop had been let to a dentist. Imagine my indignation when I woke up the next morning and discovered that all this had been happening without me as a witness!

"I remember mostly the funny side of the air-raids. There was one tremendous joke that my father was never allowed to forget. Once, as we all filed downstairs in the dark with candles in our hands, my father asked, 'Who is this hand I'm holding?' 'It's me, Mr. Trease,' answered the little maid. This almost-risque scene became an immortal family legend afterwards.

"I was about nine when the war ended. Two uncles, my father's younger brothers, died at the end of the war. One turned up missing two days before the Armistice on the Bulgarian Front and was never found. That was a great grief to my parents and family."[1]

Trease spent his time walking in the woods, writing, editing, illustrating his own magazine (entitled "British Boy's Magazine" which he sold to friends and family for a half penny a copy), and acting in the model theater in his back yard. "As a quite small boy I made up and acted plays with my friends in the backyard at home. And Bill, who was good at woodworking, made me a model theater with a proper curtain, which I played

"In another minute, me boy, I'll lose me temper!" (Jacket illustration by Louis Slobodkin from *A Thousand for Sicily* by Geoffrey Trease.)

with for hours, using the sheets of cardboard characters and scenery which you could still buy from old-fashioned toy shops . . . . I might be hopeless with a hammer, but I was always happy with pen, pencil, or paintbrush. As I pushed my characters on and off the tiny stage I muttered the made-up dialogue, speaking louder if my long-suffering mother could be enlisted as audience. Those performances were not the end of her suffering, for within a year or two I was discovering Shakespeare, learning long juicy speeches by heart, and making my poor parent listen to them. I was very fond of Macbeth's midnight soliloquy before he murders Duncan, when he imagines a dagger suspended in the air.

"'Is this a dagger I see before me?' I ranted. And Mother made the near fatal mistake of laughing in the wrong place.

"It was lucky that the dagger was imaginary or I might have made myself an orphan on the spot. As it was, my mother recounted good-temperedly later, 'Geoff took me by the throat and shook me like a rat!'[3]

Along with those theatrics, Trease and friends played cowboys and Indians, and many more imaginary games. "We flipped over tables to turn them into rafts. I remember the old-fashioned dolly-peg (an implement used to pound the washing in a tub) which we used as the helm for our ship. With a turned over table and a dolly peg, we evaded pirates and savages."[1]

A good student, Trease developed an early interest in history. "I loved it. My history master would talk through the period and leave us (like mature students) to write about what we thought fit. Then he would collect the books about twice a term and mark them. That was a great help."[1]

But at thirteen, Trease had to give up his beloved history when he won a junior scholarship to study the Classics. "I was bitter and rebellious, but I came to see the event as a blessing, very heavily disguised. For nothing could kill my love of history and it is a line of interest you can always follow for yourself, as I have done ever since. But the Classics—especially the exercise of translating Greek and Latin into good English, or turning English into a passable imitation of what Plato or Julius Caesar might have written—can, most strangely, help you write your own modern language much better. As when trying to compose verse, you learn verbal discipline. You think hard about precise meanings. Whatever their faults, the Greeks and Romans were never wooly-headed."[3]

"On the other hand, if I'd won a history scholarship, I might have gone straight into academic history—all documents and economics. I probably stopped at the right age for a future adventure story writer."[1]

"My father was not so much concerned with the money (he paid the fees into a bank for me as a nest egg for when I grew up) but he was very pleased with the honor.

"'Which would you sooner have,' he asked me, 'a bicycle or a cricket bat?'

"My answer shocked him. 'Please, Dad,' I said, 'I'd much sooner have a typewriter—secondhand would be fine.'

"He stared. I wasn't his idea of a healthy normal boy. But he was always fair and generous. I got my typewriter, an immensely heavy old machine rather like a medieval siege engine, which printed my deathless words in a rich plum purple ink."[3]

Trease continued to develop his passion for drama. "I became a great solitary theater-goer at the age of thirteen. It didn't occur to me that you needed anyone to go with. It wasn't that I didn't have friends, but if they happened not to want to do the same thing as I did, that was okay. Both my parents were very good at loving me, and at leaving me alone. They gave me independence.

"A touring company would perform a different Bernard Shaw play every night, which meant I would see five Shaws a week. I liked him immensely. The first thing I saw was 'The Doctor's Dilemma,' followed by 'Pygmalion.' As a rather politically-minded child I loved the arguments in Shaw. 'Man and Superman' in its entirety meant rushing down from school at five o'clock and sitting in the theater until eleven-thirty, but most performances were shorter than that! I would also be there for Shakespeare every night. No doubt, the standards were appalling compared to the high production standards of today, but when you're thirteen, it's the magic that matters."[1]

"I never cherished any hopeless ambitions to become an actor. My dream was now to become a dramatist. A new English teacher had come to school, young, vital, friendly, and stimulating.

"'Do any of you ever write things for yourselves?' he asked casually. 'If you care to show me your stuff . . . .' I said nothing but I pricked up my ears.

"Later that term, I was ill and missed school for several weeks . . . . During that convalescence I dashed off a full-length play in three acts and as soon as I returned to school I laid my manuscript on the teacher's desk."[3]

"The play was a wild mixture of Bernard Shaw and 'Dracula!' It took place on the Derbyshire Moors in a very haunting atmosphere."[1]

"When he had time to read it, his verdict went beyond anything I'd hoped for.

"'This isn't half bad, Trease.' (It was all surnames in the 1920s—I wasn't 'Geoffrey' for ages and he was 'Mr. Hogg' until I left school and he became 'Garry' throughout the long friendship that followed.)

"'Not half bad,' he said. 'It wants licking into shape, of course. You might tackle that in the holidays. And then—you never know—we might persuade the Head to let us produce it in the summer as an extra school play.'

"He lent me a book, *Play-making*, by a famous critic, William Archer.

"Archer was a great believer in the 'well-made play'—a concept that became unfashionable in later years. Theaters used curtains, plays were divided into separate acts and scenes, scenery was realistic, the actors moved within the frame of the proscenium. You had to look ahead and plan to get your characters onto the stage and eventually off again. They must have a good line for their exits, there must be an effective line every time the curtain comes down, a climax to each act, and a superlative climax for the 'final curtain' at the end of the play. When actors are on stage you must use them. You must give them things to do and lines to say. On no account must you forget any of the characters are present, for it is very hard to stand there, in full view of the audience, silent, with no moves, merely registering with your facial expression what you think and feel about what is going on.

Several times we thought we heard the rumble of distant cannon-fire. (Jacket illustration by Rethi from *Victory at Valmy* by Geoffrey Trease.)

"Then there was the dialogue. It must be speakable, it must fit the character . . . . Another important thing I learnt was that in real life people seldom speak in elaborate and grammatical sentences—indeed, they seldom finish a sentence, for they are either interrupted by someone else or they break off as soon as they see that their hearers have grasped the point they are making.

"With the help of *Play-making*, and [Garry's] criticisms and suggestions I pulled that play apart and put it back together again."[3]

The play was eventually produced at school. "Garry asked me if I would like to play a part or produce. I decided to produce it. Of course, we had curtain calls and so on. I got up there and made some sort of speech. I was about sixteen or seventeen by then. I just remember the one comment of my father, with tears of laughter in his eyes, 'The cheek of this kid!'"[1]

During that period, Trease became a pacifist. "The only adequately armed countries in Europe then were Britain and France. We couldn't foresee Hitler. It seemed so easy: if we'd only disarm, there would be no more fighting. This caused a slight friction because I was also Company Sergeant Major of the Officers Training Corps. It wasn't compulsory. About half the boys belonged. I enjoyed immensely drilling those solid ranks of people and I developed a splendid voice for the parade ground. We had a debate in the school debating society, however, in which I myself spoke against military training. 'This house believes that military training in schools should be superseded by some less war-like instruction.'

"The commanding officer called a meeting of all the non-commissioned officers and said that he was sorry to see that some members of the Corps had spoken for the opposite side. I asked what one was supposed to say if one didn't agree with military training? He answered, 'Nothing.'

"I handed in my resignation, but he didn't take it. A compromise was reached where I didn't make any more public pronouncements for the rest of the year. My duties were confined to going out and parading the company—which the theatrical side of me loved—and collecting the roll books as the different rolls were called. That was all right."[1]

"During that last year of school I had traveled to Oxford and taken the scholarship examinations, competing against candidates from every part of Britain. I was one of the lucky ones. I won an award which, with the money previously saved on my school fees, would carry me through the four years at the university. That autumn, I proudly entered one of the oldest of the score of colleges—Queen's, founded as long ago as 1340, though by now it occupied stately seventeenth- and eighteenth-century buildings on High Street. Other colleges sounded a bell for dinner. At Queen's the call of a medieval trumpet brought us hurrying through the cloisters. The scholars sat at their own long tables in the hall; we wore longer black gowns than the other students, and white surplices in chapel, when we took turns to read the lesson from the huge Bible on a gleaming brass stand in the shape of an eagle, our college emblem."[3]

"At Oxford, I felt I had to choose between the Oxford University Dramatic Society and debating at the Union Society. I thought I would get further debating.

"I loved the life and spoke in the Union quite a bit. I remember Oswald Mosley, later to be the British Fascist leader, coming in and speaking in favor of socialism because he was then a member of the Labour government. He was a magnetic speaker and a rather saturnine individual. I fully intended to vote against him, but he gave such a powerful speech that I indicated to the tellers that I wasn't voting. 'I cannot, in good conscience, vote against these arguments as they were put before me,' I thought. But I was on guard against an instant conversion. In fact, my period as a socialist came later and finished in the 1950s."[1]

After a year, Trease became disenchanted with his course of study. "I was very unfortunate in that my tutor was dry as dust and took no interest in me at all. Over the summer vacation, the feeling came over me that I didn't want to go on.

"I had gone to Oxford with the common sense realisation that it might not be easy to earn a living as a writer. I was very much attracted to teaching as a second choice. If I'd taken my degree, I'd probably have grumbled for the rest of my teaching life that I hadn't been able to write as many books as I'd wanted."[1]

"I went back and handed in my resignation. They complained that I'd wasted a hundred pounds of the college's money. I said that if I stayed I might waste three hundred pounds more.

"I expect that my parents minded. They didn't say much. I didn't want to go home because then my father would have tried to help me find a job. I didn't want to go home until I had one.

"My English Master, Garry Hogg, tried nobly to dissuade me from packing up. 'If you're determined to go,' said he, 'I have a couple of aunts in the East End of London who run a settlement. You could work for your keep and several shillings a week pocket money.'

"It was an atmosphere quite different from anything I'd been in before: they were idealistic, middle-class socialists.

"We ministered to the local population. Muriel Lester, the king-pin, had a saying which I think derived from Ghandi, 'You must approach the poor with the mind of the poor.' We couldn't just settle into the East End and run educational classes. You can't expect people who've been slaving all day in industrial jobs to come in exhausted and be interested.

"I helped run the youth club, taking the boys out on excursions, midnight walks to Epping Forest. They were tough, but I got on with them all right. I wasn't too pleased when one of them bit me, but otherwise, I didn't have any great repugnance for them. We got up plays and sang carols in the streets. Famous authors lectured—people like Laurence Housman, A. A. Milne, and John Galsworthy favoured the place and helped create money for it."[1]

Trease eventually left the settlement and went to work as a hack journalist in publicity. "During those years, I had a whole new group of left-wing friends, involved in 'The Young Prometheans' movement, which had the sympathy of such people as H. G. Wells. Still interested in pacifism, I ran a thing called the Active Peace Group. One of my fellow members and I wrote a letter to Wells suggesting that he shouldn't pay his income tax as a protest against arms. We got a very nice letter in return in which he said, 'I don't want to go to prison. I'm too busy. But I'd very much like to talk to both of you. Come to supper Sunday night.' So we had this tete-a-tete with Wells. It was quite an experience."[1]

"But I never forgot my determination to become an author . . . . I finished an eighty-thousand-word novel and started sending it round the publishers. Monotonously it came back with a rejection slip, a dozen times. Meanwhile, I was . . . selling small articles to lesser magazines and newspapers, and two obscure newspapers even allowed me to review books. Then—unforgettable moment!—a publisher (I feel sure he was the thirteenth) accepted the novel. A contract was signed. Within a few months my trembling fingers held his new autumn catalogue of forthcoming books, and there was a flattering paragraph about mine. After another few months came the news that the publishing company had gone bankrupt. My book never appeared. My typescript was sent back to me, tattered and dog-eared. For a little while it was like the end of the world."[3]

"By the time Hitler rose to power, I had quit the London scene. The old itch to teach had come back. I got a job in a third-rate prep school on the east coast at Clacton-on-Sea. My future wife was on staff there. Marian had been teaching kindergarten at her old high school but with economy cuts, she lost her job and had come to teach the smallest boys at this school.

"We didn't fall in love the first term. I was preoccupied with other things, like reviewing books for some obscure paper. One day someone suggested that I make up a four for a dance, and although I wasn't really interested, I went with Marian. By the second term, I felt differently. We actually became engaged at a Valentine dance. We got married that summer, and were lent a rent-free basement apartment in Bath to begin our lives together.

Trease back at his typewriter after World War II.

"I knew that I had to get busy and make some money. I wrote to a publisher of left-wing books (I didn't know that they were definitely Communist) and told them what a pity it was that children grow up imbued with right-wing ideas and had to be converted later. Why not have books which showed the other side, for instance, *Robin Hood*?

"I was interested in Robin Hood because I was a Nottingham boy and wanted to write a story in which the evils of feudalism were laid bare. The publishers wrote back and said they'd been looking for someone to do a job like this and commissioned it from a synopsis and three chapters. I was pretty excited, but I still had to write the book. You're always under a bit of suspense until you've finished the manuscript and they've accepted it.

"I don't know that my family was particularly pleased with *Bows against the Barons*. My father had died the year before I was married, so he never knew about it. I remember that my aunt was terribly upset when she picked the book up and saw its left-wing tone.

"I don't know what my mother thought about it. I remember, in later years, when I wrote the adult novel *Such Divinity*, I gave her

a copy. Her comment was, 'Yes, well, I read it until I got disgusted and then I went to bed.'"[1]

Bows against the Barons became Trease's first success. "It has plenty of faults . . . . It was dashed off in the white heat of emotion, the English all right, the historical details shaky . . . . I had walked in the remnants of Sherwood Forest, I had known the outlaws in my imagination. I thought I knew it all. I cannot remember doing any research, and only in later printings of the book have I been able to weed out the inaccuracies that made me wince after years.

"My next book, suggested by the publisher, was on an utterly unfamiliar subject—the armed rising of the Chartists in Wales in 1839. I *had* to learn about it, *had* to research, reading up the yellowing newspapers of almost a century ago, coming away from the public library with armfuls of books on the period.

"Ever since then, I have researched every book more and more thoroughly. My study shelves are crammed with volumes on the everyday life of the place and time concerned. Costume, armour, food—even the mealtimes, houses, ships, vehicles . . . everything. And there are always specialized books to buy or order from the library for each particular project. I aim at perfection but of course I fail.''[3]

With his first two books accepted, Trease and his wife moved to a cottage in Somerset. ''Then in 1935, we went to Russia. We were there for about five or six months. They had published my earliest children's books, and there were roubles due to me, so I went there to spend them. We got workers' visas, stayed about two months in an old log house in Moscow, and two months in Yalta, and got first-hand knowledge of everyday life. Yalta gave me the background for my story *Shadow under the Sea*.

''When we returned, we felt more optimistic about the world. Only in the way things turned out after the war came the gradual disenchantment with Stalin.''[1]

In 1936 Jocelyn was born. ''I was so pleased when I learned that my child was a girl because I thought, 'Well, now I shall be able to learn something about girls from the start!'''[1]

Trease continued to write historical novels for young people. ''I never thought I was going to be a children's author. That happened quite by accident. *Bows against the Barons* sold and they wanted another. Then I wrote several more. I did more conventional modern stories for firms like A & C Black. Gradually, I threw off the extreme propagandist tendency and

The class listened, breathless. The guide warmed to the tale he must have told so often. (Illustration by Eric Stemp from *A Flight of Angels* by Geoffrey Trease.)

developed a new attitude of detachment. By all means, I thought, open the eyes of children to the sides of history that aren't shown in school, but hold the scales fairly and give them different points of view.''[1]

Trease wrote a one-act play entitled ''After the Tempest,'' a farcical comedy inspired by Shakespeare's ''Tempest,'' which earned inclusion in *Best One-Act Plays of 1938*. He then had his satirical adult novel, *Such Divinity,* accepted by the first publisher who saw it. Following these successes, he wrote a more serious play entitled, ''Colony,'' which dealt with the terrible living conditions of the black population in the West Indies. '''Colony' was produced at a small club theater in London and met with excellent press notices. Arrangements were quickly made to put it on at one of the big commercial theaters. My novel came out at the same time and the critics were kind. It looked as though I might become simultaneously a West End playwright and a promising new novelist. There was just one fly in the ointment: Adolf Hitler. The new theater contract was signed on 30 August 1939. Two days later the Nazis had launched the invasion of Poland—and World War II had begun.

''All theaters were immediately closed for fear of air raids. Soon they reopened, but a controversial play like 'Colony,' criticising the British Empire, could not be presented when the whole nation had to unite in a common cause. Nor had many people time or inclination, at such a period of crisis, to read a satirical novel like mine.''[3]

While waiting to be called up to serve in the army, Trease wrote another adventure story. ''I am told that *A Cue for Treason* is one of my best books, full of joy and gusto, giving no hint of the shadows overhanging me as I wrote it. I had already broken the absurd convention that one wrote adventure stories only for boys. I had started giving equal share in the action to girls. But this time I was able to create a real heroine in Kit, the lively girl who runs away from her guardian to escape marrying a man she does not love, and then, disguised as a boy, joins the boys who in those days had to act all the female roles from Juliet and Cleopatra to Lady Macbeth and Hamlet's mother. So interwoven with a lot of mystery and hair-raising dangers, I could have fun with the idea of a girl pretending to be a boy pretending to be a girl.''[3]

A Cue for Treason was published in 1940 in the deceptive quiet of the early months of World War II. Suddenly the war flared up and in the blitz that followed, London was continually bombed. The warehouses containing the stock of his book went up in flames. Trease was eventually called to join the King's Own Royal Regiment, but was soon transferred to the Army Educational Corps. ''My own four years of army service proved unexciting . . . . I was sent out to India eventually, and ended my time in a beautiful spot amid the jungle-clad hills. Japan had by then surrendered. We had only to wait impatiently until it was our turn, and shipping became available, for the long voyage home through the Suez Canal.''[3]

Trease used those final months to write *Trumpets in the West* and sent it to his wife four pages at a time—the maximum weight that soldiers were allowed to send free by air mail. He did his first writing for radio, short dramas for the BBC Children's Hour. He also managed to fulfill a boyhood aspiration by visiting the Himalayas.

In 1946, he returned to his home, moving to Malvern in 1954, and has proceeded to publish at least one book every year since. ''There's never been a gap, even during the war. I always work to a plan, just as I'd plan a play, every entrance, every curtain. Very often, I'd plan backward so I'd know where I was going. I had a sort of Lewis Carroll attitude, you cut the cake, then you make it.''[1]

''Authors are constantly asked, 'How do your ideas come?' My own answer must be, 'In all sorts of ways. An item in today's newspaper or a passage in an old history book or a chance conversation with a complete stranger.'''[3]

''The 'Bannermere' series began while I was taking a book week up in Cumberland. Two girls came up to me after question time at the local library and asked, 'Do you ever do school stories?' 'Good heavens, no,' I said. 'Haven't you got enough school stories written by other people?' I thought of school stories in terms of secret passages and dormitory feeds—Enid Blyton and so on. That was not what they meant at all. School stories about real children going to a real school was what they wanted.

''Out of that five-minute conversation, the sixty thousand words were born. *No Boats on Bannermere* is about two children transported to a new English lakeland school to discover that they weren't allowed to use their boat on the lake. But they do, and sail to a little island where they find a grave with a skeleton and treasures dated from Viking times. They get into trouble with the landowner, who has forbidden them to use the lake.

'''If I start this,' I said to my wife, 'I'm not going to do any *Just William* type stories—going on and on about the same characters who never get any older. I will do, at the most, five. My characters will get older in each book and I'll stop when they've left school.' And that's what happened. I finished off when one of the two goes to Oxford.

''When I write historical fiction, I have to master that particular period. Certain periods or countries are used a number of times. I always said I could write about any period if I could figure out what made those people laugh. The wonderful thing is the way two or three threads will come together. For instance, I wanted to write a book about the Moors in Spain and I got the plot working. My story started in Nottingham. I read an article about the ceremony for the sequestration and seclusion for a leper in the English Middle Ages. A burial service was read over a living man in church. I thought it would be marvelous to start a book with a boy kneeling at the altar and listening to his own burial service. The priest shovels a few handfuls of dirt over his feet and says, 'Go forth, you are dead!'

''Of course, the boy then discovers that he's got a harmless skin disease which is cured by a Jewish doctor whom he rescues from forest bandits. But the boy has been officially secluded, and who is going to take the verdict of a Jewish doctor over that of a parish priest? At that moment, Edward the First expels the Jews from England. In the end, you get an essay on inter-racial harmony because you've got good and bad Catholics, Jews, and eventually Muslims. That's the story of *The Red Towers of Granada*.''[1]

Trease has also written nonfiction for young people, such as biographies of Lord Byron and D. H. Lawrence. ''My American publisher asked if I could write a teenage biography of Byron, because children had to study his poems but knew nothing about the man or his period. So I took the project on.

''I wanted to convey the information in a subtle way so as not to lecture the reader. As for some aspects of life, prominent in both Byron's and Lawrence's biographies, I take the view that it's not my business to be a sex instructor. If the more sophisticated child reads between the lines, fine, but I'm not going to spell out to the child answers to questions he or she has not asked.

Trajan was a fighting emperor. Never gave an inch if he could help it. (Jacket illustration from *Message to Hadrian* by Geoffrey Trease.)

''The D. H. Lawrence book led on very much from the Byron. Lawrence had gone to my school about twenty years before me, and some of the people who'd taught me had taught him. He was never mentioned in those days; his name was absolutely mud.

''I think he was a great influence, partly for good, and sometimes wrote very well. I like the writing that is not fashionable now, such as *Sons and Lovers*, more than I like the preaching Lawrence. He is one of those cases where you have to separate the writer and the man. As a person, I don't think he would have been my cup of tea.''[1]

In his roles as writer and reviewer, Trease has noticed many changes in English children's literature over the years. ''The discouragement of meagre earnings in those days was matched for the serious writer by restrictions on his themes and vocabulary. Older children's books were demarcated 'for boys' or 'for girls.' Girls, it is well known, ignored the division. Boys were less inclined to. Nurtured on 'healthy yarns' of slaughter and horror, they picked up a lot of incidental history and geography but little understanding of the opposite sex.

''As late as 1950 the editor of *John 'o London's Weekly*, Wilson Midgley, gently rebuked me in a private letter for 'spoiling' *Under Black Banner* with the hint of a budding love affair on the final page.

"Sex was only the most obvious of the taboos I remember. Liquor was another. I found the *Boy's Own Paper* very inhibited . . . [about] alcohol, so that it was, except in the historical context of rum-swigging buccaneers, almost literally unmentionable. The supernatural was out: any apparently psychic phenomenon was permissible only if a rational explanation was supplied before the end of the story. This would have ruled out some remarkably fine imaginative books published in the past few years. Authority must not be undermined: schoolmasters could be comically eccentric or pompous, tricks might be played to rob them temporarily of their dignity, but respect for the old school and the older generation should not be fundamentally impaired. Parents, above all, must not be shown with serious human weaknesses. They could be dead or abroad; they were very often one or the other, if not both, or the scope for the youthful initiative would have been negligible. If, however, parents were present they must also be correct—loving, lovable, and long-suffering.

"The list of restrictions could be lengthened. And it was matched by the limitations on vocabulary. Villains might 'mutter imprecations,' but woe betide the author who submitted a manuscript in which they were quoted . . . . Realistic working-class dialogue could not be reproduced, though as working-class settings were rare few people were conscious of the handicap. The natural dialogue of the playground had to be replaced, usually, by a stylized and obsolete slang, carefully refined to avoid offense.

"Am I piling it on? It is only because, after twenty or thirty years of freedom, we veterans wonder how on earth we found any satisfaction in writing under so many limitations. But of course we did, and, though we say it ourselves, some good books were written. The creative artist can sometimes thrive under restrictions, whether it be a question of conforming to a sonnet's rhyme scheme or the producer's budget for a television play. When the handicap is not technical, but comes from taboos, stereotyped attitudes, and accepted but questionable values, there is a similar satisfaction in probing the enemy lines to see just what advances *can* be made."[4]

Despite its many advances, publishing now provides a different set of frustrations for Trease. "There is much more editorial fussing and quibbling now. I used to send a book to a publisher and there might be one query or quibble and I would write back most gratefully and say, 'Thank you for pointing that out.' Today there is a new breed of copy-editors, not all content to check our spelling, grammar, and punctuation, our careless slips, repetitions, and ambiguities—all legitimate and much appreciated help—but some (intimidated by certain vocal pressure groups) questing for supposedly 'racist' or 'sexist' elements. Often they seem quite unable to distinguish between the author's own view and that of his deplorable characters."[1]

Trease's work was disrupted by his wife's stroke in 1987. "I'd been absolutely spoilt before. I'd never been intimately involved with bad illness. I reflect upon it with a mixture of gratitude and bitterness, at this moment, because my life has been knocked sideways. My wife and I had been married fifty-five years and we'd been lucky until the past two or three. We've had a lot to be thankful for until now, but I do feel rather, absurdly inexperienced in this new situation."[1]

Marian Trease died a few months later. Trease has found consolation in his work with which he is now fully occupied again. "Once when talking to a school audience, I was asked the question, 'Have you an ambition?' I made up a not too solemn answer: 'Yes, to leave three posthumous books.'

"Some of the children looked blank for a moment—they didn't know that a 'posthumous' book means one published after the author's death. But, when they cottoned on, they saw the implication—then if he leaves *three* he must have died in harness, as most of us would like to do."[3]

FOOTNOTE SOURCES

[1]Based on an interview by Cathy Courtney for *Something about the Author*.

[2]Geoffrey Trease, *A Whiff of Burnt Boats: An Early Autobiography*, Macmillan (London), 1971.

[3]Geoffrey Trease, *Something about the Author Autobiography Series*, Volume 6, Gale 1988.

[4]Geoffrey Trease, "Fifty Years On: A Writer Looks Back," *Children's Literature in Education*, autumn, 1983.

FOR MORE INFORMATION SEE:

White, *About Books for Children*, Oxford University Press, 1946.

Frank Eyre, *Twentieth Century Children's Books*, Longmans, Green, 1952.

Margaret Meek, *Geoffrey Trease*, Bodley Head, 1960, Walck, 1964.

M. T. Fisher, *Intent upon Reading*, Brockhampton Press, 1961.

Muriel Fuller, editor, *More Junior Authors*, H. W. Wilson, 1963.

Roger Lancelyn Green, *Tellers of Tales*, F. Watts, 1965.

Adventuring with Books, Signet, 1966.

Brian Doyle, *The Who's Who of Children's Literature*, Schocken, 1968.

Books and Bookmen, May, 1969.

Horn Book, June, 1971.

Author's Choice, Crowell, 1971.

D. L. Kirkpatrick, editor, *Twentieth-Century Children's Writers*, St. Martin's, 1978, 2nd edition, 1983.

Times Literary Supplement, July 24, 1981, April 13, 1984.

Author, summer, 1988 (p. 42ff).

Junior Bookshelf, August, 1989.

COLLECTIONS

Nottingham Central Library.
Kerlan Collection at the University of Minnesota, Minneapolis.
University of Nottingham Library.

VAUGHAN, Marcia 1951-

PERSONAL: Born April 6, 1951, in Tacoma, Wash.; daughter of Claude M. (an attorney) and Helen (a writer of children's books; maiden name, Adams) Pearson; married Richard Vaughan (a counselor and writer), November 14, 1984; children: Sam Matthew. *Education:* Attended Washington State University, 1969-70; Central Washington State University, B.A., 1974, Library Science Certification, 1975. *Home and office address:* c/o Ashton Scholastic Pty. Ltd., P.O. Box 579, Gosford, New South Wales, Australia 2250. *Agent:* Marilyn Marlow, Curtis Brown Ltd., 10 Astor Pl., New York, N.Y. 10003.

CAREER: Captain Charles Wilkes Primary School, Bainbridge Island, Wash., school librarian, 1975-80; writer, 1981—; Blessed Sacrament School, Mosman, New South Wales, Australia, school librarian, 1982-88. Volunteer school librarian at Natangiia Primary School, Rarotonga, South Pacific, 1981. *Member:* Pacific Northwest Writer Conference.

WRITINGS:

The Lucky Fun Book, Ashton Scholastic (Australia), 1984.

Who? (illustrated with photographs by husband, Richard Vaughan), Ashton Scholastic, 1984.

Wombat Stew (illustrated by Pamela Lofts), Ashton Scholastic, 1985, Silver Burdett, 1986.

Pewzer and Bonsai (illustrated by Megan Gressor), Hodder & Stoughton (Australia), 1985.

Crosby Crocodile's Disguise (illustrated by Philip Webb), Shortland Publications (New Zealand), 1988.

Still Room for More (illustrated by Craig Smith), Australasian Publishing & Century Hutchinson, 1989.

The Wombat Stew Cookbook (illustrated by P. Lofts), Ashton Scholastic, 1989.

(With R. Vaughan) *Adam's Apple* (illustrated by Coral Tulloch), Five Mile Press (Australia), 1989.

Ships, Boats and Things That Float, Harcourt (Australia), 1989.

As Fat as That, Harcourt (Australia), 1989.

There's a Bunyip under My Bed, Harcourt (Australia), 1989.

Milly Fitzwilly's Most Magnificent Mousecatcher (illustrated by Roland Harvey), Five Mile Press, 1990.

The Sea Breeze Hotel (illustrated by Patricia Mullins), Margaret Hamilton Books (Australia), 1990.

"BOOKSHELF READING" SERIES

Hands, Scholastic, 1987.

Tails, Scholastic, 1987.

MARCIA VAUGHAN

Whose Toes and Nose Are Those?, Scholastic, 1987.

A Cat's Eye Is One, Scholastic, 1987.

Hiccups, Scholastic, 1987.

Where Does the Wind Go?, Scholastic, 1987.

The Giant's Child (illustrated by Kellie Jobson), Harper & Collins (Canada), in press.

"JELLYBEAN READING" SERIES

The Sandwich That Max Made, Shortland (New Zealand), 1989.

Wake Up, Wallaby, Shortland, 1989.

At Night, Shortland, 1989.

Clouds, Shortland, 1989.

Numerals, Shortland, 1989.

Sleeping, Shortland, 1989.

T. J.'s Tree, Shortland, 1989.

Sleepy Bear, Shortland, 1989.

Monkey's Friends, Shortland, 1989.

Moonlight, Shortland, 1989.

"DANGEROUS AND DEADLY" SERIES

Dangerous and Deadly Australian Snakes, Macmillan (Australia), 1990.

Dangerous and Deadly Australian Spiders, Macmillan, 1990.

Dangerous and Deadly Australian Sea Life, Macmillan, 1990.

Dangerous and Deadly Australian Crocodiles, Macmillan, 1990.

Dangerous and Deadly Australian Insects, Macmillan, 1990.

Dangerous and Deadly Australian Plants, Macmillan, 1990.

Also author of "The Sticky Beak Mystery" series, twenty-six Easy-to-Read Mystery Books, published by Bay Books (Australia), 1988.

ADAPTATIONS:

"Wombat Stew" (cassette), Louie Braille Books, 1988.

WORK IN PROGRESS: The Adventures of Goldsworthy and Mort and *Goldsworthy and Mort Again,* both for Harper & Collins (Canada); a children's picture book about a bandit called "Dirty Bert."

SIDELIGHTS: "When I sit down to write a story I listen to the characters talking in my imagination. I write down their conversations and fill in the descriptive parts later. I often start right in the middle of a story and work my way back to the beginning, then to the end. Some stories, like *Wombat Stew,* jump right out of my pencil, while others take weeks to gel. One trick I always use is reading the story onto a cassette and listening back to it. If it sounds good to my ear then I know it is done.

"My parents tell me that when I was young I used to sit on the back porch telling my friends wild stories. I don't remember this, but I do remember how much I loved being read to and later reading books on my own. Every night I curl up in bed and read for at least an hour before I go to sleep. It is one of my favorite parts of the day. I often bring home a bag of children's books from the library to share with my son and husband.

"My fondest memories of childhood include hamming it up in my Saturday drama class. This class brought me out of my 'shy phase' and instilled in me a love of drama and storytelling. Each June my parents took my sister, Susan (now a professor of drama at the University of New Mexico in Albuquerque), and me to spend the summer on an island in Puget Sound. Accessible only by ferry, the island was only partially inhabited. Susan and I played in the woods, on the beach, and in the water *all* day. I really fell in love with nature on this island. (Even today I

One day, on the banks of a billabong,
a very clever dingo caught a wombat . . .

(From *Wombat Stew* by Marcia K. Vaughan. Illustrated by Pamela Lofts.)

fantasize about moving back and writing lots of books out on the deck while I watch my son, Sam, playing on the beach.)

"When I enrolled in college I thought I wanted to be a first grade teacher. It wasn't until my final semester of school that I finally stepped into a 'real' classroom to do my student teaching. Horror of horrors—I didn't like it. Being a teacher was not at all how I imagined it would be. I found out there were so many required subjects to teach that there was very little time left for all the creative activities I had envisioned. Worried that I had wasted four years of college I escaped to Arizona to reconsider just what I wanted to do with my life. I lived in a trailer in the desert outside Phoenix, and worked in an ice cream parlour—a delicious job! After six months a letter from my college placement office came listing job openings. The first three positions were for primary school librarians. Something clicked in my head. Here was a profession in which I could use puppetry, drama, storytelling and share my love for books with children whose imaginations were still alive! (I had majored in children's theater in college and also earned a B.A. in education.)

"Writing children's books was a natural spin-off of being a librarian. I shared so many books with children I decided (right in the middle of *Tikki Tikki Tembo*) that I wanted to write books too. I started writing in the loft of a cabin on the South Pacific Island of Rarotonga. I worked an entire year on those first two stories neither of which were ever published. I did build up my writing muscles though and shortly after moving to Australia, my third story *Wombat Stew* was accepted for publication in 1982.

"I've been writing ever since that first taste of success. I love it! It's a constant creative challenge. Ideas are everywhere. The biggest problem for me is that there is not enough time to develop all those ideas into stories . . . but it sure is fun to try."

HOBBIES AND OTHER INTERESTS: Beachcombing, traveling, baking, reading.

FOR MORE INFORMATION SEE:

The Story Makers: A Collection of Interviews with Australian and New Zealand Authors and Illustrators for Young People, Oxford University Press (Australia), 1989.

VUONG, Lynette (Dyer) 1938-

PERSONAL: Surname is pronounced as one syllable (Voong); born June 20, 1938, in Owosso, Mich.; daughter of Wilbur LaVergne (a draftsman) and Brandon (a practical nurse; maiden name, Richardson) Dyer; married Ti Quang Vuong (in business), January 9, 1962; children: Timothy Tuan, Theodore Tan, Tamara Linh, Tania Lan. *Education:* Attended University of Wisconsin—Milwaukee, 1958-61; Milwaukee County Hospital School of Nursing, R.N., 1959. *Religion:* Lutheran. *Home and office:* 15211 Morning Dove Dr., Humble, Tex. 77396. *Agent:* Gary L. Hegler Literary Agency, 17629 El Camino Real, Suite 400, Houston, Tex. 77058.

CAREER: St. Joseph Hospital, Milwaukee, Wis., and Mt. Sinai Hospital, Milwaukee, staff nurse in newborn nursery, both 1959-61; Vietnamese-American Association, Saigon (now Ho Chi Minh City), Vietnam, teacher of English as a second language, 1962-69; teacher of privately organized classes in English as a second language in Saigon, 1969-74; International School, Saigon, principal, 1974-75; interpreter and resource person assisting Vietnamese refugees and their sponsors in Greenville, S.C., 1975-80; Spartanburg General Hospital, Spartanburg, S.C., staff nurse in newborn nursery, 1977-79; interpreter and resource person for bilingual education program in public schools in Greenville County, S.C., 1977-79; teacher of Vietnamese language class to help Vietnamese children become literate in their native language, Humble, Tex., 1981-84; teacher of fiction-writing classes and workshops in Texas and South Carolina, 1983— .

MEMBER: Romance Writers of America, Associated Authors of Children's Literature, Houston (president, 1988-89), Society of Children's Book Writers. *Awards, honors:* Outstanding Woman of the Year from the Greenville, S.C. Junior Women's Club, 1976, for her work with Vietnamese refugees and sponsors; *The Brocaded Slipper and Other Vietnamese Tales* was included on the Texas Bluebonnet Award List of the Texas Association of School Librarians and Children's Round Table, 1984-85, and Georgia Children's Book Award nominee from the University of Georgia College of Education, 1985-86; Golden Heart Award from the Romance Writers of America, 1985, for unpublished manuscript *The Shadow of the Sickle.*

WRITINGS:

The Brocaded Slipper and Other Vietnamese Tales (juvenile; illustrated by Vo-Dinh Mai), Addison-Wesley, 1982.
A Friend for Carlita, Standard, 1989.

Contributor to magazines, including *Highlights for Children, Teens Today, Venture, Contact, Discoveries, Reflection, Partners, Between Times,* and *Junior Trails.*

WORK IN PROGRESS: A collection of Vietnamese sky legends; a book about dragons; other Vietnamese legends; *The Shadow of the Sickle,* a historical novel set in India in the 1920s, dealing with the confrontation between Islam and Christianity and reminiscent of recent events in Iran and Afghanistan; a novel about a Vietnamese-American boy's struggles to fit into his several worlds, for young people; a novel of romantic suspense dealing with a Vietnamese-American couple's life in and escape from Vietnam.

SIDELIGHTS: "One of my earliest memories is of my father telling me about Curwood Castle. The studio of adventure writer James Oliver Curwood, it stands on the banks of the Shiawassee River, not far from my childhood home in Owosso, Michigan. When I was seven years old, my father set me up with a 'castle' of my own: a drafting table in the one-windowed, walk-in closet adjoining my bedroom. Here I could look out on the cherry trees in our backyard as I wrote and illustrated little books of fabulous adventures of children in distant times and places.

"One of the first of these books grew out of a game I played with my older sister. We called it 'outwitting.' Each trying to be more ridiculous than the other, we would see who could think up the silliest stories. In 'The Roof and the Walls,' some children wash the walls away while their mother is gone and then discover that little stars are holding up the roof. The story ends in typical fairy-tale fashion: the king has a new wall built for them out of marble.

"Not long afterward I received my first taste of rejection. My poem was not the one selected to represent my class in the school newspaper. In a manner foreshadowing the typical 'not right for our present needs' statements of future rejection slips, my teacher told me that, although she felt my poem was the best, she had chosen another because 'I thought the other children would

LYNETTE VUONG

like hers better. She wrote about kids doing everyday things, and you wrote about fairies.'

"Undaunted by this first 'editorial' opinion, I continued to write from my heart, pursuing interests that have not changed much over the years: interests in folklore and mythology and in people throughout the world and through the ages. I wrote my first historical novel when I was ten, a fifty-page undertaking called 'The Russian Twins,' set at the turn of the century at the time of the Russo-Japanese War. Unfortunately, not yet having learned the importance of research, I had my Russian family fleeing Moscow to escape the Japanese. Only later did I discover that the war had been fought in Manchuria.

"Throughout high school I continued to write. But when the time came to decide on a career, I couldn't see myself in the deadline-ridden, 'just-the-facts, ma'am' world of journalism. So I chose nursing. In doing so, I found myself the proverbial square peg in a round hole; yet it was in this unlikely world that my writing first appeared in a national publication. One of my teachers had clipped a humorous piece of mine, 'A Medical Definition of Love,' from the hospital paper and sent it to *Davis Nursing Survey*.

"A few months later I met a student from Vietnam. It was love at first sight, and I followed him back to Saigon to become his wife. I lived there for the next thirteen years, absorbing the Vietnamese culture, mothering my three older children, and putting down roots so deep that, when we were forced to leave just prior to the communist takeover, it was almost as powerful a wrench for me as it was for my husband.

"As I learned to read Vietnamese, my interest in folklore led me to explore the world of Vietnamese legends. One of the first stories I found told of a girl—mistreated by her stepmother and stepsister—who, thanks to a fairy's help, acquires a pair of brocaded slippers. A crow flies off with one, dropping it into the prince's garden. Excited at finding the Vietnamese Cinderella, I wrote the story and sent it to *Highlights for Children*.

"From this beginning grew my desire to share more Vietnamese folklore with American readers. Over a span of fifteen years, the book that became *The Brocaded Slipper* evolved from a collection of ten stories to the present five 'counterparts of Western fairy tales.' The lessons of patience and persistence learned long before stood me in good stead while I searched for the right editor. As it turned out, the timing was perfect, both for my own situation and for the book's reception, which underscores my firm conviction that, having placed my life in God's hands, his schedule will ultimately prove the best.

"My second book has proved a refresher course in the same lessons. I first wrote *A Friend for Carlita* when I was sixteen years old, and received my first official rejection slip for it when I submitted it to the only market I knew: my church's Sunday school take-home paper. 'Unsympathetic main character' was the editor's criticism, for I had written the story from the viewpoint of the character who did not want to befriend Carlita, the new girl in class. The story simmered in my drawer and in my

Master Frog completed his education and grew to young froghood. (From *The Brocaded Slipper and Other Vietnamese Tales* by Lynette Vuong. Illustrated by Vo-Dinh Mai.)

subconscious for years until I rewrote it a few years ago from the viewpoint of the girl who did want to be Carlita's friend. Subsequently the story sold five times in magazine form and is now a picture book.

"These concepts: the need for patience, for perseverance, for rewriting and revising, and for continuing to send your work out until it is published are ones I share with students when I am invited to speak at schools. The opportunity to encourage young people's interest in books, in reading and writing, and perhaps to inspire some future author has been a most enjoyable fringe benefit of my life as a writer.

"Ultimately, the most gratifying aspect of writing, as well as of speaking, is the opportunity to share one's stories and one's ideas with others. For me the purposes of writing are—as most would agree—to entertain, to inform, and to inspire. To neglect the first is inexcusable, but I hope that anything I write will give something more: that the reader will in some way be a better person for having read what I have written, and that I will in some way be a better person for having lived with my characters or concepts long enough to write it."

HOBBIES AND OTHER INTERESTS: History, peoples, and cultures of the world, folklore, travel, music ("I play the flute"), foreign languages ("My day starts with a two-and-a-half mile walk with cassette tape player and foreign-language tape: French, Modern Greek, German, and—soon—Spanish. I've never met a language I didn't like!")

FOR MORE INFORMATION SEE:

Greenville News (S.C.), December 7, 1975, July 9, 1982.
Humble Echo (Tex.), August 19, 1981, November 17, 1982, February 29, 1984, November 5, 1986.
Romance Writers' Report, August, 1982.
Houston Chronicle, October 29, 1982.
Tomball Sun (Tex.), December 1, 1982.
Argus-Press (Owosso, Mich.), January 7, 1983.
Milwaukee Journal, January 13, 1983.
Humble Area Magazine, fall, 1985.
Brazosport Facts, April 29, 1987.
School Library Media Activities Monthly, October, 1989.

WALKER, David G(ordon) 1926-

PERSONAL: Born December 16, 1926, in Glen Ridge, N.J.; son of David (a lawyer) and Marjorie (an opera singer; maiden name, Sears) Walker; married Betty Ellison (deceased); children: Terri Walker Hetzel, Kim, Jake, Christian. *Education:* Tufts University, B.S., 1948. *Home:* 359 Meadowlakes Dr., Marble Falls, Tex. 78654.

DAVID G. WALKER

CAREER: John Wiley & Sons, Inc. (publisher), New York City, college sales representative, 1948-52; Mobil Corp., Luling, Tex., in oil fields, 1952-53; *Offshore* (magazine), Houston, Tex., editor, 1953-60, vice-president, 1960-61; Robinson-Gerrard Advertising Agency, Houston, Tex., senior vice-president, 1961-78; chief executive officer of Marketing Principle & Co., 1978-83; Walker Publishing Co., Houston, chief executive officer, 1981-83. Member of board of directors of R. P. Foundation, Houston, Tex. *Military service:* U.S. Marine Corps, 1948-52; became first lieutenant. *Member:* American Chemical Society, Mensa, Southern Rubber Group.

WRITINGS:

CHILDREN'S BOOKS

Rick Goes to Little League (illustrated by Mike Dick), Caroline House, 1982.
Rick Heads for Soccer (illustrated by M. Dick), Caroline House, 1982.
Rick Tees Off (illustrated by William Van Sandt), Professional Golfers' Association, 1985.

WORK IN PROGRESS: The Art of Technical and Industrial Writing; a romantic novel; a western.

HOBBIES AND OTHER INTERESTS: Travel (Europe), coaching boys' baseball and football.

WANIEK, Marilyn (Nelson) 1946-

PERSONAL: Surname is pronounced *Won*-yek; born April 26, 1946, in Cleveland, Ohio; daughter of Melvin M. (in U.S. Air Force) and Johnnie (a teacher; maiden name, Mitchell) Nelson; married Erdmann F. Waniek, September, 1970 (divorced); married Roger R. Wilkenfeld (a university professor), November 22, 1979; children: (second marriage) Jacob, Dora. *Education:* University of California, Davis, B.A., 1968; University of Pennsylvania, M.A., 1970; University of Minnesota, Ph.D., 1979. *Agent:* Marie Brown Associates, 412 West 154th St., New York, N.Y. 10032. *Office:* Department of English, University of Connecticut, Storrs, Conn. 06268.

CAREER: National Lutheran Campus Ministry, Ithaca, N.Y., lay associate, 1969-70; Lane Community College, Eugene, Ore., assistant professor of English, 1970-72; Norre Nissum Seminariam, Norre Nissum, Denmark, teacher of English, 1972-73; St. Olaf College, Northfield, Minn., instructor in English, 1973-78; University of Connecticut, Storrs, assistant professor, 1978-82, associate professor of English, 1982-88, professor of English, 1988—. Visiting assistant professor, Reed College, 1971-72. *Member:* Society for the Study of Multi-Ethnic Literature of the United States, Society for Values in Higher Education, Associated Writing Programs, Poetry Society of America. *Awards, honors:* Kent Fellow from the Danforth Foundation, 1976; National Endowment for the Arts Fellow, 1982.

MARILYN WANIEK

WRITINGS:

For the Body, Louisiana State University Press, 1978.
(With Pamela Espeland) *The Cat Walked through the Casserole: And Other Poems for Children* (illustrated by Trina Schart Hyman, Hilary Knight, Nancy Carlson and Peter E. Hanson), Carolrhoda, 1984.
Mama's Promises, Louisiana State University Press, 1985.

TRANSLATOR FROM THE DANISH

P. Dahlerup, *Literary Sex Roles,* Minnesota Women in Higher Education, 1974.
(With P. Espeland) Halfdan Rasmussen, *Hundreds of Hens and Other Poems for Children,* Black Willow Poetry, 1983.

WORK IN PROGRESS: Poems for children; *The Homeplace,* and *Lost and Found,* both poetry.

SIDELIGHTS: "I started writing poetry in elementary school. Or should I say elementary schools—since my father was in the Air Force we moved frequently. My sixth grade teacher, Mrs. Gray in Kittery Point, Maine, predicted on the last day of school that I would become 'a famous author.' I'm still trying to fulfill her prediction.

"My interest in writing verse for children grew in part out of my attempt to translate the wonderfully funny work of the Danish poet, Halfdan Rasmussen.

"For the last several years I've been writing poems with children, and I've learned a lot about what makes kids laugh. Once, as I read the last line of a poem, a third-grader literally laughed until he fell out of his chair! I consider that one of my greatest successes."

HOBBIES AND OTHER INTERESTS: Travel, "looking (seeing!)."

FOR MORE INFORMATION SEE:

COLLECTIONS

Kerlan Collection at the University of Minnesota.

WEBB, Kaye 1914-

PERSONAL: Born January 26, 1914, in Chiswick, England; daughter of Arthur (a journalist) and Kathleen (a journalist; maiden name, Stevens) Webb; married Christopher Brierley, 1935; married Andrew Hunter, 1942; married Ronald Searle (a graphic artist, cartoonist, designer, and animator), 1946 (divorced, 1967); children: Kate, John. *Politics:* Socialist. *Religion:* Church of England. *Home:* 8 Lampard House, 8 Maida Avenue, London W2 1SS, England. *Agent:* Jacqueline Korn, David Higham Associates, 5-8 Lower John St., Golden Square, London W1R 4HA, England.

CAREER: Picturegoer, London, England, journalist, 1931; *Picture Post,* London, journalist, 1938; *Lilliput,* London, assistant editor, 1941-47; *Leader,* London, theatre correspondent, 1947-49; Perpetua Books, London, director; *News Chronicle,* London, feature writer, 1949-55; *Young Elizabethan* (children's magazine), London, editor, 1955-58; *National Review,* London, theatre critic, 1957-58; Penguin Books Ltd., London, children's editor of Puffin Books, and publishing director of children's

KAYE WEBB

division, 1961-79; *Puffin Post,* London, editor, 1967-82; Kaye Webb Ltd., London, managing director, 1973—. Chairman and founder, Puffin Club (for children), 1967-87; director, Unicorn Children's Theatre, 1972; children's advisor, Goldcrest TV, 1978-84. *Member:* UNICEF (United Kingdom branch), Authors Society, PEN, Society of Bookmen, Women's Press. *Awards, honors:* Eleanor Farjeon Award from the Children's Book Circle (England), 1970, for services to children's literature; Member of the Order of the British Empire, for services to children's literature.

WRITINGS:

(With husband, Ronald Searle) *Paris Sketchbook,* Saturn Press, 1950, new and revised edition, Perpetua Books, 1957, Braziller, 1958.
(Editor) *An Experience of Critics by Christpher Fry and The Approach to Dramatic Criticism* (illustrated by R. Searle), Perpetua Books, 1952, Oxford University Press, 1953.
(With R. Searle) *Looking at London and People Worth Meeting,* News Chronicle (London), 1953.
(Editor) Raymond Peynet, *The Lovers' Pockebook,* Perpetua Books, 1954, reissued, 1958.
(Editor) *Penguin Patrick Campbell,* Penguin, 1963.
(Compiler) *The St. Trinian's Story: The Whole Ghastly Dossier,* House & Maxwell, 1959.
(With R. Searle) *Refugees 1960: A Report in Words and Drawings,* Penguin, 1960.
(Editor) Joan Aiken and others, *The Friday Miracle and Other Stories* (illustrated by George Adamson and others), Penguin, 1969.
(Editor with Treld Bicknell and Frank Waters) *The Puffin Annual No. 1,* Puffin, 1974.
(Editor with T. Bicknell) *The Puffin Annual No. 2,* Puffin, 1975.
(With T. Bicknell) *Puffin's Pleasure* (juvenile), Penguin, 1976.
(Editor) *The Crack-A-Joke Book,* Penguin, 1978.

(Editor) *I Like This Poem: A Collection of Best-Loved Poems Chosen by Children for Other Children* (illustrated by Antony Maitland), Penguin, 1979.

(Author of English text) Kazuo Iwamura, *Nat's Braces,* Kestrel, 1982.

(Author of English text) K. Iwamura, *Nat's Hat,* Kestrel, 1982.

(Editor) *Child's Day,* Ladybird, 1984.

(Editor) *Lilliput Goes to War,* Hutchinson, 1985, David & Charles, 1986.

(Selector) *All in a Day* (poems; illustrated by Kathie Layfield), Ladybird, 1985.

(Selector) *I Like This Story: A Taste of Fifty Favourites* (illustrated by Anthony Kerins), Puffin, 1986, new edition, Viking Kestrel, 1987.

WORK IN PROGRESS: Birthday Book of Six, an anthology of stories and poems; *I Like These Too,* similar to *I Like This Story* for younger readers, for Puffin; *The Family Book,* an anthology, for Hamish Hamilton.

SIDELIGHTS: ''I arrived inconveniently in the middle of a winter night the same year the First World War broke out. So, my father left for the army while my mother took me and my brother, Bill, to live in Hove, Sussex, until the hostilities ceased. Then, we moved back to London where my younger brother, John, was born. He was a marvelous boy and I looked after him.

(From ''Supply Teacher'' in *All in a Day,* poems selected by Kaye Webb. Illustrated by Kathie Layfield.)

''As a journalist for the *Star,* my father created the first gossip column in England, 'The Star Men's Diary.' He was also public relations officer for Dame Sybil Thorndike and Lewis Casson, two of Britain's most distinguished actors. When I was nine, my father took me to visit Sybil Thorndike backstage after seeing a play called, 'Madam Play Nap,' and I wrote an interview with her for the school magazine. At that time I thought being an actress was the most exciting thing in the world; that's what I was going to be. Thirty years later I took my daughter, Kate, to meet Dame Sybil, as she had become, and *Kate* wrote an article for *her* school magazine.

''My mother was a very open, sociable person. She was a theater critic for the *Irish Times.* Before I was sent to boarding school and then in the holidays, she used to take me along to see plays on their first night. We always stood in the back and I never saw the end of a play because she had to hurry to Fleet Street to phone in her review. Since she rarely knew how the play ended or whether or not it had gone down well with the first night audience, she had to trust her own judgment completely. She was brilliant at it. I just wished that I could have stayed just once for a curtain call.

''My mother was also very good at producing plays and every Christmas we put on a show, often written by her, with my cousins. There is one in particular about the siege of Troy that stuck in my memory. I was Prince Paris and a cousin I loathed because she could sing but not act, played Helen. I used to have to woo her on stage.

''My father moved to Dublin and went to work for the *Irish Times,* where we visited him during the holidays. I remember him taking me to Trinity College and saying, 'This library has a copy of every book that's ever been written.' I've never been so overwhelmed in my entire life. To me, the idea that one place could hold all the books in the world was total heaven.

''I read a mixture of books as a child. Since I had rheumatic fever and spent a lot of time in bed, I read whatever was in the house—mainly adult books. As babies we didn't have picture books but my aunt used to read me 'Ham, Shem and Japheth,' a strip cartoon from the *Chronicle.* I also read almost all of Kipling as a friend of my father's sent me a new one every birthday. I loved Lamb's *Tales of Shakespeare* which my cousin read to me, and was very fond of an extremely sentimental story called, *The Happy Wanderer.* But my very special book was *The Happy Prince,* a beautifully illustrated collection of Oscar Wilde short stories that my mother allowed me to choose myself in a second hand bookstore, after I had won my first elocution medal when I was eight.

''I was farmed out to a Dame School—an unofficial school run by Miss Hicks, a deeply religious woman who ended up in a loony bin. There, I was subjected to a great deal of religious teaching that influenced me to the extent that I wanted to become a priest. I used to lie in bed thinking that it was my calling to stand up and tell people to be good, and I'd pray to God to forgive my mother because she used the word 'damn.' The whole experience was certainly bad for me; I developed a great sense of sin and guilt which I kept all my life.

''I went to Hornsey High School and my brother was sent off to a boarding school in Devon, Ashburton. He was so unhappy that my mother finally decided to send me there as well to keep him company. I was bullied unmercifully in the first year because I came from the kind of school where you opened the doors for the mistresses and stood up when they came into the room. There was also a language barrier. To them I was automatically a teacher's pet, a foreign kid coming from London who seemed to know it all. In the end I learned to behave badly and speak with a Devonshire accent.

"Fortunately my brother and I were allowed Sunday afternoons together. We were both soppy about poetry and took long walks reading to each other. We got to know Palgrave's *Golden Treasury* almost by heart.

"We had quite a remarkable English master, Ben R. Gibbs, who inspired us with his passion for literature. He was in correspondence with Walter de la Mare who read some poem of mine in the school magazine and sent a letter saying, 'There is one poem I particularly like by somebody named Kaye Webb. I think she really is going to be a poet.' It was an unbelievably bad poem but I suppose he saw something in it. Years later I met Walter de la Mare and we became friends.

"I left school when I was fifteen without taking any exams. Mr. Gibbs was quite sure I was a writer and ought to go to Oxford, but there wasn't that kind of money in the house. Mother felt guilty about taking me away from school and since I had expressed a strong interest in acting, she contacted Lilian Baylis, founder of the famous Old Vic Theatre, who offered to take me as a trainee. With great arrogance I turned the offer down. I wrote my mother back and said, I'd rather write my own plays and then act in them. Of course, I never did."

Webb was sent to a finishing school in Belgium for six months and on her return was faced with the prospect of finding a job. "It was a time of high unemployment. I remember the family sitting around the kitchen table talking about trying to get work for my uncle and various cousins. I was obsessed with the idea of finding work and eventually got a position as an office girl in a publishing house for fifteen bob a week. It was awful. I had to type the labels for all the magazines going out, and was supervised by this fat white slug of a woman who covered the typewriter keys with rubber knobs to keep me from looking at them. I finally learned how to type and then was put on the switchboard. I made a mess of it until I gave notice and walked out after having been sworn at.

"My second job (which I got through my father's influence) was on *Picturegoer*, a magazine for film buffs with photographs and articles about stars. It was great fun. We got passes to all the West End cinemas and the talkies. I sometimes went to three shows a night.

"I was the editor's secretary and also 'George,' who answered thousands of inquiries from readers wanting to know every single detail about the life and work of their favorite filmstars. My job included getting filmstars to OK articles we had written about them. I met Ivor Novello whom I went to visit in his dressing room and whom I found holding hands with a man he called 'darling.' I was seventeen and very confused. I also met Leslie Howard when he was playing Hamlet."

Webb went to work for the *Broadcaster and Cinematograph Weekly*. "After a year I got bored with it and answered an advertisement for an editorial position on *Caravan World and the Sports Car*. I pretended to have experience as an editor, and certainly didn't tell them that I had never been in a caravan. I kept that job until I was twenty-one and got married."

In 1938 Webb worked on *Picture Post* and later moved to the famous wartime magazine, *Lilliput*, where she became assistant editor. "I was penniless and miserable when I heard that Stephan Lorant, whom I had worked for occassionally in the past, was starting a magazine called *Picture Post*. He gave me a job as a secretary and I again helped with the letters. After a few months,

Webb's 1979 publication. (From *I Like This Poem*, edited by Kaye Webb. Illustrated by Antony Maitland.)

they switched me to *Lilliput* magazine. I adored it. I've never known a magazine to cover everything as completely as *Lilliput* did. There were jokes and cartoons by current artists, brilliant photographs, and all sorts of unexpected contributors from H. G. Wells to Dylan Thomas. We covered such subjects as the Aeolian harp as well as how a hangman's rope is made. We were the first to include anti-Hitler material. *Lilliput* was called 'the pocket magazine for everyone' and we used to say that our readership was the 'duffel coat brigade': intelligent people who didn't have a large or very attentive time-span for reading. It was tremendously popular.

"After the war was declared, one of the people on staff moved to America, and I moved up to assistant editor. I was very involved with the 'doubles' for which *Lilliput* was famous. These were pairs of photographs juxtaposed to show their similarity. For instance, we had a picture of prime minister Neville Chamberlain opposite one of an ostrich, or a jolly publican beside one of a pear.

"I was terribly busy at this time because not only was I working on the magazine, but I also wrote two articles a month, a 'London Letter' for the forces magazine *Gen* and a film review for *Blighty*. I was also broadcasting regularly, and I was an air-raid warden, an ambulance driver on week-ends and used to wash up one day a week at the Charing Cross Canteen, and I was politically an active socialist like my father."

In 1946 Webb married cartoonist Ronald Searle and left *Lilliput* when her twins, John and Katie, were born the following year. "Ronald was one of the cartoonists we published in *Lilliput*. He'd already sent us the first St. Trinians drawing before he went overseas. We published it while he was in a Japanese prison-camp after the fall of Singapore. I had not met him, but he had built up an idea of me in his mind, because I had been the one who was buying his jokes and writing him encouraging letters about his work. After his release from prison-camp, he spent some time in the hospital where he was given a pile of *Gen* magazines to read. I think he felt as if he really got to know me through reading my 'London Letter' section."

Between 1947 and 1949 Webb contributed the showbusiness column for the *Leader* magazine. "I had a two-page gossip column and other theatre related subjects I wanted to write about. I could see every play and met most of the top theatre people. Christopher Fry's 'The Lady's Not for Burning' absolutely bowled me over. His writing flowed like a river of beautiful words. An actress friend of mine arranged for us to meet in a pub and he came with a bunch of anenomes. He was an extremely attractive, gentle, and interesting man, and we became friends. He lived around the corner from us and driving back at night from the theater I'd see him sitting reading by the window. I could never pass without going in for a chat."

Webb joined the *News Chronicles* as a features writer; her weekly articles were accompanied by Searle's illustrations. "Ronald was wonderful to work with. I would look for something to write that would make a good drawing but was always dissatisfied with my articles. Ronald used to grab a copy of my first draft and say, 'Use this.' He was right, the first draft was often the best, but I never had any confidence in my own writing.

"We did a series on London with slightly unexpected angles. I bought a barrel organ which we played on our way home, and then wrote an article about it. For another we took a stall in Portobello Market, and I sold second hand junk while Ronald drew the market. I also spent twenty-four hours outside Buckingham Palace (in two twelve-hour stretches) that went down very well. The most wonderful piece was about the people who sell the peanuts for the birds on Trafalgar Square. I recorded it for the BBC. (The man who worked the fountains used to turn the water pressure up to give the crowds a good cool-down when they got obstreperous on celebration nights.)

"When we ran out of London places, we did a series called 'People Worth Meeting.' All these articles were collected at the time of the Coronation in a book titled, *Looking at London and People Worth Meeting*. It sold very well."

Webb and her husband founded the Perpetua Press, named after a typeface they both like, in response to Searle's dissatisfaction with the quality of reproduction of his work. Among their publications were the St. Trinian's series of books, Raymond Peynet's many 'Lovers' books, a collection of cartoons by Andre Francois called 'The Biting Eye,' and Christopher Fry's *An Experience of Critics*.

"Fry was asked by the Critics Circle to give a talk and, being Kit, he took a tremendous amount of trouble to write it. After the lecture, I rang him up to tell him how wonderful his talk was and ask if anyone was planning on publishing it. 'No, you can do it,' was his response. I thought it wasn't long enough for a book, so I asked all the critics I knew if they'd write something about their approach to dramatic criticism. I stuck all these articles together and called it *An Experience of Critics*. At the time Ronald was doing theater-card cartoons for *Punch*, and we used to go up and down to Stratford-upon-Avon for the opening nights. Most of the

dramatic critics came up on the same train with us, and we stayed at the same pub talking late into the night about the plays while Ronald sat quietly drawing caricatures."

Webb became editor of the children's magazine, *Young Elizabethan*, in 1955. "I didn't get involved with children's books until I began to work for *Young Elizabethan*, known as 'a magazine to grow up with.' Authors such as Geoffrey Trease wrote serials for us, and subscribers were members of a club. Ronald was very good at lay-outs." After three years Webb left *Young Elizabethan* rather abruptly to care for her ailing mother.

In 1961 Webb joined Penguin as children's editor, eventually becoming publishing director of their children's division, a position she held until her retirement in 1979. "I was lucky to join Penguin when I did. The year 1961 was a golden age for publishing. A Labour government was in power, and for the first time money was being made available for children's literature and for schools to buy books. Children's librarians began to be taken seriously, and many children's editors were suddenly moved downstairs from the attic rooms or upstairs from the basement. Publishers realized that there was money to be made in children's literature. At the same time a whole raft of good bright original children's authors seemed to turn up, and I realized what a brilliant list could be made out of the 'Puffin Book' series—it all seemed to come together.

"When I first joined Penguin, director Alan Lane asked me if I was prepared to publish Enid Blyton, and I said, 'No.' She was an amusing and lively writer but her books were condescending and undemanding, and the vocabulary was dull. Arthur Calder Marshall once received a letter from a child reader who said, 'I felt older when I finished reading your book than when I began it.' That's what I thought books should do: add to children's understanding of life and knowledge. I felt it a challenge to publish well-written original books with reasonable standards that would sell at the same rate as the usual lightweight reading. I got totally involved with children's books and found myself wondering why I had not worked with them before. I felt such a tremendous sense of responsibility.

"The first thing I had to do was to make Puffin known. There were about 120 first-rate titles on the Puffin list when I joined, but nobody seemed to know about them. I went around bookshops with the sales reps and used to find the Puffins looking rather drab on a shelf behind the Armada and Enid Blyton books. I had to convince people that the Puffin books were butter and eggs books they could trust, a goal I eventually achieved.

"Officially, all Puffin was supposed to do was to buy paperback rights from hardback publishers, but I soon realized there were gaps that needed filling. There was a lot of fiction for older children but little for the younger. I found it frustrating only choosing and buying ready published books, so we started originating special collections. The first was *This Little Puffin*, a collection of finger plays and nursery rhymes. I wrote to every single nursery school in the country and asked, 'What are your favorites and have you invented anything new?' It really was a unique collection; there is nothing quite like it anywhere.

"Joan Aiken and Alan Garner were among my favorite authors. Alan is a compelling fantasy writer, stylish and positive. What is stunning is the way his books are written rather than the type of stories he tells. And I was always looking specifically for people who had a way with words or a new angle on something. Unfortunately we eventually lost Alan to Collins.

"Joan's books are unlike any I've ever read. She goes much further than the average writer in inventing ludicrous situations.

And although her characters have outrageous ideas (like trying to move the Houses of Parliament by putting them over rollers), you accept everything they do because Aiken writes about them with great seriousness, and there is never anything cardboard about the wild extravagances of her imagination. It's absolutely real. I respect Joan for the trouble she takes and re-read her books many times, each time finding more in them. The test of a good children's book is to be able to read it three times with increasing pleasure.

"Keeping high standards for the Puffin list imposed a great discipline on me. The language authors used became more explicit, and some teachers, who believed in being modern and up to date, started to prefer the more violent books. That worried me. Robert Westall's *Machine Gunners,* for instance, is a marvelous book but there were five swear words on every page and I asked him if he could cut them. He cut some but subsequently said, 'I would never do it again; this is the language children speak and you are not truthful if you don't repeat it.' It's become the norm to find swear words in children's books but I felt that by printing them you condone them. It's a difficult problem.''

In her quest to capture the interest of young readers for new authors, Webb founded the Puffin Club and its magazine, *Puffin Post.* "With television, taste unfortunately declined a bit. And too often, even children who normally read, tend to go for the easy stuff tied up with TV. The best thing to do I've discovered is to get children hooked on authors. That's why I started the Puffin Club. I used to get dozens of letters from children saying things like, 'I've read all the books of C. S. Lewis. What can I read next that are like those?' Often they wanted to write themselves and sent what they had done. I wanted to give children the opportunity to express themselves and knew that the only way to run a children's magazine was to invent a club with a solid membership, as not to be dependent on the sale or return system of distribution.

"*Puffin Post* came out once a quarter, which was all we could afford. Each issue had a couple of pages for the children's own work as well as four or five competitions involving self-expression in one form or another. We'd have poetry and writing competitions and competitions guessing how many times the letter 'P' would appear in the next issue. We usually gave a prize for the first ten entries opened. Once, we ran a very easy competition and forgot to specify that only the first correct entries would get prizes. We got more than five-hundred correct replies and couldn't afford prizes for everyone. I asked Sutton's (seed merchants) to print packets of sunflower seeds especially for Puffin and sent one to every prizewinner. The next competition was titled, 'Who Can Grow the Tallest Sunflower.' That summer there were sunflowers all over England.''

While working for Penguin, Webb also toured Britain spreading the word about new children's writers on behalf of The Children's Book Federation. "It was started with the aim of getting mothers interested in the books their children were reading. I toured the country speaking for the Federation. We'd set up displays in private or leased premises to let parents know what was available. We took book exhibitions into schools.''

After she left Penguin, Webb remained an active supporter of children's literature. She became children's advisor to Goldcrest TV and a director of the Unicorn Children's Theatre. In 1985 she edited *Lilliput Goes to War,* an anthology drawn from the original magazines. "*Lilliput Goes to War* took about a year and it got good reviews, but the publisher gave a it a dreadful cover and overpriced it. It didn't sell well. I was also asked to edit *I Like This Story,* a compilation of excerpts I picked from various

books with a running commentary by me. I contributed *I Like This Poem* to the International Year of the Child. Subsequent royalties from these books have gone to the Unicorn Theatre.

"I also got involved with children's television. I was pleased with the absolutely charming adaptation of 'Totty: The Story of a Doll's House,' an adaptation of Rumer Godden's story. Peter Firmin, the creator of Basil Brush, made the dolls and the sets. Oliver Postgate directed it. The dolls were animated but the humans were done using photographs and voices. I was the Queen Mother and also the voice of one of the dolls. It was tremendous fun.

"With the exception of the drama slots on BBC and ITV, children's television on the whole is condescending, with very little quality. If only families would read together as they watch TV together, it would give them shared references and stories and by-words.''[1]

FOOTNOTE SOURCES

[1]Based on an interview by Cathy Courtney for *Something about the Author.*

FOR MORE INFORMATION SEE:

Times Educational Supplement, November 14, 1986 (p. 37ff).

WECHTER, Nell Wise 1913-

PERSONAL: Born August 6, 1913, in Stumpy Point, N.C.; daughter of Enoch Raymond (a fisherman) and Edith Casey (Best) Wise; married Robert William Wechter (a U.S. Navy officer and teacher), March 12, 1943; children: Marcia Michele Dunlap. *Education:* Attended East Carolina Teachers College, 1933; East Carolina College, B.S., 1951, M.A. (elementary education), 1952, further graduate study, 1972; University of North Carolina, Greensboro, M.A. (English and social studies), graduate study, 1958-59, 1962-64. *Politics:* Democrat. *Religion:* Methodist. *Residence:* Stumpy Point, N.C.

CAREER: Public school teacher in North Carolina, 1933-64; free-lance feature writer for North Carolina newspapers, 1943-68; *Hyde County Herald,* Swan Quarter, N.C., associate editor, 1948-50; College of the Albemarle, Elizabeth City, N.C., teacher of creative writing and English, 1972; writer. *Member:* National Education Association, North Carolina Education Association, Outer Banks Woman's Club (honorary member). *Awards, honors:* George Washington Gold Medal from the Freedoms Foundation, 1950, for play "All Aboard for Freedom''; First Place Award from the Guildford Fine Arts Festival, 1955, for essay, and 1956, for poetry; Franklin McNutt Award, 1956, for best essay about teaching the American way of life by a Greensboro teacher; Award for Best Young People's Book by a North Carolina Author from the American Association of University Women, 1957, for *Taffy of Torpedo Junction;* National Teacher's Medal for North Carolina from the Freedoms Foundation, 1958.

WRITINGS:

JUVENILE

Taffy of Torpedo Junction (illustrated by Mary Walker Sparks), Blair, 1957.
Betsy Dowdy's Ride, Blair, 1960.
Swamp Girl, Blair, 1971.
Teach's Light, Blair, 1974.

NELL WISE WECHTER

MANFRED WEIDHORN

Yeshiva University, 500 West 185th St., New York, N.Y. 10033.

OTHER

The Romance of Juniper River (novel), Times Printing, 1937.
The Mighty Midgetts of Chicamacomico (adult fiction), Times Printing, 1974.
Some Whisper of Our Name, Times Printing, 1975.

Contributor to education journals and to newspapers.

SIDELIGHTS: The Wechters live on Nell Wechter's old home plantation in Stumpy Point where they have built a new cottage facing Pamlico Sound.

HOBBIES AND OTHER INTERESTS: Sewing, canning and freezing vegetables.

WEIDHORN, Manfred 1931-

PERSONAL: Born October 10, 1931, in Vienna, Austria; naturalized U.S. citizen, 1947; son of Aron (a merchant) and Anne (a diamond cutter; maiden name, Gelber) Weidhorn; married Phyllis Greenstein (a personnel consultant), January 12, 1969; children: Aron Homer, Eric Winston. *Education:* Columbia University, B.A., 1954, Ph.D., 1963; University of Wisconsin, M.A., 1957. *Politics:* ''I'm against whoever and whatever is in.'' *Religion:* ''Still waiting for the facts.'' *Home:* Fair Lawn, N.J. *Agent:* Scott Meredith Literary Agency, Inc., 845 Third Ave., New York, N.Y. 10022. *Office:* Department of English,

CAREER: Self-employed diamond cutter in New York, N.Y., 1948-52; University of Alabama, Tuscaloosa, instructor in English, 1957-58; Brooklyn College, City University of New York, Brooklyn, N.Y., instructor in English, 1960-63; Yeshiva University, New York, N.Y., assistant professor, 1963-68, associate professor, 1968-73, professor of English, 1973—. *Military service:* U.S. Army, Artillery, 1954-56. *Member:* American Association of University Professors, International Churchill Society. *Awards, honors:* Danforth Associate, 1969-76; listed in *Outstanding Educators of America,* 1972.

WRITINGS:

YOUNG ADULT

Napoleon, Atheneum, 1986.
Robert E. Lee, Atheneum, 1988.

OTHER

Dreams in Seventeenth-Century English Literature, Mouton & Co., 1970.
Richard Lovelace, Twayne, 1970.
Sword and Pen: A Survey of the Writings of Sir Winston Churchill, University of New Mexico Press, 1974.
(With Stanley Nass) *Turn Your Life Around,* Prentice-Hall, 1978.
Sir Winston Churchill, G. K. Hall, 1979.
Churchill's Rhetoric and Political Discourse, University Press of America, 1987.

Contributor of nearly three dozen articles to scholarly journals.

WORK IN PROGRESS: Books on Faust, Galileo, and Jackie Robinson for young adults.

SIDELIGHTS: "My inclination to write began early, even before I knew any English at all. I was a storyteller at the age of nine. Fleeing from Hitler on a transatlantic boat and then living in Havana while awaiting a visa to the United States, I enthralled my contemporaries with improvised stories that went on and on. In high school, I wrote short stories in a creative writing course. I was becoming hooked on fiction writing. In the summer of 1951, having just finished my freshman year at Columbia College and not yet twenty, I wrote my first novel and entered it into a contest. Nothing came of the venture, but I was consumed by the notion of becoming a full-time writer, even of becoming the Great American Novelist. So I wrote two more long novels during my college years, besides a mass of shorter fiction and nonfiction. Since all of it remained unpublished, my mother counselled me to not risk everything on something so highly speculative as earning a living as a writer but to prepare rather for some practical career and do writing on the side. It proved to be sage advice.

"What, then, to concentrate on? The sequence of events took care of that. In order to succeed as a novelist, I had to read classics to find out how the thing was done. So at the end of college, I found myself without a novel published but with a lot of novels read. I therefore pursued graduate study in literature, became a college teacher, and began writing scholarly articles and books. So I had become a writer, after all, though not the kind I'd dreamed of being. One adjusts one's goal.

Some day, he told himself, some day he would show them how good he was. (Jacket illustration by Gros from *Napoleon* by Manfred Weidhorn.)

"My initial focus in scholarly writing was seventeenth-century English literature. But then something from my past came to dominate me: As a child fleeing the Nazis I had been aware of this great man Winston Churchill who stood up to Hitler. Perhaps I was alive in part because of this Englishman. I was now attracted to his voluminous writings. My study of these resulted in three books and many articles, all of which may now be seen as a survivor's tribute to a benefactor.

"My scholarly writings—in all, five books and nearly three dozen essays—were well received, but I became interested gradually in trying my hand at something different. Seeking a breakthrough in fame and/or money, I wrote detective novels (still unpublished) and a psychology self-help book (published). Then came the idea, obtained from a colleague, of writing books for young adults. My colleague wrote on wars; I preferred biography. My wife suggested Napoleon, and, since he was one of the most successful men in history, the project proved to be a delight to do. What next? Napoleon's fascinating personality and enormous ego in the end did become overbearing. My next subject would have to be someone more humane. That brought me to Robert E. Lee.

"Thus far, then, I have had three phases in my career as a writer. The first one resulted in a closet-full of nearly a dozen unpublished novels. The second one, as a scholar, was much more successful: One of my books, I am told by experts, is a 'must' for Churchill lovers. The third phase, of writing history and biography for young adults, is in some ways more enjoyable than the first two phases. Or maybe it just seems that way because that is what I am currently doing. I think I'll pitch my tent here for now—and perhaps for good."

HOBBIES AND OTHER INTERESTS: Travel, chess, swimming, architectural photography, painting.

WHITE, Timothy (Thomas Anthony) 1952-

PERSONAL: Born January 25, 1952, in Paterson, N.J.; son of John Alexander (an inventory foreman and assistant engineer in aeronautics) and Gloria Marie (a bookkeeper; maiden name, Thomas) White; married Judith Anne Garlan (an art director), June 28, 1987. *Education:* Bensalem College, Fordham University, B.A., 1972. *Politics:* Democrat ("left of center"). *Religion:* Renegade Catholic. *Agent:* Owen Laster and James Stein, William Morris Agency, 1350 Avenue of the Americas, New York, N.Y. 10019.

CAREER: Associated Press, New York, N.Y., copyboy, sports writer, 1972-76; *Crawdaddy* (magazine), New York, N.Y., managing editor, 1976-77, senior editor, 1977-78; *Rolling Stone* (magazine), New York, N.Y., associate editor, 1978-79, senior editor, 1979-82; host and co-producer of "Timothy White's Rock Stars," a nationally syndicated radio series, 1986—. Writer and interviewer of MTV specials: "MTV Presents John Cougar Mellencamp," "MTV Presents Sting: The Dream of the Blue Turtles," and "MTV Presents John Belushi: Rock and Roll Actor"; head writer of MTV's eleven-hour "Amnesty International 'Conspiracy of Hope' Concert Special." Lecturer.

WRITINGS:

(With Roy Blount, Jr., Charles M. Young and others) *Rolling Stone Visits Saturday Night Live,* Doubleday, 1979.
(With J. C. Suares and Judy Garlan) *Suddenly Poor! A Guide for the Downwardly Mobile,* Atlantic-Little, Brown, 1983.

TIMOTHY WHITE

Catch a Fire: The Life of Bob Marley, Holt, 1983, revised and enlarged edition, 1989.
Rock Stars, Stewart, Tabori & Chang, 1984.
(With Leroy Woodson, Jr., J. C. Suares and others) *Roadside Food*, Stewart, Tabori & Chang, 1986.

CONTRIBUTOR

George Simon and Friends, *The Best of the Music Makers*, Doubleday, 1979.
The 80s: A Look Back at the Tumultuous Decade, Workman, 1979.
The Rolling Stone Interviews, St. Martin's, 1981.
Reggae International, Knopf, 1982.
Twenty Years of Rolling Stone, Friendly Press, 1987.
A & M Records: The First 25 Years, A & M Publishing, 1987.

Contributing editor, *Musician*, 1982—, *Reggae and African Beat*, 1982—, and *Penthouse*, 1983—. Contributor of articles to periodicals, including *Rolling Stone, New York Times Magazine, Washington Post, Boston Globe, Los Angeles Times, Los Angeles Weekly, Chicago Tribune, Detroit Free Press, Miami Herald, San Francisco Chronicle, USA Today, Spin, New Musical Express, Time Out, Elle, Harper's Bazaar, Cosmpolitan, GEO, New England Monthly, L.A. Style, Village Voice*, and *Playboy*.

WORK IN PROGRESS: A social history of Southern California for Summit Books; a collection of profiles and interviews done from 1975 to 1990, for Holt.

SIDELIGHTS: "I have always tried to stay true to the *original* tenets and philosophies of early *Esquire/Rolling Stone*-style magazine journalism, which I see as maximum legwork, maximum new information, and allowing the story to tell itself, plus permitting emotional movement and depthful occurrences to unfold through an unsentimental atmosphere of mutual trust. In books, I hope to write the kind of social history that restores mystique to even the so-called 'ordinary' aspects of modern culture. I concentrate on nonfiction, social history, biography, and profiles, because in the accomplishments of anyone there is hope for everyone."

"I changed schools often in my youth either because my parents were constantly having conscience pangs about a lack of traditional parochial school education for myself and/or my other four brothers and two sisters, or because we moved from Paterson, New Jersey to Montclair, New Jersey.

"My ethnic heritage is Irish, Welsh, Scottish and a bit of French-Canadian. Grandpa White worked for the police telegraph and Grandpa Thomas was a manager at a Wonder Bread plant (he began as a driver). My father was a talented athlete and amateur inventor, and my mother is gifted as a painter and writer, seeing her earliest prose published in such places as the bygone *Liberty* magazine.

"My mother, an avid fan of William Saroyan and a friend of Allen Ginsburg's father (he was her English teacher at Central High School in Paterson) encouraged me to write. My father, a suporb figure skater who landed a spot in the chorus of Sonja Henie's Hollywood Ice Revue (but gave it up to raise a family) encouraged me to rock.

"I shovelled snow and raked leaves to earn the money for my first set of drums, and played in numerous grammar school, high school, and college bands with ill-chosen names like the 'Mont-a-Rays' and 'Uncle Bumps and the Midnight Taxi.' While a senior editor at *Rolling Stone*, I formed an awful band with the various editors and writers that I dubbed the 'Dry Heaves.' We performed at the legendary *Rolling Stone* Christmas party of

Cover of the 1983 paperbound edition. (Cover illustration by Daniel Maffia from *Catch a Fire: The Life of Bob Marley* by Timothy White.)

1979, and guest Mick Jagger offered the following critique: 'If only these guys could write as well as they play.' In 1984, the 'Dry Heaves' reunited for a November 14th performance/party telecast on MTV, for which I wrote our most notorious song—since released by another artist, singer Woodie Garrett as a single—'If You Won't Get Out of My Life, I'll Find Somebody Who Will.'"

Of White's book *Catch a Fire* Joel Selvin of the *San Francisco Chronicle* wrote, "Probably the finest biography ever written about a popular musician." Of his book *Rock Stars* Michael Goldberg of *Rolling Stone* wrote, "The writing ranges from interesting to inspired."

HOBBIES AND OTHER INTERESTS: Caribbean history, culture, folklore, and music; playing the drums; dancing.

FOR MORE INFORMATION SEE:

Ward Just, "Newspaper Days," *Atlantic Monthly*, October, 1979.
Neil Tesser, *Chicago Daily Reader*, June, 1984.
Penthouse, March, 1988.
The Reggae and African Beat, Volume 7, number 3, 1988.

WILLIAMS, Jenny 1939-

PERSONAL: Born March 22, 1939, in London, England; daughter of Leslie (a local government administration officer) and Eleanor (a medical social worker; maiden name, Moor) Roberts; married Andy Hewson (a designer/manufacturer), July 5, 1969; children: Rowan, Bonnie Kate. *Education:* Attended Wimbledon School of Art and Institute of Education, 1958-61. *Home:* Ffynnon Wen, Capel Isaac, Llandeilo, Dyfed SA19 7TU, United Kingdom.

CAREER: Free-lance commercial artist and illustrator. *Awards, honors:* Esther Glen Award from the New Zealand Library Association, 1970, for *A Lion in the Meadow*.

WRITINGS:

JUVENILE; SELF-ILLUSTRATED

Uncle Bumble, American Heritage Press, 1970.
(Adapter) *Jenny Williams' First Fairy Story Book* (contains "Little Red Riding Hood" and "The Three Little Pigs"), Collins, 1977.
(Adapter) *Jenny Williams' Second Fairy Story Book* (contains "Goldilocks and the Three Bears" and "The Brave Little Tailor"), Collins, 1977.
(Adapter) *Jenny Williams' Third Fairy Story Book* (contains "Cinderella" and "Rumpelstiltskin"), Collins, 1977.
(Adapter) *Jenny Williams' Fourth Fairy Story Book* (contains "The Story of Aladdin" and "Rapunzel"), Collins, 1977.
Alphabet Adventures, Collins, 1978.
Here's a Ball for Baby, Dial, 1987.
One, Two, Buckle My Shoe: Counting Rhymes, Dial, 1987.
Ride a Cockhorse: Animal Rhymes, Dial, 1987.
Ring around a Rosy: Action Rhymes, Dial, 1987.

ILLUSTRATOR

Douglas J. Kirby, *The Silver Wood*, Constable, 1966, Four Winds Press, 1967.
My First Book of Nursery Rhymes, T. Nelson, 1967.
Margaret Mahy, *A Lion in the Meadow*, F. Watts, 1969.

David MacKay, Brian Thompson, and Pamela Schaub, *Things I Can Do*, Longman for the Schools Council, 1970.
D. MacKay, *Breakthrough to Literacy*, Red Series B, Longman for the Schools Council, 1970.
M. Mahy, *The Boy with Two Shadows*, F. Watts, 1971, reissued, Lippincott, 1988.
Margaret Sperry, translator and adapter, *Scandinavian Stories*, F. Watts, 1971.
Janet Lynch Walson, *Ben's Giraffe*, Abelard, 1973.
Marguerite Patten, *The Play and Cook Book*, Collins, 1973.
M. Mahy, *Rooms for Rent*, F. Watts, 1974 (published in England as *Rooms to Let*, Dent, 1974).
Helen Young, *Wide-Awake Jake*, Collins, 1974, Morrow, 1975.
M. Mahy, *The Witch in the Cherry Tree*, Parents Magazine Press, 1974.
Frances Hodgson Burnett, *The Secret Garden*, Dent, 1975.
Geoffrey Broughton, *Go*, three volumes, Longman, 1975-77.
Martha Shapp, Charles Shapp, and Sylvia Shepard, *Let's Find Out about Babies*, F. Watts, 1975.
Deborah Manley and Diane James, *On Holiday*, Dent, 1975.
Dorothy Edwards, *A Wet Monday*, Methuen, 1975, Morrow, 1976.
David Grant, *Favourite Fairy Tales*, Collins, 1976, published as *Fairy Tales*, 1979.
Kathryn Jackson, *The Joys of Christmas: Christmas Customs and Legends around the World*, Golden Press, 1976.
M. Mahy, *Leaf Magic*, Dent, 1976, Parents Magazine Press, 1977.
D. Edwards, compiler and editor, *The Read-Me-Another-Story-Book*, Methuen, 1976.
Helen J. Fletcher, *Picture Book ABC*, Platt, 1978.
Shiela Parsons, *My First Reading and Writing Book*, Longman, 1979.
Hans C. Andersen, *The Ugly Duckling*, Troll, 1979.
The Fisherman and the Mermaid [and] *The Brothers*, Collins, 1980.
The King and the Fishes [and] *The Magic Lime Tree*, Collins, 1980.
The Magic Kettle, The Golden Fish, [and] The Fairy Hill, Collins, 1980.
Poor Man's Kingdom [and] *Snake Prince*, Collins, 1980.
John G. Evans, *Llyfr hwiangerddi y Dref Wen* (title means "Dref Wen Book of Nursery Rhymes"), Gwasg y Dref Wen (Cardiff, Dyfed, Wales), 1981.
Dorothy F. Richards, *Pray in This Way*, Dandelion House, 1983.
Bruce Wannamaker, *Fixing Fences*, Dandelion House, 1984.
Pamela Oldfield, *Barnaby and Bell and the Birthday Cake*, Piccadilly Press, 1985.
P. Oldfield, *Barnaby and Bell and the Lost Button*, Piccadilly Press, 1985.
Jane B. Moncure, *Mousekin's Special Day*, Child's World, 1987.
J. B. Moncure, *What's So Special about Fall? I'm Going to School*, Child's World, 1988.
J. B. Moncure, *What's So Special about Lauren? She's My Baby Sister*, Child's World, 1988.
J. B. Moncure, *What's So Special about Today? It's My Birthday*, Child's World, 1988.
Jenny Hessell, *Staying at Sam's*, Collins, 1989.
Lynne Bradbury, *The First Christmas*, Ladybird, 1989.
Sandra Ziegler, *Understanding*, Child's World, 1989.
P. Oldfield, *Sam Sue and Cinderella*, Methuen, 1990.
Tony Bradman, *This Little Baby*, Frances Lincoln, 1990.

ILLUSTRATOR; "FIRST NURSERY TALES" SERIES; ALL BY TONY BRADMAN

The Gingerbread Man, Methuen, 1990.
The Ugly Duckling, Methuen, 1990.

The boy did not like to argue with a witch.
"All right," he said, "but hurry back, won't you?"
The witch bared her teeth in a witch smile, which was quite
wicked-looking though she was trying to be pleasant.
"If you look after my shadow properly," she promised,
"you shall have a whole magic spell of your own.
I'll choose a good one just for you."

(From *The Boy with Two Shadows* by Margaret Mahy. Illustrated by Jenny Williams.)

Goldilocks and the Three Bears, Methuen, 1990.
The Little Red Hen, Methuen, 1990.

Also illustrator of Anetta E. Dellinger's *Hugging,* Child's World, and of book jackets; contributor of illustrations to periodicals.

SIDELIGHTS: "I try to put as much detail in pictures as possible as I now know from experience (reading with my own two small children) that kids appreciate plenty to look at and that they have very sharp eyes. They love fantasy, of course, but I think very young children prefer to pick out details that they recognize from their own home environments. Very simplistic pictures are out, I

believe. Adults often think they are suitable, but they actually bore children.

"When designing a book, I always map it out in thumbnails first to ensure a balance of action. I wait till things crystallize in my mind, then plough ahead and always find that, if I have waited till the moment is right, then the book sort of illustrates itself. And everything falls into place.

"I have no preferred subjects as each new book is a fascination for the moment. But I do love drawing children, more so since I have had my own."

ZIEGLER, Jack (Denmore) 1942-

PERSONAL: Born July 13, 1942, in New York, N.Y.; son of John Denmore (a sales representative) and Kathleen Miriam (a teacher; maiden name, Clarke) Ziegler; married Jean Ann Rice (a teacher), April 20, 1968; children: Jessica, Benjamin, Maxwell. *Education:* Fordham University, B.A., 1964. *Politics:* Unaffiliated. *Home and office:* 61 Prospect Hill Rd., New Milford, Conn. 06776.

CAREER: Columbia Broadcasting System (CBS-TV), New York, N.Y., network traffic, 1967-69; KTVU-TV, Oakland, Calif., program researcher, 1969-70; free-lance writer, 1969-72; free-lance cartoonist, 1972—. *Exhibitions:* Bethel Gallery, Bethel, Conn., 1977; International Tennis Hall of Fame, Newport, R.I.; Washington Art Gallery, Washington, Conn., 1978; Nancy Roth Gallery, New York, N.Y., 1978; Foundry Gallery, Washington, D.C., 1984; Master Eagle Gallery, New York, N.Y., 1984, 1985, 1987; Artspace, New Haven, Conn., 1987. *Military service:* U.S. Army, 1966-67. *Member:* Cartoonists Association (founding member; member of board of governors, treasurer, 1981-82).

WRITINGS:

Hamburger Madness (cartoon collection), Harcourt, 1978.
Filthy Little Things (cartoon collection), Doubleday, 1981.
Celebrity Cartoons of the Rich and Famous, Warner, 1987.
Marital Blitz, Warner, 1987.
Worst Case Scenarios, Simon & Schuster, 1990.

ILLUSTRATOR

Brian McConnachie, *Lily of the Forest,* Crown, 1987.
B. McConnachie, *Flying Boy,* Crown, 1988.
Barbara Brenner, *Annie's Pet,* Bantam, 1989.

Regular contributor of cartoons to *New Yorker.* Contributor of cartoons to periodicals, including *Esquire, New York Times, Cosmopolitan,* and *Playboy.*

WORK IN PROGRESS: Mr. Knocky, a children's book.

SIDELIGHTS: "I'm a cartoonist whose work appears mainly in the *New Yorker.* I've been doing this for about seventeen years. I try to do cartoons that are hopefully funny, rather than clever. I would rather have people laugh than say 'Oh yeah, I get it.' I try to do work that would make *me* laugh if I ran across it in a magazine or book. My theory is that cartoons should be little surprises that seem to pop up out of nowhere and trigger a not altogether unpleasant reaction in the reader."

HOBBIES AND OTHER INTERESTS: Music, painting.

FOR MORE INFORMATION SEE:

Washington Post Book World, December 10, 1978, June 28, 1981.
Time, January 8, 1979.
New York Times Book Review, February 17, 1980, August 30, 1981.
Connecticut, September, 1980 (p. 62ff).
Village Voice, December 16, 1981.
Artist's Magazine, January, 1986 (p. 52ff).
Cartoonist Profiles, March, 1989 (p. 18ff).